LAW, INSTITUTION AND LEGAL POLITICS

Law and Philosophy Library

VOLUME 14

The titles published in this series are listed at the end of this volume.

OTA WEINBERGER

University of Graz, Austria

LAW, INSTITUTION AND LEGAL POLITICS

Fundamental Problems of Legal Theory and Social Philosophy

KLUWER ACADEMIC PUBLISHERS

DORDRECHT / BOSTON / LONDON

Library of Congress Cataloging-in-Publication Data

Weinberger, Ota.
Law, institution, and legal politics : fundamental problems of legal theory and social philosophy / by Ota Weinberger.
p. cm. -- (Law and philosophy library ; v. 14)
Includes bibliographical references (p.).
ISBN 0-7923-1143-4 (HB)
1. Sociological jurisprudence. 2. Jurisprudence. 3. Legal positivism. 4. Justice. 5. Law--Philosophy. I. Title. II. Series.
K370.W445 1991
340'.115--dc20 91-7704

ISBN 0-7923-1143-4

Published by Kluwer Academic Publishers,
P.O. Box 17, 3300 AA Dordrecht, The Netherlands.

Kluwer Academic Publishers incorporates
the publishing programmes of
D. Reidel, Martinus Nijhoff, Dr W. Junk and MTP Press.

Sold and distributed in the U.S.A. and Canada
by Kluwer Academic Publishers,
101 Philip Drive, Norwell, MA 02061, U.S.A.

In all other countries, sold and distributed
by Kluwer Academic Publishers Group,
P.O. Box 322, 3300 AH Dordrecht, The Netherlands.

English translation of: Ota Weinberger,
Recht, Institution und Rechtspolitik;
Stuttgart, Franz Steiner Verlag Wiesbaden GmbH, 1987.

Printed on acid-free paper

Printed in the Netherlands

TABLE OF CONTENTS

C. TREATISES ON LEGAL POLITICS AND THEORY OF JUSTICE

FOREWORD

It gives me great pleasure to offer this foreword to the present work of my admired friend and respected colleague Ota Weinberger. Apart from the essays of his which were published in our joint work *An Institutional Theory of Law: New Approaches to Legal Positivism* in 1986, relatively little of Weinberger's work is available in English. This is the more to be regretted, since his is work of particular interest to jurists of the English-speaking world both in view of its origins and in respect of its content.

As to its origins, Weinberger war reared as a student of the Pure Theory of Law, a theory which in its Kelsenian form has aroused very great interest and has had considerable influence among anglophoone scholars - perhaps even more than in the Germanic countries. Less well known is the fact that the Pure Theory itself divided into two schools, that of Vienna and that of Brno. It was in the Brno school of František Weyr that Weinberger's legal theory found its early formation, and perhaps from that early influence one can trace his continuing insistence on the dual character of legal norms - both as genuinely normative and yet at the same time having real social existence. Here, the Brno approach to legal theory has in its content an interesting affinity with British work in the Hartian style, although each appears to have developed quite independently of the other; the former, certainly, had temporal priority, but was of relatively little general influence owing to the relative isolation of Czechoslovak scholarship through the War years and under various periods of repressive communist rule thereafter.

Ota Weinberger has had great scholarly achievement through many works published variously in Czech and in German. His achievement is the more remarkable for the adversities he has suffered, as a survivor both of the nazi concentration camps (he is of Jewish family origin) and of the years of stalinism and repression in Czechoslovakia, which he left at the time of the crushing of the 'Prague Spring'. The circumstances of his life are no doubt partly responsible for the focussing of his earlier publications very considerably on logical studies, with special reference to the problems of norm-logic; in such fields one effectively eludes the censor's interference, since after all there is a limit to the intelligence and understanding of censors. However that may be, the very substantial contribution of Weinberger to the development of norm-logic and deontic logic is undeniable and a contribution which one can welcome as heartily as one deplores the possible underlying causes of his delayed opportunity to contribute also at the level of substantive value theory and studies in the normative politics of law.

That logical studies can have profound significance for legal theory is in any event a point which his work (together with that of others) has put well beyond doubt. In the present volume, chapter III deals with this issue. The setting is in Weinberger's theory of action, also discussed in chapter II. Action is here represented as behaviour guided by thinking, while thinking itself is defined as a processing of information. Fundamental to practical (action-guiding) thought are goals and values, and therefore fundamental to the analysis of practical thought must be some sort of formalisation of teleological reasoning. One of the author's most significant contributions has been his attempt to develop a 'formal teleology' (the special subject-matter of the present chapter II); this is distinct from deontic logic, which formalises the treatment of norms as possible action-guiding thought contents. It is here that their character as *practical* and *normative* is identifiable (see chapter III).

The other main point of Weinberger's 'institutional legal positivism' (a point which we fully share, as our *Institutional Theory of Law* makes clear) is that norms also have a real existence as 'thought objects', belonging among the 'institutional facts' of our social existence. The stress upon the institutional character of legal norms marks his own highly original development of the general themes inherited from Weyr and other teachers and colleagues. His account of the basic elements of this institutional approach is the opening chapter of the present book, where the thesis is advanced that a legal system is both a system of norms and a part of social reality. This may seem to involve a confusion of 'ought' and 'is'; for how can one assert the being-in-existence of a legal 'ought' without illegitimately leaping the is/ought gap? The answer offered avoids some of the notorious difficulties into which Kelsen found himself driven farther and farther; it achieves this by insisting on the necessity to pursue our understanding of normativity through action-theory, while also keeping in view the functional links between normative judgement and actual social processes.

These are the themes of Part A of the book, dealing with theoretical foundations. If the theoretical position is well grounded, one thing which has to follow from it is that there can after all be greater common ground between legal theory and the sociology of law than is sometimes supposed either by legal theorists or by sociologists. Part II pursues this thought by offering a series of studies in legal theory and the (theoretical) sociology of law. Here, chapter IV explores the ontological insights of institutional theory, reflecting from an 'internal point of view', or at least in the perspective of a hermeneutic understanding, on the idea of the 'binding quality' or 'validity' of legal norms which are in force somewhere. Chapter VI applies the formal-teleological account of action to some problems in criminal law. Chapter VII examines and defends the sense of 'legal positivism' upheld by the Weinberger version of the 'Institutional Theory'. Here I have to confess that my own recent work may have somewhat distanced the MacCormick version of the theory from the arguably more robust rejection of cognitivism on which my colleague builds. However that may be, it remains for both of us fundamental that our approach to the theory of institutions and of law is a normativist one. The contrast between this and certain sociological approaches is made plain by the critique of Helmut Schelsky's sociological theory in chapter VIII - not that our theory is anti-sociological; on the contrary, we think that a sociological approach to law has also to be normativist in the relevant sense.

Weinberger's disbelief in an objective realm of values directly discoverable by some form of cognition (his noncognitivism) does not for him entail any kind of ethical or political irrationalism or even nonrationalism. Far from it - he considers the rational analysis of problems in legal politics quite possible; and not only possible, but one of the most important tasks for jurisprudence. The point of his noncognitivism is that values cannot be the subject of pure cognition, but depend finally on the value-stances to which we ultimately commit ourselves. There is nothing in this which denies or belittles the possibility of reason in practice as a means for rational analysis of policy pursuit and normative evaluation. All this becomes very clear from chapters XI and X, which constitute the concluding Part of the book.

I have very greatly valued the warm association which has arisen between Ota Weinberger and myself since we first discovered, at the IVR Congress in Basel in 1979, how remarkable a parallelism of views we had together arrived at albeit each working quite independently of the other. Our sense of this was reinforced at other conferences in Helsinki and Edinburgh in the following months. But the project of bringing our work together for joint publication, first in German and later in English, came about entirely through the generosity and goodwill of my senior colleague. In acknowledgement of that indebtedness, and in salutation of a major scholar, I have great pleasure in offering these few words as prefatory remarks to this distinctive and distinguished book. My pleasure is the greater for the fact that two Edinburgh friends, Anne Bankowska and Ruth Adler, untertook the first stages of the preparation of the present translation, which has now been brought to completion by other hands.

Neil MacCormick

AUTHOR'S PREFACE

The legal-philosophical conception developed simultaneously by D.N. MacCormick and myself will be referred to as 'Institutional Legal Positivism'. This theory rests on a number of simple basic ideas which, nevertheless, have not altogether unimportant consequences for the treatment of crucial fundamental questions of jurisprudence. The law is, on the one hand, a social reality, on the other, a system of norms. This situation results in the problem of the specific mode of existence of normative regulatives - especially of the legal system - as integral parts of social reality. This problem - it might be condensed into the question "How is the existence of the legal 'ought' (the legal norms) to be explained without infringing the semantic distinction between 'is' and 'ought'?" - is rendered more accessible to a solution if the law is seen from an action-theoretical perspective and the institutions are regarded as the social structures where the functions of normative provisions and actual social processes combine.

Institutional Legal Positivism provides a theoretical basis for the norm-logical and the dogmatic analyses of the law as well as for the study of legal phenomena from the socio-legal point of view. It is a positivist theory in as far as it rejects the possibility of establishing "proper" law purely on the basis of cognition and without the intervention of volition based on evaluation. It distinguishes between law and morality as between two separate normative systems which, nevertheless, combine in determining human behaviour. From its point of view a rational analysis of legal-political problems not only appears possible, but it is seen as one of the major tasks of jurisprudence.

In a book written by MacCormick and myself we introduced the program and the basic characteristics of this theory in its chronological development.[1] Now this theory has to be developed and its theoretical foundations as well as the legal-philosophical implications have to be extended. The work that has been collected in this volume serves this purpose. It contains papers from three areas: In Part A the theoretical foundations of Institutional Legal Positivism are expounded; in Part B contributions to legal theory, legal sociology and general sociology are brought together; and, finally, in Part C two papers dealing with legal politics and the theory of justice are presented.

Some chapters were published earlier (see "Original Sources", pp. 289 f.); Chapters I and II were written for this volume. As a result of the chapters having appeared as separate treatises certain repetitions cannot be avoided; this particular defect of this book is compensated by the advantage that all chapters can be read independently and in any order. Those wishing to gain a clear picture of the legal-philosophical conception as advanced in this volume are advised to pay special attention to Part A.

---

1 D.N. MacCormick/O. Weinberger, *An Institutional Theory of the Law. New Approaches to Legal Positivism*, Dordrecht 1986; German version: the same, *Grundlagen des Institutionalistischen Rechtspositivismus*, Berlin 1985.

In Chapter I of Part A "Building Blocks of Institutional Legal Positivism" the fundamental characteristics of an institutional legal theory are outlined. Under the heading "Towards a Formal-Teleological Theory of Action" Chapter II deals with a specific approach to the concept of action and with the methods of analyzing action. I regard this approach as an integral part of Institutional Legal Positivism in the same way as the norm-logical conceptions presented in Chapter III of Part A ("The Significance of Logic for Modern Legal Theory"). In other words, all the fundamental philosophical elements of the normative institutional theory of law are discussed in Part A. The four chapters of Part B, on the other hand, select only some specific problems of legal theory and legal sociology; they are intended to demonstrate the theoretical applicability of the normative institutional conception to jurisprudence and sociology. Part C is meant to show that institutional jurisprudence is capable of treating legal-political questions on a non-cognitive basis and of making a contribution to the theory of justice. In this context I should also like to mention that not all the theses presented here with reference to the problem of justice are inevitable implications of Institutional Legal Positivism.

Some knowledge of how Institutional Legal Positivism evolved will, I believe, facilitate the reader's access to this theory and to this book. I shall, therefore, outline briefly the development of this conception from my own subjective perspective.

MY PATH TO NORMATIVIST INSTITUTIONALISM

While it is of considerable interest to me personally to cast my mind back over the path on which I reached my present legal-philosophical stance for the reader wishing to understand and assess my teachings the systematic explanation of the foundations and of the building-blocks of my theory will be of greater importance than the autobiographical perspective of its genesis.[2] I shall, therefore, give only a brief account of the developmental phases of my conceptions allowing far more room for setting out and discussing the basis and the fundamental philosophical conceptions on which the theory rests.

It would be wrong to assume that the author knows the developmental history of his thoughts with clarity and certainty and that he is consequently able to present it authentically and without inner doubts. In reality, an autobiographical account of this kind is a reconstruction in retrospect in the course of which we cannot by any means be certain whether we are judging correctly what the vital steps of the development were and what influences were at work. I would want my retrospective review to be understood as a hypothetical reconstruction, as a subjective image of myself which I myself don't regard as more than approximately valid.

The milieu in which I grew up was of the kind that was likely to induce a tolerant and undogmatic attitude to life as well as democratic convictions. My

[2] A detailed autobiographical account is contained in vol. I "Problemas abiertos en la filosofía del derecho" of the periodical *Doxa - cuadernos de filosofía del derecho*, 1984, pp. 257-263.

youth was spent in Brno a town where several languages were spoken and where the separate groups of the population coexisted without strict segregation. I did not enjoy any systematic religious education nor did my upbringing instil any national or ideological prejudices in my mind. The spreading nationalist movements were alien to me.

I am a doubter by nature and the childhood question "why?" has continued to determine my attitudes in adulthood. In the course of my studies I have always been particularly interested in problems of methodology and the connections linking separate elements of substantiation.

Moral questions have always been a major concern and stimulus for me. Doubts and inner uncertainties in the moral sphere lead me to pursue rational analysis to the furthest limits of the practical sphere. I believe in the power of reason. Rational analysis has a place also in practical philosophy; nevertheless, I have never thought that we can gain answers to moral problems simply by the use of rational analysis.

František Weyr, the founder to the Brno school of pure jurisprudence[3], not only stimulated my interest in the structural theory of the law; it was as a result of his question whether there are inferences with normative members that I became aware of the problems of the normative logics which have occupied me ever since. Even as a student I had an ambivalent attitude to pure jurisprudence: while appreciating structural theory and accepting non-cognitivism I object to the exclusion of sociological considerations.

It was also through the Brno school that my attention was drawn to teleology (*Karel Engliš*, *Jan Loevenstein*[4]) as well as to the connection between the teleological and the norm-logical approach.

While I have never been a faithful adherent of any one philosophical school the influences of *Kant*"s philosophy and of the kind of program of logical analysis that was evolved by Neo-Positivism are unmistakable. The fact that I studied Marxism and dealt with different elements of this system has also left its mark on my thought processes. I have firmly refused to regard cognition and thinking as processes doing no more than reflect reality. *Hegel*"s dialectics which are not greatly improved by being reversed in accordance with the Marxist recipe have been the object of my severe criticism.[5] I have rejected the thesis that the material aspects of life (economics) ultimately determine everything, pre-

---

3 See V. Kubeš/O. Weinberger, *Die Brünner rechtstheoretische Schule (Normative Theorie)*, Vienna 1980.

4 K. Engliš, Nástin národohospodářské noetiky [Outline of the Noetics of the National Economy], *Sborník věd pravních a státních*, Prague 1917, pp. 274-300, 1918, pp. 29-55. J. Loevenstein, *Velká teleologie. Konstrukce hospodářské noetiky* [Comprehensive Teleology. Model of a System of Economic Noetics], Prague 1933.

5 O. Weinberger, Der Relativierungsgrundsatz und der Reduktionsgrundsatz - zwei Prinzipien des dialektischen Denkens. Eine logisch-methodologische Studie, *Rospravy ČSAV*, 75/H. 5, Rada SV, Prague 1965; the same, Dialektik und philosophische Analyse, in: E. Topitsch (ed. with P. Payer), *Logik der Sozialwissenschaften*, 10., revised edition, Königstein/Ts. 1980, pp. 278-309.

ferring a conception of mutual effects.[6] I have been unable to accept the largely repressive Marxist conception of the law resulting from the theory of the class-struggle in both state and law.

For some years, especially during the second world war, I thought a great deal about the fundamental problems of the normative logic. In retrospect I greatly value the fact that I was not able to draw on a specific training in logics for my reflections at that time; it meant that I was able to analyse the problems without bias and without being weighed down by the prevalent views. At the same time, the fact that I later engaged in the study of logic (gaining even the *venia docendi* for this subject) was of equal importance for my intellectual development. I was then able to work with a certain professional competence in the field of normative logic and to base my advocacy of the potential existence of and need for this logical discipline on theoretically founded arguments.[7]

In view of the fact that the entire structural theory of the law is based on norm-logical connections my view of the need for a genuine normative logic to exist side by side with the logical systems of the descriptive language represents the aspect of my approach to jurisprudence that integrates all others.

Under the influence of the methodological distinction between *de lege lata* and *de lege ferenda* considerations I have called for two areas of the normative logic to be evolved in order to deal with two kinds of substantiating relations within which norms exist: (i) the theory of the structure of norms and of norm-logical inferences, (ii) the norm-logical theory of substantiation (which has to elucidate the form of these argumenations).[8]

My first and, in my view, my crucial step toward normative institutionalism was achieved by the realization that we have to distinguish clearly between regarding the norm (a) as an ideal entity and (b) as a social fact.[9] Logical relations and norm-logical deductions can only be dealt with in the realm of ideal normative entities. The social existence of norms, on the other hand, has to be regarded as a sociological fact which can be indentified only empirically. This juxtaposition of the two approaches to norms leads to the task of explaining the nature of the social existence of norms and the functions norms have in social reality. Normative institutionalism tries to provide an answer to this problem.

---

[6] O. Weinberger, Rechtstheorie jenseits von Idealismus, Realismus und Materialismus. Ein Plädoyer für den normativistischen Institutionalismus, in: K.A. Moltnau (ed.), *Materialismus und Idealismus im Rechtsdenken. Geschichte und Gegenwart, ARSP*, Supplementa No. 31/1987, pp. 16-26.

[7] O. Weinberger, *Die Sollsatzproblematik in der modernen Logik*, Prague 1958; republished in: the same, *Studien zur Normenlogik*, Berlin 1974, pp. 59-186.

[8] See O. Weinberger, Zwei Bereiche der Normenlogik, in: the same, *Studie zur Normenlogik* (Czech), Prague 1960, German version in: Studien zur Normenlogik und Rechtsinformatik, *op. cit.*, p. 17 ff.

[9] O. Weinberger, Die Norm als Gedanke und Realität, *ÖZÖR* 20, pp. 203-216 (English version "The Norm as Thought and as Reality", in: N. MacCormick/O. Weinberger, An Institutional Theory of Law, *op. cit.*, p. 31-48.

Where these problems are dealt with explicitely this happens as a rule under the heading "legal validity". None of the current theories of validity appeared satisfactory to me. I rejected the theory of the fundamental norm on the basis that the existence of a social reality cannot be proved sufficiently by mere assumption, and the approach of legal realism was unacceptable because it excludes or, at least, suppresses the normative element. The introduction of natural law as an element in the substantiation of validity in the manner of various theories concerning the justification of legal validity appeared to me to be inappropriate on account of the fact that it is possible for an "immoral" law to be valid due to the vagueness of the moral criteria for the substantiation. Only the functional connection between the norm and social processes and institutions appears to me to be a suitable criterion to determine the validity of social norms.

The normative institutional conception took shape when I encountered and examined *Searle*'s theories. *Searle* undertook the much-discussed attempt to prove on the basis of analysing promises - of the promissing-game, as one might say - that ought-conclusions can be derived from purely descriptive premisses.[10] He returned to the problem in his book "Speech Acts"[11] where he demonstrated that the deduction of the ought-conclusion can be inferred from the constitutive rules of the promissing-game. In doing so he himself has, in my view, provided the crucial argument for the refutation of the proof he offers for his claim that "ought" can be inferred from "is". Despite the fact that they also take the form of definitions in the promissing-game in a certain sense - constitutive rules comprise, in fact, the general norm "Anybody receiving the promise from person *P* that *P* is going to do *A* has the right to demand from *P* that *A* ought to be done". Consequently, we are not dealing with the deduction of an ought-consequence from purely indicative premisses. From the critique of *Searle*'s theory I moved on to the more general question what kind of connection there is between institutions and norms (or practical informations in general). These investigations resulted in normative institutionalism. In sharp contrast to some other institutional theories which tend on the whole to be anti-normative in their approach normative institutionalism advocates the thesis that institutions always contain a core of practical informations.[12]

The substantiation of this conception rests on action-theoretical reflections. I regard action as behaviour determined by information; the nature of the action reflects the structure of the information processes determining the action. The processing of the information determining the action inevitably contains descriptive as well as practical informations. Institutions as frameworks for

---

[10] J. R. Searle, How to derive "ought" from "is", *The Philosophical Review* 1964, pp. 43-58.

[11] J.R. Searle, *Speech Acts. An Essay in the Philosophy of Language*, Cambridge 1969.

[12] D.N. MacCormick/O. Weinberger, *An Institutional Theory of Law: New Approaches to Legal Positivism*, Dordrecht/Boston/Lancaster/Tokio 1986; German version: the same, *Grundlagen des Institutionalistischen Rechtspositivismus*, Berlin 1985.

action, therefore, necessarily comprise practical informations, especially normative regulatives.[13]

At the same time as developing the normative conception of the institutions I have presented a conception of the theory of action which was motivated by other problems in addition to those arising from legal theories. I have described it as the "formal-finalist theory of action".[14] This theory of action and the normative theory of the institutions are closely bound up with each other.

My approach to the problems of the theory of action was determined by two factors[15]: (i) as a logician I was very critical of attempts to substantiate principles of justice on a purely formal basis; (ii) as a result of action-theoretical considerations I came to the conclusion that our actions are always determined by considerations of utility as well as of justice, and that the analysis of justice has essentially a critical function; it is not its task to present social-political programs, or to come up with generally applicable criteria for social justice - as *Rawls* believes.[16]

ACKNOWLEDGEMENTS

I should like to express my thanks to my colleagues, Professors Dr.Dr. Peter Koller, Dr. Alfed Schramm and Dr. Peter Strasser for their help with the corrections of the book, to Mrs. Gabriela Taucher for her care in the preparation of the German manuscript. My thanks also go to the *Österreichischen Fonds zur Förderung der wissenschaftlichen Forschung*, which has funded part of this work and supported the publication of both books (the translation as well as the original edition) and to the *Landesregierung of Steiermark* for providing financial support for the translation. The translation into English was undertaken with great care and sensitivity by Dr. Christiane Brown and by Mag. Christine Peutsch-Moore. It incorporates some preparatory work by Dr. Ruth Adler and Mrs. Anne Bankowska. I wish to express my gratitude to Dr. Dorothea Mayer-Maly for the extraordinary care, skill and knowledge she proved in preparing the camera-ready manuscript of this book.

---

13 O. Weinberger, Eine Semantik für die praktische Philosophie, in: R. Haller (ed.), *Beiträge zur Philosophie von Stephan Körner, Grazer Philosophische Studien* 20, 1983, pp. 219-239.

14 O. Weinberger, *Studien zur formal-finalistischen Handlungstheorie*, Frankfurt a.M.-Bern/New York 1983.

15 O. Weinberger, Analytisch-dialektische Gerechtigkeitstheorie. Skizze einer handlungstheoretischen und non-kognitivistischen Gerechtigkeitstheorie, in: I. Tammelo/A. Aarnio (eds.), *Zum Fortschritt von Theorie und Technik in Recht und Ethik, Rechtstheorie*, Supplementary vol. 3, 1981, pp. 307-330; the same, Jenseits von Positivismus und Naturrecht, in: *Contemporary Conceptions of Law - 9th World Congress (Basel 1979), ARSP* Supplementa, Vol. 1, Part 1, pp. 43-56.

16 J.R. Rawls, *Eine Theorie der Gerechtigkeit*, Frankfurt a.M. 1975 (Engl. original 1971).

A. THEORETICAL BASES

I. ELEMENTS OF INSTITUTIONAL LEGAL POSITIVISM

1. THE ONTOLOGY OF NORMATIVE INSTITUTIONALISM

Ontology is usually regarded as a philosophical discipline with the task of representing the major categories of being. The modes of existence as well as the fundamental relations between different categories of objects. In principle it is conceived of as an identifying discipline with the task of characterizing what exists in itself. *Nicolai Hartmann*, for instance, takes this view ascribing to ontology the tasks of acquiring knowledge of being as being, of defining the different modes of being and of revealing their relations.[1] In this way it is possible to achieve the kind of categorisation of observable objects expressed in *Hartmann*'s layer-ontology (or, in complete analogy, in *Popper*'s Three Worlds Theory[2]). In contrast to these identifying object-metaphysics and to the categorisation of objects I should like to advance a different conception of ontology which emphasises the stipulating character of ontology. The ontological principles and categories are entities which determine the fundamental framework of our world view or of certain disciplines by stipulation. In the spirit of criticism this conception of ontology is based on the view that our cognition and cogitation take place necessarily within a framework of fundamental structures and that the experiential material is shaped, processed and categorized in accordance with this system of fundamental structures. *Kant*'s tenets accepted these forms as necessarily *a priori*; by contrast, the - as one might say - neocritical conception postulates the possibility of establishing a variety of frameworks of our thinking and understanding.[3] Nevertheless, the fundamental critical thesis insisting that our thinking and our cognition always take place on the basis of a metaphysical-ontological conception remains valid. Consequently we are faced, on the one hand, with the task of defining an appropriate ontological framework - a typically philosophical task -, and on the other hand, with the need to acquire and process experiential material on the basis and in accordance with the structure of ontological systems.[4] Such a conception of ontology as the task of providing a

---

[1] Compare the classical characterization of ontology by *Nicolai Hartmann*: "It is the first and foremost concern of ontology to clarify the question of 'being as being' in the broadest and most general sense, as well as confirming the reality of being in principle. This is the fundamental concern of ontology. In addition, there is the secondary problem of the modes of being (reality and ideality) and their relations to eachother." (N. Hartmann, *Der Aufbau der realen Welt*, Berlin 1940, p. 1)

[2] K.R. Popper, On the Theory of the Objective Mind, in: the same, *Objective Knowledge. An Evolutionary Approach*, Oxford 1973 (first published in 1972), pp. 153-190.

[3] Compare St. Körner, *Categorical Frameworks*, Oxford 1974; the same, *Experience and Theory. An Essay in the Philosophy of Science*, London/New York 1966.

[4] The question is left open at this point whether it is possible to return to *Kant*'s conception by way of a metaontology, as it were, by uncovering common (and, therefore, necessary) traits of every possible ontology. One result of reflections of this kind is the thesis proposing that cognition always requires a metaphysical and ontological framework and that thinking means

fundamental framework for cognition, thinking (in the realm of cognition and application) on the basis of stipulation is in a sense also related to the ideas of constructivism.[5] In that case the definitions are, however, to be understood as dependent on cognitive situations, practical tasks, in short, on the world and on the *conditio humana*. This dependence expresses itself in the demand for the construction to prove itself in this task and to be tested by being corroborated in this way.

The kind of ontology which I have in mind is an ontology of communal beings with the capacity to act. The structure of cognition is of the kind that allows cognitive insights to be applied to processes of deliberation preparatory in actions.[6] Cognition is, therefore, directed to the strictest possible objectivisation (not to be replaced by group-consensus) as well as striving for causal knowledge on the basis that the determination of means and methods (programs) assumes knowledge of causal relations and laws, the validity of which implies not only a statistical summary of prior experiences but also a general applicability transcending experience and facts, i.e. a validity for the future and validity not only for factual processes but also for potential ones. One might, in this context, use the term *epistemological primacy of practice* demanding a structure of cognition of the kind that renders possible in principle its application in the realm of action. The objects of our consideration are not only observable objects and systems, their trajectories of behaviour and their regularities understood as objectively as possible, but also the institutional elements of our world view. We are not just dealing with the actual world as a system of physical objects but also with the different realms of ideal entities as institutional and cultural components of the world we live in. The world we inhabit does not only comprise objects in the positivist-reist sense but also institutional and cultural structures; furthermore, - and this appears to me to be of particular importance - in our view of the world objects in the sense of physical objects which in principle can be perceived either directly or with some assistance acquire the character of institutional objects, institutional relations or institutional facts in addition to their physical existence. A chess-board, chess-figures are objects that can be described in physical terms; but they are also institutional objects, things with an institutional function whose role in a game - a system constituting a framework for possible actions - is characterized by rules. The objects of our experience have their place in our image of the world not only according to their physical properties; they are also defined according to their institutional attributes, depending on their function in our environment. In other words: ontology perceives objects not merely in their brute-fact-relations, but it represents a world view comprising among its elements institutional facts, too.

---

an operation within a structural framework by which empirically or otherwise posited, possibly postulated data are processed.

[5] Compare for instance H. Grimm/A. Mohler (eds.), *Einführung in den Konstruktivismus*, München 1985.

[6] Compare the following reflections about the structure of information-processes determining action as well as Ch. II "Towards a Formal-Teleological Theory of Action".

From its evolution-theoretical point of view comparative ethology has proposed the thesis that every living being develops forms of cognition which enable it to live in its biological niche.[7] The structure of the world has evolved in such a way as to constitute a relatively adequate basis for the life of each organism. From the point of view of evolutionary theory cognition and cogitation appear necessarily as instruments for the control of behaviour or action since this is the only way of explaining that they were able to evolve in an evolutionary process. Evolutionists and ethologists, therefore, advocate the epistemological primacy of practice as the inevitable consequence of their approach. Equally it is self-evident to the human ethologist that human thinking has the task of performing information-processing operations in the course of determining actions: it has, therefore, not only a role in the processes of cognition but also in the processes determining action: it is in equal measure theoretical and practical thinking. Human ethology is in this respect in accord with the key conceptions of normative institutionalism. The ethologist also points out, in fact, that man as a being living in groups lives and acts in an interplay of individual activities and communal relations. These relations can be grasped only, however, with the help of an institutionalist conception based on a certain institutionalist ontology. Its concrete form depends on the way the theory of action is conceived. In any case, one thing is certain - and in this ethology is in agreement with the normative theory of the institutions. The human view of the world does not only consist of descriptions of behaviour trajectories and insights into their regularities; it also comprises practical informations and the determination of institutional facts; and human thinking moves in ways that are necessary for operations determining our actions.

2. THE LANGUAGE OF PRACTICAL REALMS

Action is behaviour governed by information. The information-processes determining and governing actions can be distinguished from other information-processes by specific characteristics. As a first approximation - and expressed in the common language of every-day life - one might say that action is behaviour controlled by the will, i.e. behaviour determined, above all, by goals and purposes. In view of the fact that a scientific analysis cannot rely only on the immediately experienced familiarity with the phenomena of volition the implications of this statement can be explained, however, precisely by expounding the information-processing operations corresponding to the will.

---

[7] One of the fundamental ideas of evolutionary epistemology is this: The realm and structure of our cognitive faculty, i.e. the faculty to absorb and process informations which contribute to the preservation of life are constituted in a way that is specific to the respective species. Compare K. Lorenz, *Die Rückseite des Spiegels. Versuch einer Naturgeschichte menschlichen Erkennens*, München 1973; the same, *Vergleichende Verhaltensforschung. Grundlagen der Ethologie*, Wien/New York 1978. Ch. Weinberger, *Evolution und Ethologie. Wissenschaftstheoretische Analysen*, Wien/New York 1983; G. Vollmer, *Was können wir wissen?* Vol. 1: Die Natur der Erkenntnis, Stuttgart 1985.

It is a characteristic feature of these information processes - in other words, of the thinking which determines actions (or practical thinking) - that two fundamentally different kinds of information of totally different meaning occur in them which we might describe as 'theoretical' ('descriptive') and 'practical information'. This aspect is shown up even by a simple analysis of the structure of action-determining information processes. It appears that action is possible only if the subject of the action is in possession of certain factual informations, above all: informations about the situations wherein an action is to be realized; informations about nomic causal relations (be they determinist or stochastic); an understanding of the procedures for solving certain technical tasks (programs, know-how). Furthermore, the control of the course of action requires information about the intermediate results achieved by the realization of an action (feed-back). The entirety of descriptive informations, however, does not provide a sufficient basis for the processes determining action: in addition to the descriptive (cognitive) informations informations expressing an attitude to the different cognitively ascertained possibilities of action have to be taken into account, because the determination of action consists of a choice between possible alternatives of action. It is only if we have goals in view, only provided we take into account informations concerning values and preferences or/and norms of behaviour for the information-process, that it is possible to establish an information process capable of determining actions. We can conclude, therefore: *actions - and consequently all practical spheres - depend on theoretical and practical informations*. The language applied to these areas (including the respective scientific and philosophical disciplines) must provide means of expressing both kinds of information, as well as comprising theoretical and practical sentences, and it must distinguish clearly between these two categories of sentences. We refer to this kind of language as to one based on *epistemologically differentiated semantics*.

In the following the practical sentences will be characterised briefly in comparison with the theoretical, i.e. declarative sentences.

(i) The crucial difference in their meaning lies in the fundamentally different pragmatic function of the two kinds of sentences. By theoretical sentences we understand sentences describing objects. We endeavour to adjust them to the world, in other words, to achieve such declarative sentences as correspond to the facts of the world. We adapt the theoretical sentences to the world by applying processes of verification and adaptation. The situation is different in the case of practical sentences: norm sentences, sentences expressing purpose, preference and value standards. They have the pragmatic function of determining directly or indirectly the kind of world we want and the way it is to be changed and shaped through action. This difference between the pragmatic function of the theoretical and practical sentences is closely related to *Searle*'s juxtaposition of assertive acts of speech (descriptions, assertions, statements) with "word-to-world direction of fit" and directive and commissive acts of speech (directives, commands, requests, promises, vows), in the course of which "world-to-word direction of fit" takes place.[8]

(ii) Practical sentences are in principle relative to a system. A normative sentence is regarded as part of the normative system. A preferential sentence expresses a relative evaluation from the point of view of the subject (of a system). Purposes are the attitudes of a system, not objective facts which might be valid irrespective of the subject's volition.

However, the fact that they relate to systems by no means that practical ideas, 'ought', purposes, evaluations, preferences etc. are not to be conceived as intersubjectively understandable or that they cannot be treated rationally as intelligible and communicable thoughts (in the non-psychological sense).

The fact that they relate to a system makes it possible for practical sentences (such as 'ought'-sentences) to be valid in one system while they have no validity in another one.

While logical incompatibility (for instance, between the 'ought'-sentences '*p* ought to be' and 'non-*p* ought to be' may also exist between the practical sentences of different systems; the simultaneous presence of incompatible practical sentences (e.g. ought-sentences) is a logical deficiency in the case - and only in that case - that these sentences are posited as appertaining to one and the same system.

(iii) Practical sentences don't have truth values in the sense in which declarative sentences have them. They cannot be proved by experiment and observation; they cannnot be tested against the reality of the world. Their substantiation is always dependent on other postulated (accepted) practical sentences (possibly in connection with cognitive knowledge): *there is no such thing as the purely cognitive substantiation of practical sentences*. This, at least, is the non-cognitivist thesis, which, however, does not by any means preclude other than purely cognitive substantiations of practical theses. Experience, too, that is, evaluating experience, can be integrated into practical substantiations. It is possible, for instance, to prefer hypothetically, i.e. in advance of the moment of choice, object *A* to object *B* (for instance, this apple to that pear) and to test this relative evaluation (by tasting both apple and pear).

The epistemologically differentiated semantics also affect the constitution and analysis of concepts. Concepts, too, are gnoseologicallly differentiated. They can be purely descriptive concepts or have a normative, evaluative character, or they can be mixed concepts.[9] It is the task of philosophical analysis to clarify the epistemological character of concepts.

---

[8] J.R. Searle, *Intentionality*, Cambridge et al. 1983, p. 7; the same, A Taxonomy of Illocutionary Acts, in: the same, *Expression and Meaning*, Cambridge et al. 1979, pp. 1-27.

[9] Ch. Weinberger and O. Weinberger, *Logik, Semantik, Hermeneutik*, München 1979, p. 108 ff., p. 183 f.; O. Weinberger, *Rechtslogik*, 2nd ed. Berlin 1989, p. 374 ff.

3. THE LOGIC OF PRACTICAL THINKING

Human-ethological, action-theoretical and methodological considerations converge in the view that cogitation is not restricted to the realm of cognition but affects in its function the entire field of rational information processing. In the sense of the primacy of practice, i.e. of the principle that cognition serves action, the acquisition of knowledge and the purely cognitive thought processes appear as subordinate to practice (in the philosophical sense). Knowledge and science with the related purely cognitive thought processes can be seen as separate areas to be considered independently in order to achieve the highest possible degree of objectivity.

Logic as a theory of thought structures and formal operations has - in terms of intellectual history - developed as a theory in the field of cognition; for about 2000 years it has been dealing almost exclusively with sentences capable of conveying the truth and with deductive relations with descriptive members (premisses, conclusions).

In essence two factors have prevented the idea of developing logical systems for action-related thought-processes:

(i) the system-relativity of practical sentences;

(ii) the impossibility of ascribing truth values to practical sentences in the same way as it is possible to describe declarative sentences as true or false.

Deduction (inference) is - according to the traditional conception which is concerned purely with cognitive sentences - a formally necessary way of determining the truth of the conclusion in dependence on the truth of the premisses. By this we mean a conditional and formal dependence which is independent of the actual truth of the premisses: it is logically impossible (on the basis of formal relations, i.e. for every conceivable model of the form of the members occurring in the deductive relation) for the conclusion to be false (i.e. not true) provided all the premisses are true (whether they are de facto true or false being irrelevant of course). The determination of the truth of the premisses - as long as they are not true as tautologies in every possible world - rests on an objective relationship to the world, that is, on the facts that the states of affairs presented in the premisses are actual facts. Many thinkers regard the objectivity of this relationship determining the truth as the basis for the validity of the logical deductive relationship. There is, however, no reason to assume that the deductive relations depend on the existence of an objective basis of the premisses. In logical calculi the truth is something like a counter in a game which is not based on the existence of the objective relationship between the factual situation as it is described by the sentence and the respective reality. Nobody doubts the validity of deductions in possible worlds, the possibility of a logical theory of contra-factual deductions, or the validity of deductions based on assumptions.

The objective validity of the entailment relation is based on the relations between premisses and conclusions determined by their linguistic structure; for this relation there is, however, no need for the positing of the premisses to be objectively founded. Nor is an objective basis always present in the declarative-logical realm or in the deductive process undertaken in the descriptive language. The fact that practical sentences are system-relative and, therefore, do not possess an objective basis, does not preclude the possibility of deductions with practical sentences as their members.

The conflict between the traditional concept of conclusion (inference, deduction) in the field of logic which is defined as truth relation, and the validity of deductions with practical members was expressed as early as in the nineteen-thirties by *J. Jörgensen* in his famous dilemma.[10]

If one accepts the usual definition of inference and of the inability of normative sentences (imperatives) to be true then there is no such thing as inferences with normative members. However, this definition conflicts clearly with the practices of life and with the normative sciences which have no doubt about the validity of normative inferences.[11] In view of the fact that not only our practical experience of life suggests the validity of certain normative inferences but that they can also be substantiated theoretically and constructively a suitable conceptual generalisation of the inference concept will have to be agreed on. This could, for instance, be realized in the following manner:

Stipulation 1: Sentences are either declarative sentences or normative sentences. (Compound sentences consisting of both descriptive and prescriptive clauses may also be taken into consideration, but the rule that compound sentences belong clearly to one or the other sentence category always applies.)

Stipulation 2: The 'positing' of a sentence means:

(a) its truth if the sentence is a declarative sentence;

(b) its validity (within a certain system) if the sentence is a normative sentence.

We are now ready to introduce the definition of the extended inference concept which can have deciarative as well as normative members.[12]

A sentence C is the consequence of the premisses $P_1,\ldots P_n$precisely when it is logically impossible for C not to be posited if all premisses $P_1,\ldots P_n$ are posited.

For the conceptually extended inferences two meta-theoretical principles apply which can be described as *'postulates of non-inferability'*. They represent demands which must be accepted in the light of the epistemologically differentiated semantics, in view of the fact that there could be no categorial distinction between the two types of sentence if normative sentences could be logically inferred from declarative sentences (or vice versa). These postulates

[10] J. Jörgensen, *Imperatives and Logic*, Erkenntnis (1937/38), pp. 288-296.

[11] Hardly anybody doubts, for instance, that the premiss "Everybody ought to love his neighbour" leads to the inference "Franz Müller ought to love his neighbour" (provided that Franz Müller is an element of the universe that corresponds to "everybody".

[12] In the case that all the members of the inference are declarative sentences the new concept of inference coincides with the traditional one.

which must be complied with by every normative system of logic can be defined as follows:

(1) No informative normative sentence can be inferred from a class of purely descriptive premisses.

(2) No informative declarative sentence can be inferred from a class of practical (especially normative) premisses.[13]

As a result of the thesis of non-inferability (1) leading to the conclusion that there is no normative conclusion to declarative premisses it is possible to define a norm-logical deduction as an inference that results in a normative sentence as a conclusion (which can be the case only if there is at least one practical sentence among the premisses).

It must be our next step to introduce a system of structures for normative sentences and an appropriate definition of the norm-logical incompatiblitity of normative sentences as well as rules for norm-logical deductions. In doing so we are presenting a genuinely normative logic with a structure that has to be substantiated by philosophical and methodological reflections.[14] There is a real possibility that structural analogies with other systems (i.e. with modal logical systems) may emerge; the forms and rules of other systems are, however, no criterion for measuring the correctness of analogous rules in the normative logic.

Elementary normative sentences are formed by a normative operator and a description of a state of affairs as its argument. It is advisable to start from two fundamental normative operators: an 'ought'- and a 'may'-operator. 'Ought'-sentences alone can exert a regulative function (since 'may'-sentences do not exclude any alternative of behaviour) 'ought' is the basic notion of every normative system. 'May'-sentences have merely a secondary function: they express a restriction or cancellation of an ought.[15]

There has to be made a distinction between open and closed normative systems; it is only in the latter that the rule: 'What is not forbidden is permitted' applies, provided we assume the system to be logically consistent. Strong and weak permission has to be differentiated, too. p is strongly permitted if it has

---

[13] The imposition of this restriction to informative conclusions is necessary considering that descriptive language allows tautologies as non-informative sentences to be added to any system of sentences without changing its informative content. Tautological inferences can be deduced from any - even the empty - class of premisses. In analogy the same can be postulated for normative sentences. Non-informative normative sentences can, for instance, take the form of '$(p \vee \neg p)$ ought to be', or 'If $(p \wedge \neg p)$, then q ought to be' (as it is impossible to fulfill the condition, no actual 'ought' can ever be inferred from such a normative sentence).

[14] O. Weinberger, Versuch einer neuen Grundlegung der normenlogischen Folgerungstheorie, in: W. Krawietz et al. (eds.), *Argumentation und Hermeneutik in der Jurisprudenz, Rechtstheorie* (1979), Beiheft 1, pp. 301-324; see also Ch. Weinberger/O. Weinberger, *Rechtslogik*, 2nd ed., op. cit., Chap. 10.

[15] In open normative systems they can under certain circumstances resolve the uncertainty about whether something is prohibited or permitted. This is also why they are used to state freedoms.

been explicitely permitted or even obligatory; *p* is weakly permitted if no prohibition of *p* exists in the system.

The incompatibility of normative sentences must not be based simply on the definition of the contradiction in the descriptive language; it has to be defined specifically: '*p* ought to be' is incompatible with 'non-*p* ought to be'; incompatible are also '*p* ought to be' and 'non-*p* is permitted'.[16]

Compound normative sentences are formed by means of norm-forming functors which, of course, are not truth-functors; they are defined by rules of inference applicable to them. In this way the functor of conditional norms can be defined as follows:

(i) by the norm-logical rule of separation "From 'If *p*, then there ought to be *q*' and '*q*' follows '*q* ought to be' ";

(ii) by the rule: "If *p* ought to be' is valid and '*q*' is true, then it follows that 'if *q*, then *p* ought to be'" is also valid.

The rules of inference are first introduced for ought-sentences by the following reflection: To an ought-sentence corresponds a class of duties. From ought-sentences posited as premisses exactly those ought-sentences can be deduced as consequences which express a subclass of duties stated by the ought-premisses.[17] Only then inferences for permitting-sentences are introduced. From '*p* is permitted' those permitting sentences can be inferred which exclude the same class of ought-contents or a subclass of this class of ought-contents. If '*C(p)*' denotes the class of the consequences of '*p*', then the prohibition of every element of *C(p)* is excluded by the permitting sentence '*Pp*'. From the permitting sentence '*Pp*' every permitting-sentence 'Pp_i' can, therefore, be inferred, if 'p_i' is an element of *C(p)*. These remarks about the consequences of ought- and may-sentences can, of course, determine only the general concept of this theory of inference; other rules have to be taken into account, too, such as, especially the norm-logical rule of detachment as well as rules arising from the relations between normative operators.[18]

Different ways have been used in the attempt of getting to grips with the problems of the normative logic by applying the logical systems of the descriptive language, above all by the use of analogies with the systems of modal logic.

---

16 Here 'permission' is conceived of as 'strong permission' in view of the fact that it would be *ex definitione* out of place to speak of weak permission of non-*p* if *p* is commanded.

This is not the place to discuss the somewhat more complicated questions concerning the incompatibility of complex normative sentences, especially of normative conditionals. The reader will find a discussion of these questions in the works referred to in ftn. 14.

17 Caution is required in the case of the inner complexity of 'ought' (duties). If the ought-sentence '$(p \wedge q)$ ought to be' is valid, then there is a duty to fulfill the bracketed expression. This can doubtlessly only be done if *p* comes into existence. It would, however, be a mistake to regard *p* on its own (without *q*) as a duty. See also the critical comments in the text (p. 26) with reference to the standard systems of the deontic logic, which accepts inferences of this kind.

18 For instance the rule "From '*p* is commanded' there follows the inference '*p* is (strongly) permitted' ".

Without much success. The so-called 'standard-systems of the deontic logic' are discussed most widely.[19]

They are problematical in various ways: They treat the deontic sentence as a kind of declarative sentence. They employ sentences expressing 'ought' ('may') as arguments of truth-functional functors. They hesitate between two forms of expressing the conditional normative sentence: 'If *p, q* ought to be' is represented by $'p \rightarrow Oq'$ or $'O(p \rightarrow q)'$. In my view neither of these forms is adequate, nor is the deontic logic capable of representing conditional normative sentences, because it is impossible to perform this task on the basis of a truth-functional logic. The deontic standard logic recognises conclusions which, in fact, are invalid.

1. *Ross*'s paradoxon, according to which 'post the letter' $('Op')$ leads to "post the letter or burn it" $('O(P \vee q)')$. If the command stated in the premiss is not fulfilled, than a duty arises which can be fulfilled by the behaviour *q*, wherein *q* can be any kind of behaviour - even *non-p*.

2. From $'O(p \wedge q)'$ $'Op'$ and $'Oq'$ are inferred which is contra-intuitive. For instance: from the normative sentence 'Keep the window shut and play the piano' one cannot infer the normative sentence 'Play the piano'. If a conjunction forms the content of a command then the coexistence of the parts of the content is ordered; not so, however, in every case the continued existence of the individual parts. The command 'Play the piano' cannot be extracted from the conjunction of the two normative contents. If the other part of the conjunction is not fulfilled, the playing of the piano may even be prohibited, i.e. apart from the norm we have considered 'Leave the window shut and play the piano' it is possible for another norm to be valid at the same time: 'If the window is not shut you must not play the piano'.

In conclusion of this section I should like to add, that other logical systems of practical thinking also have to be developed (especially formal teleology, the logic of preference and the logic of values).[20]

4. WHY DO I CONCEIVE OF THE THEORY OF ACTION AS FORMALIST AND WHY AS FINALIST?

My conception of the theory of action is formalist in two respects:

(i) it characterises action as an information-processing operation which can be applied to any subject - not only to psychophysical persons -, provided these subjects are capable of carrying out the respective transformation of the information;

(ii) it rests on a theory of finality (teleology) which defines the teleological thinking in formal terms based on the given concept of causal rela-

[19] I am assuming the reader to possess, at least, a vague knowledge of the standard deontic logic. If necessary he will find basic information on the subject in the works referred to in ftn. 14.

[20] See O. Weinberger, *Rechtslogik*, op. cit.

tion; this concept of teleology abstracts from goal-contents and preferences which apply in concrete systems.

It is, in my opinion, necessary to relate the concept of action not only to psychophysical subjects of action, considering that man and human society are constituted in such a way that other, institutional subjects of action, as one might say, also exist. There is collective action, there are actions undertaken by corporations and realized by their organs. Actions can be performed in the name of and in accordance with the purposes of somebody else. Actions undertaken by a proxy or curator for the person being represented and in accordance with his interests obviously cannot be regarded as mere modes of reaction by a living being. Phenomena of this kind are only conceivable if the action can be based on a rationalised process, and the theory of action can explain these relations only if it is conceived as a theory of formal information-operations on the basis that in their case the thinking determining the action has to be an information-process which can be interpreted as inter-subjectively understandable.

A theory of action to be used in jurisprudence and in the social sciences has to be conceived of in formalist terms as it is only a theory of this kind that can be applied to the actions of non-psychophysical persons and of explaining the nature of actions performed by organs or by proxies.

Neither can the psychology of the actions performed by human individuals be developed on the basis of generalising the results of introspective and extraspective observations. Instead, it ought to proceed by modelling the relevant process. While being able to use the general structure-theoretical constructions of formal teleology it must, of course, also determine the respective data relating in the context which are necessary for the application of formal teleology in an empirical context. It has to ascertain the actual purposes, preferences and other determinants of action in concrete terms since only then is it possible to explain action by modelling the structure of ideal processes involved.

The possibility of achieving a structural theory of finality by generalising concrete volition appears impossible if for no other reason than for the fact that purposes and preferences constantly vary being dependent on the rhythms of life (the needs vary cyclically being dependent on the rhythm of the individual's development). A comprehensive theory of the relations between purpose and means and of the way we make choices cannot be gained by an analysis of factual volition. Furthermore, teleology is clearly an idealisation even as a result of abstracting from other determinants of decisions and actions than purposes, this is the way to achieve manageable schemata of teleological considerations and of choice directed by purposes. The psychological reality of the acting individual, by contrast, is a conglomerate of divers determinants of action which cannot be perceived separately in the observable phenomenon of actions. The actual processes of selection undertaken by a person often procede according to pragmatically simplified methods which do not correspond accurately to the structure of teleology. That is a further reason why the structure of formal teleology cannot be deduced from the actual psychological process.

The reason for something being a suitable means for a given purpose, lies in the fact that it brings about a factual situation which fulfills the purpose.

Consequently the teleological or purpose-means relationship is dependent on causal relations. The choice between possible means is determined by a relative evaluation, e.g. by prefering one possibility to another. The mechanism of these operations which constitute the essence of teleological thinking can be depicted as a particular kind of information-processing operation. It follows that such a theory can be applied to teleological considerations as well as to the interpretation of purposes underlying the action.

The idea of a structural theory of teleological thinking is, of course, nothing new. *J. Bentham, A. Schopenhauer, K. Engliš, N. Hartmann*[21] - to mention only a few - have made major contributions to this theory. It has to be said, though, that the theory of teleology is in danger of being misinterpreted: (i) sometimes it is presented as a mode of interpreting events, as an alternative to the causal explanation as it were;[22] (ii) frequently it is conceived psychologically as a description of specific phenomena of consciousness; (iii) it is understood as a purely ideal way of schematising rational actions at the exclusion of the question of structure and of the explanation of factual and extra-rational actions.

In my view formal teleology[23] is a rationally based theory of relations and operations of practical thinking which does not offer an alternative to the causal explanation of the world, no more than it is a theory for certain phenomena of consciousness. Neither does it constitute a theory of idealised (rational) action in the sense that it might describe the correct way of deciding and acting which man's real actions ought to aspire to as to an ideal; instead, it provides a schematisation founded on causal relations which finds application in the theory of action. In the context of a series of further reflections it is not to be regarded merely as a system of postulates for rational decisions and actions but as a fundamental schematisation of the analysis of action in general.

The central role of the theory of action has by now become largely established in the general consciousness; in order to characterise the outlines of my conception, i.e. the formal-finalist theory of action, I want to place some of its points into contrast with other conceptions of action.

---

[21] J. Bentham, *Introduction to the Principles of Moral and Legislation*, ed. by J.H. Burns/ H.L.A. Hart, London 1970 (1780); A. Schopenhauer, *Über die vierfache Wurzel des Satzes vom zureichenden Grunde*, Rudolstadt 1813; K. Engliš, Nástin národohospodářské noetiky (Abriß der volkswirtschaftlichen Noetik), *Sborník ved právnich a státních*, Prague 1917, pp. 274-300, 1918, pp. 29-55; the same, *Malá Logika* (Short Logic), Prague 1947; N. Hartmann, *Teleologisches Denken*, Berlin 1951.

[22] *Aristotle*'s theory of entelechy is of this kind. In the modern theory of science many regard teleology as a method of explication rather than the structure of the deliberation preceding action. See, for instance, W. Stegmüller, *Wissenschaftliche Erklärung und Begründung (Probleme und Resultate der Wissenschaftstheorie und Analytischen Philosophie, Vol. 1)*, Chap. 8, Berlin/Heidelberg/New York 1969; compare also O. Weinberger, Teleologie und Zeitablauf. Gleichzeitig eine Kritik an Wolfgang Stegmüllers Begriff der formalen Teleologie, *Rechtstheorie* 13 (1982), pp. 285-302.

[23] It is discussed in greater detail in Chapter II of this volume.

Every theory of action has to attempt, at least, to find answers to the following questions:

(i) What distinguishes action from other forms of behaviour?

(ii) Is action connected with the concept of freedom of action, and how are we to explain freedom of action or the determination of action?

(iii) How is the content of a person's action to be explained? What is the explication of the notion of motivation and of the realization of the decision leading to action?

(iv) How are we to interprete the influence exerted on actions by the relations between individual and society?

An outline of the answers given by the formal-finalist theory of action in comparison to other proposed possibilities might facilitate the access in this theory for the reader and - as I believe - make certain advantages of my conception plausible.

To (i): Action contrasts strongly with other modes of behaviour by organisms or other systems. But the question is this: in what way? While various factors are cited the question, which one is, in fact, the crucial factor remains open: is it the fact that it is deliberate, directed towards a purpose, controlled by norms, or that it involves free decisions by those performing the action, etc.? In my view, what is vital for the determination of the concept of action is the fact that action is determined and governed by a process of information which evaluates descriptive informations, doing so specifically from the point of view of practical informations in the role of selective functions. The fact that it is (sometimes) conscious is an additional element not a primary and constitutive characteristic of action.

I have the impression that two tendencies are confronting each other in the realm of the theory of action: one characterizing action primarily as purpose-orientated, the other, regarding it above all as rule-determined behaviour. The formal-finalist theory of action considers the teleological structure as fundamental and as a constitutive component for the concept of action. At the same time it regards fixed and habitualised forms of action and the effect of rules as constituent parts of the mechanism which determines actions. The role of these elements can be made clear on the basis of a primarily finalist explanation of action. The rules themselves can be explained by way of their purpose-function; they can be substantiated or their changes justified by teleological observations.

To (ii): In a certain sense freedom of action appears to be a constitutive characteristic of the concept of action. If it were only a question of characterizing the behaviour of a subject there would be no need to introduce the concept of action. If, on the other hand, action is seen as more than an observable trajectory of behaviour, and if action is regarded as behaviour that is determined by a special information-process, this information-process must, in fact, come into play as determination of the choice between alternative possibilities of action. Action can occur only where there is scope of action, where the subject is faced with the opportunity of choosing between different continuations of the trajectory of behaviour. On the basis that there is such a forking of the trajectory of behaviour into alternative possibilities of behaviour the choice of which is decided by the information-process, freedom comes to constitute a conceptual pre-condition of action. It is precisely the intervention of an information-process as a factor in the cognition of the scope for different actions (potential alternatives of behaviour and of programs of action) and as a factor in the determination and the realization of actions that constitutes freedom of action.

While this conception constitutes an argument for the existence of freedom of action it does not imply an indeterminism in the stronger sense. It does not regard man as *prima causa* of his actions because the information-process determining the action itself is determined by existing factors, namely: by knowledge, as well as by practical informations resulting from social influences and relations in addition to the personal attitudes of the acting individual. For the observer insight into the information system of the acting person and the factors determining the information-process remains very fragmentary. Consequently, prognoses about the nature of future actions are possible only to a limited extent.[24]

To (iii): A certain active attitude on the part of the system to which the action is ascribed always forms the pre-condition of action. Every living being contains within it some kind of activity; by analogy the same applies to social systems. This activity is reflected in the habitualised patterns of behaviour and finds expression in a rationalised form in purposes and relative values wherever action has to be taken. The information-process which, in my view, is always involved in actions does not cause the action, it only determines the content of the action, i.e. it channels the current of given activities into specific directions.

From this point of view it is possible also to throw light on the traditional controversy about the nature of the motivation of action. In speaking of motives we mean whatever it is that determines action, i.e. what we can specify by way of explanation for the subject's way of acting. As a rule motives are considered as something linked to a purpose; an indication of the purpose pursued by the acting person, his intention (pattern of this explanation '*S* has done *A* in order to ...), or a need which has had the effect of an incentive, these are common types by which motives are defined. There are, however, also somewhat different explanations of the 'Why?' of an action; for instance: '*S* murders *A* from jealousy'; here 'jealousy' does not really name a purpose but is the attribute of the elements of one class of purposes. The definition of the jealousy motives (= 'from jealousy') covers different goals, intentions and states that are aspired to: the goal of ridding oneself of the rival; of taking revenge for an (imaginary) humiliation; ...

The word 'motive' is used in the sense of 'explanatory reason for the action', or, instead, in the sense of 'teleological reason for the action'. It is merely a terminological decision whether we choose the narrower or the wider

---

24 Compare O. Weinberger, Freedom, Range for Action, and the Ontology of Norms, *Synthese*, vol. 65, No. 2, Dordrecht 1985, pp. 307-324; the same, Determinismus und Verantwortung, *Zeitschrift für Philosophische Forschung* 34, pp. 607-620 (also in: the same, *Studien zur formal-finalistischen Handlungstheorie*, Frankfurt a.M./Bern/New York 1983, pp. 115-136.

definition. What is crucial is that we understand clearly that teleological motives represent the core of the motivation while other additional determinants also enter into consideration, in particular autonomous and heteronomous norms.[25]

The key to an acceptable conception of motives is to be found in the insight, that the question dividing causalists and intentionalists is posed in the wrong way.[26] Explanation of action is, in fact, *interpretation* of motives, i.e. an attempt to reconstruct rationally and to comprehend the information-process determining the action. Motives are, therefore, essentially interpreted purposes. Consequently the interpreting explanation is not just concerned with determining the *(one)* purpose but it also involves the reconstruction of the teleological deliberation, wherein frequently several purposes occur simultaneously and preferences come into play.

From this point of view neither the causalists nor the intentionalists are right. Motives (i.e. interpreted purposes) are not observable states corresponding as conditions to the antecedent of causal laws but teleological informations. Neither are they, however, something evoking the action on the strength of its logico-semantic nature - as assumed by the intentionalists. What causes the action is the current of the subject's (the acting person's) activity which is organised in such a way that this activity transforms itself into real behaviour by means of an information-process.

To (iv): In the formal-finalist theory action is regarded as determined by an information-process linked to the subject. This connection with the subject's system of purposes conflicts by no means, however, with the view that human action depends on the relations between individual and communities as well as social institutions. These connections exist on different planes and, as a result, have to be seen as an interaction.

Habitualised patterns of behaviour and the purposes pursued by the individual are shaped not only by his inner, biologically determined needs, but to a large extent also by imitating the behavioural patterns of other individuals.

Actions take place in an institutional framework; the scope for action and to some extent the evaluation of possible alternatives of behaviour are socially determined. Action is often interaction between several subjects or it is collective action; the acts of the individual are circumscribed by norms of behaviour, and they are determined by expectations in respect of the behaviour of other individuals or of communities.

Social systems of norms intervene in the determination of actions; they exclude certain potential means of reaching stated goals, and they act as

---

[25] I would tend to use a narrower definition of the concept of motivation, mainly because the difference of opinion about the nature of this concept between the causalists and the finalists is only concerned with the concept of motivation in this particular sense.

[26] A useful explanation of this position is to be found in G.H. von Wright, *Explanation and Understanding*, London 1971: "For reasons of convenience I shall describe as *causalists* those who believe it possible that intention is - in the sense of *Hume* - the cause of behaviour and as *intentionalists* those who consider the connection between intention and behaviour as being conceptual or logical in nature."

determinants influencing the mode of action in addition to utilitarian considerations determined by purposes.

In my opinion, the action of the individual is determined by the interaction of purpose-orientated utalitarian considerations and at the same time by moral convictions, common interests, consideration for the fellow human being, for the various partners of role-relations as well as for the community as a whole form the content of moral principles; in terms of their function these have to be regarded, therefore, as an expression of the way in which aspects of the community are taken into account in actions.

5. COMMENTS ON THE DEFINITION AND THE SYSTEMATICS OF INSTITUTIONS

1. The institutional thesis of the inevitable connection between the institutions and the social existence of norms has been largely accepted in the discussions on my theory in the same way as the demand resulting from the institutional theory for a functional analysis of social institutions. What has been almost consistently queried, however, are the following three points: (a) the absence of a clear definition of the concept of the 'institution', (b) the demarcation of the realm of the institutions, and (c) the necessity of providing a clear classification or typology of the institutions.

I have, at times, countered, these objections by protesting that it is by no means always necessary to begin with a precise definition of those phenomena which one intends to deal with in philosophical analyses. While I still believe this view to be correct that does not alter the fact that there comes a point when it becomes appropriate to take steps to create conceptual clarity by way of appropriate definitions. In defending my theory I have, furthermore, pointed out that the term 'institution' describes a family concept in the sense it was used by *Ludwig Wittgenstein* which cannot, therefore, be defined in the classical manner *per genus proximum et differentiam specificam*. This defence of my theory, too, makes correct claims; however, after careful consideration I do not regard them as sound in view of the fact that the inner differentiation of family concepts as well as the concatenation of the subsumptions constituting them have to be discussed and clarified if they are to be used in philosophical analyses. This has not been done so far for the concept of the institution.

I shall have to attempt, therefore, to name the key characteristics of the concept which have induced me to use the term 'institution' as a fundamental concept for investigations into the social sciences and jurisprudence. We need to establish a factual and theoretical reason for using such a complex family concept. The linguistic assertion that the term being applied in different contexts assumes different meanings is in itself no convincing argument for working in our scientific analysis with concepts combining all the extravagant symbolic applications of the word.

Let us consider *Wittgenstein*'s famous example in the "Philosophical Investigation" where he introduces the idea of the family concept using the example of the word 'game'.[27] The crucial question is this: Can such a family concept be used as a scientific concept? It is clearly possible to have a scientific theory on the nature of game and such a theory can use a complex and ramified concept of game which would have to be characterised by some kind of typology or/and partial classifications. Phrases using the term 'game' as a mere metonym - like e.g. in German 'das Spiel des Lichts'- have to be excluded from the conceptual meaning covered by the word 'game'. By analogy the same applies to the demarcation and characterisation of the concept of the institution: a variety of things can be subsumed under this concept provided the different kinds of things can be proved to belong together and that these various objects belonging to the realm of the institutions are systematised to a certain extent.

The concept of the institution is intended to circumscribe our field of study in such a way as to make it possible to comprehend and explain human action as an interaction of the willing, doing and permitting of individuals with social factors and within the conditions of a common cultural framework. To employ such a concept of the institution makes sense, of course, if and only if this interaction between individual and society actually takes place and is such that it forms the necessary precondition for comprehending the existence and the functioning of both phenomena - that of the individual and that of society. And a second factual element has to be considered as a prerequisite to the determination of the concept of the institution: that is the social fact implied by the very term 'institution', namely that the phenomenon of institutionalisation can be found in every society. Whatever occurs as pattern of behaviour, mode of action, role relations or invented ('construed') systems of actions or interactions (as, for instance, a game, or a social institution, the use of a place for a flea market) has - under certain circumstances - a tendency toward institutionalisation: it stabilises in its form and assumes the character of a social fact with relative stability and individual existence and evolution; it becomes a pattern which contributes to the shaping of the way of life. And finally the determination of the concept attempted here and the typification of the institution will be based on the fundamental conception of my theory, in particular on the following theses:

1. The law, social structures and political events must be analysed from the perspective of the theory of action.

2. Actions, social institutions and every kind of institutional fact possess a core of practical informations; they can be comprehended only if these practical informations are grasped.

3. Human existence being the life of a communal being with the capacity to act is a process of interaction between individual and society; psyche and behaviour of the individual are functionally dependent on his relations in the community, while the functioning and the dynamics of the social institutions and their structures can be explained only by taking into account the creative influence of the individual.

---

[27] L. Wittgenstein, *Philosophical Investigation*, Oxford 1953, No. 66 ff.

Our definition of 'institution' - like any explication of a concept[28] - must satisfy two requirements: firstly, it has to refer to an established linguistic usage, sharpen and correct it, and secondly, it must constitute a useful means of representing the theory being advanced.

For our reflections about the generally accepted meaning of the term in the terminology of the lawyer and of the social sciences two different uses of the term 'institution' are relevant:

(a) We refer to the different institutions of the law like property, marriage, will, bail. (In German the terminology of scholars in Roman Law also uses the term 'Institut' in this sense.) It is all but impossible to define this concept of the institution clearly, but one thing is certain: it always refers to a factually and functionally interconnected complex of legal norms. *D.N. MacCormick* has attempted to characterise this concept of the institution more closely by distinguishing between three kinds of norms determining a legal institution: institutive, consequential and terminative rules.[29]

(b) By the term 'institution' we understand different types of social structures or establishments. *Hauriou* divided the institutions (in this sense of the word) into person-institutions and object-institutions. It is not entirely certain, however, whether this dichotomy fully exhausts the realm we are interested in of the socially established framework of action and of the institutional realities. I am not sure, for instance, how games, how money (as far as it is as part of the banking-system and not already clearly defined as part of an object-institution), how a black market in wartime would be accomodated in *Hauriou*'s scheme.

The problem we are facing is the question, whether there are convincing reasons for defining legal institutions in the sense of (a) and institutions in general in the sense of (b) by a common concept. I do believe, that such a procedure would be well-founded. There does not appear to be a clearly drawn distinction which must not be infringed between normative institutions and institutions in the sense of structures and public utilities and both are functionally linked with each other. Marriage is a normative institution; it is also a social structure - an object-institution -, comprising both persons and objects. Is it possible to consider games - i.e. football or chess - as nothing but normative institutions, in other words, as systems of rules characterising the game, or is it appropriate to regard them also as social institutions? Furthermore, a comprehensive conception of the notion of 'institution' is supported by the fact that both norms and functional interrelations of facts come into play in both areas - according to the normative institutional theory, at least. As complexes of norms the legal institutions are linked to an actual whole on the strength of their connection with an existing factual sphere or one being constituted by these norms

---

28 R. Carnap, *Meaning and Necessity. A Study in Semantics and Modal Logic*, Chicago 1970, p. 7 f.

29 D.N. MacCormick, Law as Institutional Fact, in: O. Weinberger/D.N. MacCormick, *An Institutional Theory of Law. New Approaches to Legal Positivism*, Dordrecht et al. 1986, pp. 49-76.

and they are institutionalised as social practices; object-institutions consist of a fusion of norms and realities (persons in institutional roles and objects with functions determined by norms). Both have, in fact, the same ingredients as it were.

Before attempting a definition I should like to discuss the problems concerning the limits of the concept of the 'institution'. Should the concept of the institution be introduced as a clearly delineated concept or as a concept with vague boundaries? One can be of the opinion that only what is socially established and relatively stabilised can be regarded as an institution. From this point of view a framework of action established explicitely or tacitly in individual cases would not be an institution. I would consider it more advisable, though, for reasons of research tactics to include in our considerations also *ad hoc* frameworks of action (like the rules and factual realities of a game played by a group) as a kind of institutions. Such rudimentary institutions which often show a tendency to stabilise should also be regarded as institutions. In doing so we shall find it easier, I believe, to get to grips with the development, the transformation and the destabilisation as well as the destruction of institutions.[30]

Institutions are framework-systems of human action. They have a core of practical informations. In the sense that they consist of an ordered system of practical informations which is effective in conjunction with psychological and social facts and events they are always complex objects. The system of practical informations can - but does not have to - exist in the form of an explicite formulation. If it serves in effect only as rule, guideline or/and standard of action without having been specifically formulated in a deliberate linguistic form the scientific analysis can make it its task to represent in explicite form the actually effective (socially existing) norms, value-standards and purposes.

I consider it advisable to start from the basic differentiation of the institutions into:

(i) normative institutions and

(ii) real institutions

(It is appropriate to assume this basic distinction despite the possibility that the difference may actually be caused by the approach.) What is of interest to us in the case of the normative institutions - like, for instance, a legal system, a legal institution, a professional code (such as a doctor's) - is the system of practical informations, while the established system of norms and the connection with social processes and institutional realities are useful to us merely as criteria for the determination of the actual existence of the system. In the case of the real institutions the practical informations form the nucleus, as it were, around which the institutions crystallize.

The system of practical informations can be structured in different ways. Usually it is a system of normative rules in conjunction with a complex of purposes, value standards and preferences. Depending on the circumstances the system evolves to different degrees, sometimes more as a complex of abstract

---

30 Transformations of institutions are frequently caused, for instance, by *ad hoc* arrangements taking a hold in an established institution.

principles, goals or maxims, at other times as a number of behavioural and empowering norms. The governing ideas determining the functional direction of the institution have their place among the fundamental practical informations.[31]

In order to make the general explication referred to above more intelligible some additional remarks about the concepts of 'framework-system of action' and 'practical information' are called for. Where I am referring to a 'framework-system' I am pointing to the fact that the institution is a condition for the determination of actions but that it is, as a rule, not sufficient on its own to determine the action and to provide the basis for the mode of action.

The rules and realities of the game of chess determine the possibilities of the actions of the game as well as certain duties (which arise as a result of the game being entered into with a partner), without determining, however, the actual moves of the game. The decision about how to act depends on the decision of the player who makes his choice from the class of available moves. It is important to point out that the selection of the move (of the program of moves or of a section of the program, i.e. of a three-move combination) is determined by a different type of rules, namely the strategic rules of chess. By analogy the same applies to actions within the framework of other normative systems. Legal rules and legal institutions constitute only a framework for the actions of a person. The purposes pursued by a person, their preference and the rules of the successful procedure (obviously in relation to the purposes and preferences) determine the actual decisions and the actions taken. It is the complex of practical informations and the respective institutional realities that form the framework in detail. The practical informations consist above all of normative rules which occur mainly in three functions: as rules of behaviour, as empowering rules and as socalled constitutive rules. Rules of behaviour are generally conceived as conditional ought- or/and may-regulations. Empowering rules determine positions, roles and competences within the framework of the system. A characterization of the constitutive rules is more difficult as the nature of these rules is interpreted in various ways. *Searle*, for instance, places them in contrast to regulative rules. "Regulative rules regulate an activity already in existence, an activity whose existence is logically independent of the rules. Constitutive rules constitute (and also regulate) an activity the existence of which is logically dependent on the rules."[32] The historical point of view, the criterion of the already or not yet existing practice, has little impact on the nature of the rules, that is, at least, neither on their semantic nor on their logical character. In introducing the formulation of the regulative rules in the form of an imperative *Searle*, moreover, appears to approach, at least, the view that these regulative rules have essentially a normative meaning, while the constitutive rules are defining and stipulative in character. The fact that the institutions and the rules determining them introduce institutional objects like, for instance, the chess-

---

31 *Hauriou* defines the governing idea (obviously only for the 'institutions choses') as "the idea of the work to be created"; compare M. Hauriou, Die Theorie der Institution und der Gründung, in: R. Schnur (ed.), *Die Theorie der Institution*, Berlin 1965, p. 35 ff.

32 J.R. Searle, *Speech Acts*, op. cit., p. 33.

board as the field of action for the game of chess, the law courts or traffic lights as realities of legal life[33] induces the mistaken conclusion that the rules on which institutions are based are definition-type regulations.

The framework of action, in other words, the institution according to my definition, frequently introduces objects, structures, positions and roles; it attaches names to them ('castle', 'judge', 'marriage', ...) as well as - and this is the key point - determining their functions in the respective institution by way of practical rules (norms, goals, preferences). The defined realities of the institution are important for the framework system of the actions but they form only a skeleton to be fleshed out by the development of the existing potentials for action. Not only the structural framework of the institution set by definition is constitutive for the institution but, to the same extent, at least, also the behavioural and the empowering rules (norms), the goals and governing ideas also contribute to its constitution.

The definitions of such institutional objects as the castle in chess or the traffic lights in the legal system have two defining constituent parts; they consist of: (i) a physical description of the institutional object (i.e. 'a body in the shape of a castle', 'an electrical installation with three lamps, one red, one amber, one green, arranged from top to bottom'; (ii) a functional characterisation stating the role of the object in the relations (particularly normative ones) determining actions.

Constitutive rules are consequently not a semantically separate type of rule, but a specific application of defining, normative, evaluative and purpose-determining rules.

The rules determining institutions differ also in another aspect: they may be precise and clear-cut and, within the system, exhaustive, but they do not always have those attributes. Whether or not a certain act (a certain move) in the game of chess is permissible can be decided on the basis of the rules; whether or not a sequence of English words forms a permissible English sentence, cannot always be determined with absolute precision.[34]

With reference to the typology of the institutions I should like to add just a few remarks. Having represented the institutions as a family concept there is no need for us to present an exhaustive categorisation of the institutions. Perhaps it would not even be possible to achieve this in the case of a family concept.

One important type of institution is represented by the person-institution. In contrast to the traditional juristic conception defining the person as a point of reference, as the subject of rights and duties, I should like to emphasise two aspects:

---

33 *Searle* says, for instance, on p. 51 f. of his book "Speech Acts": "Every institutional fact is underlain by a (system of) rule(s) of the form '*X* counts as *Y* within context *C*'."

34 *Snyder*'s remark that vague (not unambiguous) practical rules are also to be taken into account appears to me to be worth taking note of, although the question remains open whether it would not be possible to achieve greater accuracy in the definition of rules by closer analysis.

1. Persons are subjects of action. Consequently, it is not only the attribution of rights and duties that has to be normatively determined, but the way a person may act also has to be normed (this is done by empowering and accounting regulations).

2. Persons always come into being as institutional facts by the institutionalisation of certain normative rules. These rules don't necessarily have to be valid legal rules. The law has to decide normatively which persons capable of coming into being as social facts outside the law on the basis of their normative constitutive core are to be recognised as legal persons. (That means that collective persons, bodies etc. while not always having to be created by the law are always established by some kind of normative regulation.)

The institutions described by *Hauriou* as object-institutions ought to be divided into different types, in my view. Such a typology could only be undertaken, however, on the basis of a thorough study; that is why I cannot present it in this content.

6. SOME LEGAL-PHILOSOPHICAL IMPLICATIONS OF NORMATIVE INSTITUTIONALISM

Some of the consequences of my action-theoretical approach and of the normative institutional theory for the theory of law and for the determination of the tasks of jurisprudence are outlined briefly in the following:

1. *Legal norm and legal system.* The legal system is regarded as a complex of norms containing norms of different types: behavioural norms, empowering norms, normative standards, legal principles. According to the institutional conception the legal order cannot be understood and interpreted adequately unless it is perceived in the role it plays in setting up and determining institutions on the basis of norms. Legal norms are concerned with factual connections and personal relations; they can be grasped correctly only provided we don't just understand the behavioural instructions and the ought-consequences of the individual norm, but also take into account the actual-institutional context. The extent of our comprehension depends on how well we understand the governing ideas of the institution and of the general and specific purposes of the law or of the individual institution in question.

Our grasp of the legal norms must include insights into their functions - the jurist must always ask: How does the legal institution function as an institution? What is the effect on society of the regulation under consideration? He has to explain which spheres of action (scope of action for the individual) are created by the institution and its norms; what kind of role-interaction is permitted and intended (as well as having to determine which are actually to come into being). He has to reflect on the motivating effect of norms as well as considering the constellation of expectations on the part of the individuals involved in the institutions. Legal cognition - which I certainly conceive as understanding of normative content - must not cut itself off from the recognition of institutional facts as this recognition is indispensable for a proper understanding of valid norms.

2. *The Concept of Valid Law.* Valid law is defined as law that is in existence in the institutional sense rather than in the sense of legal realism according to which it is only the application of law, i.e. the actual judicial decisions that decides the actual existence of norms. The existence of norms means existence of normative entities; the criterion for the recognition of this entity cannot lie in the realization of that which ought to happen. It would, furthermore, be sociologically wrong to identify legal life with the taking of official judicial decisions. Only a fraction of legal processes occur in the form of official adjudication. Once stabilized, this does, on the other hand, exert a determining influence even on those legal relations which don't come before a judge. We are dealing here with the existence of normative entities (a kind of social existence). This existence is conceived institutionally: as factual influence in institutions, as functional ingredient in observable bodies and procedures. This normative existence is not constituted by the hypothesis of a basic norm (assumption of a basic norm) since the determination of facts cannot be based on assumption alone, or on mere hypothesis[35], but has to be based on ascertainable relations to legal institutions. Nor am I satisfied with the definition of legal validity by rules of recognition in the sense of *Hart*'s interpretation. Are the rules of recognition statements about a normative system, e.g. do they state observable characteristics by which we can know whether or not a norm is valid, or are they, instead, norms of the system determining the processes by which the valid norms are established? In the first case they are statements about existing normative practices, in the second case they are hardly distinguishable from empowering norms.[36] If I understand *Hart* correctly there is a fundamental relationship between the rules of recognition and the social practices actually in existence. The rule of recognition lays down practices and the acceptance of ought-rules on which they are based (cognitive conception of rules of recognition); however, if they are interpreted as a normative component of the legal system then they constitute the respective practices (or contribute, at least, fundamentally to their constitution). In regarding as an empirically ascertainable fact the view that the validity of the law is rooted in its practices *Hart*'s theory is in agreement with the institutional conception. In my opinion the actual roots of the validity of law are, in fact, even more far-reaching; they also embrace the entirety of institutional realities. It is not a question of which rules the judge and

---

[35] Even in scientific hypotheses the reason why they can be substantiated as statements does not lie in the hypothetical positing itself but in the fact that the statement is confirmed by a process of tests. The factuality of the order determined by a concrete hypothesis of the fundamental norm might possibly be taken into account as a criterion of verification although *Kelsen* like the other representatives of Pure Jurisprudence does not, in fact, use this possibility since this would make the validation dependent on sociological empiricism and thus destroy the "purity".

[36] In this case the process of determining the validity of a norm and of establishing or transforming a norm does not require two kinds of secondary norms - as *Hart* believes: the permitting norm functions as the basis for both: for the creation of the norm and as criterion of validity.

the government apparatus, in fact recognise (and therefore apply), but the judge and constitutional organisation themselves must be accepted as instituted by legal norms; and the government apparatus which functions in accordance with legal rules forms empirical proof of the real existence of order. *Hart*'s theory is rendered more precise - albeit still not entirely adequately so, in my view, - by the distinction between an external and an internal point of view for the consideration of the law. The valid legal rule has not only the character of a social custom (that is obvious even by observing it from the outside), but it functions as a norm; it has to be seen from the internal point of view where it assumes the role of laying down duties.[37] And for *Hart* the internal point of view is indispensable when considering the law. *Hart* is correct in as far as the behaviourist observation alone is unable to explain the law and legal life adequately; I would add: because they are institutions which cannot be grasped without comprehending their prescriptive meaning. I am of the opinion, however, that the alternative of "internal" and "external" point of view does not tackle the actual crux of the problem. What is relevant for me in this, above all, is the question of the normative (i.e. practical) core of the institution. The existence of the normative regulative is independent of the recognizance or the observation of the norm; also, it has to be acknowledged by being understood from both perspectives from which it might be considered: from the internal perspective of those who are beholden to the law and from the external perspective of any observer.

At this point it appears appropriate to me to introduce some remarks about *Georg Jellinek*'s famous theory of the normative power of the factual.[38] *Jellinek* conceives his thesis as a consequence of man's psychological tendency to accept established facts as the normal. What we are interested in is the question whether this theory can be reconciled with the normative institutional theory, or whether it conflicts with it. "The recognition of the normative power of the factual is of the greatest importance if we are to gain an insight into the development of the law and of morality. Initially the commands issued by the authorities of priesthood or state are simply complied with - be it from fear or from other motives; and, as a result, the belief grows that the frequently repeated command in itself and in isolation from its course constitutes - by virtue of its inner obligating power - a norm to be fulfilled *per se*, in other words, as moral norm." "For the people of any nation all law is originally nothing but factual practice. The continued practice produces the notion of the normative nature of this practice and the norm itself takes on the appearance of an authoritative dictate imposed by the community, in other words, of a legal norm. This conception also provides a solution to the problem of the Common Law. Common Law does not emanate from the soul of the people by which it is sanctioned, nor from the common conviction that something is law on the strength of its inner necessity, nor from a silent act of the people's will, but it arises from the general psychological human characteristic that regards the constantly repeated fact as normative." I do not think that this psychological inclination of regarding what

---

[37] Compare H.L. Hart, *The Concept of Law*, Oxford 1961, p. 86. ff.

[38] G. Jellinek, *Allgemeine Staatslehre*, Bad Homburg/Berlin/Zürich 1966, esp. p. 337 ff.

acutally happens as what ought to happen is the reason for the function of the factual, of accomplished facts etc. as a determinant of validity. The importance of this psychological tendency as a principle of explication is significantly limited especially by the possibility (which *Jellinek* sees, too) of making changes in what ought to happen, or, in other words: by the freedom man has of creating institutions and forms of life. It is a different aspect that is crucial. The factual element is an key element of institutionalism. It becomes an ought-standard if, and only if.

(i) the factual is conceived as having an institutional nature and a normative core, and further if

(ii) the factual practice has the character of establishing institutions or their elements.

Seen in this way *Jellinek*'s thesis accords completely with normative institutionalism.

3. *The Institutional Conception of Normative Dynamics.* To consider the legal system from the perspective of the normative dynamics is acceptable as an aspect of institutional legal theory, but legal dynamics are conceived in an entirely different way in this theory from their conception in *Kelsen*'s "pure" theory. The coming into being of legal norms is not a process occurring only in the system of norms; the substantiation of their validity rests equally on facts (that they have been established) and on already existing norms. That would appear to me to be a logically more correct conception[39], which is also closer to realistic observations. [*Kelsen*'s normlogical scepticism of his later period is not taken into consideration at all in this context, since I cannot imagine a dynamic conception at all on such a basis. How is one to substantiate dynamic processes if norms have no legal inferences (not even when factual premisses are taken into account)? How is one to define material derogation according to the *lex-posterior*-principle if no logical incompatibility between norms is acknowledged?[40]]

It also appears appropriate to me to consider this dynamics more from the perspective of content which would draw attention to the institutional impact of different factors at different levels. The various ways of determining the content - stacked one into the other by different instances from legislator to judge - constitute a certain idealisation which does not represent the institutional reality as it actually exists if one considers that the practice of judicial decisions mod-

---

[39] For the critique of *Kelsen*'s view that it is only the higher norm that forms the actual basis for the validation, without the additional facts required for establishing the legal norm see O. Weinberger, Die normenlogische Basis der Rechtsdynamik, in: U. Klug/Th. Ramm/F. Rittner/ B. Schmiedel (eds.), *Gesetzgebungstheorie, Juristische Logik, Zivil- und Prozeßrecht, Gedenkschrift für Jürgen Rödig*, Berlin/Heidelberg 1978, pp. 173-190; the same *Normentheorie als Grundlage der Jurisprudenz und Ethik. Eine Auseinandersetzung mit Hans Kelsens Theorie der Normen*, Berlin 1981, p. 130 ff.

[40] Compare O. Weinberger, *Normentheorie als Grundlage der Jurisprudenz und Ethik*, op.cit.; the same, Kelsens These von der Unanwendbarkeit logischer Regeln auf Normen, in: *Die Reine Rechtslehre in wissenschaftlicher Diskussion.* Referate und Diskussion des Internationalen Symposions zum 100. Geburtstag von Hans Kelsen (Wien 1981), Wien 1982, pp. 108-121.

ifies even the general legal rules, partly by interpretation partly by transformations on the level of the application of the law where the law is adapted to the altered social situation.

4. *Some Methodological Implications.* Many of the methodological problems appear in a different light before the background of my conception. The interpretation of the law becomes conscious of its social function, no longer restricting itself to historical arguments or to those of linguistic analysis; functional arguments concerning purposes come to the fore and can be expected to contribute to a more useful jurisprudence and judicial practice.

Gaps in the law are going to be considered as the vagueness of certain elements in the application of valid legal directives. At the introduction of a legal personality, for instance, there has to be a way of determining the manner in which legal acts attributable to this legal personality may come into existence. When an election is called it must be possible to determine the class of those actively entitled to vote and those passively entitled. Otherwise there are gaps as a result of valid norms not being realizable without additional normative determinations.

5. *The Functional View of the Law and Analyses of Justice.* One of the most significant effects of the normative institutional theory of law lies in the fact that this approach draws attention to functional analyses. Recognition of the law does not only imply that we understand the meaning of the legal rules but also that we have an insight into the impact of the law and an understanding of existing social institutions. As a result the area of investigation for the legal sciences is extended accordingly. Equally, jurisprudence must become additionally a theory of the organisation and effectiveness of institutions. The realm of legal politics necessarily also belongs to its field of interest. Obviously not in such a way as to assume the role of legislator but to the extent of revealing the functional relations, of examining the structures of argumentation in *de-lege-ferenda* considerations, of conducting discussions on values (without representing value standards as cognitive insights) and by taking on an advisory role in politics. I myself have made some attempts in this direction.[41]

The institutional theory also leads to a conception of the theory of justice which, in my view, is more to the point than the prevalent theories. It emphasises the largely critical function of analyses of justice and advocates the thesis that our actions and political decisions are in reality always determined by considerations of utility as much as of justice.[42]

---

[41] Compare Chapter VIII of this volume; also the paper "Institution, Organisation, Kontrolle" given by me in Salerno in 1985; also, "Reine und funktionalistische Rechtsbetrachtung", in: W. Krawietz/O. Weinberger (eds.), *Reine Rechtslehre im Spiegel ihrer Fortsetzer und Kritiker*, Wien/New York 1988, pp. 217-252; also, "Skizze einer funktionalistischen Theorie der Demokratie", in: J. Novak (ed.), *On Masaryk, Studien zur österreichischen Philosophie*, vol. 12, Amsterdam 1987.

[42] A more detailed account of my conception of justice can be found in Chap. X of this volume. I should like to point out, however, that my conception of the problems connected

7. WHY LEGAL POSITIVISM?

Those concerned with the legal theories of the institution partly advocate natural law (*M. Hauriou, G. Renard*), partly, they are positivists (*S. Romano*). I have to explain, therefore, why and in what way my conception is to be regarded as a positivist theory. The view adopted by many positivists claiming that social norms are created only as a result of explicite acts of will conflicts with the institutional theory. Consequently I reject such a view. Even more inacceptable to my mind is the 'act-relative positivism' (as it is advanced by *Kelsen* in his later theory) which recognises the existence of norms only where there is a real act of volition the content of which constitutes this norm.[43]

The term legal positivism means to me the conjunction of the following theses: (i) norms and values cannot be established in a purely cognitive manner - i.e. without taking voluntary decision (non-cognitivism). (ii) The regulatives on which the institutions are based are not *a priori* facts but man-made. (iii) In complex modern societies different social normative systems coexist. They have to be differentiated as a matter of principle, although they influence each other and contribute together functionally to a certain extent to the determination of actions. This is mainly a question of distinguishing between law and morality. (iv) In consequence of (iii) moral criteria cannot be used as conditions for the validity of legal norms. While the demand for the law to adher at least to a minimum of morality has to be made both from the moral and from the legal-political stand-point it would be wrong to make the validity of the law dependent on criteria of justification based on the content of the law.

Only by accepting (iv) is it possible to submit the existing law to a moral as well as to a legal-political analysis. We must not, in my view, assume without question and in every case that we have a moral duty to fulfil every legal directive; this duty is dependent on our personal moral evaluation of the law.

---

with justice in our own time is not only determined by the normative institutional theory but also depends on other convictions.

[43] See O. Weinberger, *Normentheorie als Grundlage der Jurisprudenz und Ethik*, op.cit., pp. 44-47.

II. TOWARDS A FORMAL-TELEOLOGICAL THEORY OF ACTION

1. STARTING POINTS

Theories can be regarded as instruments which allow us to master certain challenges. They arise when we are at a loss how to proceed in a given field of knowledge, action or thought, or if we do not understand things and their interconnections fully. We are looking for guidelines for action. We have not a clear insight into the field in which we are acting. At an advanced stage in our reflections we can at best pinpoint the problem or even define it.

I am convinced that the reader will find it easier to understand my theoretical conception if he has a clear understanding of the problem and the intent of the theory which I am advancing. In this section I would therefore like to draw attention to the elements which lead to the formal teleological conception of action based on formal teleology. What is at issue here are not the phases of the development of my theory of action, seen from an autobiographical perspective: it is rather my intention to give a short exposition of the fundamental ideas, insights and scientific challenges of this theory. The ordering of these different elements presents some difficulties as it is impossible to determine their relative importance or to rank them in any logical order.

(i) Man is an acting being. Almost all fundamental problems of philosophy are to be based on this basic anthropological characteristic: the way we look at the problems of knowledge, because the function and structure of knowledge can hardly be understood without taking into consideration their role for determining action; all questions of practical philosophy in the broadest sense of the term[1] are by nature dependent upon the explanation of the human capacity for action and the conception of action itself.

This may appear obvious, but it is of deep significance for the interpretation of important fundamental problems, especially for our understanding of the causal principle as the basis of empirical knowledge, and for the debate on freedom of the will as one of the essential philosophical problems of the practical philosophy.

(ii) The concept of action is often interpreted as a fundamental conceptual element of various current branches of learning - even of those not *prima facie* and traditionally viewed as sciences of action. This is the case for example for speech act theory as well as for sociology conceived as the theory of social action and of institutions (which are interpreted as frameworks for behaviour and

---

[1]According to Kantian tradition "practical philosophy" meant those disciplines which dealt with the problem of how to act correctly - i.e. with ethics and jurisprudence. Today a much broader concept of practical philosophy seems appropriate which encompasses all areas concerned with action, that is including axiology, theory of decision-making, teleology, economy, sociology etc.

action). It also applies to certain conceptions of economic theories, to the theory of norms, in which the concept of action is not only adduced as an element of the content of the norm but also as an element of explaining the essence and function of norms, and to jurisprudence (particularly in the normative-institutional conception[2]). Given the multiplicity of roles of the concept of action in such different scientific contexts, we have to ask ourselves whether the term 'action' is always used to mean the same thing, and whether 'action' in the psychological sense, that is in the ordinary every day sense, carries the same meaning as it does in different specialised contexts.

(iii) We understand such everyday terms as 'action', 'will', 'intention', 'end', 'motive' etc. We are acquainted with these expressions and other terms of the practical sphere: we are able to use them in meaningful sentences. Does this mean that we already master the notion of action and the associated thought processes in everyday life and are thus only faced with the task of revealing and expounding systematically this practical, implicit knowledge? I believe that this whole area is still in want of clarity, even if there exists an established linguistic practice which appears to function smoothly. The fact that we are so familiar with these expressions proves that they belong to everyday life: it does not, however, mean that the forms of expression commonly used in this area give a clear and adequate exposition of the relations and thought operations involved (this problem would have to be examined by a grammatical analysis of the deep structure of these terms). Our familiarity with these everyday expressions does not help us to solve problems of practical philosophy either. What does it really mean 'to act'? Does it only make sense to talk of the actions of individuals or should we also take into account collective or other forms of social action? Is the concept of action necessarily bound up with the notion of freedom of the will? What does 'freedom of will' mean? How can it be integrated into a scientific view of the world? Or is there perhaps no such thing as freedom of will? What does 'to will' mean? How is 'willing' related to 'knowing'? Is willing by definition a conscious process? What are purposes? What type of entities are they? How should the relations between ends and means be conceived of? What is the structure of teleology as a theory of thought operations? What are motives for action? How can they be recognised? How are 'accountability', 'responsibility', 'guilt' and 'evaluation of behaviour and action' to be reconciled philosophically with the theoretical conception of action? These are important questions which cannot be answered merely by reference to linguistic practice and our familiarity with the terms involved.

(iv) The well-known fact that there are widely differing theories of action in philosophical and scientific literature shows that a common sense conception is certainly not sufficient. Or was *Wittgenstein* perhaps right to say that philosophy and science merely bewitch our mind and create illusory problems in areas where common-sense understanding and ordinary language enable us to

---

[2]N. MacCormick/O. Weinberger, *An Institutional Theory of Law. New Approaches to Legal Positivism*, Dordrecht 1986, English translation of *Grundlagen des Institutionalistischen Rechtspositivismus*, Berlin 1985.

express everything clearly and to see things for what they are? It may well be that theoretical analysis occasionally produces pseudo-problems and obscures rather than elucidates the problems: however, in the present context it would be quite wrong to regard the basic problems of the theory of action as spurious and unimportant questions. If we want to conduct elucidatory rational analyses in the domain of practical philosophical thought, then we must not leave off where familiar linguistic practice or our common sense understanding take us: nor should we proceed from the philosophical-nihilist thesis that philosophical problems are only illusory problems.[3]

(v) I do not intend to give an overview of the problems and various interpretations of the theory of action. I shall instead introduce some of the main assumptions of my theory of action and, as it were, sketch a plan of how I will attempt to explain the concept of action. This preliminary sketch will show those already familiar with the relevant literature in which aspects my theory differs from others. For the reader who is less familiar with the subject, this brief outline will make it easier to follow the subsequent discussion.

I define action as information-dependent intentional behaviour. The explication of the concept of action thus rests largely on the characteristics of the information-processing operations which determine action. This leads to a constructivist rather than a phenomenal-analytical mode of exposition. My approach uses our knowledge about willing and acting, as well as about institutions and social relations. However, this approach is essentially derived from very general anthropological and epistemological theses and does not attempt to analyse and reconstruct everyday conceptions. I do not consider the usages of ordinary language about action nor the opinions of common sense as criteria by which to judge the adequacy of a theory of action.

I reject on principle the widespread view that acting and willing, intentions or motives are to be understood as phenomena of consciousness. Many theories hold that consciousness is an essential characteristic of willing, acting, intending, of teleology or goal-oriented acting (as opposed to teleonomy as mere appropriateness of behaviour or of the structure of organs).[4] Psychological experience shows that consciousness which may accompany operations or trajectories of behaviour can differ greatly in degree without altering their essen-

---

[3]Actually *Wittgenstein* himself devoted his life to analysing fundamental philosophical problems and attempted to resolve them by analyses of the relevant problem situation. Cf. O. Weinberger, Tiefengrammatik und Problemsituation. Eine Untersuchung über den Charakter der philosophischen Analyse, in: *Wittgenstein und sein Einfluß auf die gegenwärtige Philosophie, Akten des 2. Internationalen Wittgenstein-Symposiums* 1977, Vienna 1978, p. 290-297.

[4]Regarding the opposition of the concepts 'Zwecktätigkeit' (purposeful action) and 'Zweckmäßigkeit' (appropriate to purpose) cf. N. Hartmann, *Teleologisches Denken*, Berlin 1951; regarding the concept 'teleonomy' see E. Mayer, *Evolution und die Vielfalt des Lebens*, Berlin, Heidelberg, New York 1979; furthermore: Ch. Weinberger, *Evolution und Ethologie. Wissenschaftstheoretische Analysen*, Wien/New York 1983 (p. 90-125); Ch. Weinberger/O. Weinberger, *Teleonomie und formale Teleologie*, in: K. Weinke (ed.), *Logik, Ethik und Sprache. Festschrift für Rudolf Freundlich*, Wien/Munich 1980, p. 252-265.

tial structure. In my theory consciousness is regarded as something which arises under certain conditions - and which possibly fulfills particular tasks in specific situations -, it is, however, not a constitutive feature of action and does not characterise the essential nature of the operations which determine action.

I endeavor - in connection with the above - to treat the theory of action in a formalist, but not an empirical-descriptive manner. The theory therefore can be meaningfully applied also to those areas where due to the nature of the acting subject - e.g. a collective person - consciousness and a psychological process do not enter into consideration. Nevertheless, the theory aspires to serve as the basis for a psychology of action as well. I am of the opinion that a modern psychology of action has to proceed by a reconstructively modelling method, and this requires a formalistic theory of teleology. When using this theory for psychological analysis, attention will also have to be paid to the problem of consciousness as well as to the methodological problem of the relationships between self-observation, emphatic observation of others and observation of external conduct. The formalistic approach as I envisage it has the essential advantage that it aims not only at establishing a model for rational action, but that it is also open for explicating real actions including extrarational, even irrational actions as well as ethical determinants of actions and behaviour.[5]

The structural basis of the theory of action is founded on a formal theory of teleology and it is within this framework that the existence and the efficacy of norms as well as of extra-rational determinants of action is explained. This formalism becomes a theory of action only when the problem situations are taken into considerations as the context of the study of actions, and when it is made clear that actions are to be viewed from two essentially different perspectives. To both of them formal teleology is fundamental, yet under methodologically different aspects:

(i) The deliberation determining action: The information process - its core is teleological analysis - is used to determine action. It provides an appropriate analysis for the choice of the best way of action (in relation to the teleological system of the actor), or it controls action on the basis of feedback information.

(ii) The interpretation of motives: If we are faced with the task of understanding and explaining the behaviour of some person as this person's action, we have to elucidate the action by finding out his motives. This is always a process of interpretation.

We can, of course, look at action from yet other perspectives; the evaluation of conduct and actions in particular play a significant role in our daily life and in practical philosophy. It seems to me, however, that these additional reflections on actions are of secondary importance compared to the fundamental distinction between deliberation determining action and interpretation of motives.

---

[5]This is proven by the autobiographical fact that my first paper dealing with theory of action bore the title (indicating this fact) "Rationales und irrationales Handeln", (in: F. Kaulbach, W. Krawietz (eds.), *Recht und Gesellschaft. Festschrift für Helmut Schelsky zum 65. Geburtstag*, Berlin 1978, p. 59-89), and that this paper points out that a theory which solely models purely rational actions is very unsatisfactory.

2. COMMON-SENSE THEORY OF ACTION

It is hardly possible to make a sharp distinction between our everyday conception of action, which we could describe as common-sense theory, and other theoretical conceptions, because of the fact that certain elements of scientific theories enter successively into our general understanding. In general, common-sense theories do not provide an adequate basis for certain more subtle investigations which are necessary for philosophical consideration and the solution of practical problems. Common-sense theories present things in a simplified manner and as unproblematic (even though they are not unproblematic in the least). Finally, certain conceptual elements are tenaciously adhered to by everyday understanding, although they impede the construction of an effective theory.

The common-sense interpretation of action comprises essentially the following elements:

(a) Action is a succession of behavioural states in time.

(b) Action concerns a particular subject, a human being who realises the course of action (the behavioural process). What is meant by "to realise" is never examined by common-sense theory, whereas philosophical theories regard it as an especially difficult point which is in need of elucidation.

(c) The behaviour of the agent is viewed as the result of his volition. Acting is thus willed behaviour. What this means is considered to be clear enough as everyone understands what it means to will something. Volition is conceived of as a conscious process.

(d) It is well-known that action is dependent on knowledge, just as common sense knows that volition is dependent on knowledge and experience. However, a closer examination of these relations is rarely attempted.

(e) Action is set in some way in relation to freedom of will, basically because we as agents experience our actions in such a way that, if we do something, or abstain from doing something, we believe that we could have acted differently or not at all, if we had decided otherwise, i.e. if we had preferred to act differently.

(f) Common-sense - and to a lesser extent juridical analysis, although it, too, is essentially based on common-sense theory - sees a more or less direct connection between effecting something through action and the responsibility of the acting subject for the outcomes of its action. This view follows from the fact that the agent is usually aware that he could also have acted differently. This conception is obviously far too trivial to be of any use to ethics or jurisprudence.

(g) Common-sense theory contains only some rudiments of a definition of the content of action. A distinction is made between types of action (e.g. theft, letter writing, ...) and individual actions (that *N* has stolen this book yesterday). Individual action is on the one hand characterised by belonging to a type of action, and on the other by the fact that it is ascribed to an actor; it is furthermore individualised by space and time co-ordinates. The common concept of action does not offer a clear explanation of the content of an action nor a satisfactory explanation of the specific meaning of an action in a given context.

In my view, the main reason why it is impossible to use common-sense theory, as it were, as a starting point for a theory of action and to make it only more precise is that in the 'common-sense' interpretation of action terms such as 'volition', 'purpose', 'decision' are treated as if they were clear, exactly defined and generally comprehensible concepts. In reality, however, an explanation of action using the concept of volition is an explanation *per ignotius*. We know through experience what 'to will' means, although philosophically and structurally this concept is as unclear and undefined as the concept of action. In addition, certain implicit assumptions of the common-sense theory - in particular the concept of volition defined as a conscious process - greatly hinder the construction of a really elucidatory theory of action.

3. BEHAVIOUR AS TRANSFORMATION. DESCRIPTION OF ACTIONS. MEANINGFUL ACTIONS

Action is behaviour which is attributed to a particular subject, the agent (acting subject, actor). The description of action can be realised in two ways:

(i) as a description of the actor himself, the states in which he is, and the succession of these states in time;

(ii) as a description of the transformation of the object of action, on which the acts of the subject are realised.

These two modes of describing actions often appear in juxtaposition. They mean different things; yet they can often be linked in such a way as to make it evident that they are talking about one and the same situation, one and the same process of action, albeit from different perspectives. For example: '*S* aims at the hare and pulls the trigger of the rifle', is a description in mode (i); '*S* shoots the hare' describes the action by stating the effect of the action on the object of action - a description in mode (ii).

In both types of describing an action, what is at issue is an exposition of the behaviour of a particular system (of the agent or the object which is acted upon) as a succession of states in time.

The description of behaviour proceeds from a characterisation of the state of a system at a particular moment. This characterisation can be detailing features (attributes, relations to other objects), or parts (and their relations), and the parts can be described in turn by their features.

Behaviour, however, is not merely a static characteristic of a system; it can also be seen as a temporal series of states of the system. The transition from state S_1 at time t_1 to state S_2 at time t_2 is a transformation of the state of the system under consideration, provided that the rising index of t expresses the transition to a later point of time.[6] A chain of transformation is called a trajectory

[6]The temporal axis can be viewed as a continuum. Determining a course of behaviour (a sequence of states of behaviour) can be thought of as a series of states at disjoint points in time.

of states. $S_1, S_2, ..., S_i$ can be identical or different states. A transformation from S_1 to S_2, in which S_1 and S_2 describe the same state at different moments says that the present state of the system is maintained (identical transformation).[7]

The definition of the kind of action can take different forms - besides the differences following from the two methods just mentioned (description of the transformation regarding the subject; description of the transformation regarding the object), namely:

(a) The transformation can be described as the transition from state S_1 to state S_2; for example the action 'to open the closed window' 'to keep the soup warm' (= 'to effect that the soup which is warm at time t_1 is also warm at time t_2').

(b) The transformation can refer only to the final state which is effected by the action, for example the action of subject *N* 'standing'; the starting point, the initial state of the subject *N* is left open here.

If action is understood as a transformation of the type (a) the problem of the occasion for an action arises[8], because - to stay with our example - it is possible to open a window only if it was closed before. If we interpret 'to open the window' as a transformation according to (b), namely as a transformation from any state to the state of an open window, then the problem of the occasion for an action does not arise. If the window was already open, then this action can be performed as an identical transformation.[9]

Trajectories of behaviour can be simple transitions from one state to another, or more or less complicated chains of states of the system. This is not, however, a fundamental differentiation. An essentially different trajectory arises only when different results can occur at one or more points, because then the problem of feedback regulation enters into the theory of action.[10]

One and the same process (of behaviour) can be interpreted as a transformation in various ways and, therefore it can be characterised as an action in a variety of ways as well. When a subject *S* eats it stills its hunger, by one and the same process.

The agent's behaviour is often interpreted as 'meaningful conduct' and described accordingly. The behaviour 'taking off one's hat' is taken to be a form of 'greeting' and it is called so. One could think that the process is a fact in itself, the fact of the behaviour of the acting subject; and that in certain situations this fact assumes symbolic character, and that thereby the fact turns into the act of greeting. I think that this interpretation is not adequate. Behaviour of a certain

---

Approximation to the continuum can be reached by allowing for an unlimited refining of the time scale.

[7]This varying characteristic of action can apply to subject- or to object-related descriptions.

[8]Cf. G.H. von Wright, *Norm and Action*, London 1963, p. 37 *et passim*.

[9]Here, too, we can see a way how transformations of type (b) can - based on the structures - be transposed to type (a):$ES_1S_1S_2$ ('There exists such a state S_1 at the moment t_1 that state S_2 at the moment t_2 is a fact').

[10]See footnote 21 below, p. 64.

kind turns into meaningful behaviour by virtue of established institutions. The act (process) is performed with the intention of greeting someone. The meaning of a given behaviour, its being an act of greeting, is not something added to the process from outside, so to say as a secondary consequence; the behaviour is performed on the basis of and within the context of an existing institution. There are, therefore, descriptions of the behaviour 'greeting' as an institutionalised conduct which can be realised by different - and equally institutionalised - real, observable operations (i.e. various customary forms of greeting).

This result of our reflections provides an important insight: meaningful contents of actions are constituted as such through institutions. Meaning exists only on the basis of and within the context of institutions. Meaningful actions (meaningful behaviour) is an observable process, which can be described as transformation of behaviour which is perceived, understood and intended as action within the context of the institutionalised rules (or explicitely stated *ad hoc* stipulations).

4. SCOPE FOR ACTION AND FREEDOM

To say that acting is behaviour guided by information presupposes that the actor has - at least at certain moments - the possibility to choose among alternatives of behaviour. The definition of the alternative, which is realised, i.e. the path of the actual trajectory, must depend on information processing, or else one could not speak of an action as a behaviour determined by information.

How can the existence of alternative possibilities be reconciled with a causal world view, as I hold it? [11] This question can be dealt with in two phases:
1. independent of the analysis of the concept of action, we can ask in which sense and under which conditions one can speak of different possible states of a system;
2. we can treat the question by investigating how the concept of action is linked with the concept of the scope for action, and how the processing of information determines which alternative of behaviour is chosen to be actually realised.

The evolution of a system in time can be represented by a graph. Time is presented by the abscissa, and points on the ordinate are defined as states of the system. The trajectory of behaviour is then the line connecting points representing the succession of states of the system (fig. 1).

[11] See below, p. 54.

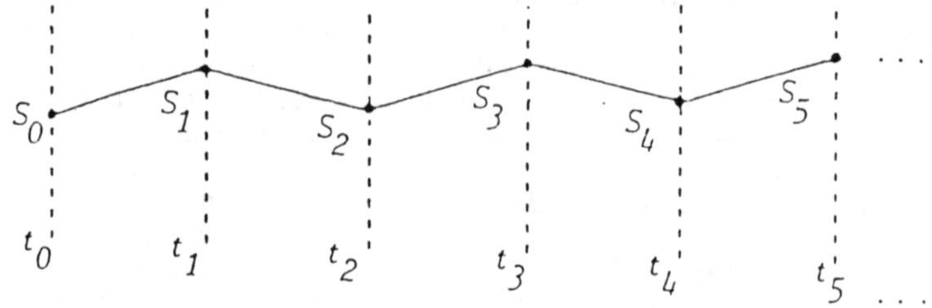

Fig. 1

Every system is at any given moment in exactly one state.[12] Why and under what kind of conditions can we speak at a certain point in time of a splitting of the trajectory into an alternativity of possible states? When can we speak of potential states of behaviour, i.e. when can we begin to consider a 'behavioural tree', a branched trajectory (fig. 2)?

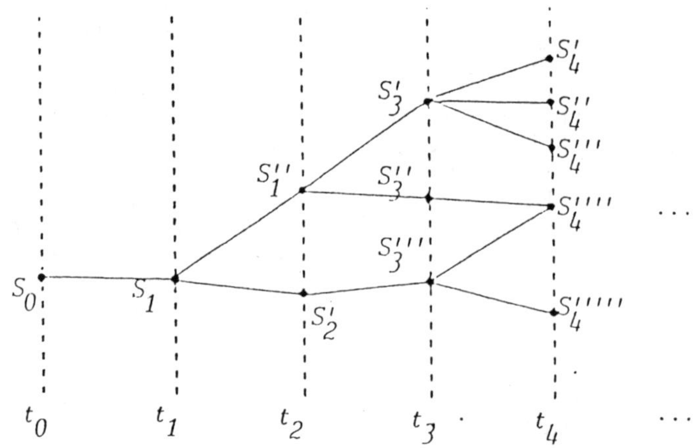

Fig. 2

The node S_4'''' shows that the concept of the "behavioural tree" allows for the possibility that a certain state can be reached by different routes. In the example of fig. 2 the different routes reach the node at the same time. Basically one and the same state can come about (be reached) by routes of varying lengths.[13]

---

[12]This assertion must be distinguished sharply from the question of being able to unequivocally establish the existence of a state at a certain point in time. It also does not express an empirical statement of fact, it is instead a prerequisite for any empirical knowledge. Therefore it is of no avail to cite *Heisenberg's* Uncertainty Principle as a refutation.

[13]The representation of the behavioural tree could express this fact so that different ordinates would be assigned to different states. The fact that S_i and S_j are the same states occurring at time t_i and t_j would be shown by them sharing the same ordinate.

In the perspective of a theological world view the branching could be interpreted as existing potentialities of the system, and God chooses to realise one of them; or a strictly indeterministic view of nature could regard the alternatives as objective characteristics of the real system, and on the basis of absolute fortuitousness exactly one of them will be realised. I reject such explanations of the tree structure of future behaviour.

The reason why the behavioural process appears to branch out into possibilities can be in my view the following:
(i) influences on the system (including varying constellations of its environment - they may be recognised or unknown);
(ii) incomplete knowledge of the system which allows for different continuations of the trajectory.

This lack of knowledge can be the result of insufficient observation or information, or if it can be a question of unknowability in principle. It could be, for example, an effect of certain modifications of the system which result from earlier influences and which cannot be noticed when observing the system in its present state, but which come to bear on the future behaviour of the system (cf. the phenomenon of memory).

Knowing the 'behavioural tree' comprises more information about the system than knowledge of the actual trajectory, because to know the possibilities of behaviour of a system caused by different inputs means to know more about the system than to know the series of its actual states. Dispositional attributes are part of those characteristics which are dependent on such different possible influences.

Let us turn now to the role of the behavioural tree (the life tree of the acting subject) within the theory of action.

1. The existence of a scope for action is, as already stated above, a constitutive condition of the concept of action. Are we entitled to assert the real existence of such a scope for action? It seems to me to be an indisputable fact of experience that we can behave differently - depending on our knowledge, our volition and on the basis of considerations and decisions.[14] It is also undisputable that we actually consider how to act, in order to reach certain goals for example, or to do justice to certain obligations. It is likewise empirically proven that knowledge (factual information about the situation, the causal relations and know-how) changes our behaviour (or can change it). From this follows that

---

[14]It is interesting that *Kant*, too, points out that practical freedom is proven by experience: "Die praktische Freiheit kann durch Erfahrung bewiesen werden. Denn, nicht bloß das, was reizt, d.i. die Sinne unmittelbar affiziert, bestimmt die menschliche Willkür, sondern wir haben ein Vermögen, durch Vorstellungen von dem was selbst auf entferntere Art nützlich oder schädlich ist, die Eindrücke auf unser sinnliches Begehrungsvermögen zu überwinden; diese Überlegungen aber von dem, was in Ansehung unseres ganzen Zustandes begehrenswert, d.i. gut und nützlich ist, beruhen auf der Vernunft." (I. Kant, *Kritik der reinen Vernunft*, hgg. von W. Weischedel, Bd. IV, Wiesbaden 1956, p. 675). His conception of freedom as causality through freedom, as freedom to act according to moral law is quite different from my concept of what constitutes freedom to act which I conceive of as the possibility of acting in essential dependence on information (see below).

our mode of action comprises - at least sometimes - alternative possibilities of acting differently. This proves two points which establish the basis of the theory of action:

(a) there exists *de facto* a scope for (possible) action, as we know from experience;[15]

(b) an information-dependent process determines (or contributes to determining) which alternative actions are chosen for realisation.

2. The scope for possible actions (and their complex, the behavioural tree) play a decisive role in the process of using information to deliberate actions and to control behaviour. The scope for action in this sense is not an objectively given fact, it is instead a constructed framework within which actions are thought up and realised. The life tree can be taken as representing symbolically the situation of the subject (or the sphere of objects of its actions); using this representation the subject develops its ideas of how to continue its life, viewing it as a field of alternative possibilities. They are those possible continuations of the trajectory, viz. those states which can be reached by the subject from its standpoint at t_0.

There exists an objective and a subjective aspect to what is possible as a future development given a certain situation. That means that there is, so to speak, an objective life tree (even if we are not able to trace it in detail) and a subjective one, which is drawn according to the ideas and beliefs of the subject. It can, of course, contain false ideas about the relevant relations; the subject can, for example, be convinced that it could make it rain by virtue of a special prayer or a magic formula. Even without mysticism there can exist false opinions, for example the idea of a man that his voice has the potential for making him an opera singer, or that his marriage to Miss N will mean the founding of a happy family. (Unfortunately such ideas often turn out to be illusions.)

Since achieving certain results depends on know-how (or, stated differently, on adequate programmes), it is sometimes the case that the construction of such a subjective life tree is in this regard a piece of invention.

The question which states are possible (attainable) in the future is of course dependent on the moment from which one looks at the tree. *N* cannot follow the news in Russian today, but he could if he had spent three years learning Russian.

There are various reasons why actions realised on the basis of an imagined behavioural tree yield results which diverge from the imagined, intended state:

α) The act (which is supposed to lead to the intended state) can fail. (I strike the match and it breaks.)

β) The causal relation which - according to the idea - should yield with a certain probability the intended result, led in this case to a different result. It is part of the nature of cognition based on probability that also the improbable result can occur. (I plant a seed, but it does not sprout.)

---

[15]The thesis that there exist scopes for acting does not imply searching for and defining such concrete areas.

γ) An envisaged alternative result can be based on wrong opinions about the causal relationship. (I avoid any movement in order to cure my heart disease, however, this worsens my condition instead, because my opinion that absolute rest would cure my heart condition was wrong.)
δ) False or insufficient information about the state of environment or about the acting subject itself can lead to alternatives of the tree which are in reality impossible; in this case the actual result of action will of course diverge from the envisaged one.
ε) The envisaged alternative result can be reached, objectively speaking, but the acting subject lacks the necessary know-how.

New aspects of the problem of freedom appear when we start with the relation between the scope for action and the concept of action: the existence of such a scope is - and I emphasise it again - a conceptual presupposition of action, just as the fact that the direction of an action (the determination of the realised alternative) depends on the processing of relevant information.

Consequently we can state: freedom of action exists insofar as the existence of a scope for action is an empirical fact, and because the behaviour realised in the action is determined by an information process which represents the volition and decision of the acting subject. This situation and the relations between possible behaviours, information process and actual behaviour can be called 'freedom of action'. This means that our practical thought is an element which determines behaviour; however, this does not entail a statement about the extent of the freedom of action, nor the thesis that human beings are in possession of a *liberum arbitrium indifferentiae*, of a free will which is indetermined. This - the central problem of the debate between determinism and indeterminism - we will have yet to discuss in greater detail. Before that I would, however, like to make a remark concerning the extent of the freedom of action. Compared with other living creatures, human beings have an extraordinary capacity to modify their behaviour. Purely genetically determined behaviour, behaviour governed by instincts, plays a minor role in human behaviour. Institutions and modes of behaving and acting which are learned in the course of our personal development dominate by far. It is possible to a large extent that human beings shape their own form of life; the question to which extent this is individually possible or mediated by social structures remains to be answered. We can, and because of our anthropological situation we need to shape the form of our lives through institutions, and every single one of us must draw up his/her life plan. A large measure of freedom exists therefore not only as the scope for action, but also as a social fact. This freedom also has its disadvantages. Mankind and every single one of us is in danger to be drawn into destructive behaviour, be it through delusions, ruinous ideologies, religious or political prejudices. History and actual events testify to these sad aspects of freedom: witch hunting, confessional wars, genocide, Holy Wars and overkill should suffice as examples. These sad historical phenomena show the ambivalence of human freedom, it is a capacity for the good and for the bad.

The conflict concerning freedom of will, the center of the philosophical dispute between determinism and indeterminism, is expressed by the different interpretations of the information process which determines action.

Indeterminists take the fact that information processes are decisive for determining action as proof of the existence of free will. The subject is free, his volition (i.e. the action-determining information process) is not determined by external circumstances, but it is a matter of free decision. The acting subject is free to act and to will: it could act differently when he chose to; he could have acted differently had he chosen another way of acting.

The determinist refuses to regard the action determining information process as *prima causa*. Freedom to act - in the sense discussed earlier - exists; what does not exist is freedom of volition in the sense that volition - interpreted as action determining information process - were separate from and independent of (other) determining elements. On the contrary, this information process is, in the view of the determinist, determined by the character of the acting subject, its attitudes, goals and preferences, and by its knowledge, opinions and ideas; that is it is determined by the effects of a totality of internal and external factors which are ordered and structured by the history of the individual personality.

Whether determinist or indeterminist, one must in either case realise that the information process of deciding is a factor by which actions distinguish themselves from other processes. It is true - as is emphasized in particular by the indeterminist [16] - that in principle the agent could also have acted differently had he decided differently. This is what I have called above 'freedom of acting'. This freedom means that the acting subject can act according to its volition and character. It is obvious that the way how the acting subject decides, is a function of its personality, purposes, values and of its personal history which formed its character. The debate determinism vs. indeterminism therefore shifts to the level of explicating the role personality plays in the decision-making process. For indeterminism personality assumes the key role in decision-making; personality is regarded here as a factor which is not shaped by external conditions and biography, but as the ultimate and essential characteristic of a person. The determinist must not disavow that the unique character of a person is the determining factor in decision-making, because he can interpret it as one of the causal factors. For him, however, the character of a person is a structure which is itself modifyable by external influences. But he emphasises that the information process determining the action is itself determined by circumstances, namely by the personality structure of the acting subject, by previous influences which formed the actor, and by the environment.

Depending on the determinist's attitude whether the mechanisms which determine volition can be known or not, he can expouse two different views:
(i) Every action (including the decision on which it is based) is determined by circumstances: by the world within which the action is performed, by the constitution of the agent, his goals, preferences and capabilities.

---

[16] I think that even a determinist ought to agree to this.

(ii) Actions are determined by conditions which are, in principle, knowable. Scientific progress will reach the point that also the information-related determination of action will be understood and consequently that actions will become increasingly predictable.

In my opinion determinism is only acceptable in the version (i), namely as a statement that volition and decision-making are subject to determinations. This kind of determinism excludes only the view of indeterminism that volition is in some way a *prima causa*; and it thinks it makes always sense to look for factors which determine volition.

I do not accept the other thesis (ii) according to which the determination of volition can in principle be known, because the information processes which determine action cannot be completely reconstructed; the ways in which these processes are determined are to a large extent inaccessible to knowledge, and to predict how someone will act is therefore possible only to a very limited extent.

5. ACTION AS A PROCESS OF SELECTION BASED ON INFORMATION

The life tree we described in the previous section forms for the subject a cognitive frame for its deliberation about how to act. The life tree is by itself of cognitive character, but its construction is of course motivated by needs, desires and goals. The subject searches for methods to reach the desired results, which become possible (i.e. can be reached) by inventing or adopting programmes of action as well as by learning skills.

The determination of actions through information processes is in essence a volitional process - when using standard terminology, and we may call it an attitudinal selection process, if we prefer to adopt the terminology of information theory. A selection process cannot be constructed on purely cognitive information. A theory which is supposed to represent intentional behaviour and the selection of modes of behaviour as an information process must use cognitively differentiated semantics which categorically differentiates between descriptive and practical sentences:

(i) cognitive-descriptive (or theoretical) information (descriptions of facts, of actual, possible or causally necessary behavioural trajectories),[17]

---

[17]From the point of view of the role which is assumed by descriptive information within the context of action, they can be divided as follows:

(a) information about situations, i.e. information about the acting subject and about the context in which the actions are to take place;

(b) information about nomic causal knowledge, regardless whether they are of a deterministic or stochastic nature;

(c) feedback information, which is in essence factual information and which can be used - within the context of certain programmes of action - to determine the goal-oriented course of the action. Feedback is a special kind of information about a situation (in the sense of (a)), in that it is so to speak information about the "intermediate results" of the action.

(ii) practical (attitudinal) information which expresses goals (purposes), standards of values, evaluations, preferences and norms.

Practical information does not describe reality, the realm of facts where actions are realised, but they express attitudes of the acting subject. They are therefore relative to a system. They express those elements of the information processes determining action which make up the volitional aspect of action. In the linguistic representation of the processes of action they are expressed by practical sentences.

The insight that there are two essentially different kinds of information in the action determining information process has significant consequences for the language of practical philosophy: this language must be based on a semantics which distinguishes clearly and sharply between descriptive and practical sentences. I am calling such a semantics 'gnoseologically differentiated'. This semantics forms the necessary foundation of the entire practical philosophy (this is a consequence of the structure of action); it agrees essentially with the semantic distinctions familiar to ordinary language and linguistic theory. And they correspond to the philosophical and methodological distinctions which are used at least since *Hume* and *Kant* in philosophy, metaethics and legal philosophy. Those distinctions include the opposition of 'is' and 'ought', of propositions and norms (declarative sentences and norm sentences), of descriptive and prescriptive language, of theoretical and practical sentences, and so on.

The semantic division between descriptive and practical sentences has logical and methodological implications. The major logical consequences are:

(a) The sentence variables of logical systems which simultaneously deal with theoretical and practical sentences, must have disjoint spheres of variability; in normative logic, for example, declarative variables and normative variables assume values from disjoint spheres of variability.

(b) The categorial distinction between practical and theoretical sentences leads to the postulates of non-derivability as a principle of construction for every logical system which is supposed to function as a normative logic:

(α) No informative practical sentence can be derived from a class of premises which includes only declarative sentences.

(β) No informative declarative sentence can be derived from a class of premises which includes only practical sentences.[18]

The most important methodological implication is the non-cognitivist thesis: Knowledge of facts (of purely cognitive arguments) alone does not substantiate practical sentences.

The semantics of practical sentences may not be conceived of reistically, i.e. as describing existing entities: the norms, values and purposes which are expressed in practical sentences, are not entities existing by themselves; they are posited by volition and an expression of attitude. Practical information therefore

---

[18]Restricting these meta-postulates to the non-derivability of informative conclusions is necessary, because tautological sentences (sentences void of information) also follow from the empty set of premises. - These postulates are a more precise representation of the usual short form of the thesis: 'Ought' does not follow from 'being'; 'being' does not follow from 'ought'.

is not knowledge about independently existing objects, it is not a kind of perception of entities existing *per se*. When an expression of will is set and is expressed by means of practical sentences then the practical information can be intersubjectively grasped on the basis of this piece of practical communication. This understanding has, of course, in a sense the character of knowledge, but it is not the knowledge of an objectively existing Platonic entity, but the understanding of a volitional intellectual creation.

The difference of the meaning and the pragmatic function of descriptive and practical sentences can also be seen in the completely different way of adapting to reality which was already noticed by Searle[19]: theoretical sentences are made to match reality, whereas in the case of practical sentences we are to make reality conform to the content of the sentence by means of our actions.

The attempt to regard comprehension of norms or values not as an understanding of specific practical entities of thought but as a process which is analogous to our acquiring knowledge of material objects mistakenly leads to a cognitivist conception of practical philosophy. Such a conception creates the illusion that a so-called practical cognition is possible and instigates concomitant metaphysical speculations. Communication is the transmission and understanding of pieces of thoughts and it does not always have to be an object which corresponds to the ideal entity. The practical sentence as the message is not a judgement about a norm, a value etc., but provides an understanding of a specific kind of thought.

If one understands action as being information-dependent then - or so it seems at least - one is faced with a dilemma. How is one to understand the realisation of an action which is based on information?

a) Are these pieces of information - in this context they are usually called motives - to be viewed as the cause of the action? (This is incompatible with the customary interpretation of causes as preceding real states, and not as information.) Or:

b) Shall information - although itself neither a physical force nor a real object - bring about logically or quasi-logically real processes? (This is hardly conceivable.)

Only a fundamentally different approach to the problem can lead to an acceptable interpretation. Information is not a cause, and it is not a moving force which itself can bring about real processes.

The acting subject, being a living creature, carries in it active tendencies.[20] The analogous holds also true for a collective action - albeit only indirectly. This circumstance can be found - expressed differently - in all modern biological, psychological and sociological theories. Life is thought of in terms of a hydraulic model of behaviour. An action does not spring from an action-determining information process, but from an active attitude as in the hydraulic

---

[19] J.R. Searle, *Intentionality*, Cambridge et al. 1983, p. 7; J.R. Searle, Taxonomy of Illocutionary Acts, in: J.R. Searle, *Expression and Meaning*, Cambridge et al. 1979, p. 1-27.

[20] The stream model does not refer only to volition and acting, but also to cognition. From perception to scientific thought, our thinking is an active process.

conception of ethology. The information process which determines the action only gives the active current a functionally adequate direction. The practical informations which enter into the information process are an expression of the active tendencies, so to speak: a rationalisation of these actual strivings. The process of deliberation, the decisions based on preferences are only mediating elements which in themselves do not give rise to real processes, but which lead existing active tendencies in relatively effective directions.

6. IDENTITY AND DIFFERENCE OF ACTIONS

In the literature on the theory of action the problem of how to describe action is discussed quite extensively particularly the fact - and the difficulties ensuing from it -, that one and the same action can be described differently. Action as a behavioural process takes place in the context of causal relations. As reality - that is as an outcome or object - it can be characterised by more or less detailed descriptions. We can describe one and the same action as 'I am writing', 'I am writing a letter', 'I am writing a letter to my uncle', or 'I am handwriting a letter of thanks to my uncle'. It is not only possible to make the circumstances, the details, the functional sense etc. more explicit, but we may use also different conceptual networks for describing an action.

Closer examination of the relation between the content of the intention behind the action and the action itself is also important. Acting is essentially the purposeful (intentional) bringing about of a desired state. However, there does not have to be congruity between what is intended and what is effected. Even if we presuppose this substantive congruity - and also for all cases where it does not exist - there is still the problem of the side- and after-effects of the action.

That actions have such additional consequences is a direct result of the network character of causality. If, for example, I apply the brakes while I am driving (to avoid a car accident), I am not only reducing the speed of my car - as was my intention -, but I am also increasing the wear and tear on my brakes and tyres. This was not the object of my intention. Depending upon the circumstances, my action has different types of after-effects. I might even cause another driver to crash into the back of my car. My action increases the time it takes to get to the station and causes me to miss the train, and so on. Are these consequences still characteristic of my action? Can we say, for example, I have carried out the action of 'causing someone to crash into my car' if the car following me crashes into mine as the result of my braking? That which was also (indirectly) intended (or at least accepted as a side-effect of the realisation of the goal) we can certainly regard as a part of the content of the action. It would, however, be absurd to declare that all the effects of carrying out my intended action are the content of my action.

This problem of the causal chain of effects of an action - as against the actually only limited content of the actor's intention - is, of course, an important and difficult problem of legal accountability, of criminal and civil responsibility. The intrinsic rigthts or wrongs of this legal problem need not concern us here, but we must ask to what extent the general theory of action provides a framework for such juridical reflections. The theory of action allows us to distinguish between effects that are part of the substance of the intention - i.e. those effects intended by the actor or accepted as a possible outcome - and causal effects which lie outside the sphere of the agent's intentions. One can furthermore say that responsibility for the results of actions is bound to the causal framework (it would not be justified to attribute responsibility in a case where there is no causal relation between the person and the effect), however, the decision as to what is attributed within this framework is based on social valuation.

To what extent is the outcome of an action which deviates from the intention to be regarded as an action of the actor? An unsuccessful action can be an attempt to carry out said action. The attempt may be incompetent if the means used (the programme of action) are fundamentally unsuited to bring about the originally intended result.

Since causal knowledge which is the basis of action is often only probabilistic, it can happen that the action has improbable, originally not intended consequences. I cross a river over a wooden bridge which by chance collapses while I cross it. The action of crossing thc river has turned into an unsuccessful attempt. But can we say I performed an action which can be described as a transformation of falling-into-the-river? Such a not intended result - even if it is a consequence of the action - will not be regarded as its outcome, even though it was an improbable effect of my action.

In view of this complex state of affairs as regards the definition and linguistic description of actions we must now ask ourselves when action A_1 is the same as A_2, that is when do 'A_1' and 'A_2' describe one and the same action and when are A_1 and A_2 different actions.

The question of identity of action varies according to whether we are discussing types of action (theft, heating a room, driving a car from London to Brighton) or an individual action, which is carried out by a particular actor at a particular time (or in a particular interval of time) and in a particular place. Whether we are talking about criteria of identity or about criteria of difference of actions, a distinction must be made between (a) the identity of the observable course of action (action as a transformation of behaviour), and (b) the identity of action which is not only the identity of observable behaviour but also the identity of intention.

The acts (sequences of acts) which correspond to actions A_1 and A_2 are identical if they are effected by one and the same actor as one and the same process with the same temporal-spatial coordinates. This can be the case even if the description of the action is worded differently; for example, '*S* is writing now', '*S* is writing a letter now', '*S* is writing a reminder' can refer to one and the same behavioural sequence. In the same way '*A* greets *B*' and '*A* raises his hat' can refer to one and the same act.

However, identity of the transformation which can be described in a variety of ways does not yet mean identity of action, for action is also distinguished by the content of the intention. One and the same observed process can be an action or not, an action of type A_1 or of another type A_2. If *S* stumbles (without intending to), this movement does not constitute an action. However, if *S* stumbles deliberately (e.g. as an actor in a film), then this is an action. When Mr. *A* gives Mr. *B* £100, he can, among other things, be giving *B* a loan, or a present, or paying a debt. The actions are different depending on the intention. Even if the observed phenomena are the same, different actions can be involved, because the intentions may be different. Identity (and difference) of actions thus does not depend only on observed facts, but also on the intention behind the action, which can only be ascertained by interpretation. Broadening the field of inquiry often can enable the observer to understand what type of intention, and thus what kind of action he is faced with. (This question of establishing or interpreting sequences of events as a type of action is in fact already an issue different than the problem of the identity of actions.)

Since the decision to behave in a particular way is the result of an information process, a particular intention can be the result of various information-based decision-making processes. For example, I can decide to give Mr. *B* £100 either to ease my bad conscience, or to give him pleasure, or to bind him to me, ... Here we have to ask whether the identity of action is determined only by the identity of the acts and the intention to carry out these acts, or whether the actions are different if the decisive elements (for example the purposes) are different. Both versions of the concept of action are possible. We will simply use different criteria of identity, or, to put it more precisely, different concepts of action, depending on the situation and task to be settled. When we are dealing with action from the point of view of morality we will not only have to take into consideration the content of the intention, but also the reasons for the decision to act in a particular way (the motives). In other contexts the action can be defined in such a way that only when taken together do identity of intention and identity of the series of acts imply identity of action.

Types of action comprise as generic characteristics always certain variables, particularly as far as the agent, the place and the time and other objective specifications are concerned. 'Theft' encompasses the variables of the person who committed the deed (the thief), the time and place of the crime, the objects stolen and their rightful owner. Identity of the type of action is determined by the description of the mode of conduct, the intention, other variables and their range of variability.

7. TELEOLOGY

A fundamental, that is to say a central element of the information processes which determine action is their intentionality. They are governed by intentions and directed towards particular goals. The information processes which determine action can be divided into two types:

(i) those which lead to the determination of the means, the programmes of action, the choice of the optimal means, and finally to the decision to act in a particular way, and

(ii) those which appear when the action is being carried out according to a particular programme.

This is not a clear-cut division, for there are programmes in which during the realisation evaluative decisions are made in the sense of (i).[21]

A theory of action which puts the determination of action by information processes at its center will first and foremost have to examine the structures of teleological thought. This theory must work with formalistic concepts - it is thus also possible to speak of a 'formal teleology' -, because it presents general schemata of these structures and operations and thus presupposes the distinction between form and content. However, I will not portray teleology as a formalised system, but rather describe the relations formally so that various modifications to the systems of formal teleology can then be introduced.[22]

Teleology is frequently regarded as a specific ontological view which says that purposes are inherent in objects and effects their development in the course of time (see *Aristotle's* doctrine of entelechy); or teleology is taken to be a mode of interpreting and explaining reality and the development of the world from the point of view of purposes.[23] This view is connected to the problematical thesis that, according to teleology what happens earlier is caused by what will happen later.[24] The teleological theory I have in mind has nothing to do with such problematical speculations. It is rather a theory of the process of deliberation about acting, represented as information processing, and of the inverse application of this formalism for the interpretation of motives.

7.1. The Relation Between Teleology and Causality

The analysis of teleological relations (the relation between end and means) is associated with causal relations. Because the following obviously holds: If there exists the causal relation '*a* causes *b*' (*a* being the cause, *b* the effect) and *b* is stated as a purpose, then *a* is a (possible) means of achieving the end *b*. One can thus arrive at a theory of the end/means relation if one takes the causal relation for granted. The teleological relation which is thus established may, however, not be described as a mere inversion of the causal relation, as

---

[21]In case of the so-called feed-back-programmes the next step of action is - as a function of the feed-back-information - predetermined by the programme. But it is also possible that in order to continue the intended action a new deliberation and decision becomes necessary: For example, I train according to a certain plan. One of the intermediate results deviates from the expected one and forces the trainer to look for new training methods, i.e. he has to redesign the programme.

[22]It can thus be assumed, for example, that there exists a system of relevant preferences, or that the relative valuations during the process are made by the acting subject. See below, p. 76.

[23]*W. Stegmüller*, for example, basically views teleology that way. Cf. W. Stegmüller, *Wissenschaftliche Erklärung und Begründung (Probleme und Resultate der Wissenschaftstheorie und Analytischen Philosophie*, vol. 1*)*, Berlin/Heidelberg/New York 1969, p. 518.

[24]Critical remarks on this view in: O. Weinberger, Teleologie und Zeitablauf, *Rechtstheorie* vol. 13/1982, p. 285-302.

would be the case if one were to equate the consequence with the end and the cause with the means. This cannot be done because the purely cognitive statement about causal relations does not in any way take an attitude of will to the terms of the relation, whereas the teleological relation is based upon the fact that the purpose is determined by the volition of a subject (the intentional agent of the teleological system). The causal relation has here only a mediatory function. It is not at all the case that every causal relation would have its teleological counterpart. In addition, the relation between end and means is only one element of the relatively complicated system of operations of the teleological information processing.

If one considers the problem of the relation between knowledge of reality and teleology from an anthropological perspective, then one will see that the structure of empirical knowledge is such that it can serve as the basis for discovering means for attaining goals, and thus as the foundation for the determination of action. The interdependence of teleology and causality then appears as functional, mutual adaptation. It can also be said that causal knowledge serves praxis - it is an instrument of praxis and is structurally suited to this task (cognitive primacy of praxis). Cognition creates knowledge which gives us orientation; this knowledge has to be more than a collection of empirical data, more than a system of sentences describing facts. Nomological connections must be discovered, for it is only this type of knowledge teleological analysis can utilise for the purpose of discovering means and methods of action (programmes). To put it another way: empirical knowledge is governed by the principle of causality; empirical knowledge is concerned with uncovering causal relations (be they deterministic or probabilistic bonds).

7.2. Some Remarks on the Principle of Causality

The principle of causality itself obviously does not constitute empirical knowledge, rather it is its precondition. The principle itself forms the framework for empirical knowledge; it is not itself an empirical sentence and cannot be proven by experience. Experience can only show us that causal relations can in fact be successfully recognised. The principle of causality is not derived from the uniformity and regularity of nature and of natural processes, it is rather that facts are analysed and categorised in such a way as to uncover regularities and causal connections. And it is assumed that the actual state of an object (or of a system) is determined by its preceding state (or, as the case may be, by its previous states) and by external circumstances and influences; this means that there is no such thing as chance in any absolute sense. In other words: the principle of causality basically rules out real miracles. This does not mean to say, however, that we know all causal relations or that we can know them completely. There are many situations whose structure is such that it is impossible to arrive at such knowledge that a cognitive determination of the processes under examination can be reached. The most noteworthy examples of this type include: the definition of the behaviour of the individual element when only statistical nomological statements are available; the determination of micro-processes; the phenomena of memory, which by definition cannot be observed, but which nevertheless determine future behaviour in unpredictable ways; and lastly: human behaviour. Human behaviour is included not because a human being as an agent is not subject to determination, is not, as it were, a *prima causa*, but because neither his attitude, the circumstances which mould a person's character, nor his biological disposition can be understood in a way that would make his behaviour predictable.

Let me elucidate the principle of causality by a simple, but important consideration: Let us assume that S_1 and S_2 are two systems which - as far as can be understood - resemble each other in every detail.[25] S_1 is at time t_i in state s, system S_2 at time t_j in the same state s. t_i and t_j can designate the same or different points in time. The systems are the same and are subject to exactly the same influences. When we show that S_1 is at $t_{i+\Delta}$ in state s' and S_2 at $t_{j+\Delta}$n state s'' - whereby $s'$is different from s'' -, then we will not say "The behaviour of the systems is undetermined" nor "A miracle has occurred with respect to at least one of the two systems", instead we will conclude from the different behaviour of the systems at times $t_{i+\Delta}$ and $t_{j+\Delta}$ respectively that, although they appeared to us to be the same, they were in fact different. 'To behave differently' is proof of 'being different'. In my view this line of reasoning is merely another expression of the principle of causality. The behaviour of each object (and every system of objects) at time t_i is determined by its proper characteristics and its relations to other objects in the period before t_i.

There are systems - for example, S_1 and S_2 - whose states at t_0 are in fact different, but this difference cannot be ascertained; however, if S_1, at least under the particular circumstances C behaves differently at a later time t_i from S_2 under the same circumstances, then we can conclude that S_1 was different from S_2 at time t_0. (Compare the concept of memory according to *Ashby*.[26])

7.3. Linear Causality and Causal Networks

Causal relations form chains of causes and effects; the consequence of a cause is the cause of further consequences. This chain-like progression of causes is a defining feature of causality. This should not, however, be understood in the sense that causality is a linear or, as it were, a one-dimensional chain of relations. Causes are more often systems of conditions of the causal effect. This is true regardless of the fact that we have a certain tendency to look for relatively simple causal antecedents, principally because this is an effective

---

[25]In case of two systems they must differ at least with regard to their spatial and/or temporal placement: For our reflections here it can be assumed that the space-time-position of the system is irrelevant for the course of its behaviour.

[26]W.R. Ashby, *An Introduction to Cybernetics*, London 1956[1], 1971[8], p. 115 and p.170. The phenomenon of memory does not, of course, contradict the principle of causality.

way of making use of causal knowledge in the sphere of action. A particular cause, or a system of causal conditions, does not only have one consequence, but it becomes part of a network of further causal consequences. Causal relations are by definition interconnected: we look in this network for such lines of causality which enable us to find an orientation and to intervene in the causal processes in order to pursue our goals. It is the interconnectedness of causality which also explains why actions usually have a host of different causal consequences and are not only the realisation of a desired goal.

7.4. Some Notes on the Ontology of Ends

What are ends (goals)? What type of objects are they? Is their ontological status adequately described by such terms as the "realm of ends" or does this Kantian concept lead to an ontological misconception, because it implicitly assumes the existence of an objective sphere of ends which is independent of a subjective volition, with ends being defined as Platonic entities?[27]

Purposes are to be regarded as expressions of a subjective volition. They are constructs endowed with meaning, of a practical nature. Their function is not to characterise an object, nor are they intended to do so. They describe a certain state of affairs which is to be attained; or they establish criteria for action, but the purpose itself is not in an object in and of itself, it is not denoted by (a referent of) the expression (the sentence), which states the purpose. Interpreting ends as objects seems to be inappropriate.

It is a constitutive element of an end that a certain content is considered desirable (intended). What this means can only be explained by reference to the pragmatic function of ends: they set the orientation for the determination of action. Any other definition of purpose merely introduces terminological varia-

---

[27]The realm of purposes is in *Kant's* view clearly separated from the teleological action-determining mechanism in the sense of formal teleology which is part of the theory of action as I developed it. Cf. the following: "Ich verstehe aber unter einem *Reiche* die systematische Verbindung verschiedener vernünftiger Wesen durch gemeinschaftliche Gesetze. Weil nun Gesetze die Zwecke ihrer allgemeinen Gültigkeit nach bestimmen, so wird, wenn man von dem persönlichen Unterschiede vernünftiger Wesen, imgleichen allem Inhalt ihrer Privatzwecke abstrahiert, ein Ganzes aller Zwecke (sowohl der vernünftigen Wesen als Zwecke an sich, als auch der eigenen Zwecke, die ein jedes sich selbst setzen mag), in systematischer Verknüpfung, d.i. ein Reich der Zwecke gedacht werden können, welches nach obigen Prinzipien möglich ist.
Denn vernünftige Wesen stehen alle unter dem *Gesetz*, daß jedes derselben sich selbst und alle anderen *niemals bloß als Mittel*, sondern jederzeit *zugleich* als *Zweck an sich selbst* behandeln *solle*. Hierdurch aber entspringt eine systematische Verbindung vernünftiger Wesen durch gemeinschaftliche objektive Gesetze, d.i. ein Reich, welches, weil diese Gesetze eben die Beziehung dieser Wesen auf einander, als Zwecke und Mittel, zur Absicht haben, ein Reich der Zwecke (freilich nur ein Ideal) heißen kann." [I. Kant, *Grundlegung der Metaphysik der Sitten*, II. Abschn., ed. W. Weischedel, Wiesbaden 1956, p. 66]
This is a Platonic-ontological view of the realm of purposes, although *Kant* sees this realm as an idea and the reasonable beings as general law-giving members of this realm.

tions or circular definitions. Ends are designed to constitute teleological relations, that is to lead to the determination of means on the basis of causal knowledge.

It would be advantageous to present a complete and systematic overview of what actually constitutes the content of purposes. However, such an undertaking lies beyond the scope of the present investigation, and a few explanatory remarks must suffice.

The content of an end can be attaining a certain state; a goal, a final state should be reached. 'Telos', 'finis', 'goal', which are frequently used as synonyms for the term 'purpose', indicate the sense of end or finality of that which is sought after. An end also can take the form of a standard which should be adhered to (see the concept of homeostasis); it can indicate a lasting state which is sought after (e.g. 'prosperity' as an end), or a goal which can only be attained after a long and difficult process (e.g. 'learning German'). It seems to me important to emphasise that it is not decisive for a purpose that it expresses the final point of the action which is intended by it, but rather the fact that a certain content is stated as desirable, as an expression of will which can be fulfilled through action.

I do not consider it important whether one views goals as a particular type of end, or whether 'end' and 'goal' are used synonymously. Because of the parallel between goal/telos/finis and the relation between 'teleology' and 'finality', it seems advisable to use the terms 'end' and 'goal' synonymously and abandon the idea that a goal has to describe an end point.

In teleological reflections there often appear ends whose suitable means cannot be determined by appealing directly to causal law (in the usual sense of the word). 'Contentment', 'general welfare' are eagerly aspired to, although causal laws as we usually understand them do not introduce these concepts as effects (consequents) of causal relations. These kinds of purposes - for want of a better word let us call them 'global ends' - are not without significance for teleological thought, although the usual causal laws cannot be used directly to determine suitable means. However, they are in a certain way selection criteria for action. If, for example, Mr. *N* is to be content, then what causes him pain according to the laws of practical experience is excluded as a means. However, it is not clear whether, e.g., going for a walk would serve as a means to achieve this particular end.

Purposes can be more or less concrete. Ends can thus be set above or below each other or ranged alongside each other.[28] The goal of satisfying bodily needs is a more general goal than the goal of allaying hunger; allaying hunger and having a suitable place to live are goals which are ranked at the same level under the abstract end of satisfying bodily needs. Very abstract goals, for example contentment and the satisfaction of bodily needs, must first be analysed by an enumeration of subordinated goals as concrete elements of the abstract

---

[28]Thinking about relationships between purposes always must take into consideration only *one* system of purposes.

purposes. The individual partial goals, as we can call the elements of the abstract goal, enter into teleological deliberations according to their relative importance.[29]

A goal G_1 is ranked above a goal G_2 if goal G_2 appears as a type of goal G_1, such that satisfying G_2 is always also satisfying G_1, but not vice versa. For example, the satisfaction of bodily needs is ranked above the goal of allaying hunger.

One could regard the abstract purpose as the set of subordinated and coordinated partial goals together with their relative weights. It must, however, also be remembered that this can only be done if there exists an exhaustive analysis of the abstract goal; in practice this is rarely the case in teleological thought.

Teleological reflection does not generally rest on a single end. The teleological systems which appear in practice generally are complex: they embrace a number of ends which are related in various ways. Generically different ends can co-exist within the same system of ends, for example, prosperity and wisdom, full employment and price-stability. It is in principle also possible that contradictory states are desired simultaneously or states whose simultaneous fulfilment is empirically impossible. I can wish at one and the same time that it would rain (because of the harvest) and that it would not rain (so that I can go for a walk). People often endeavour to achieve two accepted, conflicting goals at once: the attainment of one end limits the realisation of the other (for example, the goal 'good food and plenty of it' and the goal 'to stay slim').

A system of ends is a system of tendencies, not a description of a possible world; in a certain sense conflicts between ends are an essential part of these systems: based on the relative valuations and according to the accepted goals of the system such decisions are sought which achieve an optimum of value within the context of these many and varying aspirations, decisions which represent a balanced, relatively optimal choice. If one were to ask for a conflict-free structure of systems of ends[30], this would exclude *a limine* an essential part of teleological analysis.

Teleological conflicts are not logical contradictions, nor are they flaws in the system of purposes which would render it useless (as is the case with logical contradictions in systems of propositions), because it is not the function of such a system to describe a state of affairs. Nevertheless, the identification of conflicts in the system of ends plays an important role in teleological reflection. If *p* and non-*p* are desired at the same time, then we are forced to establish the relative value of *p* and non-*p*. I desire to stay at home and I desire to leave home. This leads to a relative assessment of values and a decision based on preference. 'Desiring' is graded according to intensity, and thus preferring *p* over non-*p* can be considered.

---

[29]Concerning the question of the relative weight of purposes and the course of the weighing functions (if need be as dependent upon relative fulfilment) see section 8 of this chapter and ftn. 47, p. 79.

[30]Some authors presuppose that the system of purpose be free of conflict, cf. e.g. G.H. von Wright, On so-called Practical Inference, in: *Acta Sociologica* 15/1, pp. 39-53.

Generically different goals are on occasion conceptually incomparable; decisions are arrived at in such cases, too, either by considering the merits of the various goals or by adopting an evaluative attitude in the actual situation. For example, 'acting morally' and 'maximising one's own advantage' can be considered as generically different ends. However, in determining how to act in an actual situation one has to decide whether to favour one or the other.

Teleology normally proceeds on the basis of a static conception of the system of purposes (and the concomitant preferences). This is entirely appropriate for the structural theory of teleological deliberation. In fact, however, systems of ends are essentially dynamic, consider, for example, the teleological attitude of the individual. New ends can appear and old ones fall by the wayside. This happens for various reasons: the biological development of the subject (in certain phases of development needs appear, in others they fade away); experiences (an imagined desirable state can in reality be quite unpleasant); imagined ends can turn out to be impracticable, etc.

7.5. Discovery, Optimisation and Choice of Means

The concept of purpose and the whole complex of the problem of teleological deliberation rest on the fact that suitable means can be found and employed for the realisation of goals or the fulfilment of ends. One can realise a final goal indirectly (or fulfil other types of ends indirectly) by employing means which bring about the desired state of affairs. As we saw above, achieving ends indirectly this way is founded on causal relations. However, this basic thesis does not suffice for an adequate explanation of the problem of means and the fulfilment of ends through means.

The search for suitable means and ways of fulfilling an end is usually not a simple process of applying causal knowledge; it is in fact a real challenge which may require skill, practice, study and inventiveness. Of course it is not always necessary to adopt an original intellectual approach; one usually gets by with the patterns which are established by social practice, or in some cases with individual ones which one has adopted before.

There is not always exactly one way of achieving a given end. It may be that no means at all exist, in which case the end is unrealisable, either in principle or at least not within the scope of possibilities open to the agent. However, one may be mistaken in believing that a goal is unattainable; it is of course quite possible that there is a way to achieve the goal, but it is unknown to the actor. There may be exactly one way or there may be several means to the particular end in mind. Then one can speak of the plurality of means; in this case a process of deliberation becomes necessary in order to choose the most suitable means.

That which was originally wanted, (aspired to or desired) is the end; volition regarding the means is derived from the original desire.[31] The relation

[31] This thesis is in no way conflicting with the fact that purposes are themselves subject to change and development (see section 8).

between ends and means leads to a transference of volition (intention) from the ends to the means. We can distinguish two phases in this process:
(i) the conditional transfer to each and every means which is suited to achieving or furthering the end;
(ii) the willing of those means selected from the class of possible means (only these are, as it were, definitively willed).

Although it is actually quite self-evident, this transference of will must be examined more closely, particularly in relation to the frequently quoted dictum from *Kant's Fundamental Principles of the Metaphysics of Ethics:* "Whoever wills the ends also wills the absolutely necessary means which are in his power (in as far as his actions are influenced by reason)".[32] Is this principle a statement of fact about the relations between acts of will, or is it an operational rule for processing of practical informations? *Kant* probably also understood this thesis in an non-psychological sense [33], as is necessary from the point of view of the formal-teleological theory of action. There is some doubt about whether this Kantian principle is actually valid, or how it would have to be interpreted to make it valid. If by 'absolutely necessary means' we understand means which are necessary for the fulfilment of the end (even if they are insufficient on occasion) then the statement is not valid. Let us say that heating is absolutely necessary in order to make a room habitable (i.e. if the room is not heated it is not habitable), and it is desired that the room be in that condition. If, for example, the windows in the room are broken, and decent windows are also a necessary condition for the room to be habitable, then heating is only wanted conditionally, that is only if the windows can also be repaired; heating is desired only in conjunction with the repair of the windows.[34] If the Kantian principle were to be correct, one would have to define the absolutely necessary means as necessary and sufficient. *Kant's* thesis is not sufficient to solve the complex problem of the relations between ends and means for it does not take into consideration the plurality of means and the thought processes which come into play in cases like these. *Kant's* thesis is indeed correct - if we take this second interpretation - but it only concerns a small area of teleology and it does not point to the necessity to develop such a theory of teleological thinking.

Although the analyses of ends with which we are confronted in our lives almost always start from a system comprising several ends and not from a single

---

[32]I. Kant, *Grundlegung zur Metaphysik der Sitten*, B 44-45.

[33]The parenthetical remark gives rise to the doubt whether *Kant* did not, after all, mean to describe here some psychological connections; in any case, he did not make explicit the purely structural character of the transfer of volitionality from purposes to means.

[34]Cf. G.H. von Wright, *Praktisches Schließen*; G.H. von Wright, Über sogenanntes praktisches Schließen, in: G.H. von Wright, *Handlung, Norm, Intention*, *op.cit.*, and my critical remarks, in: O. Weinberger, Handeln und Schließen. Überlegungen zum Begriff des praktischen Schließens, in: *The Law between Morality and Politics*, ed. by F. van Dun, *Philosophica* 23 (1979), p. 5-36, reprinted in: O. Weinberger, *Studien zur formal-finalistischen Handlungstheorie*, Frankfurt a.M./Bern/New York 1983, p. 19-58.

purpose, it is nevertheless helpful to divide our reflections into two stages in order to clarify some basic points:

(a) in the first stage we proceed on the assumption that only one end is relevant;

(b) in the second our reflections are based on a complex system of ends (number of ends $n(n > 1)$).

Ad (a): If we start from a single end E_1 (for example, the goal of living in a beautiful house), then we seek means to achieve this end. There can be (α) just one, (β) several or (γ) none. If (α) is the case, then it is clear and unequivocal how we should act (restrictions with regard to expenses do not concern us here, for 'expense' always sets limits to the realisation of other ends; this is not relevant in the case of a single end.) Case (γ) is simple, too: there is nothing we can do to achieve our end. Whether this has any influence on the continuing existence of the goal need not concern us further here.[35]

Plurality of means - case (β) - demands a relative valuation of the means (obviously from the perspective of the one particular end in question). The means M_1 can essentially be evaluated in three ways relative to means M_2:

(1) quantitatively - M_1 fulfils the end E_1 to a greater extent than (or as much as) M_2;

(2) qualitatively - M_1 fulfils E_1 better than (or as well as) M_2;

(3) it is more certain that E_1 will be fulfilled by M_1 than M_2 (or it is just as certain that E_1 will be fulfilled by M_2).

Obviously these elements of the relative valuation of means can appear in various combinations. M_1 fulfils an end to a greater extent and with a greater degree of certainty than M_2. In principle all triple options are possible. Ranking the means on the basis of the relative valuation according to the three possibilities outlined above can lead to the problem of how to establish the order of preferences. Let us suppose that M' fulfils the end E_1 better than M'', but that it is less likely (probable) that end E_1 will be fulfilled by M' than by M''. Is M' to be preferred to M'' or *vice versa*, or should M' and M'' be regarded as being of equal value? It is clear that M' would be given priority if it were to fulfil the end considerably better than M'' and only with a slightly lesser degree of uncertainty. It is, however, quite unclear how these standards are to be set, and how these factors influence the overall preference is largely a matter of attitude (decision). Even within this single-purpose model decisions are unavoidable, for it is not possible to prove rationally whether and to what extent 'more', 'better' or 'greater certainty' determines preference.

Already here we can see what will come up at other points as well: it is impossible to rationalise teleological thought such that decisions would become superfluous and could be replaced wholly by logical operations.

---

[35]One can foster unrealisable wishes, but this is more dreaming than volition striving towards realisation. Furthermore, it is possible to wish for something which is not realisable at a certain moment, but which can be realised on the basis of long-term strategies. This is, of course, not a case of 'wishing for something unrealisable'.

Teleological analysis is a rational process of optimisation, however, its standards are not rationally defined, but are attitudes. Ends are points of views (criteria), according to which the relative valuation of possible means is carried out. If a criterion for evaluation (or relative valuation, i.e. considering something preferabel or equivalent) is given - sc. on the basis of a practical decision - then the relation of preference can be cognitively determined. Methods (or operations) can be developed by which the relative valuation, relative to the assumed practical attitude, i.e. to the purpose, becomes determinable by cognition.

If we presuppose, e.g. the objective to get a calculator with a certain capacity which should be as light as possible, then the models with the required capacity can be ordered according to their weight. Preference (or equivalence) can in this case be determined empirically by help of a scale.[36]

In the case of evaluations involving taste (for example, arranging photographs according to my taste) a purely cognitive operation as above to determine the choice is not possible. (It is, however, possible to advance rational partial arguments to support the decision-making process.)

(b) Experience tells us that the systems of ends which are associated with subjects endowed with volition are complex. Human beings have various needs which exist alongside each other and which are more or less necessary for living. Therefore human intentionality is characterised by a plurality of ends. Corporations, states and other agents expressing a social will are - just as the individual - characterised by a plurality of purposes.

The relations between the various ends of a single system of ends are heterogeneous.[37] One can distinguish between conceptually superior and subordinate ends. For example, the end 'a healthy way of life' embraces subordinate ends like 'proper nutrition', 'appropriate division of one's day', etc. Means which satisfy subordinate ends are *eo ipso* also means to achieve superior ends. We can speak of generically different ends which do not admit of conceptual comparison. We can, for example, classify them as economic ends, aesthetic purposes, moral goals etc. It may be useful for the analysis of individual ends to classify them in this way; for the theory of teleology it seems to be of limited value, for generically different purposes appear side by side in teleological considerations and must be included in the determination of decisions based on the entire set of relevant preferences.

There often exists a linking of ends such that means to a particular end can themselves be attained through other means. Grain is sown, harvested, ground and further processed in order to bake bread and, ultimately, to allay hunger by means of this bread.

---

[36]Setting the purposes is relative to the system. Whether the subject desires a light or a heavy calculator, is a question of attitude of the subject's system. When the goal is stated unequivocally, then the relation of preference can be determined sometimes purely cognitively and independently of the volitional system (i.e. objectively).

[37]Differing purposes and their relations are of course especially then of interest to teleology, when the purposes belong to one and the same system.

Objects, actions and programmes of action are considered from the point of view of ends. A number of very different evaluative situations can arise. Something can be useful from the point of view of various ends simultaneously. Something can serve one end and be detrimental to another end. A resulting evaluation is worked out which cannot in principle be calculated according to a fixed rational rule. This is only possible under special circumstances (e.g. in the case of monetary evaluation). Utility and damage can be concomitants of one and the same thing when evaluated from the perspective of different objectives.

Acting can also lead to conflicts of ends in quite a different way. An action A_1can be willed (useful) from the point of view of end E_1 and harmful (not willed)[38] from the point of view of E_2 It is then not merely a question of calculating the overall usefulness from the standpoint of a complex consideration of ends, but of determining alternative programmes of action. In this case a deliberation on the basis of conflicts of ends will lead to a choice between alternative courses of action.

All teleological processes of deliberation are analyses of optimisation. They consist of rational-cognitive steps (or, to put it more accurately, they can be constituted in such a way that rational-cognitive steps are used), and they also embrace attitudinal decisions (or preferences). In cases where complex criteria, a class of different ends - one could say: a vector of criteria (of ends) - is made the basis of a relative overall evaluation, the determination of the outcome is always dependent on a decision.

An example might serve as an illustration: I use teleological analysis to determine my choice of meal in a restaurant. I lay down two criteria: (i) I should enjoy the taste of it as much as possible; (ii) it should put as small a burden as possible on my tight budget.[39] If I succeed in drawing up a clear order of preference according to my taste, and if there is a clear ranking according to cost, even then I cannot rationally derive an order - or even a semi-order - of preference according to the overall criterion "taste-cost" without making decisions that involve value judgements.

If teleology is conceived of as a theory of information processing which determines action, then valuation, and particularly relative valuation, has an important function within this theory. Teleology can then not only be regarded as a theory of the relation between ends and means, but it must also be developed as a theory of choice (of decisions leading to choice) on the basis of systems of purposes; and to this end it is necessary to include relative valuation in teleology.

By the concept of relative valuation I mean valuative acts - and the ability of the subject to perform such acts -, which produce a dyadic value relation. Relative valuation means 'giving preference to' ('preferring'). The conceptual apparatus of relative valuation can be structured in two different ways:

---

[38]'Not wanted' in the sense of 'wanted that not ...'.

[39]The reader ought to note that it is hardly possible to establish a relation of summation of these factors based on rational reasons.

(a) one can work with two predicates, the (strong) preference 'P' and the equality of values E, or

(b) with the predicate of the (weak) preference 'P_w', which holds between p and q exactly when '$pPq \vee pEq$' obtains.

For technical reasons it is often more expedient to work with the concept of the weak preference 'P_w'; closer to ordinary language and easier when considering the problem of choice is the terminology (a).[40] I therefore will use (a) as the basis for my expositions. Relative valuation is a matter of attitude, preferences are practical information relative to a particular system. The results of the valuative acts can be represented intersubjectively and formal operations can be carried out with these representations (if no further decisions become necessary). Everyone, not just the acting subject, can perform these operations. One can operate with sentences stating preferences between p and q as with declarative sentences.

For every p and q there exists a triad of possibilities: pPq, pEq, qPp. As the parity of values is symmetrical, it can also be expressed in the form: pPq, qEp, qPp.

The triad means that if relative statements of value are made about any objects or states of affairs whatsoever, then exactly one and only one of the propositions of the triad is true. It must not, however, be understood to mean that according to every criterion of value (or from the perspective of every system) exactly one of these valuations is valid. 'p', 'q' can denote objects or states of affairs which cannot be relatively evaluated according to the given criterion, or which were not actually evaluated by the system.[41]

Only when it is certain that a relative valuation of p, q is possible and exists (has been carried out or established by the subject) according to the given criterion can one conclude from the falsity of two elements of the triad that the third is valid. For example, only then is it true that 'pEq' follows from '$\neg pPq$' '$\neg qPp$'.

Establishing a (strong) preference is intrinsically related to choice: The p that is preferred to all other alternative possibilities (means) is the chosen means (the chosen alternative course of action).

---

[40]These two terminological versions are insofar equivalent as all that can be expressed in one terminology can also be expressed by the other. The following definitions hold (for each field for which all preferences (equal values) are given):

$pP_Wq \equiv$ df $pPq \vee pEq$
$pPq \equiv$ df pP_Sq & $\neg pP_Wp$
$pEq \equiv$ df. pP_Wq & qP_Wp

[41]For reasons of terminology there is sometimes unclarity in case of statements expressing equal value. For the predicate 'E the term 'indifference' is often employed. When it is indifferent for a system whether 'p' or 'q' obtains, it can mean two things: (i) p and q are of equal value; (ii) that from the perspective of the system (or according to a certain criterion) there exists no relative valuation regarding p, q or that such a valuation is not possible. (Cf. also St. Körner, *Experience and Conduct*, Cambridge et al. 1976, p. 52.)

In the case of equality of values of two or more alternatives there is no clear and unequivocal determination of choice. An arbitrary (random) choice is made between the equivalent alternatives. Seen from a psychological point of view, this could have the effect of inhibiting choice, for in addition to the teleological deliberation on preference an act of decision becomes necessary: from the rational point of view, however, this does not mean a holding back of the action, but a random choice between equally favourable alternatives.[42]

When a complete ranking of preferences is available, then the decision on choice can be worked out as a calculation. However, this is only possible in special circumstances which rarely exist. All possible alternatives would have to be given (in real life they are mostly searched for, even invented, and a complete inventory of alternatives hardly ever exists), and a determination of preference would have to be provided for every pair. The application of teleological analysis to determine action will therefore mostly turn to relative valuation - at least at certain points.

The agent often has no clear preference to begin with. An observer can sometimes determine the preferences of an agent by questioning him. It often happens (and this sometimes applies to self-analysis as well) that the observer watches the outcomes of acts of choosing (or takes as a starting point answers to hypothetical questions 'How would you decide between *p* and *q*?') and considers them as proof of the subject's preference. This analysis is not conclusive. Observation that a choice is made provides evidence only of weak preference. It could also be the case that the subject regards *p* and *q* as being of equal value (*pEq*) and has chosen this alternative by chance.

Relative valuation or declarations of preference can be arrived at on the basis of cardinal evaluations of the related elements (the number assigned to *p* by evaluation is '$W(p)$'):

(i) from '$W(p) > W(q)$' follows 'pPq';
(ii) from '$W(p) \geq W(q)$' follows 'pP_wq';
(iii) from '$W(p) = W(q)$' follows 'pEq'.

On the other hand, a cardinal evaluation of the related elements cannot in general be derived from the proposition of preference. However, when the related elements read 'p' and '$\neg p$' then the following is valid:

(a) from '$pP\neg p$' follows '$W(p) > 0$';
(b) from '$pE\neg p$' follows '$W(p) = 0$', '$W(\neg p) = 0$';
(c) from '$pP_w\neg p$' follows '$W(p) \geq 0$'.

---

[42]The image of the ass of Buridan who starves standing between two equal bundles of hay at equal distance from him, because the forces which motivate him cancel each other out, is wrong for two reasons: (a) motives are not forces which could cancel each other out by being in equilibrium; (b) equal value of alternatives does not mean refraining from action but means random choice of *one* of the optimal alternatives.

From a certain view one can - on the basis of complex systems of ends [43] - introduce the concept of *expenditure*. Expenditure is that damage (loss of utility) in relation to other purposes of the system which is associated with taking a particular alternative course of action. When I use an egg for breeding hens then I lose the possible use of this egg as food. When I use the next hour for learning German then I lose the opportunity to work out a clear answer to a particular philosophical problem in this time. The problem of expenditure in relation to the attainment of goals is obviously discussed principally in connection with goods in short supply (i.e. in economic analyses). However, I believe that it has a more general significance. The agent to whom a complex system of ends is attributed, always moves in a field of limited possibilities for action. This is caused by at least two circumstances: the fact that (a) 'bringing something about' is always a kind of work (consumption of energy), and (b) that the possibilities for action are limited, because time is scarce and does not allow for undertaking too many things at once.

If we use the concept of expenditure in teleological analysis, we can express the problem of teleological optimisation in the following way: maximum fulfilment of the purpose at a minimum of expenditure. These two requirements do not conflict with the principle of choosing the best possible means by teleological analysis; rather, for technical reasons, it is useful in some cases to consider these two aspects separately.

8. ON THE PROBLEM OF THE DYNAMICS OF THE SYSTEM OF ENDS

Teleology, as we have understood it up to now, proceeds on the basis of the existence of a particular system of ends which is taken as basis for teleological analyses. This system may be taken as a supposition or as the expression of the will of an acting subject. The attitudes towards purposes in real systems - whether of human individuals or of social agents of teleological systems - are certainly not immutable. On the contrary, it can be taken as a psychological and social fact that systems of purposes are as a rule dynamic. We must therefore ask ourselves two questions: 1. What are the essential elements which cause these changes? 2. How can we deal with the dynamics of the system of ends in an analytical way?[44]

The teleological systems of real life are part of a field of actual processes in which the agent takes part. His activity, which is set by the action-determining operation, leads to events which in a certain way supply the agent with experiential material. Verification processes are set in motion. Experience not only provides a test for the utility of the means and the programmes of action

---

[43]This is not valid - as already mentioned above - in case of a single-purpose-system.

[44]This question I can only answer partially and approximately. See also: O. Weinberger, Zwecke, Normen und Werte in dynamischer Perspektive, in: A. Grabner-Heider/K. Weinke, *Lebenswerte im Wandel*, Graz 1990.

employed and for the underlying causal laws; the goals, which have often figured in teleological deliberation only as imagined use (enjoyment), are also subjected to a verification test.[45] Experiences of this kind can obviously lead to modification of the system of ends.

Wilhelm Wundt was one of the first to draw attention to an important socio-psychological fact of the dynamics of ends.[46] His concept of the heterogony of ends points to the fact that while pursuing hitherto accepted ends people conceive of new ends, expand and re-shape their aims, either on the basis of experience or due to a new set of circumstances and new technical and social possibilities.

Of course, change can also occur in the system of ends associated with a person as a consequence of the development of the individual or of the corporate body (or another communal entity). A young man has different goals from a person of advanced years. The aims of a small firm will alter considerably if it develops into a large corporation. The change in the teleological perspective either proceeds inexorably and irreversibly as time unfolds, or occurs, as it were, in a cyclical pattern. Figuratively speaking, the intensity of purpose varies according to the degree to which it is satisfied, according to changes of the agent as a consequence of physiological processes or as a consequence of the fact that needs depend on the rhythms of nature (day/night, summer/winter) etc.

The structure of needs changes through learning, and the system of ends changes accordingly. (Once a person has learned to read that person will probably want books). The acquisition of knowledge or skill also puts within reach what was previously unattainable. The scope for action also changes and opens the possibility of setting new goals.

How can teleology and the theory of action accommodate themselves to the fact that ends are constantly changing? One possible answer - admittedly a rather incomplete one - is the following: we can try to approach the problem with a sequence of teleological systems which follow one after another. However, this is certainly only a partial answer: it provides no explanation of the transformational relations between the elements to the progression of the system, nor how consideration of later systems influences the analysis of ends in the actual teleological system.

9. REDUCING THE COMPLEXITY OF TELEOLOGICAL REFLECTION

The structure of teleological reflection outlined above, i.e. based on a complex system of ends, is very complicated. Every decision concerning action would demand a very extensive and complex evaluative procedure, which would

---

[45] This empirical test of purposes and goals I have called elsewhere "rectification of purposes" (sc. as opposed to verification of empirical knowledge). Cf. Ch. Weinberger/O. Weinberger, *Logik, Semantik, Hermeneutik*, Section 8.7. Teleologie und Bewährung, p. 147; O. Weinberger, *Rechtslogik*, 2nd ed., Berlin 1989, Duncker & Humblot, p. 295 ff.

[46] W. Wundt, *Ethik*, vol. 1, p. 284 f.

have to be repeated every time the circumstances or/and attitudes of the subject change. The actual thought processes which determine action certainly do not function like that, and cannot do so. The model of teleological deliberation is more properly to be regarded as a regulatory apparatus which shows how an analysis which determines action is structured and how decisions concerning action can be arrived at and tested rationally. Teleology also points out that the information processing which determines action comprises cognitive as well as practical information and that at several points teleological reflection involves acts of subjective attitudes.

Subjective decision is necessary at least at the following points:

(i) How a person evaluates the relative importance of the qualitative as against the quantitative fulfilment of ends is a purely subjective matter. Whether one opts for the more certain (or more probable) outcome as opposed to choosing less certainty, yet greater possible satisfaction is a matter of personal preference and not of rational analysis. In economic theory this is known as different degrees of 'preparedness for risk'. However, the extent to which the average individual is prepared to accept risk and to what extent accepting risk is economically desirable need not concern us here. The real issue here is: It is not a question of logical practical reasoning, nor a question which can be decided cognitively, at which point greater degree of fulfilment (greater gain) at a lesser chance of success is to be favoured over lesser degree of fulfilment (lesser gain) at greater chance of success. In the final analysis it is a question of attitude, a discretionary issue.

(ii) There are numerous possible ways of devising procedures of relative valuation in accordance with individual criteria of purpose, in order to give them a cognitive form so that they can be tested. However, relative valuation as a complex evaluation on the basis of two or more partial criteria always requires that the relative importance of the partial criteria be established.[47]

(iii) The influence of time on valuation cannot be logically determined; it is a purely subjective matter: Whether - and by how much - the fulfilment of an end (a pleasure, a gain) today is to be preferred to the fulfilment of the same end tomorrow can in the last resort only be decided by a subjective decision of the person concerned.

Reflections about acting in everyday life are based on methods which considerably reduce the complexity of this information process.

Preference on the basis of teleological evaluation is primarily conceived as establishing an order; it is an ordinal consideration. Time and again, however, the attempt is made to ascribe fixed values to objects or states of affairs, because it is easier to work with numbers and quantitative relations.

The difficulties which arise from the fact that the preferences which determine action are established on the basis of various co-existing purposes which are difficult to compare can, in many instances, be mastered by em-

---

[47]The relative weighing cannot always be solved by assigning constant factors to individual partial criteria, because the relative relevance of the criteria does not have to remain constant over the entire field of observation.

ploying a device which functions as a common evaluative standard. Money fulfils such a function (even if it leaves much to be desired because of various distorting economic factors).[48]

The most important devices for reducing the complexity of deliberation about action are: (a) pre-established decisions which are incorporated into the analysis as a whole and which are only in exceptional circumstances - when special problems occur - subjected to a critical analysis and newly appraised; (b) fixed intentions which form the basic framework of a life-plan and are only put in question under special circumstances. The manner in which certain activities are carried out and their evaluation are "pre-fabricated", they appear as relative totalities and programmes or partial programmes of actions. If, for example, I am to write a letter, not every single element of the activity (paper, typewriter, ...) is deliberated upon and the means selected: what in fact happens is that a ready-made programme of action is taken, only partially adapted, evaluated and then it enters into the decision-making process leading to action; (c) in most cases it is not the entire field of possibilities which is scrutinised and subjected to a relative valuation, but only a subset which encompasses a satisfying possibility (if I want to decide which car to buy I will not investigate all cars of the intended class, but only a subset); (d) it is also the case that not all aspects of the intended alternatives are analysed, but only such characteristics which are deemed necessary in the first range (thereby reducing the number of alternatives in a first step); then additional elements enter into consideration.

We live within a system of action that is built up successively during the course of our life and comprises a reservoir of preformed - but adaptable - elements.

It must also be remembered that making choices and deciding what to do not only relate to individual actions (e.g. 'going for a walk this afternoon') but also represent lasting intentions (e.g. 'next year I will take French lessons once a week') and establish forms of life.

10. REMARKS ON THE METHODOLOGY OF THE ANALYSIS OF ACTION

According to the formal-teleological conception, analyses of action are based on the following principles:

(i) Depending on the situation, what we are concerned with is either reflection which determines action or an interpretation and explanation of ob-

---

[48] I cannot enter here into the complicated question of purely monetary economic analyses in the context of teleological deliberation. In essence we can say that in relation to the total teleological valuation economic analysis plays mostly the role of a partial information; that means that elements which cannot be measured in money (e.g. 'quality of life') also play a part.

served actions.[49] Both forms of analysis are essentially based on the formal theory of teleology.

(ii) Teleological reflection generally takes place in reduced fashion. It seems essential to reduce the complexity of teleological analyses (see section 9). It is usually unavoidable to work with pre-established blocks, and to enter into teleological analysis only if need be.

(iii) The action of the individual or of subgroups of a superior communal body is not independent of social relations, interactions, reciprocal expectations, and normative co-ordination. Action is thus not only determined by teleological reflection and fixed autonomous intentions; it is also determined by heteronomous norms which assign the agent his place within the social relation.

In my view, every interpersonal interaction and every social structure stands and falls with normative regulations and other systems of practical information upon which they are founded.[50]

Internalised heteronomous norms operate as determinants of action together with teleological reflections on utility. It is extremely difficult to give an accurate explanation of the process through which action is determined by these two determinants. We can give an approximate description of this process in the following way:

(a) Internalised heteronomous norms sometimes operate in such a way that they are put before all considerations of utility: to do one's duty takes precedence; reflections about ends are admissible only in situations where the norm does not yet determine the behaviour.

(b) A balance is sought between a heteronomously imposed ought and personal utility. The question of the degree to which social (i.e. heteronomous) postulates are valued and acknowledged is of course very important here.

The system of heteronomous social norms has its own view of purposes which is generally different from the conception of ends held by the acting subject. There is thus a certain degree of overlapping of various purposes, those of the acting subject and those of the community.

(At this point we can ask the moral question of whether (a) or (b) is preferable. Absolute subordination of social obligation or balancing of social obligation and personal utility? I do not think that these should be viewed as strict alternatives. The desire to achieve a balance as in (b) in no way means that social obligations are not duly observed. But can heteronomous norms require absolute precedence without an autonomous vote of assent? This - apparently strictly moral - attitude has not always lead to moral results.)

(c) Institutions which are constituted by social norms - that is the normative institutions (e.g. property, marriage, contract of purchase) as well as the organisations and establishments (e.g. schools, courts, associations, political

[49]The methodologically fundamental opposition of deliberation about action and the analysis of motive has already been dealt with in section 1; p. 48.

[50]Cf. ch. I of this book, particularly pp. 31 f. Concerning the purpose of the nature of social norms and the character of the processes by which norms get institutionalized see also ch. IV of this book.

parties) - form frameworks of action for the modes of conduct of the acting subjects which belong to that particular society. The choice of the mode of action within the institutional framework is largely determined by considerations of personal utility.

(iv) Teleological analyses are mostly conducted on the basis of a system of ends which is regarded as relatively stable. However, it must not be overlooked that systems of ends are often dynamic entities, and that when analysing some problems this must also be taken into account.[51]

According to formal-teleological theory motives are elements in the explanation of action which are derived from an interpretative reconstruction of the information process which determines action. When we ask what the motive of a particular action is, we presuppose that the (observable) course of a particular action can be attributed to a subject; furthermore we attempt to establish which purposes the action might serve as well as to determine other decisive elements which led to the decision to act. Those action-determining elements which we derive from interpreting the behaviour of acting subjects we call 'motives'. Motives are therefore principally the purposes of the acting subject, grasped by interpretation. In addition, internalised (heteronomous) norms or other elements can also be adduced as factors which determine action (motives in the broadest sense of the term).

Extra-rational (sometimes even pathological) fixations can also be adduced as a particular type of motive to explain action.[52]

The interpretation of motives is also partially based on the statements of the agent, but we are still faced with hermeneutical problems when adopting this approach for the interpretation of motives. The ends which a subject puts forward as his motives are not necessarily to be regarded as his "true" motives. The agent can be insincere; for subconscious reasons he may himself be unclear as to what his true motives are, etc. The agent always feels the need to justify himself, with the result that his own view of his motivation may be mistaken. These problems do not only occur when we are dealing with individual private actors, but also when we are interpreting the acts of institutional persons. For example: the material accompanying drafts of bills provide reasons, that is justifications for the substance of the bill; it would be unwise, however, to assume unreservedly that they always represent the true motives of the legislator.

---

[51]Analyses on the basis of the development of the system of purposes become considerably more complicated and cannot be easily undertaken using the instruments developed here.

[52]To the problem of extra-rational determinants of action cf. O. Weinberger, Rationales und irrationales Handels, in: F. Kaulbach and W. Krawietz (eds.), *Recht und Gesellschaft. Festschrift für Helmut Schelsky zum 65. Geburtstag*, Berlin 1978, p. 737 ff. The theory of action which I espouse can obviously serve as a basis for analyses of subconscious psychological processes and of certain areas of psychopathology, because it does not restrict teleology to consciousness alone and because it provides a reconstructive and modelling procedure for the interpretation of motives.

The Kantian idea, according to which ethics alone determine moral action means the following from the point of view of our theory: moral law should be the only motive for moral action. 'To act ethically' means to act in accordance with the laws of ethics, irrespective of whether one wants to act differently or has different goals. This interpretation is compatible with my theory of action. I have reservations, however, about whether it is in fact possible to act only on the basis of the postulates of the laws of ethics. I would argue that practical goals always play some role in determining action, so that action - even when ethical postulates take absolute precedence - is determined by morality as well as by utility.

It is quite usual to answer the question why a certain subject performed a particular action in the following way, and to regard it as an indication of the motive for action: "*S* did this out of jealousy", "*S* made that mistake, because he was careless" etc. Carelessness or jealousy are certainly not the purposes in the process of deliberating the action. These reasons describe the attitude or the present state of the subject and give an account of how the subject evaluates and makes decisions. They are thus also elements which according to our theory are part of the information process which determines action.

The following theses can be derived from my idea of the analysis of motives:

(1) Our understanding of the motives for action is an act of interpretation, an comprehending explanation of action. For this reason it is necessarily largely hypothetical.

(2) Motives are not causal determinants but explanations based on sympathetic understanding.

(3) Actions are not always determined by a single motive; for this reason a competent analysis of motives should not - as is often the case - present action as the outcome of a single motive.[53]

(4) The motivation of action must be understood as a complex structure of decision-making consisting of (a) purposeful utility which is oriented towards the goals of the acting subject, and (b) normative determination, which essentially follows socially constituted goals.

(5) Determining the motives forms the basis of justification and of moral or legal evaluation. When this evaluation is based on a simplifying analysis of motives - based on the assumption, for example, that there is precisely one motive for a person's action; or that people act either according to the law or for their own ends, whereas it is possible, and in my view expedient, to look for a symbiotic relationship between personal utility and morality - then one arrives at rigorous but hardly convincing moral or legal evaluations.

(6) In rational analyses a clear distinction has to be made between stating the reasons (motives) for action, i.e. answering the question of what the action was intended to achieve, and justifying the action. Justification attempts to give reasons for a positive evaluation of an action. Explaining the reasons behind the

---

[53]Judging and evaluating is simpler when explaining action in that one-dimensional way, but it is certainly not adequate.

action and the action itself by stating motives and evaluating actions are two distinctive processes. Motives (reasons for action) can certainly be adduced as a basis for an evaluative justification.

III. THE SIGNIFICANCE OF LOGIC FOR MODERN LEGAL THEORY FUNDAMENTAL PROBLEMS OF INSTITUTIONALIST NORMATIVISM

1. MAIN AREAS OF LOGICAL ANALYSIS IN THE FIELD OF JURISPRUDENCE

Two features characterise modern legal theory, and both are related to the problem of applying logic to law:

(a) the *structure theory of law*; since *Bentham, Austin, Kelsen, Weyr, Merkl* and *Hart* this theory is considered central to legal theory;[1]

(b) the *theory of rational legal argumentation.*[2]

1.1. *Logic as the Basis of the Structure Theory of Law*

Parallel to the linguistic turn in modern philosophy, legal theorists have been attempting to work out a formally general theory of the structure of the legal order and the processes of legal practice. This theory's aim is to find a structural explanation of the essence of law, to bring logical clarity to legal analyses, and to devise schemata which allow for a standardised representation of the entire body of law of any legal order. In addition this theory spells out what is to be determined by legal interpretation. This is meant by *Kelsen*'s statement that the theory of legal proposition provides legal dogmatics with interpretative schemata.[3]

I think it is justified to view the structure theory of law as analogous to meta-ethical investigations: using the appropriate linguistic tools for a clear scientific discourse and for arriving at cogent forms of argumentation. In addition the structure theory of law - as I conceive of it - has to provide for a formal logic representation of law and it has to explain the connection between the theoretical

---

[1]J. Bentham, *An Introduction to the Principles of Morals and Legislation*, ed. by J.H. Burns/ H.L.A. Hart, London 1970; J. Bentham, *Of Laws in General*, ed. by H.L.A. Hart, London 1970; J. Austin, *Lectures on Jurisprudence or the Philosophy of Positive Law*, London 1885; H. Kelsen, *Hauptprobleme der Staatsrechtslehre*, Tübingen 1911; H. Kelsen, (*Reine Rechtslehre*, 1st ed., Wien 1934, 2nd ed. Wien 1960, English version: *Pure Theory of Law*, Berkeley/Los Angeles/London 1970), F. Weyr, *Základy filosofie právní* (Foundations of Legal Philosophy), Brno 1920; F. Weyr, *Teorie práva* (Theory of Law), Brno/Praha 1936; F. Kubeš, O. Weinberger (eds.), *Die Brünner rechtstheoretische Schule* (*Normative Theorie*), Wien 1980; A. Merkl, *Die Lehre von der Rechtskraft*, Leipzig, Wien 1923; A. Merkl, Prolegomena einer Theorie des rechtlichen Stufenbaues, in: A. Verdross (eds.), *Gesellschaft, Staat und Recht. FS für H. Kelsen*, Wien 1931, pp. 252 ff.; H.L.A. Hart, *The Concept of Law*, Oxford 1961.

[2]Cf. R. Alexy/W. Krawietz (eds.), *Metatheorie der juristischen Argumentation*, Berlin 1983.

[3]H. Kelsen, *Reine Rechtslehre*, 2nd edition, p. 3 f.

normative description of law and the real societal processes. My theory of law which is based on a normativist conception of institutions attempts to meet these requirements.[4]

1.2. *Rational Legal Argumentation*

Everyone demands a rational legal practice and a rationally ordered legal science. And everyone agrees that this goal can only be reached by means of rationally convincing argumentation. Differences arise, however, in the explications of the concept of 'rational legal argumentation' and in the theories which claim to describe and to guide legal argumentation. Some theories include logic, other conceptions separate legal argumentation from logic and logical analysis, because they fear that logical stringency will hamper legal flexibility and will obstruct the finding of a just solution in individual cases.[5]

Logical argumentation is partly logical deduction - then it is cogent proof - and partly it is rhetoric argumentation in the sense of *Chaim Perelman.*

1.2.1. *Areas of legal argumentation.* Legal argumentation is applied in a variety of areas, in particular

(i) when supporting claims as to what is valid law in a given system;

(ii) when giving reasons for legal decisions or of opinions on legal matters independent of actual legal proceedings;

(iii) in analyses and opinions *de lege ferenda* as well as in politico-legal considerations and discretionary issues in the process of arriving at legal decisions (argumentation *de sententia ferenda* in the sense of *A. Ross*);[6]

(iv) in hermeneutical analyses of jurists.

The lines of reasoning in these areas are, of course, not interdependent; e.g., asserting what valid law is depends not only on interrelations of pedigree, but also on questions of the interpretation of legal texts.

---

[4]O. Weinberger, Die Norm als Gedanke und Realität, *ÖZÖR* 20 (1970), pp. 203 - 216; O. Weinberger, Tatsachen und Tatsachenbeschreibungen. Eine logisch-methodologische Überlegung zu einem Grundlagenproblem der Sozialwissenschaft, in: K. Salamun (ed.), *Sozialphilosophie als Aufklärung. Festschrift für E. Topitsch*, Tübingen 1979, pp. 173 - 187; O. Weinberger, Zur Idee eines institutionalistischen Rechtspositivismus. Gleichzeitig eine Auseinandersetzung mit Hans Kelsens Setzungspositivismus, in: "*Kelsen et le positivisme juridique*", *Revue Internationale de Philosophie* 35 (1981), Vol. 4, pp. 487 - 507. D.N. MacCormick/O. Weinberger, *An Institutional Theory of Law. New Approaches to Legal Positivism*, Dordrecht et al. 1986 (German version: *Grundlagen des Institutionalistischen Rechtspositivismus*, Berlin 1985).

[5]Compare the sententia: *Omnis definitio in iure civili periculosa est* (Javolenus); see also: Th. Viehweg, *Topik und Jurisprudenz*, München 1974^5 (1953^1).

[6]A. Ross, *Law and Justice*, London 1958, pp. 331 f.

1.2.2. *Various views on rational legal argumentation*. The following short overview is meant to direct the reader's attention to the various approaches to the problem of legal argumentation.

The widely known and certainly important theory of *Perelman* - which he calls "new rhetoric" or "theory of argumentation" - starts from the pragmatic aspects of the process of persuasion: A speaker faces an audience which he attempts to convince of a thesis or of an attitude (an evaluation).[7] The decisive question, namely at what point this is to be regarded as a rational process, *Perelman* explains by the regulative notion of the universal audience. An argumentation is then rational, when it presupposes to address itself to a universal audience. The process of persuasion should thereby be objectified.

German-speaking legal scientists have for decades discussed extensively the topical conception of legal argumentation, whose main representative was *Viehweg*.[8] This theory actually has little to offer, it emphasises the many-sidedness of legal reflection, but it does not offer useful rules for the argumentative process.

Today's discussion focuses on the procedural theory which follows *Habermas*' ideas and whose main proponent *Alexy* has introduced it into legal theory.[9] According to this view rationality is based on an intersubjective discourse which follows certain rules about how to conduct a discussion. This theory is based on the presupposition - which I find very problematical - that such discourses and the consensus reached through them necessarily lead to the truth and to the right conception. But the essential problem of what good reasons are, and how appropriate methods of proof and of supporting evidence can be established, is hardly considered by this theory.

I also have to mention the view of those legal theoreticians who come from the hermeneutic philosophical tradition. They are of the opinion - at least as far as legal interpretation is concerned - that legal argumentation is an extra-logical, circular process from the point of view of hermeneutics.[10]

I will attempt to put forward a conception of legal argumentation which ascribes a key role to logical analysis - together with attitudinal moments (see section 4).

2. LOGIC, LAW, AND THE PROBLEMS OF THE LOGIC OF NORMS

The fact that norms (viz. their linguistic formulations: normative sentences) are the subject of analysis lends to the question of the application of logic to law and to legal theory a special aspect. To elucidate the basic problems of the

---

[7]Ch. Perelman/L. Olbrechts-Tyteca, *Traité de l'argumentation*, Bruxelles 1970^2 (Paris 1958^1).
[8]Th. Viehweg, *op. cit.*
[9]R. Alexy, *Theorie der juristischen Argumentation. Die Theorie des rationalen Diskurses als Theorie der juristischen Begründung*, Frankfurt/Main 1978; English translation:
[10]H.-G. Gadamer, *Wahrheit und Methode. Grundzüge einer philosophischen Hermeneutik*, Tübingen 1972^3; K. Larenz, *Methodenlehre der Rechtswissenschaft*, Berlin/Heidelberg/New York 1975^3, pp. 183 ff.

logic of norms turns into a precondition of defining the role of logic within the area of law.

2.1. *The Semantic Basis of the Logic of Norms and Action-related (or Practical) Disciplines*

At least since *Hume* and *Kant* the semantic characteristics of normative sentences - especially as opposed to descriptive sentences - are philosophical common currency.[11] The difference between sentences whose function it is to describe facts - descriptive sentences - and sentences which exercise a rogatory, imperative or evaluative function - practical sentences - seems to have been a part of linguistic consciousness from time immemorial.

We are now faced with the following questions:

(i) What is the philosophical basis for the categorical semantic distinction between descriptive and practical sentences?

(ii) How can we arrive at a theory of the logical connections between practical sentences and of the logical operations of practical sentences, or of how practical and theoretical sentences actually work? Our main concern here is to lay the philosophical foundations of the logic of norms.

(iii) What is to be understood by the actual social existence of normative regulations, particulary of legal orders?

(iv) Under what methodological assumptions is a formal logical analysis in practical disciplines possible?

Answers to these questions are based on anthropological considerations. Two essential features of human beings are relevant here and form the philosophical basis of an appropriate semantics for practical disciplines:

1. Man is an acting subject,[12]
2. Man is a *zoon politikon.*[13]

Action is information-oriented behaviour controlled by information. It only makes sense to speak of *action* if there exists a range for action, i.e. when it can be assumed that the acting subject can, at certain times and dependent on the processing of relevant information, adopt several different modes of conduct. Room for choosing a specific conduct means that in the course of a subject's conduct there are points where alternatives of possible conduct open up. The existence of such points cannot be fixed absolutely, they depend on the particular time of consideration and, on the other hand, on institutions, knowledge etc.[14]

---

[11] D. Hume, Hamburg 1973, 2nd book, p. 211; I. Kant, *Grundlegung zur Metaphysik der Sitten*, 2. Abs. III 34.

[12] A. Gehlen, *Der Mensch. Seine Natur und seine Stellung in der Welt*, Bonn 1955.

[13] Aristoteles, *Politics*, 1st and 3rd book.

[14] O. Weinberger, Eine Semantik für die praktische Philosophie, *Grazer Philosophische Studien*, Vol. 20, 1983, pp. 219 - 239; W. Weinberger, Freedom, Range for Action, and the Ontology of Norms, in: R. Haller (ed.), *Beiträge zur Philosophie von Stephan Körner, Grazer Philosophische Studien* 20 (1983), pp. 219-239.

The information processing which determines action is based on two different kinds of information: on purely *descriptive information* (descriptions of facts: information about the situation in which the action takes place, causal information based on causal laws), and on *practical information*, such as goals, ought-determinations and information about what is permissible, relative evaluations etc. Descriptive information alone is not sufficient for information processing for determining action. This finding of the theory of action is in my view the true reason for the categorial differentiation between theoretical (descriptive) and practical sentences, as well as for the differentiation between 'is' and 'ought', i.e. for that semantic conception which I have called *gnoseologically differentiated semantics*.[15]

I want to emphasise that this fundamental difference is to be understood only as a semantic one (or as pertaining to *information theory*); we are not speaking here of ontologically different realms of entities. Terms such as 'the realm of purposes' and the 'world of norms' are to be eschewed or to be understood figuratively only.

In this sense a norm is an ideal entity which can be put into words, which is examined as a thought content *sui generis*, and which is an element of logical relations. These relations exist independently of the fact whether the norms in question have a social existence. From the point of view of information processing the existence of logical relations of normative elements is as unproblematical as applying the rules of deduction to practical sentences. The dichotomy of truth of facts vs. truth of reason is replaced by conceiving of reasoning as the capacity for logical analysis and for operating within the field of descriptive and practical information.

The logical relations and operations refer to ideal entities and/or to their linguistic formulations.

2.2. *The Existence of Normative Regulations and the Institutionalist Conception of Law*

The problem of the social existence of normative regulations is a crucial basic question when considering man as an agent, social relations and when considering legal science as a social science.

There exists an intrinsic connection between human action, society, cooperation with institutions and practical information, particularly normative regulations. According to the institutionalist-normativist conception which I espouse institutions and practical informations (especially normative regulations) are essentially linked.

(a) Institutions are constituted by normative regulations; *no institution without normative regulations.*

---

[15]Ch. Weinberger/O. Weinberger, *Logik, Semantik, Hermeneutik*, München 1979, p. 13, p. 109; O. Weinberger, *Rechtslogik*, 2nd ed., Berlin 1989.

(b) *The socially real existence of a normative regulation* - e.g. of a legal system - *is based on the interplay of the system of norms as comprehensible ideal entities and observable processes of the social reality.*

Cicero's *"ubi societas, ibi ius"* essentially expresses this idea.

Thus institutionalist normativism represents a specific conception of legal reality, i.e. of legal validity, which is seen as the connection between normative regulations as ideal entities and observable social processes. And this conception likewise views the dynamics of law as a totality of complex processes in the area of the system of norms *and* of the associated real and observable processes (see section 4) - as opposed to *Kelsen* who regards the dynamic of law essentially as processes within the world of norms.[16]

The institutionalist-normativist theory is in accord with a broad conception of law as a social phenomenon: law is not only the system of rules of conduct and their generation, plus the totality of their normative consequences (including, as the case may be, sometimes findings of facts as premises) - i.e. individual legal norms, obligations, demands etc. -, law also includes the more abstract rules of law (i.e. basic legal principles), the teleological background of law as well as the entire body of institutions of the legal system including also jurisprudence and legal dogmatics.

Forms of life and the sense of human modes of conduct actually exist only within an institutional framework. According to the institutionalist view human reality is more than what can be learned from observable facts, i.e. more than externally observable human behaviour; and this institutional reality can only be grasped and described when practical sentences, or descriptions embracing practical conceptual elements are taken into consideration. Institutions form the frameworks of our lives by establishing how we ought to behave and act and by determining - together with other factors - our expectations of how our fellow human beings and immediate associates will behave.

2.3. *Institutionalist Normativism and the Logic of Norms*

Institutionalist normativism is based on the idea of a *genuine logic of norms*.

Normative information, just as information about facts, are pieces of communication, that is specific mental contents which can be intersubjectively conveyed by means of a string of linguistic signs. It must be presupposed that norms can always be expressed by virtue of an appropriate linguistic system; but it should not be assumed that all norms which exist in a society are explicitely stated.

Legal norms are in practice usually expressed in colloquial language, sometimes partially in a fixed technical language. The formulation of a norm as it appears in the legal texts cannot be taken as the basis for logical operations. Logical rules are applied only to a *standardised form*; the actual legal material has first to be interpreted. Then it is presupposed that the legal contents are repre-

---

[16] H. Kelsen, *Reine Rechtslehre (Pure Theory of Law)*, 2nd edition, pp. 196 ff.

sented in standardised formulations; strictly speaking the logical rules relate only to norms in such a formulation. (The same holds also for the application of logic in other domains.)

The normative system is a control system, i.e. it is supposed to determine in a certain way the actions and the behaviour of the persons involved. Hence it follows that *ought-sentences express the primary normative determinants, and sentences about what is permissible only play a secondary role*. Control always means a restricting of possibilities, and only the 'ought' can express a restriction of the scope for possible conduct, because the 'ought', but not the 'may' can be infringed upon.[17]

Institutionalist normativism starts from a fundamental category of the norm, or the normative sentence. *A uniform conception of the normative sentence is possible only if the meaning of the normative sentence is distinguished from its pragmatic functions. One and the same sentence can - depending on the situation and circumstances - serve different pragmatic functions without changing its meaning*. This is not only true for normative sentences, but for other sentences as well. For example: "Water freezes at 0°C" is a true statement; the sentence can, however, serve the function of establishing the zero point on the Celsius scale.

When my companion says "It is red," as we approach the intersection, the sentence certainly is a statement about the actual condition of the traffic light, but it can serve as well the function of a warning or a request to stop.

The distinction between the meaning and the pragmatical function of a sentence is particularly important for the analysis of normative sentences. *One and the same normative sentence can - without altering its meaning - serve different pragmatical functions*.

By means of a certain speech act, i.e. the use of the normative sentence in a given real situation, a legal norm can be generated by this act, or information about the content of a legal order can be conveyed, or the sentence can be stated for the purpose of linguistic analysis only, etc.[18]

---

[17]Ch. Weinberger/O. Weinberger, *op. cit.* pp. 114 ff.; Ch. Weinberger/O. Weinberger, Versuch einer neuen Grundlegung der normenlogischen Folgerungstheorie, in: *Argumentation und Her-meneutik in der Jurisprudenz, Rechtstheorie*, Beiheft 1 (1979), pp. 301 - 324; O. Weinberger, *Rechtslogik*, 2nd edition, *op. cit.* pp. 231 f.

[18]O. Weinberger, *Eine Semantik für die praktische Philosophie*, op. cit., pp. 232 f.

3. THE IDEA OF A LOGIC OF NORMS REMARKS ON A FEW FUNDAMENTAL PROBLEMS

Looking at the history of ideas there are principally two factors which have led to the development of research into the logic of norms:

(a) the necessity to establish a theory of thought operations for all fields of practical philosophy, particularly for ethics and jurisprudence;

(b) and the research of the logicians who noticed parallels between the (alethic) modal logic and other areas, particularly the domain of norms, and who began to study them in detail (*A. Höfler, G.H. von Wright, G. Kalinowski, O. Becker*).[19]

3.1. *The Semantics of the Normative Sentences*

It seems that even today the semantic problems of normative sentences has not been solved entirely, although distinguished thinkers have for more than half a century conducted intensive research on the logic of norms.[20] The semantic peculiarity of normative sentences as opposed to descriptive ones is almost universally recognised and presupposed in practical philosophy, yet there are at least three problematical areas in the semantics of norms:

(a) Many writers only consider the categories of normative and descriptive sentences; in my opinion, however, it is necessary to consider the category of *descriptive (or theoretical) sentences* over against the general category of *practical sentences*. Normative sentences are only one kind of practical sentences, other kinds being evaluative sentences and sentences expressing a purpose (a demand).[21]

(b) Time and again the opinion is voiced that there are ought-sentences (or normative sentences) of a descriptive and ought-sentences of a prescriptive nature. This duality of the object of the logical analysis of norms takes two

---

[19]A. Höfler, Abhängigkeitsbeziehungen zwischen Abhängigkeitsbeziehungen, in: *Kaiserliche Akademie der Wissenschaften in Wien, Philosophisch-historische Klasse, Sitzungsberichte* 181, vol. 4, 1917, pp. 1 - 56; G.H. von Wright, Deontic Logic, *Mind* 60 (1951), pp. 1 - 15; G. Kalinowski, Théorie des propositions normatives, *Studia Logica* 1 (1953), pp. 146 - 182; O. Becker, *Untersuchungen über den Modalkalkül*, Meisenheim /Glan 1952. Cf. also: O. Weinberger, *Die Sollsatzproblematik in der modernen Logik*, Praha 1958, reprinted in: O. Weinberger, *Studien zur Normenlogik und Rechtsinformatik*, Berlin 1974, pp. 59 - 186; O. Weinberger, Theorie des propositions normatives. Quelques remarques au sujet de l'interprétation normative des systèmes K_1 et K_2 de M. Kalinowski, *Studia Logica*, Vol. 9, 1950, pp. 7 - 25, reprinted in German translation in: O. Weinberger, *Studien zur Normenlogik und Rechtsinformatik*, pp. 187 - 212; O. Weinberger, Probleme der normativ-juristischen Deutung des Modalkalküls von Oskar Becker, *Conceptus* 4 (1970), pp. 22 - 31.

[20]Cf. the bibliography of works on the logic of norms by A.G. Conte/G. Di Bernardo, 1973, and J. Berkemann/P. Strasser, in: H. Lenk (ed.), *Normenlogik*, Pullach/München 1974.

[21]O. Weinberger, Versuch einer neuen Grundlegung der normenlogischen Folgerungstheorie, in: W. Krawietz/K. Opalek/A. Peczenik/A. Schramm (eds.), Argumentation und Hermeneutik in der Jurisprudenz, *Rechtstheorie*, Beiheft 1 (1979), pp. 306 f., pp. 315 f.

forms: either one and the same linguistic formation is ascribed simultaneously a descriptive and a prescriptive meaning; or two different - in some way correlated - sentences which express an 'ought' or a 'may' are distinguished: one of them is conceived of as descriptive, the other as prescriptive. The essentially analogous distinctions of such pairs carry various names: *Kelsen*'s distinction between *Rechtsnorm* and *Rechtssatz* is one of the best known; in the area of the logic of norms, for example, *von Wright* distinguishes between 'norm-formulation' and 'normative statement'.[22]

Kalinowski suggested a terminological distinction between *normative* and *deontic* sentences, where the latter are defined as descriptive sentences about norms.[23] Actually it would be better to define the deontic sentence as a proposition about a system of norms (which could include a single norm only) than to define it as a descriptive sentence about a norm. These sentences are not always propositions about single given norms of the system of norms, instead they are propositions about some elements of the set of consequences following from the given norms (using occasionally also factual premises).

It seems to me to be a necessary precondition for the development and the application of a logic of norms to distinguish between the normative sentences and its various pragmatic functions. A logical analysis of the normative realms means to analyse normative sentences as expressions of normative thoughts (of 'ought' and 'may'). *The illusion to arrive at a sound logic of the area of prescriptive language through "descriptive normative sentences" must be abandoned*, regardless whether we call these sentences "Rechtssätze", deontic sentences or by another name.

Note:

Of course it is possible to form descriptive sentences about norms or descriptive sentences about normative sentences. These propositions can say very different things about norms and normative sentences, they do not concern always the validity of norms or normative sentences. The logic of norms is neither a logic of the descriptive sentences about norms nor of the descriptive sentences about normative sentences.[24]

Kelsen provides a striking example of how an analysis of descriptive sentences about norms can lead to conclusions which are misleading and false in the context of a logic of norms. In the 2nd edition of his "Pure Theory of Law" he attempts to base the principle of contradiction which applies to legal propositions[25]: "Therefore, logical principles in general, and the Principle of the Exclu-

---

[22]H.G. von Wright, *Norm und Action*, London 1963, pp. 93 ff., p. 132 *et passim*.

[23]G. Kalinowski, Du métalangage en logique. Réflexions sur la logique déontique et son rapport avec la logique des normes, *Documents de Travail et pré-publications, Università di Urbino*, Nr. 48, 1975, Series A.

[24]Statements about a norm are not only the usual sentences of the type 'Norm *N* is valid', but also e.g. 'The norm, that ..., is unjust,' or 'The normative sentence *N* is a hypothetical normative sentence'.

[25]H. Kelsen, *op. cit.*, pp. 209 f. Quotation from the English translation by M. Knight, University of California Press Berkeley et alia 1967, p. 206.

sion of Contradictions in particular, are applicable to rules of law describing legal norms and therefore indirectly also to legal norms. Hence it is by no means absurd to say that two legal norms 'contradict' each other. And therefore only one of the two can be regarded as objectively valid. To say that *a* ought to be and at the same time ought not to be is just as meaningless as to say that *a* is and at the same time that it is not. A conflict of norms is just as meaningless as a logical contraction."

In my eyes this is not only a false but even a grotesque way to argue, namely because of two reasons: (i) There exists no logical contradiction between the cited propositions of law; both can be true if the legal order actually includes the two norms '*A* ought to be' and 'non-*A* ought to be'. (ii) The impression that these two declarative sentences about norms of the legal order (the propositions of law) are in logical conflict, is obviously only the result of the fact that the norms are incompatible from the point of view of the logic of norms. (iii) It is quite clearly impossible to base the definition of incompatibility between the corresponding legal norms (normative sentences) on a non-existent contradiction in the area of the quoted declarative sentences (propositions of law). (iv) It is also not possible to establish a postulate of consistency for legal norms (ought-sentences) on the basis of the relationships between legal propositions, because the legal propositions cited are in fact compatible.

(c) Some writers - particularly *Gardies* - doubt that there exists a sharp separation between normative and descriptive sentences.[26] There can hardly be a doubt, however, that the meaning of 'You are doing *A*' and 'You ought to do *A*' is fundamentally different. Even *Gardies* will agree to that. He supports his argument by pointing out that there are mixed sentences, i.e. sentences which consist of descriptive and normative partial sentences, and that these mixed sentences lie somewhere between normative and descriptive sentences. I agree with *Gardies* that there are mixed sentences and that they are of great importance for the normative disciplines, and that therefore they must be taken into account by every practicable semantics of norms. In order to grasp their nature we have to look at the construction of mixed sentences in general: A mixed sentence is formed by a sentence-forming operator. A sentence-forming operator is defined by the following elements:

(i) the determination of the arguments (their number; the semantic-categorial characteristics of each argument),

(ii) the successive order of the arguments, and

(iii) the determination of the semantic-categorial character of the sentences which can be formed by means of the respective operator.

The semantic character of compound sentences is defined as a functional (i.e. unequivocal) determination.

The following semantic definitions are pertinent to the characterisation of compound sentences formed by a given operator:
(a) it is a descriptive sentence;

---

[26] J.-L. Gardies, Le problème logique et le problème philosophique du passage de l'être au devoir-être, *ARSP 68* (1982), pp. 281 - 298.

(b) it is a normative sentence;
(c) it is a semantically new type of sentences which is neither a descriptive nor a normative sentence.

The third assumption (c) which *Gardies* obviously supports, leads to a complicated system of types of sentences, because the compound sentence can - of course according to particular rules - lead to yet more complex sentences. (This also would mean that ever more new types of sentence-forming operators would have to be introduced, since their arguments would be of different types.) It is clear that such a semantics is very difficult to handle, and one would choose it only as a last resort.

I think that descriptive and normative sentence-forming operators with semantically mixed arguments can be introduced without such difficulties. In practice the most important operator of this type is the operator of the *hypothetical normative sentences:* the antecedent is descriptive, the consequent normative, the compound proposition as a whole is to be understood as a normative sentence.[27]

The logical nature of the hypothetical normative sentence is thereby of course not yet determined. Perhaps a working definition can be given by establishing that a detachment rule and a rule of hypothetical extension applies to the hypothetical normative sentence, whereby it follows from " *p* ought to be": 'If *verum*, then *p* ought to be' (see section 3.6).

3.2. *Normative Sentence and Truth Value*

The categorial distinction between normative sentences and descriptive sentences is usually based upon the fact that truth values can be attributed reasonably to the latter but not to the former. I am of the opinion - as I have said in a paper in 1972[28] - that the thesis that normative sentences have no truth value is plausible within the accepted conception of semantics and of the notion of truth; however, I believe that also other definitions of the notion of truth are possible, in such a way as to allow us to classify normative sentences as true or false. This type of the concept of truth entails however a splitting of this concept into a declarative truth and a normative truth, so that the categorial distinction which corresponds to the separation of descriptive from practical information is maintained (on another level, of course).[29] The interpretation of normative sentences on the basis of a semantics of possible worlds suggested by *Gardies* can also be taken into consideration here: however, it must not be overlooked

---

[27]O. Weinberger, Teorie dusledkovych vztahu a hyposthetická normativní věta (Theory of Relations of Inference and the Hypothetical Normative Sentence), in: O. Weinberger, *Studie k logice normativních vět* (*Studies in the Logic of Norms*), Praha 1960; O. Weinberger, *Studien zur Normenlogik und Rechtsinformatik*, op. cit., pp. 20 f.

[28]O. Weinberger, Bemerkungen zur Grundlegung der Theorie des juristischen Denkens, in: H. Albert et al., *Rechtstheorie als Grundlagenwissenschaft der Rechtswissenschaft*, Düsseldorf 1972, pp. 134 - 161.

[29]O. Weinberger, *op. cit.*, pp. 52 ff.

that the postulated difference between descriptive and practical information is - and has to be - maintained here, too, since the concept of admissible worlds introduces the distinction between these two types of information.

The general postulate of the categorial distinction between information which describes facts and practical information is valid in any case. This separation can be effected in different ways in semantics and its corresponding logical systems (see the principle of tolerance in logic).[30]

The philosophical basis for demanding a cognitively differentiated semantics for the domain of practical philosophy rests upon an analysis of the nature of the information-processing which underlies action. There are various ways of satisfying the postulate of differentiating between descriptive and practical information. Defining the concept of truth in such a way that it approximates most closely to ordinary linguistic usage and corresponds to the accepted conceptual apparatus of the disciplines which deal with actions makes it just as meaningless to call normative sentences true or false as it would be to call prime numbers healthy or ill (*Dubislav*)[31].

I would like to note at this point that the question of the semantic definitions which decide whether normative sentences have truth value must not be confounded with the problem of cognitivism. The cognitivist view claims that an objective justification of norms is possible purely cognitively and without resort to decisions; the non-cognitivist denies this. I think that each of these conceptions can be represented within different semantic systems.[32]

The recognition of norms must not be interpreted as if there actually existed objectively valid normative entities which would have to be apprehended in a fashion analogous to the way in which the material world is apprehended through sensory perception. This is impossible, if only because norms are pieces of information and can thus not be observed but only understood. This has to be acknowledged even by those who for some reason - e.g. religious faith or belief in theories of evolution - suppose that there is an objectively correct 'ought'.

3.3. *Are there Normological Inferences?*

Although the question of whether there can exist at all deductive arguments in the logic of norms was formulated clearly by Jørgensen at an early stage in the research of this field, *Jørgensen's dilemma* hardly kept anyone from studies in the logic of norms.[33] Even those writers who denied that deductive arguments are possible in the logic of norms - *Jørgensen* himself, *Karel Engliš* and *Hans Kelsen* in his later work - all partially bowed to prevailing thought in

---

[30] R. Carnap, *Logische Syntax der Sprache*, Vienna 1968[2] (1934[1]), pp. 44 ff.; his thesis is: "In der Logik gibt es keine Moral" ("There is no morality in logic") (p. 45).

[31] W. Dubislav, Zur Unbegründbarkeit der Forderungssätze, *Theoria* 3 (1973), pp. 330 - 342.

[32] Cf. O. Weinberger, *Eine Semantik für die praktische Philosophie*, *op. cit.*

[33] J. Jørgensen, Imperatives and Logic, *Erkenntnis* 7 (1937/38), pp. 288 - 296.

normative research by substituting a kind of "roundabout method of deduction in norm-logic" for pure norm-logical deduction.[34]

This historical development of deontic logic has in fact simply passed *Jørgensen*'s dilemma by; as far as I know my book *Die Sollsatzproblematik in der modernen Logik* contains the first detailed discussion of the problems raised by *Jørgensen.*[35] Only recently has this question again come to be considered a serious philosophical problem of fundamental importance to the logic of norms.[36]

There is no objective reason why norm-logical deduction should not be possible, and in practice it is widely used in normative disciplines in the belief that it is obvious (with the exception of some inferential relations which may be controversial).

Norms are without doubt thoughts in themselves (thoughts in the objective, i.e. non-psychological sense), which can be regarded as the meanings of specific linguistic expressions. Practice recognises that there are obvious formal connections: incompatibilities ("contradictions") between normative sentences and normative inferences. It must therefore be possible to formulate these relations and operations as rules and develop them into a logical theory.

In the realm of descriptive sentences, too, logical relations are independent of the actual truth of the premises; and the process of deduction can be thought of as an operation according to rules, whereby the concept of truth is left out of consideration altogether. Why should it not be possible to "play a game of deduction" with normative sentences as elements? I can think of no reason for this apart from prejudices and fixed conceptual stipulations which are nevertheless not immutable.

3.4. *Logic of Norms or Deontic Logic?*

In my critical analysis of *Kelsen's* attempt to explain the concept of the contradiction between normative sentences (in his terminology 'Rechtsnormen') and to introduce a norm-logical postulate of consistency I have already demonstrated that norm-logical relations cannot be grasped by means of a logic of descriptive sentences about norms. The analogous is also true of deductive reasoning. A theory of norm-logical inference must thus be a logic of norms and not a deontic logic.

The genuine logic of norms interprets systems of norms as systems of thoughts (of sentences expressing norms), and in such a way that the logical

---

[34]J. Jørgensen, *op. cit.*; K. Engliš, Die Norm ist kein Urteil, *ARSP* 50 (1964), pp. 305 - 316; H. Kelsen, *Allgemeine Theorie der Normen*, K. Ringhofer and R. Walter (eds.), Wien 1979. Cf. also O. Weinberger, *Normentheorie als Grundlage der Jurisprudenz und Ethik. Eine Auseinandersetzung mit Hans Kelsens Theorie der Normen*, Berlin 1981, pp. 105 ff.

[35]O. Weinberger, *Die Sollsatzproblematik in der modernen Logik*, *op. cit.*

[36]Cf. e.g. Carlos E. Achourrón, Antonio A. Martino, Logica sin verdad, *Theoria*, Segunda Epoca-Año III. Curso 1987-88, No. 7-8, pp. 7-43; English version: Logic Without Truth, in: *Ratio Juris*, vol. 3, Nr. 1/1990, pp. 46-67.

relations remain unchanged even if the normative sentences fulfil various additional pragmatic functions. Figuratively speaking, the same logic governs the thinking of the legislator, the person to whom the norm is addressed and the legal scholar, and in all instances the same norm-logical deductions apply.

It is, of course, possible to develop deontic logics as logics of descriptive sentences about normative systems. However, these types of logics are to be regarded as secondary systems which reflect the logical relations of the genuine logic of norms. Deontic systems assume a different character depending on the additional postulates about the norm systems which they describe. For example, it is of crucial importance for the construction of the deontic system whether consistency of the normative system is presupposed, whether the system is considered open or closed, and whether it is supposed that the deontic subjects will always behave in accordance with their 'oughts'.

The so-called standard systems suppose that the system of norms is free of contradictions and closed, as well as that the persons to whom the norm is addressed will behave in accordance with the system. If the system were not to be free of contradictions, the interdefinition of the deontic operators could not be established. If it were not supposed that the system is closed, thc maxim "what is not forbidden is permitted" would not be generally valid. The universal good conduct of the deontic subjects must be supposed if the following deductions are considered valid:

(i) $\dfrac{Op}{O(p \vee q)}$ (*Ross'* Paradox)[37]

(ii) $\dfrac{O(p \& q)}{Op, Oq}$ [38]

If 'Op' is not fulfilled, then according to (i) there would exist the obligation to fulfil q (and q can be anything whatever), because - under the present hypothesis - only then can '$O\ (p \vee q)$' be fulfilled. But exactly this is the reason why the deduction (i) appears absurd.

It is illuminating to compare the deduction in proposition logic and the analogous norm-logical deduction at this point:

(a) $\dfrac{p}{p \vee q}$

(b) $\dfrac{Op}{O\ (p \vee q)}$

In the case of the propositional-logical deduction according to (a) it is impossible - because of the premise 'p' - to adduce '$\neg p$' as a further premise;

[37] A. Ross, *Directives and Norms*, London 1968, p. 176.

[38] O. Weinberger, Der Begriff der Nicht-Erfüllung und die Normenlogik, *Ratio* 14 (1972), pp. 15 - 32.

however, this is entirely possible in the case of the norm-logical deduction; '$\neg p$'means only that '*Op*' is not fulfilled.[39]

No less problematic than the much discussed paradox put forward by *Ross* is the rule of deontic standard systems according to which it is possible to divide a conjoined prescription in the content of an ought-sentence into two independent precepts - see (ii). Let us look at the following norms as examples:

(1) It is obligatory (to turn on the central heating and to keep the windows closed). $[O(p\& q)]$

(2) If the windows are not shut, then the central heating must be switched off. $[\neg q > O \neg p]$

It is quite usual for two norms of this type to be valid in a system of norms at the same time and no-one regards this as inconsistent. Nevertheless according to standard systems there is at least a latent contradiction between them, and an actual contradiction appears as soon as $\neg p$ is the case:
from (1) follows '*Op*';
from (2) and '$\neg q$' follows '$O \neg p$';
and these two conclusions are incompatible.

It is possible that one part of the conjunction in the content of the ought-sentence is not fulfilled; the obligation to accomplish the other part of the ordered content must not, however, be inferred from this. This partial obligation alone may - as we have shown - even be forbidden.

This is also clearly demonstrated by the relations of complementary goods: 'buy cigarettes and matches' does not allow us to infer 'buy cigarettes', for the order to buy cigarettes seems devoid of purpose if matches are not bought as well.

The logic of descriptive sentences about systems of norms is not only a secondary system in relation to the logic of norms; the standard systems - obviously seduced by analogies to alethic modal logic - even advance false theses about norm-logical relations.

3.5. *The Meta-postulate of the Non-derivability of 'Ought' from 'Is' and of 'Is' from 'Ought'*

If normative sentences (ought-sentences) could be logically deduced from declarative sentences alone, then it would be unnecessary to introduce the concept of a normative sentence, for a logical consequence cannot contain any information that is not at least implicitely contained in the premises.

The rules of inference of a logic of norms as a logical system with two categories of sentences - descriptive and normative - must contain the meta-postulate of non-derivability.

However, some caution is necessary when formulating the postulates (theses) of non-derivability. Just as there are non-informative sentences in the logic of descriptive language which also follow from the empty set of premises (e.g. sentences of the form '$p \rightarrow p$'), there can also be non-informative normative

---

[39] O. Weinberger, *op. cit.*

sentences which follow also from an empty set of premises (or premises which contain only descriptive sentences), for example the hypothetical ought-sentence 'If (p and non-p), then q ought to be' ['$(p \mathbin{\&} \neg p) > 0q$'].[40]

There can also be inferences which lead to a normative conclusion, although there are no normative sentences among the premises, but only other practical sentences, e.g. demands which express purposes.[41]

3.6. *Compound Normative Sentences, Particularly the Hypothetical Normative Sentence*

In propositional logic the sentence-forming operators are defined as truth-functions, and the compound sentences consist of descriptive partial sentences, i.e. the arguments of the operators are descriptive sentences.

There is no doubt that there are also other - so-called non-extensional - compound sentences in descriptive scientific language. I cite the following as examples: '..., because...'; or counter-factual conditional clauses (which, if one were to interpret them as conditional sentences expressing truth-functions, might never be false, but which are sometimes obviously false, e.g.: 'If Hitler had won the Second World War, he would have converted to Judaism').[42]

How can we arrive at compound sentences with normative sentences as arguments? One possible way would be to regard the matrices of the operators '$\vee$', '& ', '$\rightarrow$', '$\equiv$' as determined by neutral values (positive/negative, yes/no, 1/0), so that normative arguments and the value interpretation 'valid/invalid' could be applied to them.[43] This method does not work with mixed compound sentences, for the categorially distinctive character of the arguments must be taken into consideration, just as it is impossible to interpret *promiscue* the symbols '1' and '0' as 'true' or 'valid' and 'false' or 'invalid'. Moreover, in the case of mixed compound sentences it could not be determined whether the compound sentence as a whole is a descriptive or a normative sentence.

In practice the most important mixed compound sentence is certainly the hypothetical normative sentence (normative conditional). Its sentence-forming operator '>' obviously has to have the following properties:

(i) it is a normative-sentence-forming operator with two arguments;

---

[40] O. Weinberger, Kann man das normenlogische Folgerunssystem philosophisch begründen? Überlegungen zu den Grundlagen des juristischen Folgerns, *ARSP* 65/2 (1979), pp. 161 - 186. Cf. in particular note 28 above.

[41] O. Weinberger, Rationale und empirische Kontexte der Rechtsnorm, *Wissenschaft und Weltbild* 26 (1973), pp. 99 - 108, esp. pp. 107 f.

[42] O. Weinberger, Kontrafaktualität und Faktentranszendenz. Versuch, die Logik der faktentranszendenten und kontrafaktualen Bedingungssätze mit den Mitteln der extensionalen Logik zu behandeln, *Ratio* 16/1 (1974), pp. 13 - 28.

[43] I. Tammelo, *Outlines of Modern Legal Logic*, Wiesbaden 1969.

(ii) the first argument (the antecedent) is a descriptive sentence (it would also be possible to introduce normatively conditioned normative conditionals, but we will not persue this possibility any further here[44]);

(iii) the second argument (the consequent) is a normative sentence. I see no difficulties in introducing this type of operator; it certainly would have to be characterised by certain logical rules which determine its meaning. Since it is to express a conditional clause, it is appropriate to define it by a rule which allows the detachment of the fulfilled condition:

$p > Oq$
p (*norm-logical rule of detachment*)

Oq

Another rule must be established which permits the transition from an categorial normative sentence (*'Oq'*) to a hypothetical normative sentence with a true condition:

Oq

$(p \vee \neg p) > Oq$ this rule could also take the form:

Oq
p

$p > Oq$

4. THE INSTITUTIONALIST STRUCTURE THEORY OF LAW

The normative-institutionalist conception corresponds to a structure theory of law which deviates from traditional opinions. It takes certain elements from normativism, particularly from *Kelsen*'s Pure Theory of Law, from *Weyr* and *Merkl* as well as from *Hart*;[45] in a certain respect, however, it is closer to the moderate legal realism of *Alf Ross* and *Aulis Aarnio*.[46]

Legal validity is interpreted as a pedigree relation[47], with the main emphasis placed on the logical basis of the processes by which the norms are

---

[44]O. Weinberger, Teorie dusledkovych vztahu a hypothetická normativní věta, [Theory of Entailment Relations and the Normative Conditional] *op. cit.*

[45]Cf. note 1

[46]A. Ross, *Law and Justice*, op. cit., pp. 42 ff.; A. Aarnio, *On Legal Reasoning*, Turku 1977; A. Aarnio, The Foundation of Legal Reasoning, *Rechtstheorie* 12 (1981), pp. 423 - 448.

[47]R. Dworkin, *Taking Rights Seriously*, London 1977, p. 17.

generated. The pedigree relation is drawn up in standard logical form, starting from the principle of co-validity, according to which in every normative system the class of valid norms CN entails simultaneously the validity of the class of its consequences, and of those inferences which can be derived from CN by adducing true determinations of fact.[48]

The power-conferring norm, on which the normatively conceived generation of norms is based, is understood as a particular type of normative conditional sentence. Its distinctive quality resides in the fact that the antecedent set as condition of subsumption is an act of creating a norm, and that the content of this act forms the content of the *consequent* of the power-conferring rule.[49]

The validity of a legal norm is not grounded in its reference to another norm only - as in *Kelsen* for example [50] -, but in two indispensible elements: the normative basis and the actual occurrence (e.g. of the process of generation) in reality.

According to the institutionalist view legal dynamics is a mesh of observable facts, institutionalised norms and legal relations of various types.

The mere assumption of a basic norm or a corresponding axiomatic definition (*Kelsen* varies his definition of the basic norm in several ways [51]) cannot be accepted by institutionalist legal theory as the final and complete grounds of validity. The validity of a norm is in fact grounded in the sociologically identifiable involvement of the system of legal norms with institutions and their working, and in the actual role this system of norms plays in determining the actions of the members of the community. It is at this point that the similarities between my conception and the legal realist approach become apparent. However, I reject the view of the legal realists that the only essential criterion for the existence of law is the conduct of the legal apparatus, as I reject their view of legal source which defines as law that which the judge adduces as a basis for his decision.[52]

Since the institutionalist view seeks to examine sociological relations realistically, it encompasses the full scope of effects of the law; it rejects interpretations which only recognise threatened sanctions and - in exceptional cases - rewards as motivators.

---

[48] O. Weinberger, Die normenlogische Basis der Rechtsdynamik, in: U. Klug et al. (eds.), *Gesetzgebungstheorie, Juristische Logik, Zivil- und Prozeßrecht, Gedächtnisschrift für Jürgen Rödig*, Berlin, Heidelberg 1978, pp. 173 - 190.

[49] O. Weinberger, Die Struktur der rechtlichen Normenordnung, in: G. Winkler (ed), *Rechtstheorie und Rechtsinformatik*, Wien/New York 1975, pp. 110 - 132, esp. p. 120 f.; O. Weinberger, *Normentheorie als Grundlage der Jurisprudenz und Ethik*, *op. cit.* pp. 60.

[50] H. Kelsen, *Pure Theory of Law (Reine Rechtslehre)*, 2nd edition, pp. 196.

[51] H. Kelsen, *op. cit.* pp. 45 f., 51, 206 ff., 209, 204 ff.; H. Kelsen, *Allgemeine Theorie der Normen*, op. cit. p. 205.

[52] A. Ross, *Law and Justice*, op. cit., p. 42.

5. THE PLAUSIBILITY ARGUMENTATION AND LEGAL HERMENEUTICS IN THE CONCEPTION OF LOGICISM

In my view a satisfactory theory of plausibility argumentation must make clear which operations are of a purely logical character and at which points attitudes (decisions) intervene in the argumentation.

Plausibility argumentation must be examined on three levels:

(i) as a way of reasoning which endeavours to provide good reasons for plausibility and offers methods of analysis how the plausibility of theses and attitudes can be tested;

(ii) as the study of the pragmatic processes whereby people try to persuade each other rationally;

(iii) as questions about the pragmatic attitudes and procedures most likely to produce the best possible opinions.

According to the view of logicism (i) forms the core of the theory of plausibility argumentation.

Postulates like *Descartes' 'clare et distincte'*[53] and the postulate of logical consistency also apply to plausibility argumentation. It must not, however, be presupposed that only clear assertions should be made and that only proven opinions should be represented. This would paralyse both practical reasoning and scientific work.

There are several bases of plausibility. In many cases established probability is a good reason for the plausibility of a thesis. As far as legal reasoning is concerned, it seems to me advisable to adopt a tentative approach, in which alternative theses (e.g. alternative interpretions in hermeneutics) should be stated and logically developed, evaluated and compared.[54] Concerning this approach three theoretical points must be emphasised; (a) to find out the alternatives is partly a matter of invention (as indeed invention plays just as important a role in the plausibility argumentation as, for example, in proofs in the deductive disciplines), and partly a matter of applying combinatorial methods; (b) each alternative has to be logically analysed, by adducing the relevant knowledge; (c) based on these analyses, the optimum of plausibility is won through a comparison and relative evaluation of the alternatives.

The subjective elements play an important role in this procedure. They can be combined with intersubjective opinion-forming processes and then they represent, as it were, an optimum social plausibility, but of course they lead not necessarily to true or correct results.

---

[53]R. Descartes, *(Regeln zur Leitung des Geistes*, translated by A. Buchenau, Leipzig 1920, Regel II, pp. 6 ff.)

[54]O. Weinberger, Jurisprudenz zwischen Logik und Plausibilitätsargumentation, *Juristische Analysen* 1971/6, pp. 553 - 574.

Perelman has contributed more than anyone else to the study of the rational processes whereby people try to influence each other through rational argumentation. I doubt whether *Perelman*'s idea of the universal audience adequately characterises the essence of the rational in the process of persuasion.[55] It is certainly a characteristic of rational persuasion that the arguments are not geared to the subjective weaknesses, prejudices and predilections of the listener, but instead cite only universally ("objectively") convincing reasons. However, since this is only a regulatory idea which cannot be effectively tested at all, it seems necessary to me to complete the characterisation of rational argumentation by adding procedural requirements. The issues raised in (iii) become relevant here: I consider it rational to hold convictions without turning them into dogmas. In my view democratic discourse is most likely to arrive at optimal and plausible opinions if it proceeds analytically, if it searches for rational reasons and if it avoids being unduly influenced by majority opinion and the latest philosophical whims.

I consider *legal hermeneutics* a very underdeveloped branch of science. It has, it is true, developed a typology of modes of reasoning, but without analysing the relevance of the different procedures; a large number of rules have been established, but the logical and cognitive diversity of the rules has been ignored. Legal hermeneutics usually does not even make a clear distinction between the interpretation and the solution of problems, such as double interpretation, gaps etc.

The minimum conditions for legal hermeneutics to become a science which could meet modern requirements are:

(i) Interpretation must be recognised as a necessary component of every communication in pragmatic languages; hermeneutics is to be regarded as a systematic further development of "natural" interpretation.

(ii) Interpretation and problem-solving must be separated from one another.

(iii) The suggested rules must be studied in the light of critical epistemology and on the basis of a gnoseologically differentiated semantics.

(iv) An attempt must be made to expose and acknowledge places of voluntary decisions and not to cover them up with sophistry.

---

[55] O. Weinberger, Logische Analyse als Basis der juristischen Argumentation, in: R. Alexy/ W. Krawietz (eds.), *Metatheorie der juristischen Argumentation*, Berlin 1983, pp. 159-232.

B. TREATISES ON LEGAL THEORY AND LEGAL SOCIOLOGY

IV. ONTOLOGY, HERMENEUTICS AND THE CONCEPT OF VALID LAW

1. THE LEGAL PROBLEM OF VALIDITY

Only valid law is law; invalid law is not law. To assert that a particular norm *N* is valid law simply amounts to saying that *N* is a constituent part of the legal system under consideration. To speak of an invalid legal norm is like speaking of an 'invalid conclusion', of 'a sentence not well-formed' or of an 'invalid act in law'. An invalid inference is not an inference at all, because in this case the conclusion does not follow from the premises. A sentence that is not well-formed is precisely not a sentence in the language concerned, which is defined by its rules of formation. A legally invalid act of a particular type is, legally speaking, not an act of this type. The meaning of such expressions has to be explained by deep grammar analysis. It is always the question whether an entity which has been tentatively assumed actually is an entity of this type; in the cases cited above the answer is 'no'. It would be philosophically highly suspect to regard 'invalid law', 'not well-formed sequences of signs', 'invalid conclusions', 'invalid acts in law' etc. as special entities, so called negative objects. In fact no new (as it were negative) object is established by banishing an object from the realm under consideration.[1]

We must now ask ourselves how the important and multi-faceted problem of legal validity comes about.

(a) The validity of the legal norm is conceived of as a kind of existence. However, what does the existence of an object such as law mean? How is a legal norm recognised as existing? On the one hand this concerns the general problem of the actual existence of ideal entities, that is of objects which can be understood but not observed. On the other hand the specific question at issue is the ontological status of law.

(b) In juridical reflection the issue of the validity of law takes on yet a different aspect: It becomes a question of the basis or justification of the content of law. Some legal philosophers also ask why law is binding for the individual and why people should act in keeping with it; others are of the opinion that law is not in need of such a justification - for example by moral considerations.

(c) We must ask what elements compose law, or a system of valid law, and whether all elements of the legal system partake of validity in the same way. For example, are norms of conduct, power-conferring norms and legal principles valid in the same way or are there differences in their validity?

Opinion on this issue is extremely divided. According to *Kelsen*, only norms which address organs of the state are actually law, everything else - e.g. the legal duties of the citizen - is only the reflection of the norms concerning the

---

[1]This problem is connected to the Platonic question of the Being of the Non-Being (in the "Sophistes"), and indirectly to the genesis of dialectics. Cf. Plato, *Sophistes*, translated by O. Apelt, Leipzig 1922, pp. 108 f.; also O. Weinberger, Dialektik und philosophische Analyse (in: E. Topitsch (ed.), *Logik der Sozialwissenschaften*, 10th ed., Königstein/Ts. 1980, pp. 278-309), were I discuss the question in some detail on pp. 303 ff.

organs of state[2]; according to *Hart* the legal system is made up of primary and secondary legal norms[3]; *Dworkin* stresses the relevance of norms of conduct, legal principles and policies for legal decision-making and hence for law as a system[4]; for proponents of natural law, law consists of pre-positive and positive norms, whose interplay varies according to the conception of natural law held; according to *Aarnio*, the way of life which is expressed in lawyers' argumentation has to be considered as part of the system of law[5].

(d) It makes sense to ask whether legal norms can be valid to differing degrees. Are legal norms valid in an all-or-nothing manner? Does this hold for all kinds of norms? It is particularly important to ask this question with regard to legal principles and to provide a clear answer.

(e) Can a superior validity be attributed to some norms than to others? Why can this be the case and how does this superior validity manifest itself?

(f) Is it expedient to introduce a graded concept of legal validity, as the one for example which follows from the prognostic theory of legal validity?

(g) Are pre-positive norms valid as standards of rightness and/or as necessary preconditions for the possibility that legal norms can achieve validity at all?

(h) How is legal validity as the existence of law in social reality to be reconciled with the categorial distinction between 'is' and 'ought' and the sharp division between the two? Are we not asking questions about the existence of something, namely the norm, that is defined as not belonging to the realm of being? This is certainly an important preliminary question for any legal theory of validity; only theories which deem the normative to be a meaningless concept and set out to describe law in a purely behaviouristic way can ignore this problem.

(i) The question of what is legally valid is obviously an extremely practical question: the answer tells us how we should or may behave and what we can achieve with law. Stating what valid law is plays an important role in determining behaviour and is an essential factor in the formation of social structures and institutions. I have deliberately chosen to formulate this position rather

---

[2]The reasons for this view are weak indeed. *Kelsen* in his "Hauptprobleme" (1911) states that "an imperativistic formulation of a statement of law, in which not the conduct of the state itself is the content of the state's intention, but the conduct of the other legal subjects, is impossible" (p. 202), because the will (here the will of the state) has always to be directed towards one's own actions. Other subjects can only be motivated through motivators, especially through coercive measures. This view is bad psychology, problematical sociology and very detrimental to legal philosophy. It underestimates the organisational function of law and provides a questionable argument for the sanction theory of the legal proposition. *Kelsen*, in his late teachings (*Allgemeine Theorie der Normen*, Wien 1979), returns to the command theory of norms he had earlier contested, but he retains the sanction theory of legal norms.

[3]H.L.A. Hart, *The Concept of Law*, Oxford 1961.

[4]R.M. Dworkin, *Taking Rights Seriously*, London 1977.

[5]A. Aarnio, *On Legal Reasoning*, Turku 1977; German translation: A. Aarnio/R. Alexy/A. Peczenik, The Foundation of Legal Reasoning, *Rechtstheorie 12* (1981), pp. 113-158, pp. 257-279, pp. 423-448; Grundlagen der juristischen Argumentation, in: W. Krawietz/R. Alexy, *Metatheorie juristischer Argumentation*, Berlin 1983, pp. 9-87, especially pp. 58-87.

cautiously so as not to suggest that we can expect that people actually behave as prescribed by law. I would only go as far as to say that valid law plays a certain role in determining action: through its institutions it creates the range for action and it plays a certain determining role in the decision-making processes which govern behaviour. This role of valid law - or of its recognition - can also have the effect of making the agent "evade", or shun the law. For this reason we can say that the discussion of legal validity forms a link between a fundamental problem of legal philosophy - i.e. of the ontology of norms and the definition of the nature of legal norms - on the one hand and legal practice on the other.

(j) Law is not only valid itself, but always in conjunction with intersubjective communication processes. Law is a piece of social communication. Thus it is not possible - as I will show in more detail - to speak about legal validity in an appropriate way without taking the relevant problems of communication and hermeneutics into consideration.

(k) There is a certain relation between the temporal determinants in the content of norms and the delimitation of the duration of validity of legal norms. The concept of valid law can only be adequately analysed when the problem of the relation between temporal boundaries in the content of the norm and the period of time for which a norm is valid is elucidated.

In the present context only some of these problems can be dealt with in more detail and some can be merely touched upon.

2. 'IS' AND 'OUGHT'

The opposition between 'is' and 'ought' and the fundamental significance of this dichotomy is widely, if not universally, recognised in contemporary practical philosophy. However, the explication of the dichotomy, its methodological consequences, and the logical analysis of the relations between 'is' and 'ought' are hotly disputed.

The widely differing theories concerning the opposition between 'is' and 'ought' can be divided into two groups, according to whether they interpret this dichotomy ontologically or semantically.

The ontological view holds that there are two distinct realms, the realm of 'is' and the realm of 'ought'. The 'is'-world manifests itself in empirical experience, essentially on the basis of observation; the 'ought'-world cannot be observed but only understood as it comprises ideal entities. The world of norms is a set of ideal entities; however, systems of norms, particularly legal norms, are also social realities, to which temporal co-ordinates can be ascribed.[6]

The ontological approach seems to me to be problematic in several respects. If the world of norms comprises the totality of all conceivable norms, then it is not a world in the same sense as the one world which actually exists now, for in that case the 'ought'-world would have to encompass mutually contradictory norms. '*A world*' (e.g. in the sense of the theory of possible worlds) is characterised precisely by the fact that it does not contain any contradictory states of affairs. However, if the world of norms only comprises all

[6]*N. Hartmann* has pointed out that being in time is crucial for being real. N. Hartmann, *Das Problem geistigen Seins*, Berlin 1932.

norms which are actually valid, then it is a plurality of systems of norms, not *one single* 'ought'-world.

The ontological conception does not explain how the norm, which is by definition distinct from being, can be regarded as existing. We can try to find a way out of this by adopting a different terminology, for example by stipulating that the material world actually *exists* whereas norms and systems of norms just *subsist*. This I do not hold to be a satisfactory solution, for the material world and the world of normative systems both exist in time. I consider the theory of ontological spheres, with the world of objective reality on the one hand and the world of normative systems on the other, to be an unsatisfactory conception for the following reasons. This theory does indeed allow us to speak of reciprocal effects of one sphere on the other, but the grounds for this reciprocal influence of the ontologically divided spheres of existence remain inexplicable.[7] Some writers try to bridge this dichotomy by devising additional principles or by assuming intermediate forms between 'is' and 'ought'.[8] On closer examination, however, it becomes clear that such attempts are not well-founded. Some have also, like *Searle*, attempted to create a logical connection between these spheres by arguing that 'ought' can be derived from 'is'.[9] In my opinion we can arrive at a satisfactory explanation only if we understand the distinction between 'is' and 'ought' as a semantic and categorial one, view the existence of 'ought' (i.e. of norms) in the context of a theory of action and interpret social and legal reality from an institutional point of view. By this I mean that we look at brute and institutional facts and interprete the existence of systems of norms - particularly of law - and also that of institutional facts as inextricably linked phenomena.

I would like to mention two theories that attempt to explain the ontological division between 'is' and 'ought': (a) the conception of the norm as command, put forward by *Hans Kelsen* in his posthumous work[10] and indeed also by *G.H. von Wright* in his last works[11], and (b) the conception of norms as superstructural phenomena.

If the norm is defined as the meaning of a real act of will, whose content is aimed at the behaviour of another subject, then it is understandable that these acts cannot be characterised as true or false. However, this theory does not

---

[7]Mutual influences between elements of different spheres are for example discussed by theoreticians of ontological layers (*N. Hartmann, H. Henkel, V. Kubeš*).

[8]Such additional "bridging" principles can for example be in form of the (controversial) principle "ought' implies 'can'" (*H. Albert*); *J.-L. Gardies* assumes intermediary forms between normative propositions and affirmative propositions.

[9]J.R. Searle, How to derive 'ought' from 'is', *The Philosophical Review* 1964, pp. 43-58; J.R., Searle, *Speech Acts, An Essay in the Philosophy of Language*, Cambridge 1969. Cf. my critical analysis of *Searle*'s proof of deductibility in: D.N. MacCormick/O. Weinberger, *Grundlagen des Institutionalistischen Rechtspositivismus*, Berlin 1985, pp. 22-25.

[10]H. Kelsen, *Allgemeine Theorie der Normen*, K. Ringhofer/R. Walter (eds.), Wien 1979.

[11]Especially: *G.H. von Wright*, 'Is and Ought', Opening lecture to the 11th World Congress on Philosophy of Law and Social Philosophy, 15th August 1983; published in: E. Bulygin/ J.-L. Gardies/I. Niiniluoto (eds.), *Man, Law and Modern Forms of Life*, Dordrecht/Boston/Lancaster 1985, pp. 263-281. Cf. also O. Weinberger, 'Is' and 'Ought' Reconsidered, *ARSP*, Vol. XX/4, 1984, pp. 454-474.

explain - and *Kelsen* was partly aware of this - that the validity (i.e. the existence) of norms is not limited to the moment of their generation. In my opinion denying the existence of norm-logical relations and inferences - which is a consequence of *Kelsen's* view - causes insurmountable difficulties.[12]

When norms are characterised in terms of a Marxist theory as superstructural phenomena, then the emphasis is certainly put on the relation conceiving of norms as ultimately being the products of social and economic realities. However, the ontological, semantic and logical character of norms remains unexplained. The institutional ontology of norms would thus not be incompatible with Marxist theory, but the Marxist conception of the superstructure presents difficulties for an institutionalist and functionalist conception for the following reason: social phenomena have no beginning; institutionalist theory certainly regards institutional relations as linking observable processes with systems of practical information and it emphasises the functional relation between production, social forms and normative regulations as well as systems of values and ends. However, it considers the thesis of the primacy of economic relations untenable, because social production could not exist at all without at least an implicit normative framework. Production is a social process, and according to the institutionalist view social interaction is essentially bound to normative regulations. Moreover, especially from a functionalist perspective, it appears as an unfounded and useless dogma to claim that economic relations and processes are "in the final analysis" the basis of social norms and values - when in fact they are undoubtedly dependent on organisation and 'ought'.

I firmly support the view that the dichotomy between 'is' and 'ought' is to be regarded as a categorial semantic distinction. Reflecting on the theory of action can demonstrate that the structure of action, and consequently practical philosophy in the broadest sense (i.e. all disciplines concerned with action) needs a semantics which allows to express both descriptive and attitudinal information and to separate them.[13] I am restricting myself here to the relation between 'is' and 'ought' although this semantics is actually primarily concerned with categorising sentences into theoretical and practical ones, and only secondarily with the opposition between 'is' and 'ought'.

My semantic conception does not evade the issue of explaining the existence of norms; the answer is given by institutionalist theory. This theory does not only explain the existence of systems of norms, but also the nature and existence of institutional facts. Both problems, the question of the existence of institutional facts and the question of the existence of norms, and of legal validity in particular, are recognised as being inextricably linked and are answered together. Such a theory, however, only makes sense if the problem of 'is' and 'ought' is dealt with primarily on the semantic level.

The distinction between 'is' and 'ought' is a semantic distinction. Declarative and normative sentences are two entirely different semantic sentence categories. Their differentiation is conceived of as a difference in meanings (hence

---

[12]Cf. O. Weinberger, *Normentheorie als Grundlage der Jurisprudenz und Ethik*, Berlin 1981; and: Der normenlogische Skeptizismus, *Rechtstheorie 17* (1986), pp. 13-81.

[13]O. Weinberger, Eine Semantik für die praktische Philosophie, in: R. Haller (ed.) *Beiträge zur Philosophie von Stephan Körner*, Grazer Philosophische Studien, Vol. 20, 1983, pp. 219-239.

the fact that declarative and normative sentences cannot be substituted for one another) and is guaranteed by the theses of non-derivability: in short, 'ought cannot be derived from is' and 'is cannot be derived from ought'.

The theses of non-derivability can be explained more adequately and accurately as follows:

The two semantic categories of sentences are: theoretical sentences (descriptive sentences) and practical sentences (sentences which relate to action and in some way express an attitude towards the facts of a case). The following kinds of sentences are included in the latter category: normative sentences, evaluative sentences[14] and purposive sentences [15].

The more precise formulation of the theses of non-derivability - they are metapostulates for the construction of norm-logical systems - is as follows:

(a) Normative sentences which convey information cannot be derived from a class of premises which does not include any practical sentence.

(b) Descriptive sentences which convey information cannot be derived from a class of premises which does not include any descriptive sentence.

The restriction to informative consequences is necessary, because tautological sentences [e.g. '$p \vee \neg p$'] are derivable also from the empty class of premises (therefore from every class). (a) can thus admit of normative sentences which do not convey any information [such as for example 'if (p & $\neg p$), then q'] as the conclusions of any class of premises. In (a) I speak of 'practical sentences' as premises in order not to exclude *a limine* possible inferences with normative consequences from teleological premises (as they appear in so-called 'practical inferences' [16]).

The logical relations between norms and norm-logical inferences - which are defined as inferences with normative conclusions following from normative or from normative and descriptive premises - are to be studied on the level of the linguistic system of the logic of norms which includes the categories of descriptive and normative sentences; neither the field of acts establishing norms, nor that of norms which are actually valid are the right field for the inquiry of norm-logical relations.

The results of these logical theories are of course valid for any existing systems of norms, for it must always be presupposed that when a norm is valid within a given system the same is true for any consequences following from it. Furthermore, also valid are those consequences which can be derived from valid norms of the system, and true statements of fact (*principles of co-validity*).

The relationship between norms as linguistic entities and norms which actually exist (are valid) is as follows: the norms (normative sentences) of the language form a reservoir of possible normative regulations which are used in

---

[14]One can distinguish between absolute evaluative sentences and preference sentences which express a relative evaluation.

[15]The terminology for sentences which express teleological determinations is not uniform. *K. Engliš* calls them 'postulates'; other terms could be 'optative sentences', 'demand sentences'.

[16]Cf. O. Weinberger, Handeln und Schließen. Überlegungen zum Begriff der praktischen Inferenz, in: F. Van Dun (ed.), *The Law between Morality and Politics*, *Philosophica* 23, 1979, pp. 5-36; reprinted in: O. Weinberger, *Studien zur formal-finalistischen Handlungstheorie*; Frankfurt a.M./Bern/New York 1983, pp. 19-58.

speech acts. The normative sentences which are valid in a social system of norms represent a sub-class of all normative sentences which are linguistically possible. This is analogous to the indicative realm, where the asserted sentences are a sub-class of all linguistically meaningful descriptive sentences.

3. THE FIELD OF LOGICAL OPERATIONS

The traditional conception of logic has to be fundamentally altered. Logical operations are not only instruments of cognition, they do not serve only in the processing of cognitive material, as it was thought, but they also are operations in the process of determining and guiding action.

We can illustrate the fact that logic and logical analysis are not only instruments for the processing of knowledge, but also play a part in the information processes which determine action, in the following way:

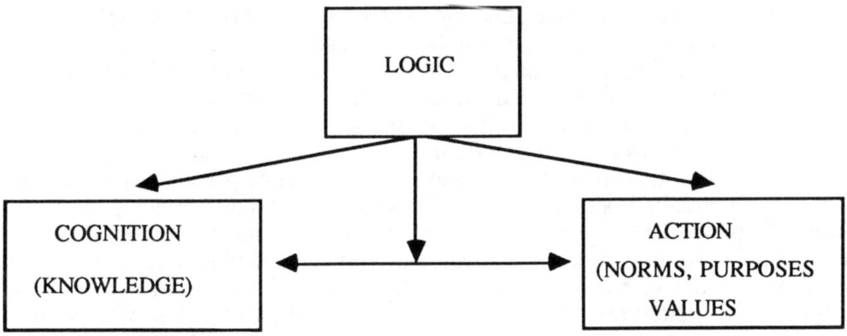

The question to ask then is: What characterises logical relations and operations, now that their field has been broadened and therefore the old definitions do not suffice any longer? According to the old definition logical relations are truth-relations determined by the form of the sentences used, and logical inferences are defined as being truth-conserving. The task of logic within this broadened conception remains the analysing of forms represented by means of logical formulae. It analyses relations which are determined by the structure of the sentences used. For example, logical incompatibility between normative sentences is defined as a structural relation just as contradiction between descriptive sentences. Or, concerning deduction, it is established that - on the basis of structural relations between the premises and the conclusion (or conclusions) - setting the premises also sets the conclusion. However, within this generalised conception not only truth but also validity (in the sense of validity of norms) can be the "heritable quality". The operations are described by means of formal schemata and formal rules.

4. INSTITUTIONAL ONTOLOGY OF NORMS

The human world view is not only a physical world view; it is not only looking at how various objects and systems function in terms of statistical regularity. Man as a social being capable of action grasps and processes facts which relate to his activities. This functional character of cognition and the view that the structure of knowledge is determined by its role in the context of action can be termed the 'cognitive principle of the primacy of praxis'. Even cognition of so-called brute facts is structured with regard to its possible role in orienting the agent in the world and of its possible use in action-determining thinking. For this reason our mind does not hold a mere collection of facts - *Popper* calls this type of conception of knowledge ironically the "bucket theory of the mind"[17] - but rather strives for the knowledge of laws, because it is only on the basis of laws that suitable means for given purposes can be determined.

Much of what we are confronted with in our experience is the work of man, the result of human willing, planning and acting. Institutions within which certain objects have a particular function evolve as a result of our activity and co-operation with others. The facts that we can ascertain are thus not only the existence of objects with their physical properties, but also institutional facts and institutional functions of objects. Institutional facts are facts which are dependent on institutions; they can thus not be grasped and understood without taking into consideration their institutional function.

I maintain that institutions always have a core of practical information. Institutions are realities situated in the context of action; they provide patterns for actions, frameworks for possible actions, and they organise the interaction between people. To this purpose it is necessary to use rules which determine what the actors should or may do, and what they can achieve (power-conferring rules). Social structures, too, are created by systems of rules of this type, whereby of course the actual behaviour of the people involved also play an important role, as well as what might be termed institutional realities. In the institution itself objects with established functions, institutionalised structures, normative rules and occasionally also objectives form a whole, whose existence and functioning can only be explained as an interplay between observable facts and practical information.

The question is therefore not only how the existence of social norms (particularly legal norms) is to be explained, but also how certain objects and institutions (for example, a chess figure or a university) can be grasped not only as physical objects but also as entities in their institutional function. A rook, a piece of paper as money, and a person as judge are objects of this type if and only if they are understood in the context of the respective normative rules. This means that the facts and processes of the human world are not only real as physical objects and their functioning, but also as institutional facts. The nature of institutional facts can only be adequately explained if one takes into account the meaning of institutions: what is immediately observed and what is understood in its institutional role, i.e. normative, teleological and axiological information concerning these facts are inextricably linked here.

---

[17]K.R. Popper, *Objective Knowledge*, Oxford 1972, pp. 60 ff.

The actual existence of norms is institutional existence. 'Ought' is reality when it is an element of the system determining action. As far as the individual is concerned, this means that norms, whether autonomous or heteronomous, are elements of the deliberation determining action; as far as the community is concerned norms establish the forms of behaviour in society, the social structures (e.g. legal persons) and human interaction.

The relative stabilisation of the forms of behaviour is regarded as the key element of the phenomenon of institutionalisation. However, in my view, it is important to emphasise that institutions are practical in character, i.e. they are frames for action and are formed around a core of practical information. From a sociological point of view, the question of relative stabilisation of course plays a vital role here. This follows already from the fact that institutions are action-related systems, and practical activity requires a certain degree of stability of its frame of reference.

I would like to illustrate with an apparently trivial example why the practical-informative core and not the stabilisation of behaviour is fundamental to institutional reality. When two children go and decide to play "soccer", their game is an interaction which is in a certain way governed and supported by a system of norms which they accept as valid for this particular situation. This situation is, as I understand it, an institution (even if it is short-lived), and it is not necessary to establish its *ad hoc* definitions and institutional realities (the size of the field and the width of the goals) as permanent or universal social institutions. Stabilisation certainly is also an element of institutionalisation in very many important instances: people need stable frameworks as the basis for their actions, for only this way can objects and practices be standardised, simplified and made customary. However, we would limit our reflections on institutions in a way that would serve no purpose if we were to consider only relatively stable institutions.

Some writers (*Luhmann* for example) consider the development of expectations in the persons concerned as the decisive element of institutionalisation. I think that on the contrary the normative core has to be considered as the fundamental element of the institution; expectations are important consequences which are nevertheless differentiated by a set of different moments, and therefore it is not to be considered an equivalent of 'ought' or a constitutive element and decisive criterion of the institution.

5. THE JURIDICAL DEFINITION OF VALID LAW

The juridical theory of legal validity rests in my opinion on the institutional ontology of norms outlined above. It is by means of this ontology that the basic problem of the normative-ideal character of law and the fact that it is also a constitutive element of social reality can be understood. Based on this conception I will now look at various specifically juridical problems of legal validity.

Modern legal practice demands a clear and definite answer to the question "What is legally valid?" Contemporary legal science therefore searches for methods by which to describe law in a generalised form and logically ordered, because only then is this question to be answered with some precision.

The problem of the exact definition of legal validity is also connected to the idea of *"Rechtsstaatlichkeit"*, the idea of the "rule of law".

The structure theory of law solves this problem by establishing rules about the generation (creation) of law, i.e. rules which allow us to discern whether a valid law has been generated. According to this conception of the *Rechtsstaat* not only human conduct is subject to normative regulation, but also the production of general rules of law itself is conceived of as a legal process and thus formally determined.

It seems to me that - strictly speaking - we are justified to call a system a genuine "Rechtsstaat" only if the creation of law is also subject to normative regulation on the legislative level. This does not mean, however, that only a system with a written constitution and with an explicitely stated regulation of the legislative process can be regarded as a "Rechtsstaat" (in this sense). It is essential only that the process of creating law is also institutionalised as a relatively fixed process determined by norms, or as the case may be, by customary law, which can only be characterised by rules formulated by legal science.

These theories can be called - in the terminology of *Dworkin* - "pedigree theories of legal validity".[18] When legal practice follows rules as outlined by these theories, then they constitute an important step towards determining what valid law is. But we cannot suppose that our problem is thereby already resolved.

The first question is: What are the elements of valid law? *Dworkin* in essence seems to say that only the rules of law - apparently meaning *Hart*'s primary and secondary rules (i.e. norms of conduct and power-conferring rules) - need to be proven legitimate by their pedigree, but not legal principles and policies. According to the institutionalist conception legal principles are elements of law, that is they, too, have to be proven valid within the system, particularly

(a) by finding such abstract rules or determinations of purpose in the texts of legal sources;

(b) by abstracting these principles from the system of valid regulations; or

(c) by proving that they are part of customary law.

To regard legal principles as elements of natural law or to assume that social (i.e. extra-legal) morality and ethics invade at this point the legal system is, I think, unfounded, although it is a view held by many a famous scholar.[19]

Are rules of competence (rules of the pedigree, power-conferring rules) purely formal or are they coupled with - or can they be coupled with - substantive criteria of validity? Proponents of natural law presuppose that the immanent ethical consciousness provides at least a filter of minimal standards which valid laws have to pass. Since, in my opinion, there exists no practical cognition - it cannot be decided on a purely cognitive level what fair law should be - I see no reason for accepting such a view. It would be very questionable for legal practice, if those applying the law were granted the substantive (moral)

---

[18]R.M. Dworkin, *op.cit.*, p. 18.

[19]E.g. *R.M. Dworkin, L.L. Fuller*; Cf. O. Weinberger, Die Naturrechtskonzeption von Ronald Dworkin, in: D. Mayer-Maly und P.M. Simons (eds.), *Das Naturrechtsdenken heute und morgen. Gedächtnisschrift für René Marcic*, Berlin, pp. 497-515.

right to examine and check the legislator's directives. It would lead to a dangerous state of legal uncertainty if the judge were to apply only that law which accords with his subjective moral convictions (in reality this would frequently mean: his political, religious etc. convictions).

In my opinion even from the standpoint of a positivist view it has to be taken into consideration that the 'spirit' of higher level norms (i.e. of constitutional principles) sets limits for the content of subordinate norms and defines criteria for their interpretation. Customarily the generation of secondary norms - which is based on competence norms and determined by the pedigree - is limited with regard to their content by certain already established determinants: namely by the field of competence and - as the case may be - also by the purpose and principles of the legislative task.

At this point we have to discuss the question whether we should suppose various degrees of validity. Legal norms (as defined by the pedigree) coming from different legal sources are equally binding; therefore it is not necessary to presuppose that they are valid to a greater or lesser degree. But a problem arises when there is a conflict between different norms, and in the case of the validity of those elements of the legal order which are not applied by subsumption, i.e. particularly in the case of the application of legal principles: When valid rules of law lead to conflicts between legal obligations - and this possibility cannot be excluded in principle - then special norms designed to solve such conflicts are used or the conflict is decided by assessing the relative legal value of the obligations.

I am of the opinion that comparative norms or legal principles are valid (or not) in the same way as norms of conduct and power-conferring norms, even though their application does not follow from a subsumption in an all-or-nothing manner.

In such cases it is not a question that a norm would be more or less valid, but that the meaning of a norm is so specific as to imply an application different from the application by subsumption. In the case of legal principles which have been abstracted from a class of norms of conduct establishing the limit of the validity of the principle (i.e. an abstract rule) can be problematical.

A dynamic view of the legal order can - according to *Merkl* - lead to placing norms in an hierarchical order.[20] In principle the *lex posterior rule* will be used as the basis for pragmatically necessary legal developments. Classes of norms (legal sources), to whom this rule applies, share the same degree of relevance; but when a norm of the type t_1 remains valid even if it is contradicted later by a norm of the type t_2, then norms of the type t_1 enjoy legally a higher relevance than norms of the type t_2. The degree of relevance (or of normative force) is thus based on the 'derogatory power' of the norm. The matter is relatively simple when a later norm does not gain any validity because its content is in conflict with an older, hierarchically superior norm. If, on the contrary, the hierachically weaker norm gains validity and can only be contested - as the case

[20] A. Merkl, *Die Lehre von der Rechtskraft entwickelt aus dem Rechtsbegriff*, Leipzig/Wien 1923; A. Merkl, Prolegomena einer Theorie des rechtlichen Stufenbaues, in: A. Verdross (ed.), *Gesellschaft, Staat und Recht, Festschrift für H. Kelsen*, Wien 1931, pp. 252-294.

may be under special conditions and in special proceedings -, then the older norm of higher relevance is only conditionally applicable.

We can now ask whether it is adequate to conceive of the annulment of legal rules - because of formal or material derogation - as the end of their validity in time, or whether it is not more appropriate to regard the temporal termination of the validity as a temporal boundary of the conditions of subsumption (because even an derogated law can in a certain way continue to be valid with regard to past states of affairs).

In order to be able to analyse clearly the two possibilities of representing temporal limits I use the general hypothetical normative sentence as the basic form of legal rule. In simplified form, without explicitly expressing quantifiers, I write, '$p >! q$' ('If p, then q ought to be'). I use indices to indicate the temporal limits. To express that a legal rule is valid for the period t_0 - $t_i$we can now write symbolically:

(1) $(p >! q)t_0 - t_i$

or

(2) $p(t_0 - t_i) >!q$

The difference between (1) and (2) can be interpreted as follows:
The sentence (1) expresses for which period the legal rule is valid; sentence (2) sets temporal limits to the class of subsumable states of affairs. On the whole both forms are equivalent except that according to (2) the norm can be applied even after t_1 to matters which occurred during the time t_o - t_i (or were completed just then), whereas this is not permitted by (1).

The most difficult problem for a pedigree theory of legal validity is to explain the fact that laws may become obsolete. According to the strict conception of the pedigree theory becoming obsolete is properly speaking inconceivable. When valid law is *de facto* not applied, this fact constitutes an infringement of the law, but not an abrogation of the respective norm. The institutionalist view does not want to relinquish the formal relevance of the pedigree theory, yet it also wishes to do justice to the reality of a decentralised dynamic of norms, and therefore there is only one way to explain the fact that formally valid legal norms may under certain conditions become obsolete: the process by which a law becomes obsolete must be at least implicitely accepted as institutionally valid. The mere fact that a rule is not applied cannot, however, be the reason for it to become obsolete, only its non-applicability according to stringent conditions and for reasons of certain derogatory moments recognised by the law can be an acceptable reason.

Legal theory will have to adduce empirical criteria for determining what constitutes valid law. Here we have to distinguish between two issues:

(1) The question of the validity of a legal order as a whole. Sociological criteria about average effectiveness will be decisive: exact criteria are not available here and cannot be expected. Special situations such as civil wars, revolutions and the founding of new states are problematic: clear-cut answers cannot be given there, they would lead to assertions contradicting the facts, because the power relations in such situations vacillate between two different orders.

(2) The validity of a single norm as an element of the legal system is to be determined primarily by criteria of the valid generation of law. This seemingly

exact determination is modified by hermeneutical problems (see section 6) and - albeit rarely - by the possibility that legal norms may become obsolete.

These reflections make it clear that even when considering the issue of the validity of law a certain measure of idealisation - as in so many areas of scientific knowledge - comes to bear and that reality deviates somewhat from that idealised picture.

6. LEGAL VALIDITY AND HERMENEUTICS

I have underlined the decisive importance of the formal determination of validity. However, this should not close our eyes to the fact that "what law is" is not only determined by defining the validity of a legal text as a binding legal source, but is also shaped by the treatment of the given normative text in the process of communication. It is thus not only a question of establishing that a normative text *N* is valid, but also of establishing what *N* means. In other words, what valid law actually is, what is binding in law is dependent on interpretation in the broadest sense of the word.

From an institutionalist perspective, the hermeneutical aspect of the problem of legal validity acquires particular characteristics which set it apart from the traditional conception:

(a) Looked at from the point of view of linguistic theory, every interpersonal communication is coupled with an active process of interpretation by the person who receives the message. Legal interpretation is to be regarded as the scientific, i.e. methodologically reflected, extension and systematisation of this immanent constituent part of every communication designed for the specific realm of law.[21]

(b) Legal hermeneutics is institutionally inextricably linked with the existence and activity of the organs of the administration of justice, for it is here that legal interpretation always takes place, and - at least in civilised society - with jurisprudential activities. What is institutionalised as valid law must be determined in the process of applying the law, taking into account the way in which normative sources are understood. The accepted methodology of interpretation in a legal system, as well as the dominant jurisprudential conceptions, must be adduced as institutionalised determinants of interpretation.[22]

(c) In *Aarnio*'s conception in particular the hermeneutic tradition, the legal way of reasoning in the process of comprehending the law is a constituent part of the form of the way of life of the respective society. Moreover, he also points quite rightly to the role of juristic systematisation in the process of legal

[21]Ch. Weinberger/O. Weinberger, *Logik, Semantik, Hermeneutik*, München 1979, pp. 159-171, pp. 185-191.

[22]This thesis is not to be understood to say that legal science has to accept the dominant juridical methodology. Quite the contrary, it is also a task of legal science to offer a critique of the dominant conceptions and - if need be - to transform them on the basis of appropriate theoretical grounds. The social task of legal science exerts - historically as well as sociologically - an influence on the conception of law as an institutional fact, and on the development of its position within society.

interpretation. From the institutionalist point of view these observations are correct. However, it must also be said that the reference to the way of life only has an explanatory function in sociology, but cannot be used as an argument in hermeneutical analysis itself.

There are significant differences with respect to the methods of interpretation which are valid in the various legal systems. The most noticeable differences concern two elements: (i) the role ascribed to the judiciary, and (ii) the question whether or to what extent purposes play a role in the interpretation and application of the law (the debate between formalism und instrumentalism in legal hermeneutics).

Legal validity of a norm is in my view based primarily on criteria of the creation of norms. However, institutionally it is also dependent on interpretative processes and on the dynamics of the process of interpretation and of attempts at systematisation of the legal material.

Institutionalisation of these processes in judicial activity and in legal scientific work are essential components of the institutional existence and effect of the law.

7. DECISION-MAKING PRACTICE AND VALID LAW

The judiciary is ascribed a different role in different legal systems: in customary law jurisdiction it is accorded the status of a source of law; in statute law it is not a formal source of law, however it is certainly of importance for the determination of legal decisions.

In any case there is an interplay between the sphere of general legal rules and the decisions in law cases. In legal systems which regard precedents as sources of law, the *rationes decidendi* of precedents are standards for future decision-making practice, with the result that here, too, general rules and principles play a part in determining the decision. The *rationes decidendi* is to be understood as a rule or legal principle; in any case it is a general normative proposition, and only because of this can it be considered the basis for justifying a decision.

In every modern legal system there is a mutual relation between the system of general rules and decisions: (1) decisions are established on the basis of general rules and principles; (2) decisions are important as elements of the interpretation, concretisation, and development of law. Besides this, in customary law systems they are also primary sources of law.

Why is decision-making practice so important for understanding law and thinking about it? The meaning of everyday expressions depends on how they are understood by those using the language. In the case of legal rules this is indicated by the judiciary, albeit in conjunction with jurisprudence and in particular with the so-called dominant theory. The role of decision-making practice in determining law is not, however, restricted to the role of linguistic interpretation; the judiciary also defines the realm of cases which can be subsumed, defines principles as a generalisation of individual determinants and establishes models for their relative importance. From a sociological and historical point of view there is no doubt that the judiciary exerts an influence on the further development of law.

This all goes to show that the question of what is valid law is not solely determined by relations of legal dynamics; the reality of decision-making practice and jurisprudence as an institution of the legal practice also have to be taken into account when answering this question.

According to the realist theory of legal validity, it is the judiciary alone which determines what is law. Only what the state apparatus decides is valid law; and to answer the question of what law in fact is can be answered only in so far as the judge's decision can be predicted. This predictive theory poses a question which is often of considerable practical significance, namely what is the probable outcome of a case under consideration. One would ask oneself this question for example, when faced with the decision of whether or not to bring an action in a particular situation. However, inferring valid law from the behaviour (or even from the predicted behaviour) of the judge is not an acceptable theory of legal validity. The point of valid law is to determine the actions of the judiciary; it is not bc understood as a mere reflex of the judiciary. The law bestows the function of legal decision-making on the organs and they arc held to decide according to the valid law; therefore they cannot be regarded as a criterion of establishing what valid law is. According to the predictive definition of valid law, legal decisions by the appropriate organ could not be criticised. The predictive conception of validity turns legal validity into a dimension which can be quantitatively graded, for it is based on a prediction, namely on the assertion of a certain probability. Moreover, this probability can hardly be determined mathematically; the outcome will often be different, depending upon which geographic area or which judge is under consideration.

I do not accept the definition of legal sources according to the principles of legal realism, namely that everything the judge adduces as argument of his decision is a legal source[23], for valid law has to be the actual basis of the decision. The decision may of course be supported by secondary considerations, in which case, however, these additional arguments have to be conceptually distinguished from the basic sources of law.[24] What is to be considered a legal source is determined by the institutionalised constitution which defines the system of the hierarchy of norms, and not by the judge's thinking and reasoning.

8. LAW AND PURPOSE: ON THE DEBATE BETWEEN FORMALISM AND INSTRUMENTALISM

The legal system serves certain purposes. This is a basic anthropological fact: social life in communities, towards which human beings naturally tend,

---

[23]Cf. *A. Peczenik*'s exposition in the article A. Aarnio/R. Alexy/A. Peczenik, Grundlagen der juristischen Argumentation, in: W. Krawietz/R. Alexy (eds.), *Metatheorie juristischer Argumentation*, p. 29.

[24]O. Weinberger, Logische Analyse als Basis der juristischen Argumentation, in: W. Krawietz/R. Alexy (eds.), *op. cit.*, pp. 178 ff.

requires rules to establish order. However, the purposes of law are fairly roughly and approximately formulated purposes such as legal peace, legal certainty etc. However, these concepts do not provide a sufficient basis for a critical examination of legal norms from a point of view of legal politics. Another possible approach would be to state the essential function which every legal order must fulfil; however, I do not believe that this type of anthropological characterisation of law can be regarded as natural law, or as a "minimal content of natural law"[25]. They are, rather, functional characterisations of the concept of legal order.

Individual institutions have more tangible purposes, functions, etc. towards which they are oriented. Some theorists of institutions, notably *M. Hauriou*, go as far as to state that institutions are created by their conceptual determinants. Admittedly *Hauriou* does not interpret the *idée directrice* as a purpose, however, I believe that it is of an essentially functional and teleological character.

It is certainly the case that the legal system pursues social goals just as individual legal institutions can be understood with regard to their function. In general one can say roughly: law and its institutions have to be viewed against a teleological background.

From the point of view of legal methodology we must now examine the consequences that arise from the relation of law to purposes.

Understanding norms and the application of the law are largely dependent on how successful we are in grasping their function. Besides, just taking the purely linguistic perspective alone, successful communication through everyday language is bound to an understanding of the teleological context of the message. Therefore teleological analyses can hardly be excluded from legal hermeneutics. Thus far everything looks simple and thoroughly convincing. In reality, however, we are dealing with one of the most difficult and contentious problems of legal methodology. And these theoretical problems relating to hermeneutics have important consequences for the character of legal argumentation and for legal practice.

The two contrasting ideal types of the role purposes play in legal hermeneutics are described as 'formalism' and 'instrumentalism'. The main issue of the debate can be characterised approximately as follows: according to the formalist view, legal rules are essentially rules of conduct which indicate what the legal consequences should be under particular conditions. Not the purpose which may lie behind the norm and may have brought it about in the first place is decisive, but solely the description of the relevant conditions of subsumption and the associated regulations of conduct. The teleological background cannot be unequivocally determined and teleological arguments cannot alter the validity of norms of conduct in any way. It is especially true that cessation of the purposes which gave rise to the legal norm do not impair its validity *(cessante ratione non cessat lex ipsa)*. To argue with teleological arguments for or against a law

---

[25]*Hart* compiled a list of those functions which every modern legal system has to fulfil. These determinants he interprets as the minimal content of natural law. Cf. H.L.A. Hart, *The Concept of Law*, Oxford 1961, pp. 189-195. In my opinion *Hart's* exposition of these features of law is more of a functional characteristic of the legal system than a piece of natural law.

gravely undermines the certainty of the law, because the intended purposes cannot be clearly determined, nor can their use in argument produce clear results which are free from subjective value judgements. Only formal relations and as literal an interpretation as possible, particularly with regard to the historical context in which the law developed, offer legally optimal solutions to problems of interpretation. They guarantee a legal practice which is characterised by legal certainty.

The instrumentalists can also put forward good reasons in favour of their view of law. It is fairly obvious that a genuine understanding of law is scarcely possible without some appreciation of the social function of law and of individual institutions. In particular, the solution of hard cases, discretion on the basis of diverging principles, and decisions which presuppose that gaps in the law are to be filled can hardly be effected in a reasonable way without recourse to teleology. It is in line with present day conceptions of law to regard the legal system less as an expression of metaphysical values but instead much more as an expedient technique of social regulation. Law is thus to be understood as a social instrument; the jurist shapes social relationships. Legal science is social engineering.[26] Therefore: purposes are to be adduced as arguments when interpreting the law and it must also be attempted to reach socially expedient solutions when applying the law. In the same way the task of legislation follows societal purposes.

How should jurisprudence and legal practice steer a course between the *Scylla* of rigid formalism and the *Charybdis* of indeterminate instrumentalism? Legal interpretation is primarily the establishment of conditionally regulated ought-conduct. The outcome of hermeneutical analysis is also to be represented essentially in the form of general rules of conduct. However, determining the meaning of the texts of legal sources cannot be accomplished without reconstructing the teleological background of the law. The transformation of the social system of purposes or the cessation of the purpose of a legal determination does not mean that it ceases to exist. It must be borne in mind that deducing the purpose of a legal institution will not always yield unequivocal results. However, there is no such thing as mathematical certainty in hermeneutical analysis. A further difficulty and source of uncertainties which must be overcome by a carefully considered decision of the interpreter or the person who applies the law is an effect of the structure of the teleological reflection. One and the same norm can have various purposes. For this reason it is often necessary in teleological argumentation to weigh the matter carefully with respect to different purposes simultaneously. These are all factors which lead to the complexity of teleological analyses and to their dependency on decisions; nevertheless, analyses of purpose seem to me to be inevitable aspects of juridical work. Up until now I have pleaded for a combination of formalistic and teleological reasoning. However, there comes a point where one has to decide in favour of one or the other position. In the debate between formalism and instrumentalism, the crucial point is the following: Are the elements which determine meaning and the "will of the historical legislator" the only decisive factors for the interpretation and

---

[26]Cf. e.g. R.S. Summers, *Pragmatischer Instrumentalismus und amerikanische Rechtstheorie*, München 1983.

application of the law? Or is the awareness of the task of shaping social relations - i.e. the politico-legal reasoning about purposes - also to be adduced for the law's interpretation and application (particularly when filling gaps and making decisions within the framework of legal discretion)?

The institutionalised legal tradition oscillates between these two poles. Austrian tradition in this regard seems to be extremely formalistic. However, I think that the retrospective argument of historicism is less important than rational politico-legal analyses and the consideration of the social consequences of the interpretation and orientation of the judge's discretion when the law is applied.

V. CONSTITUTIONAL THEORY IN THE LIGHT OF THE NEW INSTITUTIONALISM

1. PRELIMINARY REMARKS CONCERNING TERMINOLOGY

The new institutionalism is not a descendent of the classical legal doctrine of the institutions; nor is it a revised version of *Maurice Hauriou*'s or *Carl Schmitt's* theories. It has evolved independently from those theories and it expresses a largely different conception of social norms, of the law and of the institutions.

I have - or rather *D.N. Mac Cormick* and I have - given this legal theory the name 'Institutional Legal Positivism'.[1] This theory combines a normativist conception of the institutions with a particular kind of legal positivism. It is positivist in the sense that it refutes the possibility of practical knowledge, i.e. the possibility of determining the right norms and true values on a purely cognitive basis. It acknowledges, however, the possibility of rational argumentations on questions of legal policy. What this theory advances is consequently - as will be demonstrated - a modified form of legal positivism.

I shall use the terms 'New Institutionalism' and 'Institutional Legal Positivism' *promiscue* in the following chapter.

2. THE PROJECTED TASK

In this chapter the fundamental concepts of the constitutional theory are to be discussed from the point of view of Institutional Legal Positivism. Two reasons have caused me to attempt this approach: (a) I am convinced that the positions adopted by Institutional Legal Positivism can play a useful role in the process of clarifying some of the fundamental questions facing the constitutional theory, and (b) I want to put the New Institutionalism to the test. The significance of a legal-philosophical theory does, after all, express itself in the contribution it is able to make to the various jurisprudential disciplines. What we have to do, therefore, is to investigate the implications of Institutional Legal Positivism for the methodology and for legal dogmatics in an important area of jurisprudence. The question whether it is more appropriate to leave such questions to the representatives of the specific discipline - the legal constitutionalists in this case - or whether the legal philosopher ought to express his views on certain fundamental questions of the dogmatic disciplines shall be left unanswered. I myself as a legal philosopher take it upon myself to make the attempt of discussing fundamental problems of constitutional theory in the following pages.

---

[1] D.N. MacCormick/O. Weinberger *An Institutional Theory of Law: New Approaches to Legal Positivism*, Dordrecht et al. 1986; German version: *Grundlagen des Institutionaliustischen Rechtspositivismus*, Berlin 1985; O. Weinberger, *Recht, Institution und Rechtspolitik. Grundprobleme der Rechtstheorie und Sozialphilosophie*, Stuttgart 1987; the same, *Norm und Institution. Eine Einführung in die Theorie des Rechts*, Wien 1988.

3. FUNDAMENTAL PROBLEMS OF CONSTITUTIONAL THEORY

For the purpose of this investigation I want to compile a list - without aiming at completeness - of the fundamental problems facing constitutional theory. To these I shall attempt to give at least partial answers from the point of view of Institutional Legal Positivism.

i. What is the relationship between state and constitution?

ii. Is it possible for a state to exist without a constitution? In what sense is the constitution the precondition for a rational understanding of the state and its structure? In what way does the constitution depend on customs and on explicitely fixed constitutional norms?

iii. The constitution and notion of a constitutional norm in the technical sense.

iv. What in essence is the content of the constitution and what its fundamental functions?

v. What kind of relationships exist between social power and the institutionalization of areas of competences and of roles?

vi. Legality as the idea that all the setting of norms and all social structure as well as all political processes in the state should be determined by the constitution. The concept of the constitutional state and the determination of the dynamics of the law through the constitution - legalization of the institutional processes occurring in the state and in public life.

vii. The problem of social power and the relationship between this question and the legal system: problems of the division of power (analysis of the concept and examination of the effectiveness of the division of power in the state); a complex network of power as an element in the creation of a system of government and as a means of limiting as well as controlling power, the *idée directrice* of the institution and the concept of functional power.

viii. The problem of the legality of public order and of the exercise of power in the state.

ix. The relationship between constitution, constitutional state and democracy; democracy as a claim to lawful competences and democratic control as well as demand for a functional conception of social power. The democratic state and the democratic way of life as a system of interlocking competences and as a system of democratic principles.

4. THESES OF INSTITUTIONAL LEGAL POSITIVISM WHICH ARE RELEVANT TO THE CONSTITUTIONAL THEORY

First thesis:

Every institution possesses a normative core. This core is necessary for the institution to be able to exist and to function as a social framework for action. The nature of the institution does not only depend on the existence of customs and models of behaviour but, in addition, it always comprises institutionalised normative and evaluative components. In the case of institutions of a corporate nature the ought consists of norms covering both behaviour and competences.

Second thesis:

The existence of a social institution and the existence of its normative regulative are phenomena which are intrinsically connected with each other. The institution cannot function without being regulated by norms; social norms are valid - i.e. they can exist as social facts - presicely when they determine the functioning of the respective institutions in their role as regulatives. *What we mean by the validity of a social norm is the existence of a connection between the impact made by a norm and the respective institution.*

Third thesis:

The theory of law has to be constructed as a rational-analytical theory. *Institutional Legal Positivism follows entirely the tradition of analytical legal philosophy*, according to which the structural theory of the law and the theory of the structures of juristic argumentation form the basis of the entire theory of law. In contrast to other analytical theories - above all in opposition to the Pure Theory of Law - Institutional Legal Positivism does not hold that the role of jurisprudence should be limited to structural analyses. *Institutional Legal Positivism demands emphatically that jurisprudence must also investigate the politico-legal character of the institutions and their functionality.*

Fourth thesis:

In the development of the analytical-legal philosophy two phases can be distinguished: it was the preeminent task of the first phase to uncover a common basic structure of the legal sentences in order to gain formal means for the representation of every possible legal content; in the second phase important differences between the various legal structures have had to be considered - above all, legal principles have been contrasted with rules of behaviour and the different types of argumentation relating to these two elements have been shown up.[2] In addition, the specific nature of empowering norms in contrast to rules of behaviour have been clarified.[3] *Institutional Legal Positivism is an analytical theory of the second phase.* In other words, it deals both with the explicite and the implicite ideal connections between the norms of the legal system, i.e. with legal principles, the teleological background of the law and with policies in the sense of *Dworkin*. At the same time it distinguishes between the automatic development of norms resulting from observable facts and the deliberate creation of norms enabling additions or changes to be made to the contents of the legal system.[4]

---

[2] R. Dworkin, *Taking Rights Seriously*, Harvard 1978^2.

[3] See O. Weinberger, *Norm und Institution. Eine Einführung in die Theorie des Rechts*, Wien 1988, p. 91 ff.; the same, *Rechtslogik*, Berlin 1989^2, p. 64, p.91.

[4] See A. Procházka, Normative Theorie und Rechtserzeugung, in: V. Kubeš/O. Weinberger (eds.), *Die Brünner rechtstheoretische Schule (Normative Theorie)*, Wien 1980, pp. 304-323.

[5] Kelsen's Pure Theory of Law (second edition) provides arguably the most striking expression of the purely normative conception of legal dogmatics. Kelsen describes the sentence expressing the ought rule as *conditio per quam*, - or the true reason for the validity of the

Fifth thesis:

The law is a dynamic normative system. Institutional Legal Positivism has essentially adopted the dynamic conception of the law developed by *A. Merkl* and *H. Kelsen*. It has, however, fundamentally modified this conception in accordance with the institutional principle. Institutional Legal Positivism does not conceive of legal dynamics as a process occurring within the system of legal norms[5] but as an institutional process which - in accordance with its nature - has to be interpreted as an interaction of actual social processes and legal acts with the institutionalised system of norms. Consequently the theory of legal dynamics relies on normative insights and norm-logical deduction as well as on conclusions drawn from observations made of social reality.

Sixth thesis:

It is a characteristic aspect of modern society that a *multiplicity of social norm-systems exist simultaneously within it.* Some are general rule-systems relating to all members of that community, some specific regulatives applying only to certain groups.

Seventh thesis:

There are legal and non-legal institutions (obviously, the first thesis about the normative core of institutions applies to both types). Institutions may come into existence on the basis of certain legal (constitutional) norms. On the other hand, they may arise automaticly - as one might say - as a result of certain social situations. *Institutions which have come into being by non-legal means can be legalised* by integrating the respective norms into the hierarchical legal system later on.

Eighth thesis:

The demand *for legal rules to be regarded not only as individual and isolated ought-sentences but as functionally connected complex systems* is a major consequence of every institutional theory. To know what ways of behaviour are demanded, prohibited or permitted and which power-conferring norms exist is not all there is to know about the law. With reference to the normative institutions (*'institutiones'* in the terminology of Roman law) *MacCormick* distinguishes three types of rules defining the legal institution: *institutive, consequential and terminative rules.*[6] The *concept of the governing idea* plays an even greater part in providing a conceptual definition of the task layed down for the institution. From the sociological point of view the purpose which the institution is intended to serve is the nucleus around which the specific social reality of the institution crystallizes, and for those involved with the institution it is the element they can relate to in order to identify with the institution. (There is, of course, no trace left in Institutional Legal Positivism of *Hauriou*'s metaphysical speculations about the objective existence of the governing ideas,

---

normative conclusion, as one might say - while he regards the sentence stating the facts merely as *conditio sine qua non* of the conclusion. (pp. 191 f.) In view of the fact that both premisses are necessary for attaining a conclusion such a distinction is logically untenable.

[6] MacCormick and O. Weinberger, *op. cit.*, pp. 49-76 (German version, pp. 76-107).

according to which these ideas are there waiting to be discovered.[7] They are, in fact, the product of situations and needs, partly even inventions of the human mind.)

Ninth thesis:

Civilised man cannot live without institutions. *His interest in the institution and its norms is, on the other hand, frequently ambivalent.* He is interested in the existence of the institution and he identifies with it to some degree. He, therefore, feels under some obligation to it: he acknowledges his responsibilities and duties and through this sense of duty he realizes his feeling of belonging to the institutional community. There are times, however, when it is in his interest to offend against the regulative and to profit from this failure to fulfil the accepted regulative. As a result, it becomes necessary to provide a normative and actually realizable protection of the institution's rules - by means of sanctions among others. It is a fundamental mistake, however, from the sociological point of view to believe that the only way to make sure of behaviour that conforms with the rules is by introducing motivators - reward, punishment, measures of enforcement.[8]

Tenth thesis:

Institutional Legal Positivism is a positivist theory despite the fact that it rejects some assertions frequently made by positivists: It cannot be proved that anything whatever can be the content of the law there may be anthropological limits - albeit not explicitely known to us - restricting this possibility. Valid law does not only come into existence as a result of explicite decisions to lay down laws but also by practices being established, by customary behaviour, which becomes institutionalized as normative behaviour. Institutional Legal Positivism certainly rejects the extreme stance of positivism which only recognizes the existence of a norm if it was preceded by an explicite act of will with the respective content establishing the norm.[9]

In order to ensure that the variety of forms which institutions might potentially take is kept wide open and in order to avoid that limitations arising from historically accepted prejudices become fossilized *Institutional Legal Positivism does not make any assumptions based on natural law* and does not acknowledge that practical reason determines the content of law through apriori principles.

The validity of the law cannot be made to depend on evaluative criteria. If the constitutional theory is to deal realistically with the state as an existing

---

[7] See O. Weinberger, Institutionentheorie und Institutionalistischer Rechtspositivismus, in: the same and W. Krawietz (eds.), *Helmuth Schelsky als Soziologe und politischer Denker*, Stuttgart 1985, p. 150 ff.

[8] As in H. Kelsen, *Hauptprobleme der Staatsrechtslehre, entwickelt aus der Lehre vom Rechtssatze*, Tübingen 1911, p. 202. - Kelsen never abandoned that stance.

[9] This is the view taken by Kelsen in the late development of his theory. See H. Kelsen, *Allgemeine Theorie der Normen*, ed. by K. Ringhofer and R. Walter, Wien 1979; O. Weinberger, *Normentheorie als Grundlage der Jurisprudenz und Ethik. Eine Auseinandersetzung mit Hans Kelsens Theorie der Normen*, Berlin 1981.

institution it has to define the existing network of authorizations and to recognize the effective normative regulatives.

The law undoubtedly aspires in some way to conform with the morals of a given society and positive law can be evaluated from a moral point of view by any observer, but there are no prepositive (independent of the will of society) value postulates capable of defining the principles of admissible law.

In view of the fact that, among other reasons, there is no such thing as an exactly determined social morality and that all accepted moral principles are potentially contentious *Institutional Legal Positivism does not even accept the subsiduary validity of moral concepts as determinants for the law.* But all persons involved in the creation of law, the lawgiver and the whole legal staff, should be aware of the moral importance of their roles to find and apply morally acceptable legal standards.

5. COMMENTS ON THE FUNDAMENTAL PROBLEMS OF THE CONSTITUTIONAL THEORY

In this section I want to demonstrate that the implications of the theses of Institutional Legal Positivism summarized above can be of use in answering some of the fundamental questions facing constitutional theory since they introduce perspectives which, in my view, contribute to the clarification of these problems.

5.1. State and Constitution

The state can be regarded as a comprehensive situation, as an institutional whole within which the life of modern society takes place. It is on the whole appropriate to the political situation of our time to consider the state as the relevant universal institution. While it is appropriate for legal and politico-legal considerations to do so we must not forget that there are institutions which are valid and effective beyond the borders of an individual state.

In its role as an institution the state has inevitably a normative core: a legal system. The state is regarded as an entity (totality) which is structured and comprises different and relatively independent institutional systems. It is the primary function of a state's constitution to establish the basic organisation and the organs of the state. Consequently the constitution is, in the first place, that normative sphere which determines the structure of the state first and foremost, that is, by giving authority to subordinate institutions and organs of the state and by ordering the relations between them in such a way as to bring about a unified structure covering the entire system of the state. *The constitution creates a unified system for the political order*

5.2. The Indispensability of the Constitution for the Existence of the State

There are states which have a codified constitution (a written Constitutional Charter) and there are those which do not possess such an explicite constitution in form of a *ius scriptum*. From the point of view of Institutional Legal Positivism every state must necessarily have a constitution, i.e. a normative regulative turning the collective institution of the state into an ordered and unitary entity. *The constitution can be expressed explicitely or it can exist only implicitely.* In the latter case it can be drawn up doctrinally, i.e. by jurisprudence which constitutes the legal framework of the state. The reason for the validity of a doctrinal definition of the constitution does not rest, however, in the nature of the representation provided by the legal profession but it results from the *de facto* valid rules in accordance with which the state exists as a collective body of institutions. 'The doctrinal constitution' (if I may call it that) does not in itself constitute the state, but declares - more or less adequately in relation to the facts - its institutionalised constitutional situation.

No state without constitution. The existence of the state as a collective institution cannot be detached from the existence of its constitution and from the legal system thereby instituted.

The constitution (and the respective legal system) is valid precisely when it is institutionalized in such a way that the system of political institutions functions on the whole in accordance with the constitutional system.

5.3. The Effectiveness of the Constitution

The constitution is essentially a system of norms. It is, in fact, the fundamental subsystem of the legal order of the state. In looking at the constitution from the institutional point of view it is the relationship between these norms, on the one hand, and the institutions and the functions of the state, on the other hand, that is of particular interest. *The constitutional norms* - be they explicitely or implicitely (i.e. merely doctrinally) presented - *are real (or effective) when they function as a framework for the practices and the actions of society.*[10] This does not necessarily mean that the rules of constitutional law are always obeyed; but it does mean that they determine the organisation and the life of the institution. As a result, constitutional law describes the political reality of the state not as a system of observable facts and processes - its normative nature prevents it from doing so -, but it must correspond to the reality of social practices. The examination of this "correspondence" between constitutional norm and the practices of society at times leads to the conclusion that the statutes of the constitution are incomplete or that they conflict with reality; the doctrinally presented rules of the constitution may be wrong; this is the case, if they contradict the constitutional practices.

---

[10] See H.L.A. Hart, *The Concept of Law*, Oxford 1972^6, Chap. V and p. 245.

A note on the Marxist thesis concerning the withering away of the state

It does not make sense to speak of the withering of the state if one conceives of the state as a collective institution of society and if one regards the law as the basis of the state. The structure of the state and the methods of regulating as well as enforcing the law can be changed. It is inconceivable, however, that the state as the entirety of the social order with its normative regulative could disappear. That would mean men would have to live without institutions - which is unthinkable.

Marxism explains the development and the nature of state and law in terms of class-theory as being established by one class for the purpose of suppressing another one. The withering of state and law is predicted as a consequence of the removal of the class-structure of society. Changes in the structures of power, in the nature of the economy and the relations governing production are entirely feasible; they are possibly even to be expected, albeit not in the sense of the rather vague notions expressed by *Marx*. The existence of these possibilities is no reason, however, to assume that the collective institution of the state and the law as such might wither. The one-sided and problematical model used by classical Marxism as a basis for explaining this process becomes wholly unrealistic as a result of its prognosis of the withering state.

5.4. The Institutional Unity of the System of Legal Sources

My stringent claims concerning the unifying role of the constitution, resulting in the establishment of state and law as a universal institution come into conflict with certain tenets of the system theory - and of the institutional theory. The content of the legal system and the relevant processes of the law are not, in real life, created by a single normative centre, by a central creator of laws and by instances which determine the law only in the given frame. The judge, for instance, is also co-creator of general (law-like) rules.

Institutions and socially relevant norms are not always the product of the legal hierarchy. Institutional Legal Positivism emphasises the possibility of a non-legal genesis of social institutions and of the related norms. From the sociological point of view it is not right, therefore, to assume that there is a unified system of sources for social norms fed by a single original source. We have to reckon with the - as it were - spontaneous genesis of institutions and social norms. The institutions which come into existence in this extra-legal way tend subsequently to undergo a process of transformation legalizing them.

The postulated rational unitary nature of the legal system and the conflict-free development of the political order in form of a hierarchical system authorized by norms are *the product of an intellectual construction* which sets out the complex social development in a logical form.

5.5. The Legal Stabilization of the Constitution: The Law establishing the Constitution (the Basic Law, the Constitutional Charter)

The concept of the constitution is connected with the ideas of stability and with the ritual aura of festive foundations. The symbolism of stabilization is frequently coupled with the constitutional act although the act itself and its ceremonial nature are not invariably the source of the institutionalization. Nevertheless, the formal setting down of a constitution always acts as a major support for the future development of the state and the society in question.

The formal stabilization of the constitution as a system of norms which are of fundamental relevance is often strengthened by the introduction of a specific form of law, namely the constitutional law. Semantically and logically the norms of the constitution are no different from other legal rules. Since we have on the whole realized that a total petrification of the constitution is neither possible nor desirable the usual aim is to create relative stability with the help of tighter conditions for creating a new constitution or for introducing changes into the existing one.

In this way it has also been possible to protect certain governing ideas of a social system from hasty or insufficiently considered changes. Whether, however, such formal protection can be effective also against the corruption of the law, against the imposition of dictatorships or other crude forms of tyrannical rule, that remains a problematical question. I would answer it in the negative. Political systems driven by some kind of madness, brute force and similar circumstances usually overcome such hindrances with ease or they remove them with the help of force and by breaking the constitution. Our expectations of help in the battle against the corruption of the law by hindrances to change constitutional statutes should, therefore, not be pitched too high.

There is also an additional problem: Which material legal principles ought to have formal constitutional status? The ideas governing the system, of course. Yet this definition is, clearly, too vague. What we are really asking is, after all, what is to be raised to the status of the guiding principles.

It is up to us, in my view, also to warn against turning material legal principles precipitately into constitutional law. We have to remember that such formal hardening could obstruct social and politico-legal progress as well as placing obstacles into the way of updating adaptations of the law. I would like to make a strong plea for wise caution to be given its well deserved preference before propaganda.

5.6. The Essential Content of the Constitution

I consider it a not unimportant task to categorize the contents of the constitution as they have evolved. It has to be remembered that constitutional norms do not express only those elements which contribute to the development of the universal institution of the state but, in addition, there are also those norms which for political reasons are to be subjected to more difficult conditions of change.

(i) *The primary layer of constitutional norms consists of those rules which determine the organs of state and their interaction.* This layer of norms lays down the structures, competences and roles of organs of the state. The forms of and the conditions for the creation of norms and all spheres in which political activity by the state takes place have to be standardized in outline by specific authorization.

This layer of the constitutional content is not only fundamental for the constitution - the *ratio essendi* of the constitution, as one might say, - it is also that part of the constitution which - by casting it in a logical form - turns the legal system into a rationally comprehensible integrated whole. *This unity is achieved* (or, at least, aspired to) *by creating a kind of hierarchy of delegations and by avoiding conflicts of competences.*

(ii) The constitution expresses *the fundamental principles of the social system.* Using *Maurice Hauriou*'s terminology which is generally accepted in the institutional theory one might say: The constitution expresses the govering ideas of the universal institution of the state and of the social order that exists in it; usually it contains, however, not only the major governing ideas of the society as a whole, but also the governing ideas of the subordinate institutions.

Governing ideas establish themselves in conjunction with the respective institutions, both achieving their separate existence in society. Sometimes it is assumed that the constitutive governing idea is the factor which remains constant during the development of the institution. That is, however, only partially true. It must be said that it is even one of the major characteristics of the governing idea to unfold and change as the institution grows and transforms itself. All that remains in existence is an attitude which determines the general direction taken by society as a certain basic tendency embodied in the governing idea.

The governing ideas of the state and of its institutions are in essence the same as the socalled *principles of the political system or the principles governing particular institutions.*

The consequence for constitutional theory resulting from this is the need to treat the constitutional law which expresses governing ideas differently from rules of behaviour and power-conferring rules. They express abstract principles which are not always judicable. Nevertheless, they are not a nothing, but an element that is crucial for an adequate understanding of the law and for the work in the institutions.

(iii) The form of the constitutional law with its effect of relative petrification is used for the purpose of turning certain legal norms into stable constituent parts of the legal order. These then become norms of the constitutional law without, in fact, having a constitutional character in respect of content. What is introduced - largely for power-political considerations - is the constitutional form of these regulatives without their content representing the structure of the state and of the social system (i.e. the governing ideas). Whether this kind of solution is technically satisfactory and whether it serves the cause of democratic development - that remains an open question.

5.7. The Institutional Conception of Constitutional Knowledge

Among the consequences Institutional Legal Positivism has for jurisprudence the fundamental change it makes to the way the concept and the task of legal knowledge are defined is one of the most profound. For us - what I mean is, above all, in the context of Austrian law - legal knowledge means *'scire leges'*; knowing legal regulations, understanding what legal consequences (prescriptions, prohibitions, permissions, authorizations) are linked to which factual conditions. In this question about the nature of legal knowledge the conceptions of the Pure Theory of Law provide the accepted view, even among the opponents of that theory. The broadening of the approach demanded by Institutional Legal Positivism has three goals: On the one hand, it demands a broader conception of those components of the law which concern its meaning: to understand the governing ideas and the institutional connections; on the other hand, it regards the knowledge of sociological facts derived from the interpretation of observations as an integrating aspect of legal knowledge, and therefore, as a task of jurisprudencc. Legal knowledge is the knowledge of complex institutional facts, including the knowledge of the actual existence of the institutions, rather than the mere understanding of norms. We must take an interest in the way the law motivates man, in the ways of behaviour evoked by the law and by the organisational bodies instituted by the law. Nor is it true that these effects brought about by the law move simply between the poles "adherence to the norm/violation of the norm". Norms create power-constellations and effect profound changes in the situation concerning the vested interests of individuals bringing about changes also in the way they conduct themselves within the institution. That, too, has to be understood by the legal profession.[11] An evaluation, any politico-legal response to legal measures must - if it is to be well-founded - take account of the relevant facts. Even the interpretation of the legal texts themselves is dependent on actual facts and actual structures. These far-reaching theses ought to be supported by some examples, at least (in order to do this in a moderately satisfactory manner, however, one would have to write an entire book on the subject).

In the so-called Stalinist constitution of the USSR every confederate republic had the right to leave the union. It might appear that this meant free self-determination and political decentralization and that what bound them together, the union, rested entirely on a free consensus. Those reading nothing but the law might believe it, those who know, at least, a small amount about the actual reality, know that this interpretation is entirely wrong: the centralization could not have been more severe, for under Stalinist rule there was not even the possibility for such 'rights of withdrawal' of the member states which are laid down in the law to be put into practice. The abolition of these 'rights of with-

[11] One example, at least: When the career of the assistant lecturer depended crucially on the professor's goodwill and assessment, everybody adjusted their conduct to this situation. Nowadays in the universities with group-organization where the career depends on the voices of colleagues and students everybody tries to capture these voices.

drawal' in the constitution of the Gorbachev era may be regarded as a return to centralism by those who would only read legal texts without referring to factual knowledge in their interpretation.

Autonomy is undoubtedly an important postulate to be considered in the framing of a constitution. It is a democratic postulate in view of the enormous national (and other) differences within the states which are hardly avoidable in the European context. The combination of circumstances and the actual behaviour of political groups may lead to the destruction of the state, so that the autonomy clause functions only as a preparatory step for actions leading to independence.

And finally just one example of the problems we face in the interpretation of the law. Art. 18 (1) B-VG (Austrian Constitution) states the principle of legality: "The entire public administration may be carried out only on the basis of laws." An important principle of the constitutional state. But how are we to understand it? If an organ of the state has been given unrestricted powers in a certain field (let us say in the matter of policing) this instrument of public order acts formally on the basis of the law. If, however, there is a requirement for at least an outline definition of the content of the law (which appears to be the accepted interpretation) problems might arise depending on the type of administrative activity. The variety of administrative activities is such that the normative restrictions are not equally relevant in every case: in the area of economic administration, in particular, matters have to be assessed in an entirely different way from such areas where rights of freedom are to be protected. Factual knowledge of the fundamental differences in the various fields of administrative activity leads to the demand that the principle of legality must be interpreted in a highly differentiated way or - preferably - that it should be invested with differentiated norms.

6. POLITICAL POWER AND THE STRUCTURE OF THE CONSTITUTION

The conceptual triad of 'rule' (or 'government'), 'power' and 'force' implies a range of problems which are highly significant for constitutional theory.

In some sense any legal order can be regarded as a system of rules or government established by the constitution. The constitution does not only determine the structure of the state, the functions of its organs and the governing ideas of its social system, it also defines the nature of the authority in the state. Government means expressing the will of the society as a whole, determining its actions vis-à-vis other states and exercising power in the community even in regard of groups and individuals.

The exercise of government is conceived of primarily in analogy with the power a property-owner exercises over his property: government was originally domination. Under the influence of democratic ideas the concept of government has changed some of its characteristics: the state is no longer conceived of as the rule of some person or institution but as *res publica*, as a universal institution for the rule of the people. This is, however, only a vague characterization taking the form of a rough governing idea. A realistic description giving an objective definition can be reached only by discussing the questions concerning the power which determines the nature of the government. The problems of government are found largely in two areas:

(a) in the concept of the rule of law and in the relationship between those exercising power and the democratic concept of the rule of law;

(b) in the question of the constitution and the structure of power. Force being a factor in the exercise of power political theory also has to take into consideration the connection between force and tools of force in relation to power.

Men rule even after the state and other communities have ceased to be the property of a master *(dominus)*. Even after that change to rule or govern means to determine the actions of the collective institution. These acts undertaken for the community are activities within the institution: to rule or govern is to determine the functions and competences of the individuals including the potential enforcement of the respective activity; to evolve the measures needed to realize the governing ideas; further, to guide the actions of the institution in its external relations. What then do we mean when we refer to the rule of law? How can we demand that the rule of law should be established, or that the rule of law should be put above the rule of man?

"Rule of law" is not a description of the actual distribution of power in society but an ideal construct which, in my view, constitutes a pre-condition for the development of a democratic society. What we have to examine, is what exactly the implications of this construct are and whether it is realistic.

The ruler - any ruler, whether dictator or an official in a democratic system - is in terms of the rule-of-law conception somebody empowered to act in relation to his sphere of influence over which he rules. His rule is no longer the result of innate power but it is authority or competence (possibly, - as in the case of the dictator and the absolute ruler - unlimited authority) which is conferred on him. Consequently it has a social function. Even the absolute ruler is an empowered organ of the state having a social role in the institution. Where *"princeps legibus solutus"* is accepted this principle must be regarded as an element of the legal system. It does not, however, refer to the empowering norm which constitutes the (unlimited) power of the ruler. Rather, it suggests, on the one hand, a symbolic distinction between (a) the concept of rule as determined by competences which are conferred and (b) the view that the position of the ruler is God-given or the result of predestination allowing him to deal with the community as he wishes. The rule-of-law conception may be - but does not have to be - linked to a socially evaluating test of legitimacy while the dominion-conception precludes such considerations *a limine*.

It is exactly this fact that the rule of law can be compatible with dictatorial systems that demonstrates that this conception of the state and the constitution provides a necessary albeit by no means a sufficient basis for democratic systems.

Which of the constructs gives a realistic picture of the sovereign power, the dominion-model or the rule-of-law model? *De facto* any power - even that of an unrestricted dictator - is based on a whole host of relations and institutionalized elements, i.e. it has a normative and an institutional basis; this applies also, of course if it has theocratic roots. In that sense the construct of the institutional authority is more objective. It is only by disregarding the fact that "rule of law" is an ideal construct and not the description of an actual ruling power that the fictitious idea of the personified law being the actual agent of power arises. In reality the rule-of-law conception is meant to be a demand for rather than description of specific circumstances wherein government and power are exercised.

In analysing the problems of power from the political point of view and from that of the constitutional theory we have to apply the perspective of the theory of action and of institutional theory. *Max Weber*'s famous definition: "Power means the chance of imposing one's own will on a social relationship even against resistance no matter what this chance is based on"[12] is inadequate. It even appears to me that this definition places the problem of power into an inappropriate perspective: It sees power in terms of the relationship between the subject and other engaging in activity in the same sphere while - from the institutional point of view - power is, above all, competence and the actual possibility of determining and realizing the activities of the institutions. By emphasizing the imposition of one's will against the will of others in this definition of the problem of power one might interprete power as conflicting with democracy and with ideals of freedom - although that was hardly *Weber*'s intention. Is it not a shift in the meaning of the concept to define power as a chance, i.e. as a probability of achieving what is intended? Power is not the opportunity of getting one's way but the position of a subject - be it individual or collective - in a social structure which provides this opportunity.

From the point of view of the theory of action the problem of power appears in a slightly different perspective.

(a) Power is, above all, possibility for action. Powerful is whoever has a broad field of opportunities for action and is able to exert decisive influence on the actions of other individuals or collective persons. Not only the individual is an agent of power. Political theory has to take into account the power of different groups, organisations and institutions. Of special interest are the relations between the power of the individual and the power of the institutions, as well as the power of the individual within the institution and his potential advantages of power in other areas resulting from his function within the institution.

(b) Scope for action is the pre-condition of power;[13] extending the scope for action is the basis for the possibility of any extension of power. The founding of institutions creates opportunities for action, in other words, the scope for action is extended - for some subjects, at least. For instance: the introduction of the game of chess creates the opportunity to play chess. By developing the

---

[12] M. Weber, *Wissenschaft und Gesellschaft*, Tübingen 1972[5], p. 28.

[13] For the concept of the scope for action see O. Weinberger, Freedom, Range for Action, and the Ontology of Norms, in: *Synthese*, vol. 65 (1985), pp. 307-324.

institution further structures may evolve from which positions of power could grow: one might write books on chess, become a champion player, ... and in doing so gain money and other positions involving power. Something similar applies to other areas, i.e. the field of education, the arts, research. The institutions serving the purpose of learning and training extend the field of action and of work; they create social structures and the basis for the development of spheres of influence among different subjects.

(c) The institutional conception regards power above all as the prerequisite and the basis for establishing institutions; the organisation of the institution lays down power structures which are meant to fulfil a functional purpose in the service of the institution's governing ideas. Institutionalism is, however, aware of the fact that this functional power (power constituted by competences within the institutions) also creates additional social power which accrues to the official. The official acquires possibilities for action as a result of the increase in his economic means, by gaining access to informations (which are not usually generally available), by making the acquaintance of influential people, by achieving the kind of social status which is connected with the function he fulfills, etc.

(d) Power does not only mean being able to influence the actions of others; it does not only mean an increase in the possibilities for action gained by the agent of power and leading to a restriction of the same opportunities for others. Organisation and power can also contribute to increasing the possibilities for action for the members of the institution other than those of the agent of power. The power (the competence and the ability) an official has to organize cultural events provides the creative professions with increased opportunities for creative activity and audiences with additional opportunities for consuming culture. The constructive functions which power can undoubtedly have are obscured if we define power only in terms of the relationship between the agent of power and other acting persons who are controlled or, at any rate, influenced by the way he exercises power.

(e) Functional structures produce positional inequalities for men living in society. Equality as an actual state cannot exist in a functionally structured society. We can only aspire to the following two forms of democratic equality: (α) formal equality of access to functions (in conjunction with the widest possible opportunity for actually realizing this accessibility) and (β) a kind of balance between positions taking into account their objective differences.

(f) It follows that the democratic conception of power has to face the fact that there can be no question of negating control and power for the simple reason that the institutions of the state have to function and the organisation has to serve the governing ideas. All we have to be concerned about is that the institutions serve democratic governing ideas - or, at least, governing ideas which do not conflict with democratic ways of life -, that a division and distribution of power of such a kind is introduced - with, among others, the help of a separation of powers - as to guarantee democratic control and the mutual functional limitation of the power of individuals, groups and institutions.

(g) It is impossible to identify problems of power on a purely statistical basis; constellations of power can only be understood from a dynamic perspective. The balance of power evolves in processes comprising the development of institutions, their organisation and the distribution of competences. But facts are not the only thing that is crucial for the development of the seats of power. Equally important is people's understanding of or their views on the distribution of competences and of power as well as the expectations arising from these views.[14]

(h) Power is constituted by norms - legal or non-legal ones - as well as by actual relations. It changes as a result of changes in the realm of normative competences, of accompanying circumstances (resulting from the increase or decrease in the size of the institution, for instance), also due to changes in the way people perceive the relations between different spheres of influence. As a rule these perceptions of the nature of existing power-structures often act as self-fulfilling prophecies.

(i) Power has to be seen as a network of relations, i.e. as determined by a system; it is never only authority, possibility of action and opportunity to impose one's own will in accordance with one's own purposes but it is always also *"quid pro quo"*, the agent of power is always bound by his role or, at least, by the expectations of the members of society that he will produce achievements for society.

(j) On the one hand there are those who uphold the thesis that it is power that decides what the law is, on the other hand, I have tried to show that the power of the powerful is among other things also a product of the law. What then is the primary factor, the law or power? We have to ask the question in a different way. The problem is less confusing if law and power are seen from the dynamic point of view. Elements of power - including the potential use of force - are connected with elements involved in the construction of viable institutions and in the development of the value systems (or ideologies) which form the basis of the law. The structure of the universal organisation of society (the state) always has to be seen in normative terms - in the sense of granting authority -. In a certain sense we also have to see it as hierarchically structured if one considers that even in a democratic system there has to be some kind of organisation which makes it possible for intentions to be formulated, decisions to be taken and effective control to be exercised.

7. THE PROBLEM OF LEGITIMACY

The rule of law practised on the basis of the constitution determines the legitimacy of the life of the society in the constitutional state by legalizing the government and the power by way of an ordered system of delegated authority. Social theory in its critique poses the question - more often than not in the spirit

---

[14] See B. Bames, *The Nature of Power*, Oxford 1988.

of democratic ideas - about the legitimacy of the government.[15] What is crucial here is the problem of how to define the criteria of legitimacy. The fact that somebody is ruling the country is not enough; we require some kind of moral or socio-political legitimization of the ruler (or of the system of government). The actual effectiveness of the system of government, i.e. the fact that those in power are able to enforce their will (by power, force or/and on the basis of acceptance) is not sufficient - seen from this point of view - as a guarantee of legitimacy.

Whenever we use an existing system as the basis for our assessment then it is precisely the type of government which has been empowered to rule by this system that we consider legitimate and, inevitably, any movement, person or group seeking power or government without being empowered in this way appears illegitimate.

It is one of the characteristic attributes of any democractic system that it contains a realizable method as well as making provisions for a legitimate - i.e. one determined by the built-in rules of the system - transition from one authorization to govern to the next.

It is an indubitable historical fact that such an effective mechanism for the potential change of power does not always exist in a state and that corrupt legal systems and governments appear again and again, their degeneracy conflicting so markedly with all civilized moral conceptions that nobody observing the system from a geographical and/or chronological distance without, therefore, succumbing himself to the mass-delusion[16] can doubt the corrupt nature of such a system of power. Those involved in the study of social and political problems have, therefore, asked the question, when a system of government can be regarded as legitimate. It is not easy to find a satisfactory answer to this question. There probably is no exact and fully satisfactory solution which would always provide an undisputed and incontrovertible answer to the question what legitimacy is. We can only point to ways of approaching the problem and to attempts at solving it which offer at least partial definitions for the assessment of a system's legitimacy.

(1) The approach to the problem of the relationship between ruler and ruled on the basis of contractual theory - which has played an important part in the history of political theory - transforms the act of ruling from a position of subjective arbitrariness into a system where the ruler is bound to his controlling function by his responsibilities. Even if we dissociate ourselves from the image represented by the concept of the contract there remains the postulate of the social commitment and responsibility to the task of controlling society as one of the necessary, albeit not entirely sufficient, criteria for the legitimacy of government.

---

[15] See for example P. Graf Kielmannsegg (ed.), *Legitimitätsprobleme politischer Systeme*, Opladen 1976.

[16] See O. Weinberger, Angst vor dem menschlichen Wahn, in: A. Grabner-Haider/O. Weinberger/K. Weinke (eds.), *Fanatismus und Massenwahn*, Graz/Wien 1987, pp. 4-34.

(2) Legitimacy certainly cannot be explained with reference to the factual enforcement of power. After all, the definition of legitimacy is supposed to represent a value criterion to be contrasted with the purely factual situation. However, in view of the fact that the legitimate system must have (- or be capable of achieving) an institutionalized existence the actual imposition of power - or rather the realistic chance of achieving it - must, nevertheless, be regarded as a necessary precondition for the legitimacy of a system of government.

(3) The consent to a government and to a legal system on the part of the members of the society appears to be at the heart of the criterion of legitimacy. From the point of view of the democratic spirit universal consent is the crucial factor. Nevertheless we have to ask ourselves whether something like universal consent actually exists, especially whether it exists in the complex and differentiated societies underlying modern states. This is a problem in particular if we interprete consent as genuine and well-considered approval rather than merely as the sociological fact of non-explicite resistance. The concept of majority consent might be reached - possibly in two stages: overwhelming (almost universal) consent and consent by a simple majority. Partial consent lacks, however, the strength of conviction that is associated with universal consent. It is only the case of universal consent that we acknowledge a system's legitimacy purely on the strength of the fact that it is supported by the will of all members of the community.

(4) In bowing to the necessity of moving from universal consent to some kind of partial agreement - a move which is, in fact, practically unavoidable - one is faced with the question whether the concept of acceptability ought not to join or even replace the concept of acceptance as a criterion of legitimacy. It is true that acceptability, too, is a matter of approval - and with that of an evaluation on the part of the members of society -, but attention here shifts away from the mere evaluating response to the reasons for the evaluation expressed in the acceptance. The reliance on reasons for or against consent means that the mere existence of a majority - be it overwhelming or very small - ceases to be acceptable as the only criterion of legitimacy. To give a general definition of what the crucial "sufficient reasons" for an assessment of acceptability are is in all probability impossible. It will often be possible, however, to come to a broad agreement on the subject of those elements which impair the legitimacy.

8. THE CONSTITUTION AND THE GOVERNING IDEAS OF DEMOCRACY

Democracy has essentially to do with constitution: After all, democracy being the postulate and program of the rule of the people depends on common decision-making processes and these processes have to be determined by normative regulatives which ultimately have to be established by the constitution. Formal legitimacy can only be conferred on an act of the communal will by way of a normative authorization.[17] Even the attempt to invest the system of authorization itself with a democratic legitimization with the help of a primary ballot is only possible with reference to a normative regulative as a prerequisite for the ballot.

'Rule of the people' is a vague - but by no means meaningless - governing idea which finds its way to application through the medium of the constitution. The system is constituted by the structural principles determining the decision-making process, the exercise of power and the control of the social institutions. It takes account of two key points: the governing idea of the rule of the people and the postulate of the effective functioning of the institutions (assessed with reference to the governing idea of the respective institutions).

There are three fundamental demands of democracy concerning government and power. They can be formulated relatively clearly in institutional terminology:

(1) Power must be restricted to the exercise of functional power wherever possible.

(2) The effectiveness of the institutions must be safeguarded.

(3) All public functions must be subjected to democratic control while being adapted to the governing ideas of democracy and to the actual will of society.

To point (1):

The ability to act, taking decisions in the name of institutions, coordinating the activities of individuals, controlling the effectiveness of the institutions, serving the governing ideas - all these are necessary, therefore power is necessary for the realization of social goals. The individual acts largely in the sense of the institution since he identifies with the institution and wishes to contribute to the achievement of its goals. An additional controlling and coordinating power is, however, indispensable. In a democracy this power is always coupled with political responsibility vis-à-vis the community.

The law inevitably creates social positions offering additional possibilities for the exercise of power in other matters and other directions. In a democracy every effort has to be made to limit this non-functional power and to recognize only functional power.

To point (2):

There are those who believe that democracy and democratic forms are valuable in themselves however inefficient they may be in the given application. They maintain we have to put up with a degree of impediment put in the way of effective management in order to achieve the democratic life we value. I cannot accept this point of view.

---

17 See my paper "Abstimmungslogik und Demokratie" [in: B. Sutter et al. (eds.), *Reformen des Rechts*, Graz 1979, pp. 605-623] where I have attempted to show that collective decision-making processes are possible only on the basis of normative rules. In a modern state the constitution has the task of providing a normative basis for the definition of the functions fulfilled by the organs of the state as well as the competences and the decision-making processes.

It is an indisputable fact, in my opinion, that every system faces socalled frictional losses in the organisational structure; the administration always contains superfluous elements; the economy spends quite substantial sums on advertising (despite the fact that it frequently does not lead to needs being fulfilled). The democratic system also has undoubtedly inevitable "frictional losses". It is important, however, to minimize them and to keep an eye on the effectiveness of the institutions when organisational forms are being developed. In view of the fact that democracy has to compete with other forms of society it will only be viable in the long run if it proves itself functionally, too.

In acknowledging the necessity for the control of democratic institutions to be efficient we have to accept the need to use a variety of forms of organisation and of decision-making. Transparent and regulated monocratic control is no less democratic than collective decisions are. Pseudo-democratic institutions are to be avoided and the fact that correct decisions rely on information and on problem-solving ideas always has to be born in mind. This fact imposes considerable restrictions on the possibilities of direct democracy. In any case, varied forms of participation and consultation are certainly preferable to mere voting mechanisms.

The structure of the institutional functions has to be determined in such a way as to allow it to fulfil both the governing ideas of the projected work, i.e. the intended social role of the institution and also the general governing ideas of democracy. In order to be functionally efficient the institution has to have a kind of hierarchy. The following criteria in particular have to be taken into account when the structure of an institution is decided on: a) the adequate distribution of competences ensuring effective control and the democratic limitation of power, b) effective internal and external control as indispensable elements in the process of realizing an action, c) the motivating influence exerted by the structures on the behaviour of the persons involved.

To point (3):

Control is an integrating element of every action. The person engaged in the action controls his activity himself. Well-developed self-regulation is a vital aspect of civilization. Actions relevant to society - especially political and economic activity - have to be subjected to additional social controls. Depending on the circumstances hierarchical as well as consultative structures may be appropriate for this purpose. The correct timing of both decisions and controls is important. Inefficient and pseudo-democratic structures tend to produce rash decisions and ineffective controls *post factum*. It is pointless, for instance, to decide on the construction of a nuclear power plant, to build it and eventually not to operate it. Equally, control is not only useful as a final *placet* or as a reproach *ex post* but above all as a constant attendant on every kind of work that is undertaken.

In jurisprudence the processes involved in collective decision-making are frequently regarded as democratic and contrasted with monocratic processes. Formal rules regulating the decision-making processes of society must safeguard the democratic life of society and guarantee a maximum of freedom by means of the principles of majority, but formal rules alone are not sufficient to protect a democratic society.

The alternative between democratic (= collective) or monocratic control does not make a useful contribution to the theory dealing with different forms of government if one considers that, on the one hand, certain monocratic forms of government are thoroughly acceptable even from the democratic point of view and, on the other hand, there are a number of different forms which do not fit into this scheme of alternatives (especially forms of co-determination or participation).

A democratic system as such can only function if the following conditions are fulfilled: In addition to the rules which establish the democratic decision-making processes society must also broadly acknowledge a system of postulates concerning the content of those rules and it must have democratic habits as well as democratic value ideals.

The ideals of democracy constitute an open class of evaluative attitudes and postulates which are subject to change in the process of history and in connection with technical, economic and intellectual developments.

Assuming that the democratic system is based on a formal-democratic and on a substantive component two questions arise:

(a) If it is possible to determine what is right for society on the basis of the substantive postulates then there is no positive function for the process of democratic voting: if it leads to a decision that could have been reached by a rational argument, it is superfluous, if it contradicts such a decision than a bad decision comes about as a result of the democratic act of will.

It is misleading to set out the problem in this way. Firstly, the substantive postulates of the democratic world-view are not sufficient in themselves to determine political decisions; and the postulates themselves do not provide detailed definitions resulting in the need for evaluative responses where different postulates collide; and secondly, it is by no means certain which substantive principles can claim to be valid. Protection of minorities, periodicity of elections and other decision-making processes, as well religious freedom are generally acknowledged candidates for such a position in the democratic world-view. The principles are applied by deliberation rather than simply determined by subsumption; they could in many cases turn out to be very problematical if they were regarded as absolutely valid rules. In our culture religious freedom is seen as an indisputable democratic postulate. We must not forget, though, that religious systems themselves can be extremely intolerant. Enthusiasm for the faith not only leads to the idea of dissemination and mission, it also engenders contempt for non-believers or those with a different faith, leads to fighting against other religions (or against "heretics"), war and destruction often connected with particular brutality. Religious systems tend to have an ecclesiastical organisation frequently claiming not only influence over the souls and the morals of its members but also domination over public life and the state. Although religious freedom must be protected it must not be forgotten that religions and religious communities can be extremely undemocratic; they can be the cause of religious wars or of a "holy war", even of genocide. Religious freedom raised to the status of absolute principle without regard of the content of the faith and of the tolerance or intolerance of the community of the faithful may degenerate to a blank cheque against freedom and democracy.

(b) On the basis of the democratic decision-making process it is possible for decisions to come about which run counter to certain material principles of democracy. Democratic processes can be corrupted by propaganda, ideological indoctrination or rigid principles. Sometimes dictatorships are installed by democratic processes, sometimes by manipulated, and only seemingly democratic ones. It is possible for substantive democratic principles to be destroyed by democratic means. For example: The rights of the minority can be abolished in accordance with the principle of majority. Depending on the interests involved - i.e. under the threat of high unemployment - measures against individual groups (such as foreign workers - socalled guest-workers -, non-members of parties and trade-unions etc.) may occasionally be taken.

How can we prevent democratic processes from being destroyed or corrupted? Protection by way of petrification or by laying down harder conditions for the introduction of changes can hardly make an impact, especially not at crucial moments considering that such obstacles have no effect on emotionally charged mass movements. To lay down absolute prohibition of any change is neither effective nor in tune with the democratic views which do not permit that the will of the people at any given time is prevented from influencing the life of society.

The institutional approach makes it possible for a kind of answer to be found to the problem of the relationship between the forms of democratic decision-making and the material democratic ideals. The material principles of democracy can be regarded as a kind of guiding ideas of the democratic institutions. They are not strict rules of behaviour but goals and regulative ideas to be developed in the process of concrete analyses. They provide guidelines for evaluating the organisation and for assessing the functioning of the institutions. Due consideration of the material principles will be guaranteed only if we think of democracy in terms of consultation, discussion, criticism rather than seeing it only as a competition for majorities.

For highly developed democracies it is an important postulate, therefore, that they should pursue the democratic dialogue on many levels and with the participation not only of the political parties, pressure groups, individual politicians and the civil service but also of the press and the other mass media, the sciences, clubs and educational institutions etc. and that they should make provisions for this dialogue to be adequately institutionalised.

VI. THE FORMAL-TELEOLOGICAL THEORY OF ACTION AND CRIMINAL LAW*

1. SOME PROBLEMS FACING CRIMINAL LAW AND THE THEORY OF ACTION AND THE GOALS OF MY INVESTIGATION

The elucidation of the concept of action is one of the most important of the fundamental problems facing jurisprudence. In the wake of Welzel's teleological theory of action with its philosophical and dogmatic implications this concept became a key topic of debate in the context of criminological theory.[1]

The teleological theory of action has not only shed new light on a variety of familiar problems of the theory of criminal law it has also advanced a number of striking and much discussed theses of its own: It regards teleology as a constitutive feature of the concept of action. It derives the criminological concept of action from the general concept of action. It postulates that inalienable features of an action are in the legal sense the product of the structure of the action and that the different elements which can be standardized are equally produced by the conceptual-structural framework of action. In addition the teleological concept of action attempts to determine the generic concept of crime and undeavours to present an acceptable explication of the concept of omission. It makes an important

---

* The following chapter was originally composed as a contribution to a *Festschrift* for *Ulrich Klug*. It was preceded by the following dedication: "For Ulrich Klug who successfully pioneered the increasing application of modern logical analysis in jurisprudence on his 70th birthday."

I am most grateful to my colleague Dr. Manfred Proske for his critical suggestions for the first version of this paper; the ideas presented here are, however, my own responsibility.

1 H. Welzel, Kausalität und Handlung, *Zeitschrift für die gesamte Staatswissenschaft*, 51, 1931, pp. 703-720; the same, *Um die finale Handlungslehre*, Tübingen 1949; the same, *Naturrecht und materiale Gerechtigkeit*, Göttingen 1951; the same, *Aktuelle Strafrechtsprobleme im Rahmen der finalen Handlungslehre*, Karlsruhe 1953; the same, *Das neue Bild des Strafrechtssystems*, Göttingen 1961; the same, *Vom Bleibenden und Vergänglichen in der Strafrechtswissenschaft*, Marburg 1964; the same, *Das deutsche Strafrecht*, 9th ed., Bonn 1965; see also: K. Engisch, Der finale Handlungsbegriff, in: *Probleme der Strafrechtserneuerung. Festschrift für Eduard Kohlrausch*, Berlin 1944, pp. 141-179; the same, Logische Überlegungen zur Verbrechensdefinition, in: *Festschrift für Hans Welzel zum 70. Geburtstag*, ed. by G. Stratentwerth et al., Berlin/New York 1974, pp. 343-378; H.-H. Jeschek, Der strafrechtliche Handlungsbegriff in dogmengeschichtlicher Entwicklung, *Festschrift für Eberhard Schmidt zum 70. Geburtstag*, ed. by P. Poschelmann and W. Gallas, Göttingen 1961, pp. 139-155; U. Klug, Der Handlungsbegriff des Finalismus als methodologisches Problem. Prolegomena zu einem axiomatischen Handlungsbegriff, in: *Philosophie und Recht. Festschrift für C.A. Emge*, Wiesbaden 1960, pp. 34-50; R. Moos, Die finale Handlungslehre, in: *Strafrechtliche Probleme der Gegenwart*, vol. II, Strafrechtliches Seminar der Vereinigung der österreichischen Richter, print by: Bundesministerium für Justiz, Stein 1974, pp. 5-41; W. Niese, *Finalität, Vorsatz und Fahrlässigkeit*, Tübingen 1951; C. Roxin, Kritik der finalen Handlungslehre, in: the same, *Strafrechtliche Grundlagenprobleme*, Berlin/New York 1973, pp. 72-122 (*ZStW*, 74, 1962, pp. 51 ff.); E.A. Wolff, *Der Handlungsbegriff in der Lehre vom Verbrechen*, Heidelberg 1964.

contribution to the theory of forms of guilt, in particular by advancing the thesis that intent constitutes an element of the facts of the case to be taken into consideration. It further expresses noteworthy views on problems of attempt, participation and other issues.

The current *general theory of action* is characterised by diverging views, such as: the controversy between determinism and indeterminism; the debate between causalists and intentionalists[2], divergencies in the definition of the concepts of 'action' and 'motive'; disputes about the form the description of actions should/ought to take and about the determination of types of action; lack of clarity about what constitutes the meaning of actions; controversies about the relations between the theories of rational and factual decisions (actions); the problem of the origin and effect of norms as determinants of action, etc.

In view of the controversial problems connected with the teleological theory of action and with the general theory of action I want to try and examine the major theses of the teleological theory of action from the point of view of the *formal-teleological theory of action* which I have endeavoured to evolve[3] and from that of *Institutional Legal Positivism.*[4] I am convinced that this approach will be able to contribute to the process of clarifying - if not solving - the disputed problems.

2. CHARACTERISTIC FEATURES OF THE FORMAL-TELEOLOGICAL THEORY OF ACTION

The usual explanation, viz. that action is willed behaviour, has to be defined more accurately. We are all familiar with the concepts of 'action' and

---

2 G.H. von Wright *Erklären und Verstehen*, Frankfurt a.M. 1974 (1st ed. 1971), p. 92.

3 O. Weinberger, Rationales und irrationales Handeln, in: F. Kaulbach/W. Krawietz (eds.), *Recht und Gesellschaft*, Berlin 1978, pp. 721-744; the same, Handeln und Schließen. Überlegungen zum Begriff der praktischen Inferenz, in: F. van Dun (ed.), *Law between Morality and Politics, Philosophica* 23, 1979 (1), pp. 5-35; the same, Teleologie und Zeitablauf. Gleichzeitig eine Kritik an Wolfgang Stegmüllers Begriff der formalen Teleologie, in: *Rechtstheorie* 13 (1982), pp. 285-302; also Ch. Weinberger/O. Weinberger, *Logik, Semantik, Hermeneutik*, München 1979; O. Weinberger *Rechtslogik*, Berlin 1989 and Chap. II of this book, the same, *Studien zur formal-finalistischen Handlungstheorie*, Frankfurt a.M./Bern/New York 1983.

4 O. Weinberger, Die Norm als Gedanke und Realität, *ÖZÖR*, 20 (1979), pp. 203-216; the same, Tatsachen und Tatsachenbeschreibungen. Eine logisch-methodologische Überlegung zu einem Grundlagenproblem der Sozialwissenschaften, in: K. Salamun (ed.), *Sozialphilosophie als Aufklärung. Festschrift für Ernst Topitsch*, Tübingen 1979, pp. 173-187; the same, Das Recht als institutionelle Tatsache. Gleichzeitig eine Überlegung über den Begriff des positiven Rechts, *Rechtstheorie* 11 (1980), pp. 427-442; the same, Zur Idee eines institutionalistischen Rechtspositivismus. Gleichzeitig eine Auseinandersetzung mit Hans Kelsens Setzungspositivismus, *Révue internationale de philosophie* 1981, pp. 487-507; D.N. MacCormick, *Law as Institutional Fact*, Edinburgh 1973; D.N. MacCormick/O. Weinberger, *An Institutional Theory of Law: New Approaches to Legal Positivism*, Dordrecht et al. 1986; the same, *Grundlagen des Institutionalistischen Rechtspositivismus*, Berlin 1985.

'willing'. In dealing with these concepts on a scientific basis, however, we must have recourse to theories of explication which provide a formal representation of the processing of information that corresponds to the 'willing'.

The formal-teleological theory of action is based on *formal teleology*. This is founded on the assumed knowledge of causality (and of the concepts 'causal relations' and 'causal law') and it has been evolved free from psychological conceptions. Formal teleology represents a specific kind of information-processing which can be described as 'teleological thinking' provided thinking is conceived of as an information-processing operation rather than a psychological process. Apart from the setting of goals this kind of information-processing operation also deals with factual informations about the respective situation, about causal relations and laws of causality at work. Furthermore, it is involved in discovering potential means for achieving particular goals and in making relative evaluations of these means from the point of view of the intended goals.[5]

It is the means or the programs which are rated relatively above the others that are *chosen*. If the alternatives are valued equally one of them is selected arbitrarily (at random).

By *the subject of the teleological system* we mean a person or another system to which a system of goals is assigned and which is capable of conducting relative evaluations (i.e. of preferring *A* to *B* or of regarding *A* and *B* as of equal value).

By the *behaviour of a person* (or a system) we understand the sequence of states which a person (or system) pass through within a given period of time.

The concept of *action* is defined as a behavioural process which is dependent on a specific information processing operation. This operation forms the core of the teleological thinking which is represented schematically by formal teleology. Teleology is thus just as much a constitutive characteristic of the concept of action in my formal-teleological theory of action as it is in *Welzel*'s teleological theory of action.

The fact that behaviour is seen as dependent on elements of information (knowledge and goals) and the processing of information is an essential aspect of the concept of action. It is equally crucial that there are alternatives of behaviour, i.e. that there is *scope for action* so that different actions can take place according to the decision that is taken on the basis of the information received and evaluated.

Freedom in the sense of choice between these alternative possibilities, i.e. the existence of scope for action, is a precondition for the concept of action. The conceptual apparatus of the concept of action does not, however, require that an action should not be determined at all in the sense that the subject of the action would be *prima causa* and able to decide its actions free from the influence of determinants.

---

[5] Ch. Weinberger/O. Weinberger, see ftn. 3; O. Weinberger, Handeln und Schließen, see ftn. 3; the same, Teleologie und Zeitablauf, see ftn. 3.

The concept of *fixation* constitutes an important element in the formal-teleological theory of action. Teleological deliberation preceding action is frequently simplified by "prefabricated blocks" of volition. In addition there are also *fixed intentions* which enable the subject to act in a relatively constant way without having always recourse to the whole process of teleological deliberation. *Autonomous norms* may be seen as a particular type of *fixed intention*.

In view of the fact that man is a social being and that collective action and communal life are only possible on the basis of institutionalised normative regulatives it is inevitable that *heteronomous systems of norms* should also occur as determinants of action.

The formal-teleological theory of action assumes that there is a kind of interaction between the deliberations preceding action based on the system of goals and those based on other determinants, especially normative regulatives. The way normative regulatives operate is complex. Norms are partly internalised and operate as received determinants, and to some extent the person to whom the norm is addressed is moved to comply with the norm by various motivating factors (punishment, reward). It would be wrong, however, to regard the operation of heteronomous norms as no more than a utalitarian reaction to the expectations of punishment and reward.

Human being are *free* also in the sense that their actions can be influenced by norms - to some extent even against their teleological deliberations of utility.

The processing of information which forms the basis of action is concerned with determining means for given ends, programs of action and with the choice between means or programs which have been acknowledged as possible alternatives.

The realization of actions, too, involves the processing of information which governs the action (theory of feedback).

In the formal-teleological theory of action the information processing operations referred to above are not regarded as the source of action - the activities of human beings or any other acting systems being determined by their own nature -; instead, they are seen as an institution which serves to determine the direction and the control of biologically or socially constituted systems by investing them with spontaneous activity. This conception has the effect of rendering the controversy between causalists and intentionalist concerning the theory of motives obsolete.

The formal-teleological theory of action permits *several different descriptions of actions*: The action can be expressed as the description of the *sequence of different states of acting of the person* (for instance "getting up"); it can be presented as the description of the *sequence of the different states which the system undergoes which is affected by the acting subject* ("to kill a person"). Action can be defined as the transition from one state to another, or simply in terms of the final state the action aims to achieve.[6]

---

[6] O. Weinberger, see ftn. 3.

In the social context actions are often to be understood as more than just sequences of states guided by information; they also have an *institutionally determined meaning* (Sinn). The transformation of one state into another which occurs when I perform the action of raising my hat and replacing it on my head after a certain time has the additional meaning of a greeting (provided the appropriate secondary conditions are fulfilled). I have, in other words, performed the action of greeting by enacting a movement with my hat.

It is an essential feature of the formal-teleological theory of action that it distinguishes between two fundamentally different ways of applying formal teleology in the theory of action[7]:

(a) *deliberation preceding the action* leading to the selection of means or programs,

(b) *interpretation of motives* in which the phases of the action under observation are explained as actions with the help of an interpretative reconstruction of the information processing operation which guides the action. The formal-teleological theory of action regards *motives* as purposes of action which are ascertained by interpretation; they are non-observable entities, namely pieces of information.

Note on Jürgen Rödig's view of the concepts of 'action' and 'omission'

Rödig, one of *Ulrich Klug's* most important disciples defines the concept of action as follows: "If *s*1 is a particular behaviour and there is at least one *s*2 which belongs to the same range of behaviour as *s*1 and can be distinguished from it, then we can say: '*s*1 is an action'."[8] By analogy the concept of omission is defined as follows: "If *s*1 belongs to the same ranges of behaviour as *s*2 (...) and *s*1 is different from *s*2, then we may say: '*s*1 is an omission of *s*2'."[9] These definitions only refer to the alternative possibilities of action, not to the processing of information. This I believe to be a mistake. *Rödig* regards omission as a form of action. This conception is only justified as long as one remains within his conceptual framework. As soon as the fact that action is dependent on information is taken into consideration - as is the case in my conception and in the teleological theory of action - then omission has to be regarded as a form of behaviour which is not always an action.

3. THE CONCEPT OF 'INSTITUTIONAL LEGAL POSITIVISM'

On the basis of *Searle*'s distinction between 'brute facts' and 'institutional facts'[10] I describe the law as an institutional fact. However, my conception of institutional facts is not the same as Searle's. Searle introduced the concept in order to prove that 'ought' can be inferred from 'is' (facts), whereas I base my conception on cognitively differentiated semantics[11] and emphasise the

---

[7] Ch. Weinberger/O. Weinberger, see ftn. 3.

[8] J. Rödig, *Die Denkform der Alternative in der Jurisprudenz*, Berlin/Heidelberg/New York 1969, p. 98.

[9] J. Rödig, *op. cit.*, p. 85.

[10] J.R. Searle, *Speech Acts. An Essay in the Philosophy of Language*, Cambridge 1969.

[11] Ch. Weinberger/O. Weinberger, see ftn. 3, p. 109.

thesis that it is impossible to describe institutional facts without normative, teleological or (and) evaluative characteristics.[12]

Institutional legal positivism regards the social existence (validity) of legal norms as the consequence of the interaction between norms (as comprehensible ideal entities) and observable social processes. The legal norm is a fact as a result of being interwoven with real and observable processes. This kind of fact is different only on account of its normative (teleological or evaluative) core. It is, in other words, an institutional fact.

Like all other forms of legal positivism Institutional Legal Positivism denies the possibility of practical knowledge, it rejects, in fact, the idea that it is possible to determine empirically or/and logically whether a norm is justifiable; on the other hand, it treats intuitive evaluation as an empirically verifiable psychological and sociological fact. It recognises, therefore, the possibility of legal-political lines of reasoning and examines their structure; it is always at pains to separate matters of voluntary decision from cognitive arguments.[13]

Institutional legal positivism transcends the difference between normative and realist legal positivism as according to institutional legal positivism the reality of law consists of a normative order, a class of legal relations which are functionally based on the normative order and a system of institutions (in particular the government apparatus and the legal staff) including also legal dogmatics, jurisprudence and legal methodology, because these sciences contribute as institutions to the formation of legal practice.

Of the methodological implications of Institutional Legal Positivism I shall mention only some in the present context: the postulate to make a clear distinction between cognition and decision; the importance of not confining oneself to the question of observance or infringement when examining the effect of a norm but to take into consideration all the consequences it entails; the need to distinguish clearly between establishing the reasons for a sentence on the basis of legal rules and reflecting on the justification of the sentence; the fact that guilt is not simply constituted by an interrelationship of facts but is attributed in accordance with criteria laid down by norms.

4. FUNDAMENTAL PRINCIPLES OF THE TELEOLOGICAL THEORY OF ACTION IN RELATION TO CRIMINAL LAW

Leaving aside the early stages of the development of the theory [*Welzel* refers to *M. Grünhut* and *E. Schwinge* as forrunners][14] *Hans Welzel* must be regarded as the father and most important exponent of the teleological theory of

---

[12] O. Weinberger, Tatsachen und Tatsachenbeschreibungen, ftn. 4, p. 179 f.

[13] O. Weinberger, Jenseits von Naturrecht und Rechtspositivismus, *ARSP*, Supplement, vol. 1, part 1, *"Contemporary Conceptions of Law"*, 9th World Congress Basel 1979, Basel 1982, pp. 43-56.

[14] H. Welzel, Vom Bleibenden und dem Vergänglichen in der Strafrechtswissenschaft, see ftn. 1, p. 5.

action in criminal law. I want to draw attention to the following crucial features of the theory:

(i) There are *permanent structures* by which the legislator is bound. The *concept of action* with its teleological character is one of these.

"If [the law] generates neither the actions nor their teleological structure or the additional dimension of meaning opened by this structure; instead, it selects: It prohibits such actions as are incompatible with its desired social order and prescribes those which promote this order. In *this* role the law is certainly 'free' and 'creative', at least, in relation to the teleological structure of the action - whether and to what extent it is subject to other conditions remains to be seen."

(ii) The teleological theory of action is based on a homogeneous concept of action which it regards as the generic concept of crime.

(iii) Action is *ex definitione*[15] teleological (directed towards a goal). A person can be said to act if, and only if his action is purposive.

(iv) Although acting negligently is not necessarily a purposive activity it, too, is teleological to the extent that it is according to Welzel the "purposively avoidable causation" of the effect caused by negligence. In other words, this definition regards - if I interpret Welzel correctly - potentially purposive activity as a kind of finality. There is a shift of emphasis in the definition of the general nature of purposive activity from the setting and realization of goals to the regulating of behaviour with the opportunity to act being conceived of as finality.

(v) Action has a dimension of meaning (Sinn):

"*This fact* [i.e. the fact that action is an intellectual achievement] distinguishes it [the action] radically from a mere natural process: an action cannot but include 'the dimension of meaning', that is, the dimension of meaning which is *opened up* by the anticipation of the goal of the action, the choice of means for its realization etc.[16] This means that every action - in contrast to a natural process - is a meaningful entity the core of which is formed by the determination to act which brings about and shapes the action. In the same way as the law can only standardize and evaluate this teleological structure of action, rather than add anything to it or take anything away from it, so it is the primary task of the *science* of criminal law to understand the structure of action correctly and to use it as an interpretative framework for the legal concepts applicable to it."[17]

(vi) The legislator is bound by the ontological structure of the action which forms the object of his evaluation and control.

"Those wishing to establish norms for *actions* must respect the ontological structure of the actions. Even the legislator cannot alter the structure of man's purposive activities or the function of the intention underlying them;

---

[15] H. Welzel, see ftn. 14, p. 6, 8.

[16] H. Welzel, see ftn. 14, p. 7.

[17] H. Welzel, *ibid.*, p. 9.

instead, he must base his regulations on this structure when he establishes norms for them or fail to achieve their object."[18]

With this view which is, in my opinion, correct *Welzel* combines certain natural law theories. While he does not believe that it is possible to deduce the objective rightness of a norm he maintains that it is a necessary pre-condition for the setting of meaningful existential acts to acknowledge the existence of objective (objectively founded) goals of action.[19] Logical structures are a prerequisite of any positive regulation.[20] He postulates (the assumption of) a transcendental meaning of life.[21]

"The adherence of actions to structural laws and the existence of principles of guilt, these are the two stable factors which affect criminal law 'from the outside' - i.e. from within the nature of man as an *acting* being and as a being that in his actions is *bound* by an all-embracing transcendental meaning of life, and it is between these two fixed points that the historical multiplicity of regulations of the criminal law unfolds."[22]

I am unable to agree with *Welzel*'s natural law conclusions: While the ontological structure of action forms a framework for establishing laws it does not provide a framework for determining whether or not laws are fair laws in the sense of the natural law. There is no need to assume the transcendental existence of objective values in order to be able to establish values. All we have to do is to demonstrate that an awareness of values constitutes an empirically verifiable human characteristic.

(vii) A particularly striking consequence of the teleological theory of action is the fact that intention becomes part of the evidence and is not regarded as an aspect of the guilt. The teleological theory of action stresses the subjective elements in the facts of a case and results in a person-orientated conception of offence.

(viii) The teleological theory of action also has repercussions for the conception of participation and other issues of the criminal law doctrine which have to be omitted in this context.

5. 'ACTION' AND 'OMISSION' IN CRIMINAL LAW DOCTRINE

Theories of action in criminal law doctrine can be divided into the following main types: 1. the naturalistic (or causal), 2. the social, 3. the personal and 4. the teleological conception of action.[23]

---

[18] H. Welzel, Naturrecht und materiale Gerechtigkeit, see. ftn. 1, p. 197.
[19] H. Welzel, see ftn. 18, p. 196.
[20] H. Welzel, ibid., p. 198.
[21] H. Welzel, see ftn. 14, p. 16.
[22] H. Welzel, ibid., p. 25.
[23] O. Weinberger, Probleme der formalen Teleologie, see ftn. 5. pp.y 1-6; A. Kaufmann, Die ontologische Struktur der Handlung. Skizze einer personalen Handlungslehre, in: the same. *Schuld und Strafe*, Köln et al. 1966, pp. 39, 65.

The *causal-naturalistic conception* is unsatisfactory since 'the will' is not an observable factual circumstance which could be presentend as a cause. As a result this concept cannot be used to provide a causal explanation of an action. The concept of 'will' itself needs elucidating, and this cannot, in my view, be done by describing directly observable processes and causal laws but only by adopting a theoretical approach to the processing of information appropriate to the phenomena of volition.

The *social concept of action* as defined by *Maihofer*: "'Action' is behaviour directed toward the violation of social goods"[24] likewise fails to be satisfactory: 1. The nature of action is not adequately explained due to the absence of reference to the information processing operation that precedes the making of decisions and guides the action which is a characteristic feature of action. 2. If the term 'directed towards' is interpreted as conveying an intention then the concept of omission is no more part of the social concept of action than it is of the teleological concept. 3. If 'directed towards' means no more than bringing about, then the concept of 'behaviour' becomes the generic term for the system of crimes and is designated by the author as 'action'. What is entirely missing from *Maihofer*'s conception is the necessary definition of the concept of action - which must express the fact that the modes of behaviour commonly regarded as actions are contingent upon intention and information. 4. Referring only to illegal behaviour the definition makes no distinction between 'acting' and 'acting illegally' or between 'behaviour' and 'illegal behaviour'. It appears essential to me to find a neutral concept of action which - being free from any evaluation - allows the legislator to determine what constitutes illegal modes of behaviour on the basis that they violate what he considers social goods.

The *personal concept of action* is defined by *Arthur Kaufmann* as follows:

"Human action is the responsible and meaningful shaping of reality with causal consequences (in the broadest sense of the word) which can be controlled by the will (and can, therefore, be attributed to the agent of the action)."[25]

This definition of the concept makes a constructive contribution by highlighting the key role played in action by the will; it stresses both the element of meaning as a component of action in the legal context and the fact that the consequences of actions are conceived of as governed by the will. On the other hand, it has to be said, that the role of the will is not adequately explained and that *Kaufmann* does not make any distinction between the definition of the concept of action and legal evaluations of action.

The *teleological concept of action*, in my view, gets to the heart of the concept of action by emphasizing its intentional character. Nevertheless, it has to be supplemented, in my view, by a theory which explores in depth the way in which action is guided by information. The teleological theory of action can only remain consistent if, and only if, it acknowledges that not every kind of omis-

---

[24] W. Maihofer, *Der Handlungsbegriff im Verbrechenssystem*, Tübingen 1953, p. 72.
[25] A. Kaufmann, *op. cit.*, p. 65.

sion constitutes an action and if it desists from making the concept of action out to be (postulating) the generic concept of crime.

The formal-teleological theory of action tries to use a structural theory of teleology as the basis for a theory of action. In doing so it integrates elements of fixation (autonomous, heteronomous norms and possibly pathological elements) into the processing of information which governs action. As a result, it achieves a more subtle analysis of motivation. The problem concerning the awareness of teleological elements in an action[26] can be resolved adequately on this basis: the formal-teleological theory of action does not postulate awareness of goals, but it permits reference to it as to the characteristic of a particular form of intention. Unlike the teleological theory of action the formal-teleological theory of action does not regard every omission as an action. It rejects, consequently, the postulate of 'action' as generic concept of crime.

What do we mean when we say: 'Action *A* has been omitted'? 'Omission' is a complementary concept. By complementary concepts we mean concepts which are constituted as follows: 1. We are presented with a generic (universal) concept *U* and a concept of a species of*U* - let us call it: *A*. 2. The complementary concept *'non-A'* is defined as the concept which comprises precisely those elements which are *U* but not *A* [i.e.: 'Non-smoker' is defined as a person (universal concept) who is not covered by the concept 'smoker'].

In the case of complementary concepts used in everyday speech it is often not obvious which the relevant universal concept is as it is usually not referred to explicitely. In my example, for instance: Is a 'non-smoker' a human being who does not smoke, or is he a man who does not smoke?

In the case of omission we have to decide between 'action' and 'behaviour' as possible universal terms. There is no doubt that a person who omits to perform an action is not always carrying out an action (in the sense of a teleological theory). Even *Welzel* writes (1965):

"From an ontological point of view omission being the omission of an *action* does not constitute an action itself." ... "The truth of the matter is that *action* and the *omission of an action* are two independent variants of human 'behaviour' which is governed by a purposive will."[27]

Consequently 'action' must be defined as complementary concept to the universal concept of 'behaviour'.

---

26 W. Platzgummer, *Die Bewußtseinsform des Vorsatzes. Eine strafrechtsdogmatische Untersuchung auf psychologischer Grundlage*, Wien 1964; A. Pöhl, Böser Vorsatz und unbewußtes Wissen, *ÖJZ* 16, 1961, pp. 66-67; G. Stratenwerth, Unbewußte Finalität? in: *Festschrift für Hans Welzel zum 70. Geburtstag*, ed. by G. Stratentwerth et al., Berlin/New York 1974, pp. 289-305.

27 H. Welzel, *Das deutsche Strafrecht*, *op. cit.*, ftn. 1, p. 180.

6. THE GENERIC CONCEPT OF CRIME IN CRIMINAL LAW

It is useful to make the attempt to base the system of criminal law on a general concept which is homogeneous and comprises everything for which punishment can be set and their imposition threatened.

Punishment being considered as a means for motivating action there can be no doubt that the person threatened with punishment has to be a subject who is capable of action.

From the point of view of structural theory a juridical person, too, - being capable of action and of being motivated by means of its organs - could be the recipient of threats of punishment and of punishment. [The closing down of an association on account of activities contravening its constitution could be seen as a punishment imposed on the association.]

The fact that punishment can only have a motivating effect on subjects who are capable of action has led some commentators to jump to the conclusion that only actions are punishable. As a result, they regard the concept of action as the generic concept of crime they are looking for.

A legal system which recognises both delicts caused by negligence and genuine delicts of omission as an offence should not postulate the concept of action as the generic concept of crime. Negligence certainly has to do with potentialities of action but negligent behaviour need not always take the form of an action. To be more precise: If subject S by negligence produces a result R and he was not allowed to do so, or was obliged to prevent it then he is not performing an action the intention of which might be characterised by the goal non-R, indeed, his behaviour need not be an action at all in this case. Where genuine delicts of omission occur we are certainly dealing with modes of behaviour of subjects capable of action, not, however, always with actions.

Punishment laid down for negligence or for a genuine omission can undoubtedly have a motivating effect. It can induce the subject to take the required care, or to perform the postulated action if its omission stands under the threat of punishment despite the fact this is punishment for behaviour which does not necessarily constitute an action.

If the teleological nature of 'action' is seen as one of the constitutive characteristics of the concept of action - be it in the sense of the teleological theory of action or the formal-teleological one - 'action' cannot be the generic concept of crime we are looking for. Instead, the generic concept of crime ought to be defined as *'behaviour which is susceptible to being governed by the will'*.

What we generally understand by behaviour is a trajectory of states characterised by the states of the subject or (and) of the system which is affected by the subject's action. Not everyone of these states of the subject can give rise to punishment; only those modes of behaviour are involved which are susceptible to the impact of the will and which in principle can be influenced by human actions. [The progressive hardening of the arteries is a behaviour of a subject in the sense of the above definition, it does not, however, constitute reasonable grounds for a punishment because it is not a behaviour that is susceptible to the subject's will.]

It is therefore possible to arrive at a narrower definition (although too broad a class of potential grounds for punishment has no effect on the structure of criminal law): *Behaviour in the sense of criminal law is behaviour which is susceptible to being governed by the will.*

The borderline between behaviour that is and is not susceptible to the will depends on the respective situation. It is, therefore, difficult to define it with any precision. If I have not learned to swim then saving a drowning man in difficult conditions is not a mode of action open to me; if I have learned to swim and have possibly even had lessons in life-saving then I am in the position to perform such an action.

7. THE CONCEPT OF GUILT

In principle it is possible to conceive of criminal law in (a) a purely causal-objective way, or (b) by taking into account criteria of subjective blameworthiness.

If the legal system contains a rule prescribing an ought which states that nobody should drive faster than 70 mph (primary norm of prohibition) it follows that a punishment norm may be introduced laying down that punishment *P* for everyone driving faster than 70 mph. According to the causal-objective conception the imposition of the punishment is justified by the fact that the observable factual situation is caused to occur.

Modern criminal law is concerned with guilt. It does not only introduce forms of guilt as a condition of blameworthiness - and hence of punishment - but it also takes into consideration other elements which preclude blameworthiness - and consequently liability to punishment - such as diminished responsibility, admissable self-defence etc.

'Guilt' is a concept that has no place in the realm of brute facts. 'Guilt' is a normative concept since it results from a normative attribution based on facts which are considered blameworthy. The norm determines: (i) when guilt is attributed, (ii) what facts (circumstances) prove the guilt, (iii) what punishment is to be imposed on the guilty party. The elements determining the attribution of blame - (i) and (ii) - are based on facts which can be established. There is as a rule a causal relationship between the person who is blamed for something and the facts of the case; the individual has caused these by behaving in a particular way or could have averted them by behaving otherwise. Nevertheless, the guilt of this individual is not determined on the basis of causal relations but by the application of norms which in some way relate to natural causality. The facts of the case - the objective representation of the facts as well as the subjective elements which constitute guilt - are descriptions of circumstances. It does not make sense to attribute blame if the basic facts of the case are not known (or, from the point of view of the court, if the factual circumstances have not been established).

Considering that an imputation of guilt arises from the violation of a primary behavioural norm the attribution of guilt always depends on the violation of a primary norm. However, it is not by the objective violation of primary behavioural norms alone that guilt as defined by criminal law comes about; for someone to be guilty certain subjective criteria have to be fulfilled as well. Legal systems recognise various forms of guilt which are standardised by the introduction of particular criteria for the definition of specific forms of guilt. The different forms of guilt can be divided into two categories, into (i) deliberate guilt and (ii) guilt arising from carelessness (guilt resulting from the failure to fulfil an obligation to exert care). In the discussions held by the theoreticians of criminal law the distinction between 'intention' and 'culpable negligence' corresponds to these categories. It will be expedient to work with my more general terms in our reflections since we intend to leave aside specific varieties of the definition of intention as set down by the legislator in a particular legal system as well as the various types of intention or (and) culpable negligence which could be introduced (cf. *dolus* - *dolus eventualis* - "knowingly"; voluntary - involuntary negligence, and other differentiations).

In the case of deliberate guilt the intention of the acting individual (in conjunction with the legally established qualifications - such as awareness of the motive, certain knowledge of the consequences etc.) forms a constituent part of the facts of the case. The legal proceedings have to establish that the outcome - possibly in a qualified way - was intended.

In the case of guilt resulting from carelessness an intention aimed at a particular outcome is, of course, not a characteristic of the offence; what has to be established is only the causal effect of the lack of care. The process of establishing it involves a legal evaluation. The much discussed question whether the intention (the intentional guilt) forms an aspect of the facts of the case or of the assessment of guilt is posed in the wrong way, in my opinion:

(i) What is to be regarded as guilt is determined by the normative definition of the criteria of guilt for the relevant form of guilt. Consequently the process of finding an individual guilty constitutes an evaluation of facts based on those criteria.

(ii) The conclusion that these criteria have been fulfilled in the case which is being judged rests on the knowledge of the facts; it forms, therefore, an integrating part of the process of establishing the facts of the case.

Guilt can be imputed only on the basis that the relevant facts of the case have been established. This means in fact: assessment of guilt is part of the findings of the case under consideration.

In the case of guilt resulting from carelessness it will be necessary for the behaviour which is deemed to be obligatory to be susceptible to the will, in other words, the guilty person would have been able to avert the socially undesirable outcome if he had acted differently (possibly by acting with greater care).

8. NOTES ON THE METATHEORY OF SUBSUMPTION IN CRIMINAL LAW

The metatheory of any particular realm of human activity is faced with the task of laying down rules of rational procedure in the relevant realm and to justify them. (Cf. the concepts of 'metamathematics', 'metalogics', 'meta-aesthetics'). The metatheory of subsumption in criminal law is concerned with the question of how the conditions of subsumption ought to be represented in legal terms. It also deals with the question how subsumption is to be carried out under the norms of criminal law. These two questions are obviously interrelated.

Assuming we have gleaned from the relevant regulations prescribed by the law all the criteria of subsumption for a typical case we are able to propose the following formula for the criminal law

(1) $\mathrm{A}x_1\ (f_1B_1x\&f_2B_2\ x\&\ldots\&fnBnx)\ >!Sx$

where the points f_i ($i\in\{1,2,\ldots,n\}$) are either empty or filled up by a negation sign '$\neg$'.

For every x which fulfills the conditions of subsumption $B1, B2, \ldots, Bn$ (these conditions can on occasion be negative conditions) x must be punished with punishment P.

The setting of the punishment is valid precisely when the conditions of subsumption '$(f_1B_1x\&f_2B_2x\&\ldots\&f_nB_nx)$' consisting of a conjunction ('and' connection) of conditions are fulfilled for a particular subject.

The law as well as the theory introduce for the sake of convenience particular types of negative conditions of subsumption. The current theory divides the characteristic features and - the respective reflections on subsumption - into the following categories: (i) establishing the facts, (ii) establishing the illegality and (iii) establishing the guilt.

If confusion is to be avoided we have to distinguish between two different notions of the 'facts of the case'

1. The totality of the conditions causing the facts as represented in the paranthetical expression, - F_1 ('all the facts of a case'); 2. the factual characteristics of the offence as defined in criminal law - F_2 ('factual information about the offence').

F_1 comprises the totality of the conditions of subsumption, all those facts which have to be established in order to form the basis of the subsumption and of the conclusion leading to the punishment.

F_2 comprises only some of the conditions of F_1 since certain of the negative conditions are not mentioned when the facts of the offence are defined. Their existence must, however, always be considered, in view of the fact that it becomes impossible to conclude [from (1) and from the identification of the facts of the case] that x has to be punished as soon as even a single one of these negative conditions is fulfilled.

Illegality is positively determined by the characteristic features of the offence, it is, however, limited by so-called excluding circumstances such as self-defence, consent of the injured party, social adequacy. When illegality is examined the key issue is the question whether there are any elements which would rule out illegality (in other words, negative conditions of subsumption).

Likewise, to examine guilt means in this context finding out whether there are any subjective negative conditions.

The view has been put forward that the steps (i) to (iii) taken in the process of establishing the facts have to follow each other in the order given above.[28] While this may be convenient from the point of view of work practice it is irrelevant from the point of view of logic since the conditions in T_1 occur as conjunctions.

A distinction has to be made between two different effects exerted by negative conditions: (a) those, which lead to a mode of behaviour appearing permissible although the facts of the case are in accordance with T_2 (i.e. self-defence § 3 (1) Austrian StGB, or social adequacy), and those which result in non-punishability.

'Legally permissible' and 'non-punishable' are two terms which clearly do not carry the same meaning. It appears advisable to distinguish between 'grounds for justification' and 'grounds for excuse', the first leading to an act being permissible, the second one only to freedom from punishment.

There are obviously some modes of behaviour which are prohibited without being punishable. Can there be any doubt that a child contravenes the law if it shoots and kills somebody? Where there are grounds for excuse but not for justification the behaviour is not permitted although it is not to be punished. In the case of self-defence or so-called socially adequate behaviour things appear to me to be different. Such actions are not to be regareded as unlawful.

---

[28] i.e. D. Kienapfel, *Österreichisches Strafrecht. Allgemeiner Teil*, Wien 1979, pp. 242 f.

VII. INSTITUTIONAL THEORY AND INSTITUTIONAL LEGAL POSITIVISM

1. THE PROGRAM OF MY INQUIRY

Institutional theories were developed by *B. Malinowsky, H. Schelsky* and other sociologists. The philosophy of law has produced one interesting and important school of thought in the field of institutional philosophy which is represented preeminently by *M. Hauriou, S. Romano, G. Renard* and *C. Schmitt.* On its basis *D.N. MacCormick* and I independently from each other evolved a legal ontology and a legal-philosophical conception. This will be known under the name 'Institutional Legal Positivism' (abbr. ILP).[1] Our conception is not based on the sociological theory of the institutions, nor is it in terms of the history of ideas an off-spring of *Hauriou*'s theory of law. Our reflections were motivated by different questions from those which led to *Hauriou*'s investigations, in particular the question: "What means social existence of a norm or of law as a system of norms?[2]; furthermore, there was the problem of different types of facts confronting man.[3] In this point both *MacCormick* and I were influenced by *Searle*'s and *Anscombe*'s juxtaposition of 'brute facts' and 'institutional facts'.[4]

In view of the fact that my discourse will, as I hope, contribute significantly to the clarification of ILP it is a challenging task for me to be writing about the relationship between the institutional theories of sociologists and legal sociologists - mainly those of *Helmut Schelsky* -, as well that between Hauriou's approach on the one hand and ILP on the other.

Werner Krawietz' interesting study: "Begründung des Rechts - anthropologisch betrachtet: zur Institutionenlehre von Weinberger und Schelsky"[5] has demonstrated to me the importance of such a comparison. His study has laid the foundations which have significantly facilitated the writing of this treatise.

---

[1] See D.N. MacCormick/O. Weinberger, *Grundlagen des Institutionalistischen Rechtspositivismus*, Berlin 1985.

[2] E.g. expressed in brief by the title of my paper "Die Norm als Gedanke und Realität", *Österreichische Zeitschrift für Öffentliches Recht*, 20, 1970, pp. 203-216.

[3] Compare D.N. MacCormick, *Institutional Facts*, Edinburg 1973; O. Weinberger, Tatsachen und Tatsachenbeschreibungen. Eine logisch-methodologische Überlegung zu einem Grundlagenproblem der Sozialwissenschaften, in: K. Salamun (ed.), *Sozialphilosophie als Aufklärung, FS für Ernst Topitsch*, Tübingen 1979, pp. 173-187.

[4] G.E.M. Anscombe, On Brute Facts, *Analysis* 18, 3, 1958, pp. 69-72; J.R. Searle, *Speech Acts. An Essay in the Philosophy of Language*, Cambridge 1969.

[5] W. Krawietz, Begründung des Rechts - anthropologisch betrachtet: zur Institutionentheorie von Weinberger und Schelsky, in: W. Krawietz/H. Schelsky/G. Winkler/A. Schramm (eds.), *Theorie der Normen. Festgabe für Ota Weinberger*, Berlin 1984, pp. 542-556. (I am, of course, very grateful to my friend Werner Krawietz for the publication of this "Festgabe" and for this contribution which was particularly stimulating and instructive for me.)

In the course of it I intend to present observations concerning the following three interlinked problem areas:
a) fundamental problems of jurisprudence,
b) questions concerning the ontology and logic of norms, and
c) questions related to the theoretical basis of sociology where it is concerned with group phenomena, social structures of an organisational and/or intellectual kind, as well as with the relationship between individual and collective action.

With reference to the problems of jurisprudence I wish to investigate the following areas:

1. a concise definition of ILP and of the implications arising from this ontology for the theory of law, for the theory of legal argumentation and for the sociology of law;
2. a comprehensive survey of institutonalism from the point of view of legal theory, including the diverging views within this school of thought;
3. a critical juxtaposition of ILP and the conceptions of the *Hauriou* school emphasising both the major differences and the common ideas.

My observations about the ontology and logic of norms are intended to expound the anthropological pre-conditions for ILP and to demonstrate to what extent the ontology of norms is rooted in the theory of action and in what way - according to ILP - the existence of normative regulatives and of institutions relate to man's role as *zoon politicon* with the capacity to act.

With reference to the realm of sociological problems I want to advocate a thesis which in this point is comparatively close to *Schelsky*, namely that sociology in the above sense is not possible without reference to the ontological ideas of ILP, in particular those concerning the essence of sociological facts and their dependence on institutionalised practical informations. I wish to demonstrate that it is only on this basis that sociology can be simultaneously an empirical, a comprehending and an explanatory science.

In implementing this program I shall procede in the following way: I shall begin by characterising ILP, the assumptions on which it is based and its implications (Paragraph 2). In order to explain my conception of ILP it appears to me to be necessary to add some remarks about my theory of action and about the semantic foundations of practical philosophy (Paragraph 3). I shall attempt to complement this exposition with remarks about a typology of institutions (Paragraph 4). Following these I intend to sum up the central concepts of the legal and sociological institutional theories (Paragraphs 5 and 6). The next part of my reflections is going to deal with the divergences between institutional theories and ILP and with the overlap between these theories. In view of the not inconsiderable differences between them the nature of this paragraph is going to be predominantly critical (Paragraph 7). In the final part (Paragraph 8) I shall touch on the relevance for sociology and legal sociology of the fundamental views underlying the ontological and methodological approch of ILP.

2. A CHARACTERISATION OF INSTITUTIONAL LEGAL POSITIVISM

ILP is a form of normativism: it regards the law as a system of norms and legal life as a series of processes occurring on the basis of norms (and observable facts) and creating their own dynamics. The legal system of norms consists of general rules and individual norms. Their dynamic force, i.e. the evolution and abolition of norms, depends both on acts of will and on other observable facts as well as on relations established by the inner logic of the norms. Consequently ILP can be described as a *normativist logicism*. ILP is not only interested in the formal structure of the legal order and the logical form of juristic argumentation - which distinguish it as an analytical theory of the law -, but it also makes it an objective of legal theory to provide a logically based depiction of the legal order and legal processes.

In my conception this area of logical connections and logical conclusions forms the object of a specific field of logic, *the normative logic*. It is my view that the norm-logical relations and operations (especially the logical inferences with normative members) cannot be reduced to the logic of the descriptive language. Instead, a genuinely normative logic has to be evolved.[6]

ILP is based on certain - very general - anthropological insights (or assumptions) and it is on this basis that it explains its conception of the ontology of norms as well as of the language and logic of practial philosophy. Two human characteristics - questioned by hardly anyone - are of vital importance for this approch:
(i) man is a being with the capacity to act, and
(ii) man is a communal being.

These are the foundations for a specific theory of action which I want to describe as a *formal-finalist theory of action* and it is this that provides the framework for the *gnoseologically differentiated semantics* necessary both for practical philosophy[7] and an ontology of norms.

Human action is either individual, cooperative or collective. It is action that takes place not only in the natural world but also in the man-made world of the institutions. According to ILP the existence of the institutions is linked fundamentally with normative regulatives and other types of practical data (intentions, values and preferences). The existence of institutions and that of social

---

[6] The systems proposed by the deontic logic and other attempts of establishing a theory of normative logic indirectly on the basis of the descriptive language fail in their attempt in my view. Compare O. Weinberger, Die Sollsatzproblematik in der modernen Logik, *Rozpravy Ceskoslovenské akademie věd*, 9 (1968), Rada SV, Praha 1958; reprinted in: O. Weinberger, *Studien zur Normenlogik und Rechtsinformatik*, Berlin 1974, pp. 59-186; Ch. Weinberger/O. Weinberger, *Logik, Semantik, Hermeneutik*, München 1979; O. Weinberger, Der Begriff der Nichterfüllung und die Normenlogik, *Ratio* 14, 1972, pp. 15-32; the same, Kann man das normenlogische Folgerungssystem philosophisch begründen? Überlegungen zu den Grundlagen des juristischen Folgerns, *ARSP* 65, 1979, pp. 161-186; the same, The Expressive Conception of Norms - an Impasse for the Logic of Norms, *Law and Philosophy* 4, 1985, pp. 165-198; the same, "Is" and "ought" reconsidered. Comment on G.H. von Wright's lecture "Is and ought", *ARSP* LXX, 1984, pp. 454-474.

[7] O. Weinberger, Eine Semantik für die praktische Philosophie, in: R. Haller (ed.), *Beiträge zur Philosophie von Stephan Körner, Grazer Philosophische Studien*, 29, 1983, pp. 219-239.

norm-systems can be understood only by regarding them as interconnected entities. Observable social processes and the respective practical informations (normative regulatives, goals, values and preferences) are connected in such a way as to prevent one from being understood without the other. It should be remembered that the views on ILP expressed in this chapter are by no means as indisputable as the anthropological characteristics of man listed under (1) and (2).

3. MY CONCEPT OF ACTION AND THE SEMANTIC FOUNDATIONS OF PRACTICAL PHILOSOPHY

Action is behaviour determined by information. The behaviour of a system can be characterised as a sequence of states in time (behaviour trajectory). The behaviour of a subject can be described
(a) as the chronological sequence of states of the subject of the action or
(b) as the trajectory of the states of the system which the subject is acting upon.[8]

Behaviour can be conceived as an action only if different alternatives for the continuation of the behavioural trajectory are possible at certain moments and if the choice of the realised alternative from the possible ones is made by the subject on the basis of processing descriptive and practical informations.

The justification for the use of the term action rests, therefore, in *the existence of scope for behavioural alternatives* open to the subject and *the availability to the subject of a system for the processing of informations* as a basis for the determination and selection of behavioural alternatives. In the course of the data-processing operation by which actions are determined two types of informations are involved:

(a) *descriptive (theoretical) informations* on the subject's circumstances e.g. the system within which he lives and which is to be influenced, on causal relations as well as knowledge of potential programs of action for the purposes of specific aims (technical knowledge, know-how);

(b) *practical informations* (aims, value standards, preferences, norms).[9]
The postulate of the theory of action demanding the separation of theoretical and practical informations forms the philosophical backbone of the *gnoseologically differentiated semantics* (see below) as does the *metalogical postulate stating that theoretical and practical sentences cannot be inferred from eachother.*

No restrictions are laid down with reference to *the subjects of action.* In the context of this theory of action any system capable of realizing the data processing operations relevant to the action can be considered to be a subject. This

---

[8] Compare the sentences '*S* makes writing movements with his right hand' - '*S* is writing (= producing a piece of writing)'. The first sentence sets out the subject's behavioural trajectory, the second one the system with the help of which the subject of the action *S* achieves a purpose.

[9] For my conception of the theory of action see: O. Weinberger, *Studien zur formal-finalistischen Handlungstheorie*, Frankfurt a.M./Bern/New York 1983, and Chap. II of this volume.

conception permits us to refer not only to the actions of individuals but also to collective actions.

The processing of information leading to the determination of actions corresponds to what we commonly describe as willing to do something. Despite the fact that we are familiar from everyday life with the notion of volition a theory of action has to provide an explicite depiction of the data processing operations involved. It is, in fact only in this depiction that the foundations for a theory of action (and by implication the foundations for a structural theory of volition) are laid.

To every subject of action a teleological attitude, or teleological system is attributed; *in principle action is purposeful behaviour* - although also other determinants of action have to be taken into account. The basis for the theory of data processing as determinant of action is formed by the theory of final structures and of choice (of decision) in accordance with goals.

Such a teleological theory can be developed formally provided the notion of causal connection is assumed as given;[10] on this basis it is possible for a theory of action to be evolved from the formal teleology. In view of the fact that it is based on the formal theory of teleology I have termed it a *formal-finalistic theory of action*. The fundamental concepts of this theory can be summed up in the following points:

(i) We may distinguish between direct acts and indirect action. Subject *S* of an action realizes an intention (potentially a system of intentions) if *S* brings about a state or a trajectory of states. In principle an intention can be realized either directly or indirectly. The direct realization of an intention means that the intended state is realized. [I want to lift my arm, this intention is realized by lifting my arm.] The indirect realization of an intention consists in the (direct) realization of states as means which will bring about the intended result.

(ii) The theory of action distinguishes two methodologically different problem situations: *the deliberation determining the action* and *the interpretation of the motives leading to an observed action*. Formal teleology forms the basis for both analyses.

(iii) The determination of action on the basis of complex goal systems is often very complicated; this complexity is often mastered with the help of fixed programm blocks which represent global acts with inner complexity.

(iv) The fixing of attitudes and of certain behaviour-patterns means, on the one hand, reducing the complexity of the pre-action deliberation (as a result

---

[10] How this can be achieved I have broadly outlined elsewhere (compare ftn. 9). A great many problems remain, however, concerning the details of such a theory.
I am fully aware, of course, of the many problems connected with the depiction of causality itself and of the fact that the conceptual explanation of 'cause', 'effect', 'causal relation' is dependent on the application of these terms in the context of action, i.e. as information for the determination of actions. Compare G.H. von Wright, *Erklären und Verstehen*, Frankfurt a.M. 1974, pp. 67 ff. Taken as a whole, this thought process is not, however, circular, in my view. It merely reflects the intrinsic structural link between the realm of causal cognition on the one hand, and teleology and the theory of action, on the other.

of the situation not having to be reconsidered each time it occurs), on the other, it broadens the potential for action considerably (for instance, on the basis of practice and learning).

(v) The fixing of attitudes etc. referred to in (iv) also forms the basis for the generation of autonomous norms. The content of those autonomous norms which determine the subject's actual behaviour depends in its genesis largely on interpersonal and general social relations.

(vi) The fact that man in his capacity as the subject of action is a communal being is reflected in the theory of action on different levels:

a) The individual's actions are determined by social norms and by the reality of the social institutions coupled with normative regulatives as well as social value- and goal systems.

b) For the determination of autonomous norms, too, a communal orientation is provided by way of example and imitation, education and inherited social institutions (childcare, the caring for fellow-men in the cycle of generations, man-woman provisions etc.).

c) We are capable of introducing interactive actions of different kinds. The sources of such actions may be biologically programmed; the modes of action may be institutionalised by the prevailing culture or they may be constituted by the implicit or explicit agreement of the partners.

d) We create institutions with the capacity to act as specific subjects by empowering their organs to perform acts in their name. Such actions in the name of institutions are structurally analogous to the actions of individuals in the sense that they, too, are determined by intentions, norms and preferences. However, the intentions, norms and preferences of institutions are not identical with those of the individuals involved, not even those acting as organs for the institutions. Actions in the name of a body or institution (as its organ) can be instigated in different ways: by empowering the organ, by collective processes of decision-making etc.[11]

Apart from the facts which since *Anscombe* and *Searle* tend to be described as *brute facts*[12] in analytical philosophy there are also facts in this world which concern man as an acting being, the institutions and communities, those, in fact, which are described as *institutional facts*.

Institutional facts are no less real constituent parts of the world as we understand it than the brute facts are. They have time co-ordinates and they constitute determining elements in observable processes. They serve as indispens-

---

[11] It is a positive aspect of the formal-finalist theory of action that it can also be applied to actions of this kind (collective or other communal actions). One might also say that it is precisely because human actions occur in the form of data processing which can be formally rationalised that this opens the way to collective action and to a variety of possibilities of 'actions in the name of other', be it as representative, be it as organ, or as adviser (although the adviser does not realize actions in the name of others, he undertakes the deliberation from the point of view of goals which are not his own).

[12] Compare ftn. 4, p. 163.

able elements for the description and explanation of the phenomena which make up our, the human world; they cannot be reduced to brute-fact descriptions.

The fundamental thesis underlying the ontology of ILP is this: *There is an essential link between institutions and institutional facts on the one hand and practical information (norms, goal-systems and values) on the other.* The institutions are functionally connected with real systems of practical informations (especially normative regulatives); institutional facts and their observable processes can only be understood if they are interpreted in the context of normative regulatives which means in the final analysis that they have to be considered within the context of action. It is precisely when they are aspects of institutions and because they are institutionally effective that normative systems can lay claim to real existence. This results, on the one hand, in *an explanation of the real existence of the law* (and of other normative systems in the social sphere) which bases the validity of the legal system on its strong links with institutions, and on the other hand, on the *view that legal and social institutions as well as their organisation are founded on norms and must not be regarded as mere regularities of behaviour.* The institutionalised normative regulatives provide the scope for institutional action, they establish the duties, demands and expectations of the individuals involved.

While normative rules determine what ought to be done, possibly what may be done, this task does not exhaust their social function. It is on the basis of norms that responsibilities are assigned, that the power of the law is constituted, organisations are formed, scope for action is provided, especially where the behaviour and the actions of the individual take place in an institutional framework. [I can only marry if the legal institution of marriage exists. I would not be able to buy rolls if the contract of purchase, money and trade did not exist as norms and as institutions.]

The social processes, that is, what sociologists are able to observe and note, become intelligible and meaningful only if they are not interpreted as mere sequences of behaviour but as institutional processes shaped by normative regulatives.

The concurrence of observable social processes and of the law as a system of norms is important in more than one way from the point of view of ILP: it provides a basis for an answer to the problem of validity, as well as for the theory of legal dynamics and for observations on the impact of the law. However, the impact of the law, should be acknowledged not only in the normative consequences of the law - like, claims, offences, the imposition of legal penalties etc. - but also in the broad field of non-normative effects such as economic, psycho-sociological ones etc.

4. THE CONCEPT OF THE INSTITUTION AND ITS TYPOLOGY

Although the juxtaposition of brute facts and institutional facts is in some way connected with the concept of the institution, this can be understood quite well without the concept of the institution having been clarified entirely and without a complete grasp of the nature of institutions or of the variety and types of institutions in existence. Even the mere distinction between two types of fact permits different theories of institutions, all the more so since even the juxtaposition of brute facts and institutional facts can be defined in different ways. The sciences dealing with institutions and institutional facts, and in particular the development of an institutionally based theory of law, do, however, require a more detailed analysis of the concept of the institution. It is inevitable, therefore, that the demand for a typology of institutions should emerge in the realm of legal theory.[13]

The term 'institution' denotes a family concept of a particular kind: wherever we refer to institutions, the reference infers something that contains the same essential ingredients: namely, relations between individuals and a community, relations with a certain tendency to permanence, relative regularity and normative order. Nevertheless, the institutions are so varied that it is impossible to set down a unified class of attributes to define all of them.

A certain vagueness, perhaps even confusion about the concept of the institution results from two matters: the variety of areas where we refer to institutions, and the differences between the theoretical constructs attempting to explain the phenomenon of the institutions.

I shall attempt in the following to provide an approximation of the concept's nature as it presents itself to me from the standpoint of ILP. In other theories and in discussions on other problems it may well be advisable to work with a modified concept of the institution.

The crucial elements leading to the definition of the concept of the institution are the following:

(i) Human life and actions are characterised by the relationship between the subject's individual acts and the communities. The behaviour of the individual depends on communal relationships: his individual conduct is determined by inherited, learned or otherwise internalised behaviour patterns. This does not, however, preclude his freedom to modify and shape the modes of his behaviour creatively. Any form of communal action, be it co-ordinated, confrontational, the mixed interplay of actions by two or more persons or the collective actions of bodies (institutionalised non-psychophysical personalities), it is always the product of the personal behaviour and actions of individuals within an institutional framework. *This interplay between individual and society - always understood to take place in the context of action - is the place of the institutions: institutions make this interplay possible, and the institutions are the result of the interaction between individual and society.*

(ii) To some extent the concept of the institution is connected with the concept of institutionalisation. Institutions indicate a degree of stabilisation, the setting up of patterns, standards or/and ways of life to which a kind of relative continuity adheres, albeit by no means permanence. They (the institutions) constitute orientation for actions, a vital factor in the constitution of action potentials for the individual, his standards for goals and values and for the form of actions. In addition, they constitute elements of social reality and the basis for

[13] See Chap. I, Para. 6.

every kind of social action. According to my conception of action the practice of data processing as a determinant of action requires at least a partial stabilisation of behavioural patterns and value judgements. The institutions are the places where the fixing of these patterns occurs as a result of a certain concatenation of individual and communal elements.

(iii) *Institutions contain within them systems of practical informations.* They are unthinkable as realities without this core of informations to draw on. It is not an easy task to provide a clear definition of the relationship between the institutions as observable social realities and their respective norm- and value-systems. Whether individual or collective every subject with the capacity to act has certain values and is able to make preferential decisions. Effective actions, learning processes, and all forms of communal action rely on the premise that intentions and norms of behaviour are fixed to a certain extent. Consequently, institutions are not merely systems safeguarding regular behavioural processes and regular de-facto interaction between individuals within communities, but they are always linked with the setting of ought-rules. Every human being as an individual has practical attitudes and every communal situation, albeit a transient constellation, gives rise to more practical attitudes and norms,[14] in particualr, obviously, where stable social structures are involved.

(iv) The development and the social existence of institutions result from human interaction, the constitution of roles and the concurrence of values among the acting individuals. The term 'fundamental consensus of value standards' is frequently used in this context. It is quite possible, though, for human beings with diverging values and very different ways of life to live together reasonably and to form relatively harmonious social structures - provided there is tolerance and tolerant forms of interaction emanate from it. Consequently, it would be wrong to assume that consensus of values among all those involved - a fundamental consensus - is necessary for institutions to constitute themselves, let alone, that institutions come into being on the basis of this fundamental consensus. There is, in fact, a possibility that an institution can only exist on the basis of a variety of attitudes. A historical example: in a Christian world which has prohibited the charging of interest the institution of the Jewish money lender could only come about because they believed the charging of interest to be legitimate (as everybody does nowadays). Modern life would be all but unthinkable without occupational differentiation, a variety of views on preferred leisure activities, as well as the resulting differences in value standards.

(v) *Institutions exist* in the form of *socially institutionalised normative rule-systems* (for instance, as legal institutions, i.e. as complexes of rules which are instrumental in the creation of prototype institutions and in the introduction of the relevant concepts) or/and they exist as *actual specific instances of the*

---

[14] Whenever people come together in an unexpected situation which is new to them (for instance, when there is an accident) everyone of them is confronted with a problematical ought-situation as well as the ought of interaction.

particular institution.[15] [Compare: (a) marriage as a legal institution defined by rules which can be applied to every possible individual case, and (b) a specific marriage as a social and legal relationship between a particular man and a particular woman.] It is precisely because of the existence of a body of normative rules applying to this type of institution and because the individual case is subsumable under these rules that the individual case is covered by the institutional type.

(vi) *As a rule institutions have a certain organisational structure. The organisation points to the eixstence of personal and factual elements which are linked with eachother through their functions.* For instance, a university as an organisational body consists of buildings, furniture, implements, books, a teaching staff, civil servants etc. In this body objects and human beings are linked by interactive relations and bound together in a system which finds its expression in behavioural regulations and ought-relations (i.e. regulations controlling the conduct of its members and a prescribed order for their interrelations). Organisation is also an institutional fact. Whatever is integrated in the organisation gains institutional status, while the processes occurring among the elements of the organisation can be explained only on the basis of the institutionalised relations within a set order.

(vii) According to ILP an institution is either institutionalised as no more than a system of rules - in which case it is part of the law or some other normative system -, or it is an entity of social reality consisting of persons in social relationships and objects related to the institution as such or, as the case may be, to the persons involved in the institutions in question. *These relations between the human and the material foundations of institutions are, however,* - and it is this that is crucial for the ontology of ILP -, *not only behavioural relations in the behaviourist sense but they are always additionally determined by practical information, ought-rules and value standards.* Consequently an institution as an entity in the conext of action can be fully grasped only if its core, i.e. the relevant normative informations, is understood and treated as part of the institution.

(viii) Figuratively speaking one might say that *institutions achieve something like an "independent" existence.* In this sense we are justified in regarding them as objective realities *sui generis*. What is it that constitutes this "independent existence"? It is all but impossible to define this condition exactly as general terms; what we mean by it can only be explained with the help of examples. For instance: a certain inherent *"element of inertia"* is at work in institutions which has the effect that institutionalised forms - such as legal

15 The legal system contains institutions like marriage, property, contract etc. by setting out the conditions for the genesis of an institution of this kind, by determining which relations establishing duties, permissions and authorisations apply in this particular case, and finally, by defining the way the existence of this individual case of such an institution is to be ended. Compare D.N. MacCormick, *Law as Institutional Fact*, Edinburgh 1973, pp. 5 ff., where the author distinguishes between 'institutive', 'consequential' and 'terminative' rules of a legal institution.

institutions - remain in existence long after their meaning and purpose have disappeared. Also, institutions continue to evolve internally. An institution can, for instance, expand, the number of people involved in it can grow; changing circumstances within which an institution exists can lead to its modification; quantitative changes within the institution can make changes in its organisation necessary.

(ix) *Institutions* are associated closely - especially so under the influence of *M. Hauriou*'s theory (see Paragraph 5) - with a *key concept* which the institute serves. It is this that gives it its character and *"une idée directrice"* determines its existence and its development. A central - as it were global - concept of this kind can frequently be drawn on in order to gain a fundamental characterisation of the institution; it must not be assumed, however, that the character and development of an institution can, in fact, be deduced and determined entirely on the basis of such a slogan-type characterisation. The function of the key concept can change as a result of outer and inner developments. Companies are founded for the purpose of making profits by fulfilling economic needs. There is always a chance, however, that a company might become a vital social or power factor. The "independent life" of the institution precludes the fossilisation of its key concept.

My approach is based on the view expressed above: while all institutions share certain characteristics they can be of varying types otherwise. This means that the concept of the institution constitutes a family of concepts rather than a single unified concept. What is common to all institutions is the reference to a context of actions, in other words, it is their function to determine individual or/and communal actions; and they form the link between the actions undertaken by individuals and by the communities to which they belong; furthermore, they depend on a core of socially constituted practical informations, especially normative regulatives. *Institutions are ontologically complex insofar as they possess one ideal side - expressed in form of normative, teleological and evaluating information - and one side consisting of a material substratum.* As a result institutions have to be seen, on the one hand, as symbolic structures and, on the other, in their relations to observable objects and behavioural processes.

It is a common demand, as well as my own, that we should distinguish between different types of institutions. There is, however, no commonly accepted view of what kinds of institutions exist, or what a typology of institutions ought to look like.

A typological distinction between *normativ institutions* and *real institutions* which is fundamental, at least in terms of ILP, might be placed at the beginning of such a typology. Normative institutions like 'property', 'marriage', 'testament', 'contract' etc. are notional building blocks of the legal system.

There are different ways of defining units of content in norm-systems. The normativist theories concentrate on the definition of

(a) the substantial elements of the law as prescribed or prohibited types of conduct depending on a variety of conditions and

(b) of the authority to produce norms in accordance with certain conditions.

According to the institutional conception certain groups of normative regulations form a kind of entity which is usually defined by a name and constituted as a result of factual connections. This entity is a more or less independent element of social reality which can be relatively easily isolated.

The normativist approach which believes that behavioural regulatives constitute the decisive building blocks for the substance of a legal system does not, in my view, conflict with the view of the legal system as a complex body of normative rules. My reason is this: the construction of the legal system as a system of institutions forming the building blocks of the legal order perceives only additional connections in the social reality and recognises the need to combine separate legal regulations in functionally linked norm-complexes, because such a conception alone can provide a legal and socially functional substantiation of the law, or more specifically, of legal institutions.

One might hold the view that it is unnecessary to introduce terms for legal institutions and that to assume the existence of certain ideal entities - like "property", "marriage", etc. - is merely to pretend that such separate entities exist, while in reality there are only certain normative relations (duties, claims, authorisations) between one person and another person or persons.[16] It would, in fact, be theoretically conceivable to characterise the whole of human behaviour and the legal situation entirely in terms of behavioural norms and of authorisations. In fact thought processes and substantiations in the realm of the law are determined by reflections about institutions as the building-blocks of the legal system. In practical terms it would be all but impossible to provide norms which take account of all possible situations or to determine the legal consequences of every single one of those situations; furthermore, it is only from the institutional point of view that the peculiarities arising from unusual constellations of circumstances can be analysed in such a way as to allow for justifiable normative conclusions to be drawn even in such special cases. In other words: In view of the fact that it is impossible to take into account the entirety of all possible situations and to regulate them the possibility of reducing the law to a set of norms of behaviour and authority-conveying norms explicitly ceases to exist.

Constructive legal thinking is always based on certain factual units which are introduced normatively with reference to social realities. The social basis of marriage rests on certain actual constellations, for instance: the relationship between man and wife, the relations among the generations (parents - children, education, the passing on of property) which make it possible - and in some ways necessary - to introduce marriage as an institution. The normative manner in which this takes place, is an aspect of every-day life having to cope with a host of actual practical conditions. It is only from the institutional perspective that the politico-legal analysis can be understood properly and conducted rationally (that is when society and jurisprudence reach a state where they can engage in systematic *de-lege-ferenda* deliberations).

---

[16] Compare A. Ross, Tû-Tû, *Harvard Law Review* 70, (1956-7), pp. 812-825.

Legally an institution - such as marriage, property, divorce, juridical personality, pledge etc. - is determined by the respective normative rules being in effect precisely what these rules circumscribe. In their role as socially relevant constructs, however, we can understand the institutions only if we see them as functional units forming the building blocks which constitute the content of the legal system. It is only on the basis of an institutionalist approach that we can say, for instance, that the institution of property continues to exist even if certain rules and duties connected with property are changed. The functional concept of the institution also provides the basis on which it is possible to refer to different forms of the same institution within different legal systems. This is a significant factor providing, as it does, the basis for comparative law and being effective in many areas of international civil law.

In respect of most - if not all - normative institutions it is advisable to introduce the typology of rules determining them proposed by *MacCormick: institutive rules* covering the conditions which apply to the formation of individual examples of a particular type of institution; *consequential legal rules* which lay down the normative consequences for existing individual examples of the institution - frequently with reference to additional circumstances; and finally, *terminative rules, i.e. rules covering the end* of the actual existence of an institution.[17]

By dividing the rules in this way it is possible to introduce conceptual building-blocks of the legal system as well as to hold the view that an institution as a whole is not dissolved as soon as individual rules determining it are updated to some extent, but is merely altered and adapted in response to social developments. While the *normative change of the institution* can, of course, be reconstructed logically in terms of a succession of norm-complexes, in the application of the law the manner of representation based on the institutional conception is easier to handle.

It should be pointed out that the normative institutions previously mentioned are on the whole described as 'legal institutions' in Roman law.[18]

In ILP normative institutions are considered from the perspective of the theory of action: it stresses the fact that above and beyond the legal relations, legal duties, claims and opportunities for action resulting from the institutions there are also other, psychological and social consequences which occur in the realm of evaluation. Institutions open up scope for action, they raise expectations in respect of their fellow-men's conduct; they are of consequence for the interaction of the members of society even outside the law. I consider it essential, therefore, not to limit our understanding of the law to the understanding of normative relations - or in other words to the legal consequences of facts and actions -, but to take account of other consequences, too (i.e. economic effects,

---

[17] Compare ftn. 15, also D.N. MacCormick/O. Weinberger, *Grundlagen des Institutionalistischen Rechtspositivismus*, Berlin 1985; English version: *An Institutional Theory of Law. New Approaches to legal Positivism*, Dordrecht et al. 1986.

[18] Compare F.C. von Savigny, *System des heutigen Römischen Rechts*, Heidelberg 1814, p. 9.

expectations, duties, moral evaluations). We shall understand the existence and the impact of the law fully only if we are aware of both the legal consequences and the others - namely the psychological or/and social consequences of the normative process.

Real institutions consist of a combination of norms and observable facts: of 'ought' (normative regulations), human behaviour and the objects which have a certain role or function in the framework of the institution. An actual marriage consists of a human couple - this being in this particular institution a husband and wife rather than just a man and a woman -, and certain specific relations to objects, especially with regard to the constituent parts of the conjugal property, are constituted therein.

In some institutions the factual and organisational elements are more prominent than in others. Institutions like schools, corporations etc., are man-made, artefacts, as one might say, with a factual, organisational and functional basis. In the way they are organised and function as well as in the social tasks they are determined by norms (of conduct and competence) and by their objectives.

Institutions like these where organisation and concrete artefacts play a key role as well as juridical personalities and object-based institutions[19] should, in my opinion, be seen first and foremost from the perspective of the theory of action. From this point of view the organisation appears not only as a system of directives possibly a hierarchical one and as representative of a function, not merely as a regulator of behaviour, but also as determined by norms and objectives.

In the institutional conception the person in the general legal sense is regarded not only as a point of normative imputation who is invested with rights and duties but also as the subject of actions, as an entity with its own system of goals and to some extent with the capacity to act in such a way as to engender legal acts to be performed by organs and recognised as acts of the person in question.

In the case of so-called natural personalities this view appears obvious to us: they are human beings and as such have the capacity to act. In what sense is it feasible to say that other - non-psycho-physical - personalities act or have the capacity to act?

Let me mention, to begin with, that the capacity to act does not always exist as a manifest fact in human beings. The *nasciturus*, the infant, the person who is sick in some way or another, they are human individuals who have not (or only to a limited extent) either factually or legally the capacity to act. It is true to say, therefore, that a certain normative decision determining the relevance of the natural capacity to act comes into play in any case. This capacity can be limited or precluded even in the case of subjects who are without doubt physically fully capable to perform legal acts (e.g. under Roman law in the case of personalities under the *patria potestas*).

---

[19] Compare *Hauriou*'s well-known division of the institutions into 'person-institutions' and 'object-institutions' which I shall be dealing with in Para. 5 of this Chap.

To a certain extent the forms of action of all institutionalised personalities are regulated in a way that takes into account the goal-system of the institution. Among non-psycho-physical subjects actions are in principle always performed by organs. Nevertheless it is a common feature of person- and object-based institutions (e.g. foundations) that they have their own system of objectives (in terms of a framework at least) which differs from the system of objectives of the person acting as an organ of that institution.

Non-psycho-physical personalities are possible and can exist as social factors because man is a social being and acts communally.

Communal action can take the form of cooperative action of different kinds or of collective action.

Cooperative action differs according to the structure of the purposes of the persons involved, however, whatever the institution may be - no matter whether the goals of the participants diverge or their interests even conflict with eachother - there is always a common purpose, i.e. the purpose of putting the cooperative enterprise into practice.

The borderlines between certain types of cooperative and collective action appear not to be sharply drawn. We shall refer to collective action whenever there is a body structured in a certain way with an inherent organisation and organs to execute the actions ascribed to this body. The collective personality exists as a complex structure consisting of physical elements, individual persons, normative rules governing prescribed behaviour and attitudes relating to purposes and values. This intricate web of constituent parts exists as an institutional fact.

In the sense of the formal-finalistic theory of action which I am advocating man is capable of acting as the organ of a body (i.e. of the collective subject of an action) for the following reasons: the control of an action is an information process which can be executed by rational operations; furthermore, the human individual is capable not only of putting into practice his own subjective goals and values in his own personal actions, but also of processing communal aims and values of collective action and realizing the corresponding acts in the name of a collective or organisation.

This relationship can exist independently as a sociological fact: in certain circumstances man forms collectives and acts as their organ (i.e. in the name of the collective and in accordance with its intentions). In contemporary legal culture the development, organisation and the attribution of the organ's acts as acts of the collective are all legally controlled, that is, they are legally recognised precisely when the appropriate norms for his authorisation have been fulfilled.[20]

In all cases, - even where the subjects of the collective body is not legally controlled - the organisation and the functioning of the body is dependent on - at the very least - implicite normative systems for the normative constitution of the order and the forms of collective action.

---

[20] Which does not mean that from the sociological point of view collective action can only take place in the general legal framework. From the sociological point of view collectives can exist without being noticed by the law and being accorded the status of a legal personality.

5. INSTITUTIONAL THEORY IN MODERN JURISPRUDENCE

The tenets held by the representatives of the institutional theory of law differ so radically from each other that one can refer to them only loosely as a school of thought: *Maurice Hauriou*, for instance, advocates natural law, *Santi Romano* is a positivist, *Carl Schmitt* glorifies power as the key factor in the constitution of an order. Consequently, we have to ask ourselves whether there is, in fact, a common core to all these various theories which would justify classing them under a common concept. The mere fact, that all these authors use the term "institutions" does not offer sufficient reason for doing so. What appears to me to be a common characteristic is the fact that they don't see the law - or, at least not exclusively, - as a system of norms endowed with institutional existence. Instead, they regard the institutions in some way as actually existing entities in their own right constituting, as it were, the origins of the law. In this sense the above authors have an anti-normativist approach - although they certainly recognise that the norms have a role to play. For them the norms are something like the epiphenomena of the institutions rather than the vital foundations and constituents of any institution which they are in the conception of ILP. This applies even to *Santi Romano* despite his statement: "Any legal system constitutes an institution, any institution constitutes a legal system; the equation of the two concepts is essential and absolute"[21], since, in his view, the law constitutes order, structure and the basis of society even before it becomes norm. To *Romano* the omnipresence of the legal order does not suggest the institutional existence of norms - as it does in ILP - but the presence of structures with an independent existence of their own which in the last analysis engender the law.[22]

The best-known representative of this school of thought is *Maurice Hauriou* (1856-1929). His work on "The Theory of the Institution and of its Foundations" with the peculiar subtitle "Essay on Social Vitalism" offers a reasonably systematic account of his teachings.[23] For him the institutions constitute the true realities of the law. The law as an institution is simultaneously a social reality and something ideal, an entity determined by ideas. This is reflected in the fact that the *idée directrice form the key concept of this theory.*

Hauriou opposes the legal theory of volition whether it occurs in the form of *Rousseau*'s social contract and the *volonté générale* or in the shape of the theory of the collective consciousness advocated by the *Durkheim* school.[24]

[21] S. Romano, *Die Rechtsordnung*, ed. by. R. Schnur, Berlin 1975, p. 32.

[22] S. Romano, *ibid.*, p. 23: "Seen in this comprehensive manner the legal order is an entity which moves in accordance with the norms. Above all, though, the legal order itself also moves the norms similar to figures on a chessboard. Consequently, the norms are objects and tools in the activities of the legal order rather than elements of its inherent structure."

[23] M. Hauriou, Die Theorie der Institution und der Gründung. Essay über den sozialen Vitalismus, in: R. Schnur (ed.), *Die Theorie der Institution*, Berlin 1965, pp. 27-66.

[24] See M. Hauriou, *ibid.*, p. 29, p. 44.

According to *Hauriou* there is a conflict between objective and subjective views in the theory of law. His explanation regarding this subject appears somewhat obscure to me. If I understand him correctly his views can be characterised broadly in the following way: While it is the normal assumption of jurisprudence that the subjective law derives from a conscious act of will made by individuals and that the objective law exists without such individual acts of will, *Hauriou* believes that subjectivity is sustained by our deliberate expressions of intention, while the ideas present in our subconscious are the basis of objectivity.[25] He does not regard the objectivity of the legal system as the objective existence of the legal norm. Instead, true objectivity adheres to the key ideas, the concepts of the enterprise which is to be realized. These form the basis of the institutions and, by taking root in a certain social milieu, generate institutions.

Hauriou aims at overcoming both subjective and objective legal theories as well as the theory of the subjectivity of the law by using a concept of the institution which he defines as follows: "[A]n institution is the idea of an idea which finds realization and existence in law in a social context. For the purpose of converting this idea into concrete facts a power evolves which furnishes the idea with organs. Among the members of the social group participating in the process of putting the idea into practice expressions of communality develop under the guidance of the organs and in accordance with certain rules."[26] In terms of this view it is the subjective elements that provide the creative thrust and action while the objective elements contribute the legal norm, the social context and the public order as an organisation providing stability and continuity.[27]

With reference to the founding of institutions *Hauriou* says: "... the founding of the institution has legal character and (...) from this point of view even the basis for the duration of the law's existence is of a legal kind, too." ... "Institutions come into being, live and die in accordance with the rules of law. They come into being as a result of the founding procedures which establish the legal basis for their existence and thereby ensure their survival. They live both objectively and subjectively thanks to repeated legal acts on the part of government and administration, performed in accordance with prescribed procedures. Finally they die as a result of legal decrees for their dissolution and abolition."[28]

Institutions are, consequently, social entities of relative duration, with an abstract structure, expressed in the governing idea, and they come into existence through the law and legal provisions with legal norms playing a secondary role: "It is the institutions which create the legal norms rather than the legal norms which create the institutions."[29] Not the legal system is the true (primary) objective element, but the institution.

---

[25] M. Hauriou, *ibid.*, p. 28.
[26] M. Hauriou, *ibid.*, p. 34.
[27] M. Hauriou, *ibid.*, p. 33.
[28] M. Hauriou, *ibid.*, p. 34, p. 35.
[29] M. Hauriou, *ibid.*, p. 65.

Hauriou draws a distinction between two kinds of institutions: object-institutions (institutions-choses) and person-institutions (institutions-persones, associative institutions), but he focusses his attention on the person-institutions. It is *Hauriou*'s purpose a) to show where in society the creative forces are to be found, b) to reveal their dependence on ideal elements, and c) to explain the processes leading to the founding of institutions and throw light on their "lives".

Question a) is answered univocally by *Hauriou* the primary importance rests with the force which creates institutions, controls society and constitutes the origins of the law on the basis of the governing ideas. "This is precisely, however, where the problem lies: what one wants to know is where in society the creative force is to be found, whether, in other words, the legal norms have created the institutions, or whether it is not rather the institutions which create the legal norms thanks to their inherent powers of leadership. It is in this question of the initiation and creation of the institutions that the system of objective legal norms fails. To concede the creation of the social institutions to legal norms would mean indirectly to admit their creation by the social milieu which for its part is assumed to be a product of the legal norms. This approach clearly constitutes an all too obvious misjudgement. No more than an element of inertia ought to be ascribed to the social milieu which feeds in augmented form into every individual initiative where it appropriates the same. Alternatively the social milieu becomes a troublesome handicap where it rejects the initiative. But it neither possesses any initiative of its own nor has it any creative power. It is, therefore, out of the question for it to produce a legal norm which for its part is creative, and which would assume to precede the institution."[30]

The governing idea, i.e. the concept of the enterprise that is to be realized, does not merely constitute the link to vitalist ideas;[31] it is also the most characteristic attribute of this institutional theory.

For *Hauriou* the governing idea is that element which creates the institution as a functioning and relatively stable social reality and which for this purpose invests the institution with power. It is the governing idea that justifies the organised power in its service and that constitutes the source of the sense of community within this society. The power in the service of the governing idea represents the creativity of society. This central notion is the ideal element which constitutes the institutions. While its nature is in principle directive and teleological it must not be equated with goals in the usual sense. There is something mystical about the governing idea (compare the quotation referred to in ftn. 31). For Hauriou the governing ideas have an existence as something like an ideal

---

30 M. Hauriou, *ibid.*, p. 32.

31 "Admittedly, it is *Claude Bernard*'s famous 'idée directrice' that is interpreted here in the vitalist sense, and, I am certain, that this will be noticed also by the biologists. On the other hand it is especially among them that vitalism has its supporters, and in the end there is always this basic fact: when it is projected onto the social level the governing idea appears as objective in the acutally palpable phenomenon of this association; it is the governing idea that influences its members and its mysterious effect that stirs the masses into action." M. Hauriou, *ibid.*, p. 47.

creative force above and beyond their significance as functions of social volition and as the expression of social constellations and objectives. "In fact, ideas cannot be created, one can only chance upon them."[32]

Other constituents of associative institutions apart from the idea of the project that is to be created, are those of the organised power in their service and the expression of a sense of community within a social group.[33] Not only the members of the group supporting the institution submit to the power and to its organisation through the manifestations of the sense of community, the leadership itself is subject to the authority of the governing idea. The organisation which owes its existence to power is morally upgraded by the phenomenon of the institution.[34]

(Communal-)personalities evolve in *three steps: incorporation, embodiment and personification.* In this way a *personalité morale* comes into existence on the basis of which a legal personality can be introduced. It is only when the sociological actuality of the communal personality has been established that the foundations are laid for the possibility of legally introducing juristic personalities.[35]

Hauriou is an exponent of natural law, his tenets of the natural law are, however, not entirely obvious. His thinking is influenced by the Thomist school[36], but to what extent, remains uncertain. "The law is a kind of program which is set up in such a way as to be aiming simultaneously at establishing social order and justice."[37] Natural law continues to develop without being adaptable; it is individualistic and anti-socialist; furthermore, it is an ideal concept of the law as the originator of the social order and of justice both *ars boni et aequi* and *ars stabili et securi*.[38]

Georges Renard is *Hauriou*'s most important disciple to continue his work. In his book "La Théorie de l'Institution. Essai d'ontologie juridique" he proposes a specific institutional ontology describing his theory emphatically as catholic and Thomist. It is constructed in terms of the tenets of natural law, or, to be more precise, as a special kind of Thomist-religious natural law. For his institutions are psychological and social actualities at the same time as pieces of

---

32 M. Hauriou, *ibid.*, p. 39.

33 M. Hauriou, *ibid.*, pp. 35 f.: "As we know, every associative institution contains three elements: 1. the idea of a project to be achieved in a social group; 2. the organised power in the service of this idea for the purpose of realizing the idea; 3. the expressions of communality occurring within the social group with reference to the idea and its realization."

34 M. Hauriou, *ibid.*, pp. 42 ff.

35 See J. Delos, La Théorie de l'Institution, *Archives de Philosophie du droit et de Sociologie juridique* 1931, pp. 119 ff.

36 G. Renard, *La Théorie de l'Institution. Essai d'ontologie juridique*, Paris 1930, p. XIII.

37 M Hauriou, Sozialordnung, Gerechtigkeit und Recht, in: R. Schnur (ed.), *Die Theorie der Institution*, ibid., pp. 67-95; p. 91.

38 M. Hauriou, *ibid.*, p. 95.

natural law. The institution is imposed on us by the nature of the situation;[39] natural law being based on observation this concept is a purely scientific one.[40] The founding of institutions is an essential aspect of human nature. Man has a fair amount of freedom in the setting up of institutions[41], albeit only in as far as man's natural inclinations are sanctioned by natural law, e.g. by the critique of reason.[42] Natural law is the organic law from which we derive our personalities and our nature; God is the ultimate origin of the institutions since "rien n'existe, hors Dieu, qui est sa raison en soi-même".[43] Consequently the hierarchical conception of the institutions which will be referred to later has its foundations in God.

His institutional theory is meant to take up the middle-ground between individualism and sociologism.[44] The dualism of person and institution forms the metaphysical basis of the ontology of institutions.[45] According to *Renard* institutions are the communities which human nature enables man to found. He establishes institutions on the basis of existing institutions not created by him.[46] There are not only different levels of existence but also different levels of institutions; institutions can be elements of superior institutions; there is a tendency in society for institutions to spread.

In the legal context ideas are of two different forms; they are rules or they form institutions. Every institution arises from a basic creative concept. The institution is the seat of the legal system and of authority.[47]

Certain psychological and sociological characteristics which *Renard* discusses at length determine not only the concept of the institution but they also form the basis of institutional legal theory: he names the following as basic elements of the institutions: permanence, authority, the continuity of the institution, the close relationship between individuals and the institution, identification with the institution *(consortium)*, the objective existence of the institution with internal and external relations etc. The institutions create a status for man to

---

[39] "L'institution s'impose par la force des choses; elle fait partis de ces notions de droit naturel qui rentent par la fenêtre lorsqu'on les chasse par la porte." M. Renard, *ibid.*, p. 281.

[40] M. Renard, *ibid.*, p. 391.

[41] M. Renard, *ibid.*, p. 360: "La loi naturelle laisse au discernement de l'homme le soin d'en choisir et de varier les formes, indéfinement; son engagement n'est pas étroitement borné à l'exécution d'un programme tracé point par point."

[42] M. Renard, *ibid.*, pp. 389 f.: "le droit naturel sanctionne les inclinations humaines, en tant qu'elles sont gouvernées par la raison; or il existe dans la nature humaine une inclination à ce dépassement de soi que traduit le formule de la fondation et de l'institution; donc la fondation institutelle est sanctionnée par le droit naturel moyennenant satisfaction donnée aux exigences de la raison."

[43] M. Renard, *ibid.*, p. 390.

[44] M. Renard, *ibid.*, p. 13.

[45] M. Renard, *ibid.*, p. 47: "L'ordre juridique repose sur un double support: la personnalité humaine et l'institution."

[46] M. Renard, *ibid.*, p. 109.

[47] M. Renard, *ibid.*, pp. 120 f.

maintain within them which is to be distinguished, however, from subjective right.[48] Also of interest in *Renard*'s theoretical juxtaposition of contractual and institutional elements of legal life is his view that the contractual elements tend to transform themselves into institutional ones.[49]

Renard's institutional ontology restricts the concept of the institution essentially to the person-institutions in *Hauriou*'s sense. He demonstrates that the institutionalist approach makes it possible to analyse interesting sociological and politological aspects of the law.

Two tendencies dominate legal life according to *Renard*: the 'justice' factor and the 'certainty' factor (here clearly in the sense of 'legal certainty').[50]

I should like to conclude with a passage which from the point of view of its relevance to the institutional theory comes close to my semantic conception although its author is otherwise an anti-normativist like all representatives of this school: "L'ordre est un système de règles indicatives en tant qu'elles s'addressent à la matière brute ou aux êtres privés de raison, règles imperatives en tant qu'elles s'adressent à l'homme et aux sociétés humaines, - loi morale et loi juridique."[51]

It is likely that the teachings of *Santi Romano* (1875-1947) evolved in relative independence from *Hauriou* and *Renard*, but in the confrontation with the normativism of Pure Jurisprudence. His reference in the French school of institutional jurisprudence appears to me of minor importance. In any case, the intellectual basis of *Romano*'s approach differs fundamentally from that of the two French authors.

Romano develops his concept of the legal system in opposition to the approach of pure normativism according to which the legal system is simply a system of norms. The legal system is an entity, an undivided whole, not only however, an entity of norms[52], but a complex order[53] an organic whole existing objectively and producing norms which regulate the development of this organic system.

Central to *Romano*'s theory is the thesis of the identity of legal system and institution: "If this is true, the concept of the institution apppears to be both necessary and sufficient for a precise account of what constitutes the 'law'. What is meant by the law in this context is the legal system in its *entirety* and seen from the point of view of its unity. Every legal system is an institution and vice versa, every institution is also a legal system: the equation of the two

---

48 M. Renard, *ibid.*, pp. 330 ff.

49 M. Renard, *ibid.*, p. 426.

50 M. Renard, *ibid.*, p. 49: "le droit n'est pas seulement facteur *de justice* et par consequent de moralité; il est facteur de sécurité; et c'est l'union de le justice et de la sécurité qui en fait une discipline originale."

51 M. Renard, *ibid.*, p. 94.

52 Compare the concept of pure jurisprudence and those of other analytical theories of the law. *Romano* quotes the relevant works by *F. Weyr* (Zum Problem eines einheitlichen Rechtssystems, *Archiv für öffentliches Recht* XXIII/1908) in addition to *Kelsen*'s.

53 See S. Romano, *Die Rechtsordnung*, ed. by R. Schnur, Berlin 1975, pp. 27 f., 26, 75.

concepts is necessary and absolute."[54] ... "Furthermore, we do not regard the institution as the source of the law nor, consequently, the law as a result, a product of the institutions; instead, there is, in our view, complete identity between the concepts of the institution and of a legal order which is conceived of as one. This conclusion can, however, only be reached by abandoning the traditional doctrine of the law as a mere norm or a complex unity of norms."[55]

According to *Romano* there are historical examples of legal systems without either written or unwritten norms. In such cases the law has to be seen as vested in the power of the judge who expresses the objective social consciousness.[56] This appears highly problematical to me as it poses the question: what is it that makes the judge a judge. Surely, a constitution which has to be seen as normative, but is made up of laws which have to be institutionalised even without obviously having been written down. Apart from that, I doubt that institutionalised courts (judges) can exist without, at least, common law norms developing. A judge does not merely make decisions, he will always attempt to substantiate this decisions, i.e. he will decide on the basis of normative standards which he will, if necessary, set himself.

Romano presents a brief definition of this concept of institution supplementing it with some comments: "As an institution we regard any concrete social something, every actual social phenomenon."[57] The institution must exist objectively and materially, it must be "corpo sociale". It is the expression of man's social nature and it serves specific interests and tasks. An institution can consist exclusively of persons, or it can be a combination of material as well as immaterial, personal or factual elements. "The institution is a self-contained something, which being endowed with its own individuality can be considered on its own, separately." There are also "institutions of institutions".[58] Institutions are "antithetical" if they are illicit from the point of view of other institutions. The institution is a fixed, durable entity which does not lose its identity even when its individual elements change - such as its members, property, means, objectives, those gaining advantages from it, its norms etc. It is also possible for it to renew itself while remaining true to itself and preserving its individuality. On this basis it is possible to regard it as self-sufficient and not to identify it with the elements of which it is formed."[59]

By identifying the institution with the legal system the author reaches the distinction between inner order (this is identical with the respective institution) and such rules as might be valid for the institution as a result of a different (superior) system.

---

54 S. Romano, *ibid.*, p. 32.

55 S. Romano, *ibid.*, p. 37.

56 S. Romano, *ibid.*, p. 27.

57 S. Romano, *ibid.*, pp. 38 ff.

58 S. Romano, *ibid.*, p. 40. In this there appears to be an echo of *Renard*'s concept of the institutional hierarchy.

59 S. Romano, *ibid.*, p. 41.

It is hardly surprising that he rejects *Kelsen*'s conception which identifies the state with the law (in the sense of a system of legal norms). State equals institution. "The genesis of the state is not a process regulated by legal norms: it is a purely factual process, as has been shown repeatedly."[60] ... "Contrary to a widespread formulation the law cannot be identical with the norm laid down by the social organisation; instead, the law itself constitutes the organisation, manifesting itself externally by, among other things, the setting of norms."[61]

In his theory of the juridical personality *Romano* opposes the dualism of associations of persons and foundations (object-institutions). "The basis for a juridical personality is, consequently, provided by an institution in the sense of the conception which I have developed above. The essence of the juridical personality is not constituted by the persons involved - this applies even to personal associations -, nor by the assets underpinning it, nor the organs, offices, or the objectives it pursues, the essence always and exclusively rests in the legal order that binds the person together, invests the assets with a specific purpose, determines its organs and coordinates the whole in the direction of a specific goal. And in regarding the legal system as the essence of the juridical personality we are referring to its 'inherent' order rather than to the rules which have been established for juridical personalities by a higher, more comprehensive order than, for instance, the state."[62]

As a result of identifying institution and legal system *Romano* arrives at the thesis of the variety of legal systems. In my opinion this kind of conceptual structure does not provide the right sort of support for important considerations of the problem of the legal system as a logical whole (in the normative sense).

Romano also attempted to present a typology of institutions.[63] It has been summarised by *M. Fuchs* in the following outline:

"1. original - derivative institutions
2. institutions with universal/limited objectives
3. composite - simple institutions
4. perfect - imperfect institutions
5. institutions with/without the attributes of the juridical personality
6. dependent - independent institutions."[64]

A good deal in this remains obscure. In any case, I don't believe that this "systematic" approach contributes much to the advancement of the institutional theory.

Carl Schmitt (born 1888) has a special place in the context of institutional theory for the following two reasons: because he submitted an interesting juxtaposition of three fundamental juristic approaches with one of them being close to the institutional conception, and, furthermore, because it is an interesting ques-

---

60 S. Romano, *ibid.*, p. 49.
61 S. Romano, *ibid.*, p. 50.
62 S. Romano, *ibid.*, p. 69.
63 S. Romano, *ibid.*, pp. 112 ff.
64 M. Fuchs, *Die allgemeine Rechtstheorie Santi Romanos*, Berlin 1979, p. 67.

tion to what extent the thinking in terms of concrete systems which he advances is fundamentally and inevitably connected with the Nazi ideology and its legal conceptions of which *Schmitt* was the most important protagonist.

Within the framework of this treatise I shall, of course, restrict myself to dealing only with *Schmitt*'s connection with *Hauriou*'s and *Romano*'s institutional theories without attempting a complete interpretation of his legal and political theories.

Schmitt's three juristic thought models are normativism, decisionism and the theory of concrete order *(das konkrete Ordnungsdenken)*. *Schmitt* regards *Hauriou* and *Romano* as predecessors of his conception, i.e. the theory of concrete order.

In the context of normativism the law is an impersonal and suprapersonal system of norms. The law must rule, not man.[65] The juristic essence of normativism is characterised aptly by *Schmitt* when he says: "The strict normativist with his constant reference to the norm as basis for his juristic thinking reduces king, leader, judge, state to mere normative functions to the point where the highest or lowest norm, the law of laws, the 'norm of norms' in its purest and most intensive form becomes nothing but a norm or law. In concrete terms this achieves simply that the norm or law is played off politically and polemically against the king or leader; through this 'domination of the law' the concrete system of kingship or leadership is destroyed by the law; the masters of the *lex* subjugate the *rex*. This is, in fact, usually the concrete political intention behind the manoeuvres of playing off the *lex* against the *rex*."[66]

Decisionism believes the law and the reasons for its validity to be established by processes of the will leading to sovereign decisions. "The ultimate legal basis for all legal meanings and values is to be located juristically in a process of volition, in a decision which by its very nature is in fact what creates 'the law' and the legal validity of the decision cannot be derived from the legal validity of rules of decision." ... "For the jurist of the decisionist type what represents the source of all 'laws' i.e. of all norms and systems derived from it, is not the command as command but the authority or sovereignty of an ultimate *decision* expressed in the command."[67]

The two approaches mentioned here allow a connection which could be equated in essence with the legal positivism of the nineteenth century. It is the law established as a result of authority that forms the basis of decisions. "The positivist does not represent an independent and therefore not a permanent type of juristic thinking. He submits - decisionistically - to the *decision* of the respective law-giver currently in possession of the power of the state since he alone can guarantee actual enforcibility; at the same time he demands that this decision should continue to have definite and absolute validity as a *norm*, in other words, that even the official legislator himself must submit to the law passed by himself

---

[65] C. Schmitt, *Über die drei Arten des rechtswissenschaftlichen Denkens*, Hamburg 1934, pp. 13 f.

[66] C. Schmitt, *ibid.*, p. 15.

[67] C. Schmitt, *ibid.*, p. 25.

and to its interpretation. This kind of system of legality alone is described by him as a 'constitutional state' *('Rechtsstaat')*, although it is, in fact, precisely the 'state of justice' *('Recht'staat')* (the state based on the concept of justice) that this system replaces with a statutary state (state based on laws) and the interest of justice with the interest of legal certainty."[68]

The theory of concrete order postulates that it is not the norm or rule that creates an order but that the rule is merely an aspect and a tool of the order. Not the law rules but human beings exerting power. The judge is not subordinate to the norm but to a concrete order. He himself forms part of a system of order. However, the concept of order is explained only in negative terms and quite insufficiently by Schmitt, or at least, that is how it appears to me. Order cannot be reduced to a system of norms. Normativism demotes the heads of the system, such as the guardian of the constitution (state presidents[69]) or the leader of the movement and others to mere organs of the state; incompatibilities are fixed in accordance with norms; at the same time *Schmitt* regards those wielding power in the concrete order as rules rather than as organs of a normed order whose authority is subject to restrictions imposed by normative regulations. His concept of order itself he explains most clearly with the help of a quotation from *S. Romano*'s L'ordinamento giuridico: "'The legal order (l'ordinamento giuridico) is a unified being, an entity moving partly in accordance with rules, above all, however, itself moving the rules like figures on a chess-board; the rules, therefore, represent the object or the tool of the legal order rather than an element of its structure.'"[70]

It can be said, therefore, that *Schmitt* like *Romano* and the other representatives of the institutional theory of law defines order as an entity *per se* which *de facto* precedes the normative rules.

This conception forms the basis for rulers to disengage themselves from the law and the normative order. It is an ideology, in other words, which while not, in my view, inevitably leading to Nazi views, certainly opens the door to such ideas and to a dictatorial way of life.

It has to be pointed out as well, though, that there are meaningful ideas contained in *Schmitt*'s conception. The existing order as actual social constellation is a framework within which legislation and any new norms have to be embedded. The normative order - forming as it does, in my view, - implicitely, at least, the basis of every order - is more comprehensive than can be expressed in terms of law. It must be said that there are - even for the adherent of the democratic order - situations when in the course of founding new institutions new laws are institutionalised without the support of a given authorising framework.

---

68 C. Schmitt, *ibid.*, p. 35.

69 See C. Schmitt, *Der Hüter der Verfassung*, Tübingen 1931; also W. Mantl, Hans Kelsen und Carl Schmitt, in: W. Krawietz/E. Topitsch/P. Koller (eds.), *Ideologiekritik und Demokratietheorie bei Hans Kelsen, Rechtstheorie*, Beiheft 4, 1982, pp. 185-199.

70 C. Schmitt, *ibid.*, p. 24. Schmitt refers to p. 17 of Romano's work "L'ordinamento giuridico".

6. INSTITUTIONAL THEORIES IN SOCIOLOGY

It is not my intention, nor is it necessary in this context, to discuss at length the various sociological institutional theories. In view of the key position of the concept of institutions it would be necessary to take into account almost the entire field of sociology and possibly even to analyse discourses which deal with the problems under discussion without even using the term institution. I am confining myself to giving a brief outline of three important contributions to the institutional theory by German sociologists[71] on the basis that their connection with ILP appears to me to be of particular interest.

The sociological theories of institutions are intended to determine the structure and the mechanics of every kind of social institutions. They respond to this task in various ways: from the socio-holistic perspective, from the point of view of system-theory, from the functionalist standpoint or from the anthropological and ethological perspective, etc. What is of particular interest to us is the way in which the nature of the relationship between social institutions and normative regulatives is defined, or, in other words, the approach to the ontology of norms and the weight given to social norms in explaining the constitution and the mechanism of institutions.

According to *Arnold Gehlen* (1904-1976) the institution broadly plays the same role as behavioural determinant in the human sphere that instincts play for animals. For *Gehlen* man is a naked ape barely protected by now by his physical attributes and inherited patterns of behaviour. His behaviour is guided only to a very small extent by those life-preserving instincts which safeguard the animal's chances of survival in the animal realm. The instinct-guided behaviour which proved itself in the development of the species has been replaced in man by a considerable openness and adaptability of behaviour. The fact that human behaviour is not determined by instincts is compensated by institutions taking on the role of behavioural determinants. "It is, in fact, possible to say that much in the same way as animal groups and symbioses are held together by instinctual and trigger responses their human counter-parts are held together by institutions and by the quasi-automatic habits of thought, feeling, evaluation, action which become simplified, habitualised and thereby stable only as a result of their institutionalised conception."[72]

It is true to say, therefore, that *Gehlen* regards the institutions from the point of view of the theory of action and interprets them as objective constellations which determine man's individual and collective behaviour.[73] Man

---

[71] The reader will find a more detailed account of the sociological theories of the institution, for instance, in H. Schelsky, Zur soziologischen Theorie der Institution, in: H. Schelsky (ed.), *Zur soziologischen Theorie der Institution*, Düsseldorf 1973, pp. 7-26; also in H. Schelsky, *Die Soziologen und das Recht*, Opladen 1980.

[72] A. Gehlen, *Der Mensch. Seine Natur und seine Stellung in der Welt*, Bonn 1955, p. 84.

[73] See for the following: A. Gehlen, Probleme einer soziologischen Handlungstheorie, in: A. Gehlen, *Studien zur Anthropologie und Soziologie*, Neuwied - Berlin 1971, pp. 196-231.

establishes institutions because he has the necessary scope to do so being open, adaptable and largely free from instinctual control and because his communities have to be organised and stabilised somehow.

We live in a multiplicity of institutions. Each one develops its own autonomy leading to unforseen and potentially unintended results for the persons involved. According to *Gehlen* the institution implies mutually obligatory modes of behaviour. He also recognised the link between the institution as a social structure where authority and power have their place, too, and the normative regulatives which are connected with them. Institutions provide a subjective scope for action, or, as one might say, potentials for action, models for action and possibly pre-established decisions determining actions.

Actions cannot always be rationally explained on the sole basis of their intention. Consequently it is advisable to distinguish between the concepts of purpose and motive. Motives - seen by *Gehlen* apparently as anything that might determine an action - are not only determinants rationally defined by their purposes but they also contain other elements. They have, for instance, an ought-content (convictions) and various internalised behavioural patterns.[74]

The concept of the institution held by *Helmut Schelsky* (1912-1984) is more than a mere synthesis of the tenets advocated by *Gehlen, Malinowsky* and other representatives of an anthropological and functional explanation of the institutions; what appears to be especially significant in *Schelsky*'s theory, is the fact, that he gives particular weight to the law as a normative principle of organisation.[75] "*The law* is first and foremost a social mechanism with the help of which individuals find their bearings in their social interaction"; in addition, it fulfills the function of stabilising the achievements reached in earlier developments and to provide the means for planned social change.

Like *Gehlen*, *Schelsky* interprets the relationship between individual and institution in the context of action. He does, however, interpret it in a different way from *Gehlen*, that is, as "circular processes" where, on the one hand, the institutions contribute to the control of individual behaviour and, on the other hand, acting individuals with their ideas, impulses and intentions - one might say, with their systems of motivations - establish institutions and determine their nature.[76]

With this approach *Schelsky* expresses his opposition to the view that it is inevitable for man to be absorbed by the institutions, for him, in contrast, it is a political postulate that the individual, his freedom and his ability to act independently must be protected. *Schelsky* accuses *Gehlen* of deserving the accusation of having emphasised the role of the institution at the expense of the

---

[74] In the formal-finalist theory of action I have defined the term 'motive' as 'interpreted purpose', while taking into account other fixed determinants of action apart from motives. See O. Weinberger, *Studien zur formal-finalistischen Handlungstheorie*, Frankfurt a.M./Bern/New York 1983. Basically this is a matter of terminology rather than a factual divergence of opinion.

[75] See especially H. Schelsky, Die Soziologie und das Recht, *loc.cit.*, pp. 77-146.

[76] H. Schelsky, *ibid.*, pp. 77 f.

individual's position, on the other hand, he accepts the possibility that Gehlen had intended to underline the role of the individual personality rather than restricting it. This ambiguous interpretation of *Gehlen*'s work is reflected in the following two quotations: "*Gehlen* himself has caused these misgivings [e.g. on the part of *Habermas* who fears that subjectivity must be prepared for the institutions to destroy it, O.W. note] and along with them the protests of those advocating subjectivity that he has failed to notice and point out in his concept of the institution the individual's influence on the institution: e.g. on the one hand, by passing laws, in other words, by founding institutions and by introducing planned changes into their objective structures, on the other hand, by preserving the individual's rights, as for instance, through constitutional proceedings. The view that the law means freedom from the social influence of the institutions was for Gehlen an all too frequently neglected position." ... "In respect of the rights of the institution the assessment of the liberal American journalist *Walter Lippmann* may still be quoted in response: Civilisation and culture flourish and continue in innumerable private spheres. Without the last reserves of personal habits, energy and adaptability the mistakes of the great leaders of humanity would long since have proved irreparable. In view of the possibility that *Gehlen* intended to strengthen the personality of the individual in his institutional theory rather than destroying it I believe it to be entirely feasible that he would have agreed almost entirely with *Lippmann*'s assessment."[77]

Schelsky's theory of institutions taken as a whole can be summed up in the following points:

(a) Both the life of the individual and the make-up of the institutions must be considered from the point of view that both have the capacity to act and that their actions can be understood only as a mutual relationship, "motivations for the actions of the individual as a factor determining the institution/institutional control of the individual".

(b) The institutions are based on ideas and controlled by a kind of ideas that were described by *Malinowsky* as "charter" and by *Hauriou* as "idée directrice". Institutions can and must be explained as much with reference to the ideas which guide and control them as to the *structure of human needs* and to *the rules governing their social organisation.*

(c) The institutions have, on the one hand, stabilising properties, on the other hand, they are subject to *social change*. In terms of institutional theory social change can, therefore, be described as *a process wherein the institutions of the highest grade in each case (the others, too, by the way) produce new needs which demand to be satisfied institutionally, thereby producing more and more institutions and in turn again more needs*. In addition, the human need for critical self-examination comes into play in this process. It is correct, therefore, to refer to functional changes taking place in institutions.

---

[77] H. Schelsky, *ibid.*, pp. 82 f. While *Gehlen* may not have discussed the individual's influence on the institution in greater detail, compared with other sociologists there are, in my view hardly any of those tendencies to see the individual as being submerged in the institution present in his work.

(d) The most characteristic feature of *Schelsky*'s institutional theory is the part, he assigns to the law in respect of the material existence of both individuals and institutions. For *Schelsky* the law is not only the subject of a separate discipline, i.e. legal sociology, but it also constitutes a social phenomenon to be taken into account in the general field of sociology. Present-day sociological theory will only be able to shed its one-sidedness. Schelsky believes, if it acknowledges the importance of the law for the structural laws of society more adequately than this is the case of the moment.[78] Sociology has to recognise the law as a constitutional element of the institutions. And finally, the law is more than a tool of social control and for the solving of social conflicts in *Schelsky*'s eyes; it is also, - especially so in the present political situation - the basis and guarantee of human freedom. The emphasis on free will and on the individual's independence within the framework of the law is his central concern. *Schelsky*'s tenets are more than a theory, they represent an approach which encapsulates political postulates. "The law does not only link inherited stability with permanent social change, not only the personal right to freedom with the acceptance of duties imposed by society but, what is more, in the context of this institutional tension between subjective freedom and objective social obligation it is also the only political mechanism capable of mediating between the domination inevitably imposed by others and the self-determination constantly aspired to by the individual. By obeying the law I acknowledge the will of an older generation from the past; by renewing it I determine the future conduct of our heirs who in turn will treat it as a relevant aspect of their past. The passing of laws as a task of the present ensures - similar to biological continuity - the permanent survival of the subjective and the social will from one generation to the next. It appears to me that the law provides the practical basis for the reconciliation of subjective freedom and independence with the obligation inherent in the social existence of both individual and institution."[79]

(e) Not surprisingly *Schelsky* shows little sympathy for *Luhmann*'s system-theoretical approach which limits itself to defining formal properties like the increase and reduction of complexity, decision, selection, data processing: "In Luhmann's system of categories all cats turn a functional grey."[80]

(f) The three personal guiding principles of the law: permanent mutuality; equality despite dissimilarity; integrity and autonomy of the individual vis-à-vis the organisation *are regarded by Schelsky as central to his conception of the law. This approach simultaneously determines the sociological nature of the law in its content, characterises Schelsky's view of the institutions as social elements dependent on the law and expresses his system of political postulates.*

For *Niklas Luhmann* (born 1927) the theory of social systems and within its context the problem of institutionalisation take the place of an institutional

---

[78] H. Schelsky, *ibid.*, p. 95.

[79] H. Schelsky, Soziologie - wie ich sie verstehe, in: H. Schelsky (ed.), *Die Soziologen und das Recht*, op. cit., pp. 26 f.

[80] H. Schelsky, *Die Soziologen und das Recht*, p. 93.

theory.[81] His approach is dominated by the concept of the system, by the functions and mechanisms involved in the forming of systems as well as those elements which are crucial for the organisation of systems and for the conduct of the subjects within them: complexity, contingency, selectivity etc. These concepts are treated as determinants for contexts of action, albeit in a different way from the ones used by most other institutional theories where the institutions are seen as building-blocks of social reality and as meaningful human creations as well as the element linking the individual in his actions with communities and institutional bodies. Due to his different approach Luhmann does not deal with the systematic analysis of institutions or with their more general typology. Instead, he provides this concept merely with an approximate definition by way of a partial sociological characterisation: "In sociological terms this concept [of the institution] does not simply denote a complex of norms but a complex of actual behavioural expectations which are activated in the context of a social role and, therefore, always able to count on social consensus."[82] Here as in many other places, especially in his legal sociology[83], he analyses the problem of the institution in descriptive terms taking into account the subjects' behavioural expectations and the social consensus.

He rightly doubts that institutionalisation is sustained mainly by a consensus of values and patterns of behaviour. As he puts it pointedly but appositely: "Institutionalisation serves the purpose of successfully overestimating consensus."[84]

Institutionalisation means that expectations are consolidated, made anonymous, generalised and made to be expected. While he also connects the question of norms with institutionalisation, he does so in a different way from the normativists of every description, that is, not in terms of internalisation and social impact of normative rule-systems but as a special kind of organisation of expectations. This view results from *Luhmann*'s - to my mind rather peculiar - interpretation of the norm-concept based on the distinction between cognitive and normative expectations.

"Cognitive expectations are, consequently, marked by a willingness, albeit not necessarily a conscious one, to learn, while normative expectations are characterised by the determination not to learn from disappointments. While the possibility of a disappointment is anticipated in the awareness that man inhabits a complex and contingent world where others may act in an unexpected way this is regarded in advance as irrelevant to the expectation." ... "Norms are accordingly *contra-factually stabilised behavioural expectations*. The meaning of the

---

[81] N. Luhmann, Institutionalisierung - Funktion und Mechanismus im sozialen System der Gesellschaft, in: H. Schelsky, *Zur Theorie der Institutionen*, Düsseldorf 1973, p. 23: "We shall assume in the following that it is not the concept of the institution but the concept of the social system which defines the realm of sociology"; see also pp. 36 f.

[82] N. Luhmann, *Grundrechte als Institution*, Berlin 1965, pp. 12 f.

[83] N. Luhmann, *Rechtssoziologie*, 2 vols., Hamburg 1972.

[84] N. Luhmann, Institutionalisierung - Funktion und Mechanismus im sozialen System der Gesellschaft, in: H. Schelsky (ed.), *Zur Theorie der Institution*, p. 30.

term implies that its validity is unconditional in as much as the validity is experienced as independent from the actual realization or non-realization of the norm, and it is institutionalised in this sense. The ought-content symbolically expresses first and foremost the expectation of the contra-factual validity without putting the nature of the expectation itself into question. This is what constitutes the meaning and the function of the 'ought'.

Despite its contra-factual orientation the meaning of 'ought' is no less real than the meaning of 'being'. All expectations, whether fulfilled or not, are factual. Their factual nature comprises their normative nature within it. Consequently, the usual juxtaposition of factual and normative ought to be abandoned."[85]

Using adapted concepts taken from the behaviourist psychology of learning *Luhmann* reinterprets the essence of the norm-concept as a kind of expectation which seems to me very problematical.

The relationship between norm and expectation is extremely complex. While a norm (like not being unfaithful in marriage) may exist, psychologists and sociologists may, nevertheless, expect human conduct not to comply with this norm. The approach taken from the psychology of learning has nothing to do with the actual questions concerning the concept of the norm. Having chosen the learning process as the basis of one's approach it is surely nonsensical to be determined not to learn from experience.

Considering that the norm is regarded as no more than a particular type of expectation it is hardly surprising that *Luhmann* does not distinguish as essentially different between what is factual (I would say empirically observable) and what is normative.

7. INSTITUTIONAL LEGAL POSITIVISM CONTRASTED WITH JURISTIC AND SOCIOLOGICAL INSTITUTIONAL THEORIES

It is my intention to demonstrate that the institutional theories which I have described in the preceding pages fail although they doubtlessly cover certain aspects of the institutions and their role in the realm of individual and social action; that they fail, nevertheless, on account of having neglected to clarify the fundamental semantic and ontological problems. The following analysis of these problems will also constitute a juxtaposition of ILP and the other institutional theories.

The central divergence of opinions between ILP and the traditional institutional legal theories arises from the normativist approach of one side and the anti-normativist conception of the other side. It appears necessary, therefore, to examine the origins and foundations of anti-normativism.

The normativism of the analytical schools of jurisprudence was based on the perception by *Hume - Kant - Poincaré* of the semantic as well as logical peculiarity of ought-sentences compared with purely descriptive sentences. The -

---

[85] N. Luhmann, *Rechtssoziologie*, vol. 1. p. 43.

as it were - pure normativists understood the norms as idealities *sui generis*.[86] The realist opposition to normativism drew on neo-positivist doubts about the meaning of the norm sentences (norms) arising inevitably from the point of view of a theory of the verification of meaning (*A. Hägerström*), while on the other hand, it recognised that the validity of the norm is coupled with the sociologically observable human behaviour and with the existence of institutions.

The representatives of institutional jurisprudence justly maintained that certain social realities, such as collective personalities, social institutions, exist objectively, i.e. they are social facts as such. They recognised that there is some kind of connection between these institutions and legal norms. They believed, however, that the institutions could not have been established as social facts by the norms; that the opposite is the case, instead, and that the legal norms are generated by the institutions as tools for granting their function. Admittedly these conceptions are not always formulated in this way by the representatives of institutional jurisprudence. *Romano*, for instance, identifies the legal order with the institutions and regards the norms as the emanation of the legal system (= institution).

The insight that the system of rules which are formulated explicitely as laws and other regulations does not constitute the entirety of the law also leads to anti-normativism with its claim that the law is not a mere complex of norms but a product of the institutions. And, finally, anti-normativism also results from the conviction that it is structured power organised on a conceptual background of the type provided by the *idée directrice* and applied in its service that constitutes the source of both the law and social organisation.

ILP deals with this problem in an entirely different way, accepting as it does only some of the individual theses of traditional institutional jurisprudence without embracing its fundamental position or its overall interpretation.

According to ILP there is no institution as a social reality which is independent of practical informations; whether implicitely or explicitely formulated this fact inevitably comes into play when institutions are constituted. The question whether it is the law that creates the institutions or the institutions engender the law is misleading. In reality a social institution never exists without the relevant system of norms, neither does such a system of norms exist without the relevant institution.[87] A community, a collective personality, or a social institution are real in the social world if they exist as elements of interactive connections, if they are not only regularities of behaviour but contain also ought- and may-rules, as well as empowering rules. Institutions do not consist only of actual modes of behaviour and rules for their control, they always also comprise normative and evaluating responses to potential alternatives of behaviour; in other words: they comprise normative as well as evaluating rules. As elements in

---

86 Conceptions tending in the direction of the institutional ontology of norms really don't occur before *Hart*. See H. Hart, *The Concept of Law*, Oxford 1961.

87 While a norm sentence (a norm) can be grasped and understood whether or not the respective norm has an institutionalised existence, valid norms can be grasped as such only in relation to institutions and only on the basis that their institutional existence is recognised.

the context of action they are associated with informations reflecting a particular point of view (practical informations).

These theses require some elucidation: There is, of course, no need for the practical informations referred to in connection with the constitution and the mechanisms of institutions to take the form of explicitely formulated norms, postulated goals or preferences. It is quite feasible for rules to be institutionalised and followed in the belief that the ensuing behaviour and actions comply with their intentions even without the subject always being able to refer to explicit rules. They are, nevertheless, institutionalised elements of the social reality of the respective domain,[88] and as such they have to be taken into account in a complete, rationally reconstructed description of the institution. In contemporary legal life specialised organs for the generation of law have evolved: organs of jurisdiction - which frequently generate general normative rules, as well as organs of legislation. There can be little doubt, however, that the institutional existence of normative rules does not begin with the development of such specialised organs.

The institutions have an essential core of elements (those sustaining the institutions and ensuring their function, in fact) and as constituent parts of the institution these elements fulfil certain roles. They attract a certain institutional status and a web of structures evolves consisting of these elements and the fixed interrelations. The personal and material core elements together with the fixed interrelations form an order. This order is not something, however, that is capable of existing ontologically independent of the rules determining the relations, goals, behavioural programs or scope for actions for those involved and a corpus of ought-determination.

The extent to which order and practial information are ontologically interwoven emerges when one examines power and authority. The power of the individual is not only a function of physical or mental power - *de facto* not even primarily - but it denotes a certain status brought about by rules and institutional relationships. Authority as an exercise of power within society is above all, therefore, an institutionalised constellation determined by the web of normative, functional-factual and ideal (possibly ideological) factors.

While *Hauriou*'s thesis of the institution as controlled by governing ideas and goal-determinants appears to me to offer an important sociological insight, I would want to strip these ideas and programmatic conceptions of the mystique that attaches to them in the theory of the French scholar. Social reality is more than a system of personal and factual-material relations; it is surely also a product of the mind considering that social existence means existence in a context of action, and that man and human communities have at their disposal a scope for

---

[88] With reference to this point the comparison with language (e.g. some kind of colloquial language) is instructive. There is no need at all for the rules of language to be formulated explicitely; nevertheless, they exist and are *conditiones sine qua non* of the language and for the possibility of using it in the reality of the social context. See also *Wittgenstein*'s analogous statements in respect of language rules in: L. Wittgenstein, *Philosophische Untersuchungen*, Oxford 1953.

action and opportunities of varying degrees of freedom for organising themselves.

At this point I should also like to comment on *Schmitt*'s juxtaposition of 'Rule of Man' and 'Rule of Law'. There is no such alternative. There is no such thing as the rule of law separate from man, only the legally ordered and more or less legally controlled rule of man - this control being what democrats are concerned about -, and in the political reality there is no rule of man other than what is founded on the social constellations and norms which constitute the power of individuals and the structures of authority within society.

It is, of course, possible to norm and establish systems of allegiance if power is idolised and identification with the leader is seen as the highest emotional and moral achievement and - this being commonly associated with it - domination over other peoples as the ultimate goal. Those structures, too, are, however, normative structures.

ILP as a form of normativism which regards norms as elements of institutional reality does not regard the three juristic thought models as in opposition to each other. Instead, it considers the normative approach, the level at which the juristic decision is viewed and the consideration of the institutional order as different aspects of juristic perception. For me, however, order does not constitute an aim in itself, nor does identification with the community mean allegiance to a leader with the purpose of dominating others and of consolidating the friend-enemy constellation.[89] Far from being the goal of political organisation the power of the individual is a factor necessary to accomplish the task assigned to him within society. It is for this reason that I insist on a determination of the powers vested in organs, of controls and norms of incompatibility, all of which are rejected by *Schmitt* as infringements of the leadership's power. Binding normative ties are essential for a communal organisation unless the intention is - as in the case of *C. Schmitt* - an allegiance identification within the organisation without legal protection or freedom for the individual as a precondition for war outside it.

Gehlen's, *Schelsky*'s and *Luhmann*'s theories are related to my own approach in as much as they start from the theory of action and interpret the problem of the institution i.e. of institutionalisation as a reflection of the relationship between individual and social action.

It seems to me that *Gehlen*'s and *Schelsky*'s theories complement the theses and conceptions of ILP to a large extent, that is, their findings do not conflict with the ontology of norms and legal theories of ILP although they view

---

89 See *Schmitt*'s political theory which is based on the concept of the friend-enemy distinction as the central content of politics, in: C. Schmitt, *Der Begriff des Politischen* (1932²), Berlin 1963. The fact that politics are also meant to create cooperative structures, a balance of interests and constellations for peace as forms of life in a society does not seem important to *Schmitt*. In my view politics concern both: friend-enemy structures and strategies as well as cooperative efforts and the creation of structures to ensure peace. I personally rate the peace-construction more highly and assess friend-enemy considerations from the point of view of peaceful and cooperative objectives.

the problem of the institutions from points of view which are different from those held by ILP.

The thesis of the institutions taking the place of instinctive behavioural control seems to me to be in need of amendment by a theory of structural systems provided by practical information forming the framework for the institutions.

On the basis of its formal-finalistic theory of action and its particular ontology of norms ILP is in the position of contributing the foundations for such a reassessment.

The sociologist takes note of situations where roles and obligations evolve, the proponent of the analytical norm-theory, on the other hand, takes an interest above all in the ideal structures and operations and occupies himself with their analysis. I, for my part, regard the sociological method and the norm-logical analysis as interlocking approaches to the same problem-complex.

The structural theory of action is ideally suited to providing the common point of departure for the investigations of both domains, legal theory and sociology. On this basis the sociological explanation of the phenomena adhering to institutionalisation would become an integral part of the juristic explanation of the existence and the mechanisms of the law while the analysis of normative processes would form an element of the sociological understanding of the institutions.

In two points *Schelsky* is even closer to ILP than *Gehlen*:

1. *Schelsky* devotes explicit attention to the interaction between the volition and the action of the individual and the constitution and the activities of the institutions. ILP is inclined to go even further in this respect: instead of characterising the structures of the respective argumentation as a circle of action it would wish to study them in more detail.

2. *Schelsky* regards the law as a constituent aspect to be taken into consideration in every sociological study. This position is close to the ontological conception of ILP. While *Schelsky* considers the legal normative element as a real constituent of the institutions and of all social phenomena ILP prefers a broader formulation for its thesis of the internal interaction of institutions and social phenomena, on the one hand, and normative rule-systems, on the other: it points to the contribution made by practical informations to the constitution and the structuring of the institutions. In the opinion of ILP, it does not always, therefore, have to be the legal system that plays the leading part in the regulation of the institutions, other normative rules can form the basis of an institution equally well. This broader conception by ILP implies that it is important also to consider the relations between different systems of practical informations which might become simultaneously relevant to the functioning of the institution under certain circumstances (for instance, the law and the ethos of the judge in the administration of justice).

Although *Gehlen* and *Schelsky* did not develop an ontology, semantics or logic of norms or, as it were, of the law, it appears to me that their theories are in essence compatible with the respective conceptions of ILP. Clearly, the same cannot be said to apply to *Luhmann*'s tenets. His attempt to explain the norms with the help of purely descriptive concepts leads inevitably to his denial of the semantic distinction between 'is' and 'ought'. In this respect his views are not compatible with ILP; in fact, any explanation of the institutions with its central thesis of the interdependence of the personal and material essence of the institutions, on the one hand, and their practical information system, on the other, is opposed to *Luhmann*'s theory. Nevertheless, his system-theoretical observations are certainly of interest even to ILP in as far as they refer to the origins and the function of the interplay between the actions of individuals and those of complex systems. In brief, one might say: the system-theoretical approach becomes compatible with ILP and appears useful from the point of view of its theory as soon as the system-theoretical analysis adopts the semantic differentiation of descriptive and practical informations which is vital for the entire context of action and integrates it into its theoretical system.

8. INSTITUTIONAL NORMATIVISM AND SOCIOLOGY

I am going to conclude my analysis of the relations between ILP and the institutional theories of jurisprudence and sociology with a very general thesis concerning the dependence of the whole of sociology on the fundamental theses of institutional normativism.

Undoubtedly, certain elements of the institutional ontology of norms are already firmly established as constituent parts of various sociological theories. Among these are, for instance, the thesis of the inextricable link between individual and communal actions, the thesis of the dependence on institutionalised rule-systems of the relationship between man and social institutions, as well as the thesis suggesting that the existence of symbols and their psychological and sociological functions is grounded in institutionalised rule-systems.

My own postulates regarding sociological theory which are derived from the institutional ontology of norms are more far-reaching, however, they are summed up in the following theses:

Sociological questions, whether directly or indirectly, always refer to a context of actions. While it may appear that certain questions have the character of straightforward statistical and behaviourist description (as in the case of crime statistics), the purpose and the function of studies of this kind, possibly even the methodology of the analysis and of the explication of phenomena are, in my opinion, to be found, at least, implicitely, in the realm of action.[90] We must proceed, therefore, from a theory of action, which takes into account the following theses[91]:

---

[90] To show this in detail would go beyond the natural framework of this discourse.

[91] See O. Weinberger, *Studien zur formal-finalistischen Handlungstheorie*, Frankfurt a.M./Bern/New York 1983; also, Eine Semantik für die praktische Philosophie, *Grazer philosophische Studien* 20/1983, pp. 219-239; also, Freedom, Range of Action and the Ontology of Norms, *Synthese* 65 (1985), pp. 307-324.

(a) Action must be seen as information-dependent behaviour, and specifically as intended for a particular purpose in an area where there is scope for action alternatives.

(b) Systems of action determine a subject's actions on the basis of two kinds of criteria: first, on the basis of finalistic utility-analyses and, secondly, on the basis of fixed programs of action, fixed goals, autonomous or heteronomous norms and others. This means that various and often complex connections exist between the two kinds of determinants.

(c) The actions and the principles which they are based on (rules of behaviour), are, at least partly, socially orientated. The individual acts *sua sponte* as *zoon politicon* while the content of his intentions and principles frequently results from the internalisation of social norms and standards engendered by imitation and education.

(d) There are communal actions of a variety of structures (to set up models of these structures must be seen as an urgent task for sociology) which are essentially analogous to individual actions. The fundamental prerequisite for a potential introduction of the concept of collective action and for the organs to be regarded as those who perform the collective actions is a formalist theory of action. Only by conceiving of actions as rational acts of information-processing can a subject be said to act as an organ in accordance with the intentions of the collective, i.e. in accordance with intentions other than his own.

(e) Sociology must not restrict itself to describing behavioural processes and noting their statistical regularities. The following requirements indicate clearly that sociology cannot get along with descriptions in a purely descriptive language: the need to have regard to the contexts of action which implies the necessity of focussing on practical informations (norms, values, goals); the task of understanding social events as well as analysing linguistic and other symbolic communications as determining elements of social events.

(f) In this sense sociology belongs into the sphere of action related disciplines. It requires a linguistic equipment capable of coping with the duality of theoretical (purely descriptive) and practical informations (principles, concepts).[92] Like every action-relative discipline it requires gnoseologically differentiated semantics.

(g) The problem of the institutions - as places where individual and community are in essential contact - as well as the processes of institutionalisation are key questions for every kind of sociology. In this context institutionalisation must not, however, be regarded as a mere matter of customs and statistical regularity. Instead, it must be emphasised that institutionalisation has to do in essence with ought-, value- and goal components. It is not only observable behaviour but also the practical attitudes connected with it that sociology must give account of. In respect of the momentum of institutionalisation it is important to

---

[92] Compare my comments in the works mentioned in ftn. 91 and: Tatsachen und Tatsachenbeschreibungen. Eine logisch-methodologische Überlegung zu einem Grundlagenproblem der Sozialwissenschaft, in: K. Salamun (ed.), *Sozialphilosophie als Aufklärung, FS für Ernst Topitsch*, Tübingen 1979, pp. 173-187.

take account of the interplay of rational argumentation and social interests. It is essential for the process of institutionalisation which aspires to relative permanence while also being subject to evolution and transformation that there should be cooperation between the individual (his attitudes, concepts and programs) and the communities as those responsible for the process of institutionalisation.

(h) In the realm of sociological problems which is largely concerned with the interrelationship between individual and social acts, i.e. institutional relations, the approach of the theory of action entails the additional need for system-theoretical considerations. In my view, these have to be conducted in such a way, however, as to prevent the fundamental connections between pure description which is vital for the practical sphere and practical informations, especially normative regulatives, from falling victim to a behaviourist reductionism.

VIII. SOCIOLOGY AND THE NORMATIVE INSTITUTIONAL THEORY
REFLECTIONS ON HELMUT SCHELSKY'S INSTITUTIONAL THEORY FROM THE POINT OF VIEW OF THE NORMATIVE INSTITUTIONAL ONTOLOGY

INTRODUCTION

I should like to make some observations about the theory of the institutions, about theoretical sociology and the system-theoretical approach to social and legal problems from the point of view of my theory of action and my ontology of norms.[1]

I shall also deal with the role of the law in *Helmut Schelsky*'s teachings as well as with the relationship between his theory and Niklas *Luhmann*'s system-theoretical approach to the problems of legal sociology.

1. BEHAVIOUR AND ACTION

The concept of behaviour can be defined so broadly that it is possible to speak not only of the behaviour of a certain person or of a collective, but also of the behaviour of any system. The behaviour of a system is characterised by descriptions of states as well as by the representation of chronological sequences of states, i.e. behaviour trajectories. Descriptions of behaviour in the above sense can be interpreted mainly as statements of the results of observations. On the basis of the behaviour trajectories of an observed system - or of a class of the same kind of systems - it is possible to ascertain correlations of the frequency of states and other peculiarities of the behavioural process - like, for instance, cyclical recurrence .

Our understanding of the observed behaviour can, however, go beyond the framework of such descriptions. Behaviour is observed in its dependence on a variety of potential influences on the system. Depending on the preceding input different branches of the behaviour trajectory can be reached. Reality as an object of cognition is not only made up of what is actually in existence but also of the potentialities connected with this existence. Beyond mere statements of what

---

[1] For my conception of the theory of actions see: O. Weinberger, *Studien zur formal-finalistischen Handlungstheorie*, Frankfurt a.M./Bern/New York 1983, also Chapter VI of this volume; for the ontology of norms and the legal-theoretical conception resulting from it compare: O. Weinberger, Ontología de las normas en la perspectiva de la theoría de la acción, in: *Akten des ersten Internationalen Kongresses für Rechtsphilosophie in La Plata,* vol. 2, La Plata 1982, pp. 544-566; the same, Eine Semantik für die praktische Philosophie, in: R. Haller (ed.), Beiträge zur Philosophie von Stephan Körner, *Grazer Philosophische Studien*, vol. 20, 1983, pp. 219-239; D.N. MacCormick/O. Weinberger, *Grundlagen des Institutionaliustischen Rechtspositivismus*, Berlin 1985; English version: *An Institutional Theory of Law. New Approaches to Legal Positivism*, Dordrecht 1986.

actually exists descriptions of behaviour are also able to encompass potential behaviour, dispositions and characteristic aspects of behaviour under contrary-to-fact conditions. The justification for statements of disposition, contrary-to-fact theses - as well as their refutation - are based on the premise that nomic relations are valid in the real world.[2] The same applies to prognoses. A view of the world which encompasses nomic connections in its events must inevitably transcend facts, being founded on theoretical construction and empirically tested hypotheses. The scientific conception of life rather than being a mere statement of reality provides access to a cognition of reality in a comprehensive fact-transcendent sense: reality is also what is empirically possible and empirically necessary, namely the nomic relations in the world recognised by science in a process of approximation.

Behavioural laws are constructed in such a way as to assign empirically necessary concommitant circumstances or resulting conditions to certain systems of basic conditions which are depicted in descriptions of behaviour.[3] The system of behavioural descriptions is closed: nothing but factual description can occur in it.

The behaviourist approach in psychology and sociology ought to be aware of this fundamental limitation: In this point of view there is no room for anything other than descriptions of behaviour and what relates to these. Traditional psychological concepts linked with experience, understanding, intention, functionality of purpose or interpretation of meaning have no place at all in it. The same applies to sociology: meaning, function, social acts, norms, values, institutions etc. cannot be constituted conceptually in a view of the world consisting of nothing but descriptions of behaviour and their interrelations. Neither is there any room in the straightforward observation of behaviour for a concept of action as purposeful behaviour dependent on informations, evaluating responses and acts of decision.

The concept of action cannot be defined by mere descriptions of behaviour. Not even the additional reference to contrary-to-fact moments is sufficient to determine the concept of action. We may, indeed, speak of an action of subject *S* only if the contrary-to-fact claim that the result of the action would not have occurred unless *S* had behaved in a particular manner[4] is proved correct;

---

[2] Compare O. Weinberger, Kontrafaktualität und Faktentranszendenz. Versuch, die Logik der faktentranszendentalen und kontrafaktualen Bedingungssätze mit den Mitteln der extensionalen Logik zu behandeln (English version: Contrary-to-fact and Fact-Transcendent Conditionals. An Attempt to Deal with the Logic of Fact-Transcendent and Contrary-to-fact Conditionals by Means of Truth-functional Logic), in: *Ratio* 16, 1974, pp. 13-28 (English edition pp. 15-32); the same, Faktentranszendente Argumentation, *Zeitschrift für allgemeine Wissenschaftstheorie* 6, 1975, pp. 235-251.

[3] Compare N. Rescher, Lawfulness as Mind-dependent, in: the same (ed.), *Essays in Honour of Carl G. Hempel*, Dordrecht 1969, pp. 178-197; O. Weinberger, Der nomische Allsatz, in: *Grazer Philosophische Studien*, 4, 977, pp. 31-42.

[4] G.H. v. Wright, Handlungslogik. Ein Entwurf, in: the same, *Handlung und Intention. Untersuchungen zur deontischen Logik*, Berlin/New York 1977, pp. 87 ff.

but in this instance we are dealing merely with a necessary condition, not with a sufficient one. If driver *D* passes out because of a heart attack and his resulting behaviour *B* causes a collision with another car, it would be correct to make the contrary-to-fact statement: "If the driver *D* had not behaved in the way *B* the collision would not have occurred"; to claim, however, that driver *D* had taken an action leading to the collision is by no means justified. - It may be true to say that action is behaviour - it is, after all, possible to characterise it as behaviour-trajectory - but such a representation is only partially true. A behavioural description of this kind represents that aspect of action which is accessible to external observation, not, however, the action as a whole; for that the data-related constituent which determines the manner of action by a data-processing operation is of the essence.

In principle there is fairly general agreement on the view that action is behaviour directed by information. It is, therefore, in the structural theory of the information operation on the basis of which the action is performed that the essence of the concept of action is to be found. In detail the views of those advancing theories of action are considerably at variance.

I would like to distinguish between three types of approach to the problem of action:

(i) the intuitive approach, according to which we are immediately familiar from every-day life with actions and the processes of volition determining them; all we have to do, therefore, in order to be able to formulate a theory of action, is to examine our intuition analytically and present it systematically.

(ii) the explication of the phenomena of action based on a theory of learning with its tendency toward behaviourist reductionism;

(iii) the formal-finalist theory of action, with its starting point in an information-theoretical analysis of the operations determining and guiding actions and its basis in the fundamental thesis that these data-processing operations deal with semantically different informations, e.g.:

1. factual informations and
2. practical informations expressing selective functions, evaluations, attitudes, purposes, guide-lines, norms, preferences etc.

In my view the third way alone leads to a useful theory of action and to an adequate conception of practical philosophy.

A theory of action must not be psychologically defined; instead, it has to be founded formalistically, as it is on this basis alone, that the informational structures and the operations determining the actions can be properly clarified. In addition, there are other important reasons for a formalist foundation of the theory of action. A theory of action ought not to be just a theory of individual actions, but it must also provide the basis for the explication of social actions, the actions of collectives, of juristic personalities and of various other institutionalised systems. This cannot be achieved by a psychologically based theory. It is only on the basis of a formally conceived theory that it is possible to explain actions performed in accordance with the purposes of others, in other words, phenomena like the actions performed by organs and by proxy in the name and the interest of other subjects.

The intentionality of action has to be regarded as its essence. Action pursues purposes; this has to be regarded as the fundamental characteristic of action, even where additional elements, such as habits, norms and others have to be taken into consideration as determinants of action. Causal and system-theoretical theories - despite rejecting on principle a finalist conception of action - also implicitely employ concepts of a teleological kind: purposes, goals, intentions, motives etc. (interpreting them, though, as a kind of cause).

The explication of action has to avail itself, above all, of a formal teleological theory which analyses the relationship between purpose and means as well as alternatives of choice on the basis of relative evaluation. Far from being concerned with the psychological or physical attributes of men as subjects of teleological systems and as acting personalities this formal theory determines what attributes a subject has to have in order to be regarded as the subject of a teleological system or an acting personality; such a subject must have the capacity to realize the relevant information-processing operation.

From the point of view of a formal theory of finality it is of no consequence whether or not the data and the operations are consciously experienced processes. Depending on the application they may be; otherwise their role is only that of thought-models which grasp the teleological background of actions by comprehending it.

Formal teleology - which cannot be depicted even in outline within the present framework - is based on evaluative functions: the capacity to plan toward purposes, to make relative evaluations and the associated ability to make choices.[5]

In proceeding from the formal theory of action it is possible to consider action from a variety of perspectives. The following problem situations are of fundamental importance in this respect:

(i) the deliberations preceding the actions, in the course of which alternatives of behaviour are determined and programs as well as choices are fixed in accordance with purposes;

(ii) the interpretation of motives seeking to grasp the behaviour of the acting subject as intentional actions from the outside, as it were.

(iii) the need to explain the interplay of various factors determining the action, in addition to purposes, especially normative regulatives, as well as both seemingly and actually irrational elements;

(iv) the question, when an action appears to be justifiable, having to be asked, on the one hand, from the perspective of a moral consideration, on the other hand, on the basis of assessing the action from the point of view of a heteronomous system of norms.

The problem of the time factor is of particular interest in teleology. The program, like the question what is realizable, what purposes can be achieved,

---

5 An approximate characterisation or formal teleology is to be found in: Ch. Weinberger/O. Weinberger, *Logik, Semantik, Hermeneutik*, München 1979 (Chap. 8. "Formale Teleologie"); or O. Weinberger, *Rechtslogik*, 2nd ed., Berlin 1989, Chap. 11; compare also Chap. II of this volume, pp. 63 f.

and similar questions have to be analysed in relation to time factors by their very nature. In addition, even the goal-systems themselves, the fixing of purposes and their importance which varies in accordance with their place in the time sequence also have to be studied more closely. This constitutes one of the necessary bridges between the purely formal teleology and its practical application for the purpose of analysing human actions and social relations.

2. THE LANGUAGE OF PRACTICAL PHILOSOPHY

The term 'practical philosophy' implies more for me than theories attempting to answer the question how man should act; it goes beyond ethics and jurisprudence, in other words. The term comprises, in my opinion, the entirety of philosophical analyses and scientific disciplines central to which is the concept of action. I, therefore, class economics and sociology among aspects of practical philosophy.

In order to represent the information processes underlying actions we have to work with two kinds of informations:

(i) factual informations and

(ii) practical informations expressing value standards, preferences (the results of relative evaluation), goals, purposes and norms.

The proof for this important thesis is easily provided. *Ex definitione* action exists only where behavioural alternatives, i.e. a scope for action[6] exists. Subject *S* acts, and acts only, if the behaviour of *S* determines on the basis of the information processing operation which one of the potential behavioural alternatives is to be chosen and realized. This cannot take place on the basis of a mere statement of facts, but clearly only with the help of some kind of evaluative information .

The fact that information-linked operations for the purpose of determining and directing actions comprise two categories of informations means that practical philosophy requires a language which distinguishes clearly between factual and attitudinal sentences in order to express the respective informations. It is customary to place these disjointed sentence categories into juxtaposition as theoretical and practical sentences. I shall refer to the semantics based on such a categorical distinction between sentences as 'gnoseologically differentiated semantics'. These are non-reist semantics, e.g. semantics which do not assume every linguistic expression to refer to an existing object or to a factual situation consisting of objects. Reist semantics constitute a point of view which does not lead only to the hypostasation of pseudo-entities - as does, for instance, *Meinong*'s ontology[7] - but gives also support to a totally misconceived conception

---

[6] For the problem of scope for action see: O. Weinberger, Semantik für die praktische Philosophie, *op.cit.*; the same, Freedom, Range for Action and the Ontology of Norms, *Synthese*, 65 (1985), pp. 307-324.

[7] A. Meinong, Über Gegenstandstheorie, in: the same, *Untersuchungen zur Gegenstandstheorie*, Leipzig 1904; the same, in: R. Schmidt (ed.), *Die Philosophie der Gegenwart in Selbstdarstellungen*, vol. I, Leipzig 1922, pp. 101-160.

of practical philosophy. In the basis of this kind of semantics values, norms, purposes are regarded as objects per se, to be examined, assessed and acknowledged; in reality they are not objects as such with an objective existence and relevance but specific meanings playing a part in practical thinking without a referential character, i.e. a character designating objects.

This results in significant consequences for certain norm-logical and legal-methodological conceptions. (i) Assessments of norms don't express perceptions of normative entities existing per se, instead, they constitute either meta-linguistic sentences about normative sentences or, having to be individualised (albeit *modo obliquo*), they represent an inadequate way of expressing normative contents. (ii) Theories like Kelsen's juxtaposition of 'legal norm' *('Rechtsnorm')* and 'legal sentence' *('Rechtssatz')* are ill-conceived considering that to grasp a norm is to understand a normative sentence, not to judge it or to express an opinion on a norm (on an ought-reality).[8]

The gnoseologically differentiated semantics distinguish between (a) a meaningful norm (as the correlative meaning of a normative sentence well-formed in the language system) and (b) norms which are given an existence, i.e. validity in a certain system. Valid norms belong, of course, to the class of norms which are linguistically meaningful, i.e. have a potential existence. However, in neither of the two perspectives the norm is an object that exists per se or is recognisable as such; instead, the norm is always an ideal entity capable of being grasped only by comprehending it.

Norms which are valid (in existence) in a system do not have to be present in a linguistic formulation. It must be possible in principle, though, to express them linguistically as meaningful normative ideas. It is generally accepted that normative rules of conduct can be effective and determine actions without the subject of the action being explicitely conscious of them.[9] If that is the case they can be represented in an interpretative reconstruction under certain circumstances.

This fundamental semantic conception is faced with the task of explicating the different basic principles of language expressing attitudes or that part of the language that expresses practical information. It is the theory of the operations underlying the determination and the control of actions that clarifies the meaning of 'value', 'purpose', 'norm' ('ought', 'may'), and how these concepts relate to each other.

---

[8] O. Weinberger, Intersubjektivität, Kommunikation, Normenlogik und Normendynamik, in: *Rechtstheorie* 8, 1977, pp. 19-70; also reproduced in: I. Tammelo/H. Schreiner (eds.), *Strukturierungen und Entscheidungen im Rechtsdenken*, Wien/New York 1978, pp. 235-263.

[9] Compare L. Wittgenstein, *Philosophische Untersuchungen*, in: the same, *Schriften I*, Frankfurt a.M. 1969, pp. 82 ff.

3. NORMATIVE INSTITUTIONAL ONTOLOGY

The general conception of the institutions forming the basis of my reflections can be characterised briefly by the following points:

(i) *The Action-theoretical Explication of the Institutions*

Institutions can be understood only if regarded as elements in a context of actions. They determine the framework for possible actions, they create forms of action and interaction, and they play a part as determinants of action.

(ii) *The Institution acts as a Link between Individual and Community*

Man is a communal being; institutions provide the context for the interaction of individual and community. Collectives, communal action and various forms of interaction only exist as institutions. The actions of the individual, his way of life is, at least partially, determined by an institutional framework of action even where he acts in isolation as an individual like, for instance, when he is learning, playing patience or jogging.

(iii) *The Dependence of the Institutions on Practical Informations*

It is impossible to define the nature of the institutions by mere descriptions of behaviour. Behavioural processes and their regularities or statistical frequency cannot fully and appropriately characterise the institutions. Institutions like, for instance, the law, the family, money, a company, the university or certain games can only function in the context of the normative regulatives they are based on. This thesis is what I regard as key sentence of my conception of the institution. I, therefore, describe my approach as a 'normative institutional theory'. As structures of action the institutions can only function on the basis of the respective practical informations. The institutional theory cannot characterise the objects of its investigation appropriately and sufficiently by descriptions of behaviour; instead, it must expose the practical informations as the substance of the institutions and present them in an explicite form.

The law, like other social normative systems, is an institutional fact. To them - trivial as it may appear - the key sentence of my conception is applicable: they are normative systems not systems of actual behaviour. My conception, therefore, conflicts with the view of some legal realists suggesting that the law sets out prognoses about the future conduct of the legal staff. Social norms have to be accorded an institutional existence on account of their effective connection with the real systems of actions (possibly potential actions). Institutions in the usual sense - *Hauriou* distinguishes between 'institutions-personnes' and 'institutions-choses'[10] - are complex: they are based on a system of normative rules which determines their structures and regulates, on the one hand, the actions of the institutions (of a corporate body, for instance), and, on the other, the behaviour of the persons within the institutions in relation to each other as their members; furthermore, they have a material and a personal core content. Institutions serve a purpose; they can, consequently, be explained by expounding their functions.

---

[10] M. Hauriou, Die Theorie der Institution und der Gründung. Essay über den sozialen Vitalismus, in: the same, *Die Theorie der Institution*, ed. by R. Schnur, Berlin 1965.

I shall use the typical example of the game of chess in order to demonstrate the fact that the normative conception of the institutions does not only rest on a fixed concept in accordance with which institutions have to comprise practical informations on account of their action-related function, but that it is also possible for the essence of the practical significance of institutions to be shown in concrete terms:

Games are institutions; frameworks for a certain activity or a regulated interaction between players introduced on an *ad hoc* basis - or most often - on a relatively permanent one. The rules of the game of chess are defined by its basic conditions: chessboard, figures, starting positions, rules of operation etc. We might ask whether these rules should be regarded as normative rules or as definitions. If they were mere definitions the person who does not adhere to the rules would not be seen as infringing the "duty of the chess-player", but simply as not playing chess.[11] It is true that nobody is obliged to play chess; the rules of chess apply to the players not as a system imposed by society but only as a result of a voluntary participation in the game; but they are relevant for the possibility of setting acts since they lay down a behaviour in accordance with a duty and define the class of possible results of the game: the game which is won (or lost).

I should like to emphasise that no description of the chess-player's behaviour (in the past, present or future), however complete, will ever define the essence of the game of chess. Only by comprehending the rules is it possible to understand the game as an institution with a specific structure.

In analogy with other institutions - like, for instance, the law - the normative regulative of the game of chess determines the framework of the actions taken in the game, the intentions of the players - e.g. to checkmate the opponent -, not, however, the actions themselves; that is a matter for other - socalled strategic - rules. The actions taken in the game are subject to the decisions made by the player and they depend on his inventiveness and strategy. In everyday life, too, it is not the legal rules alone that determine how best to conduct oneself in the framework of the law.

(iv) *Roles and Institutions*

Roles may be regarded as elements of institutions. They are more than just modes of behaviour put into practice, as a rule, by people in certain positions: they constitute patterns of behaviour in two ways: (1) as the usual modes of behaviour of certain types of people in a particular role, and (2) as rules stipulating how these people are to conduct themselves in their roles.

Roles are not only patterns for the normal behaviour of role-players but they also encompass ought, may and can, as well as goals and role-related value standards. Consequently, roles have a connection with practical informations in

[11] There is no logically clearly defined distinguishing line between the defining framework and the rules of the system. It is more of a useful distinction for the manner of representation to differentiate between definition and normative rules in the constitution of games (or other institutions). In any case, it has to be stressed that the rules of games also comprise normative provisions (apart from definitions). For this problem see Chap. I of this volume, pp 36 f..

particular, mainly with legal as well as moral postulates. Role-players are not merely be expected to adhere to specific modes of behaviour, but it is also demanded of them.

Role-consciousness implies more than a system of specific patterns of behaviour; it also means the awareness of a task, of duties and of responsibility.

The analysis of roles and role-consciousness has a number of different aspects. From the psychological point of view the consciousness of role-related duties is not only a constituent of the individual's way of life but also the basis for a contented life. Role-consciousness and role-behaviour are vital building-blocks of social relations. The evaluation of balance in the interplay of roles constitutes a decisive factor in the analysis of justice.[12]

(v) *Institution, Institutionalisation; Stability and Change*

Action is, in fact, only possible within the context of an, at least, relatively stable framework and on the basis of stabilised patterns of behaviour. Action shows a certain tendency to evolve certain forms of behaviour. Procedures which have been tested, learned and practised tend to be retained as long as there is no motive for modifying them. While action has to be regarded in principle as goal-directed, neither the teleological consideration nor the determination of the mode of action requires the repeated reopening of the teleological analysis; instead, they put into practice blocks of well-rehearsed procedures in a combination suitable for the solution of the tasks in hand.

There is a fundamental tendency in the realm of the institutions and the social relations connected with them to adhere to forms of interaction and to live by the models of behaviour which have become habitual. To examine the precise way in which the process of institutionalisation takes place is the task of sociology. The course of events central to this process is based on the fundamental tendency to repetition and stabilisation which we have already referred to; otherwise the process of institutionalisation can be expected to occur in a variety of ways depending on the kind of institution and the given situation.

Institutionalisation implies a certain stabilisation of institutions, roles, modes of action and interaction. It may appear - and, it is true to say, that the problem is, indeed, frequently seen in this way -, that institutions can be defined as the products of institutionalisation. I myself tend to the view, however, that the essence of the institution and the social process of institutionalisation ought to be treated as two separate, albeit usually related, questions. Even in individual situations it is possible for a system of rules of interaction to evolve which can be considered as an institution, no matter whether or not it becomes a stable and permanent institution. Interactions and *ad hoc* communities should not be excluded from institutional theory - considering that they constitute frameworks of action in a similar way to established institutions. In addition, they occasionally provide the basis for permanent institutions.

No doubt, tendencies to stabilise institutions do exist in society; and the question of stabilisation is doubtlessly important in terms of legal policy. How-

---

[12] Compare Chap. X. Para 8 of this volume.

ever, stable and unstable institutions ought to form the object of the institutional theory in equal measures.

In some legal-political and system-theoretical approaches the attainment of stability of institutions or systems is regarded as the crucial criterion for the successful functioning of an institution. Other scholars emphasise instead that institutions must have a capacity for internal change. I am of the opinion that it is an essential aspect of effective and especially of democratic institutions that they realize such changes as an internal process within the institution. I am aware that institutions have a certain ideal basis in the sense of an *idée directrice*, that the governing idea usually remains in existence and that it is frequently only the tactics of its implementation that change. Despite the tendency for the governing idea to resist superficial changes in the institution it appears, nevertheless, possible and at times necessary to me that institutions including their governing ideas are completely changed.

(vi) *Institutional Realities*

Institutions create new facts, in part, that is, in the form of real objects with specific functions (for instance, money, chess figures, schools), partly as normative rules concerning behaviour and authority, partly as modes of behaviour, or, in other words, as elements of a way of life. Other facts come into being which cannot be adequately presented by physical or chemical descriptions: I am referring to institutional facts.[13] Institutional facts are elements of human reality.

(vii) *The Institutional Existence of Social Norms*

The validity of social norms rests on their relationship with the institutions. A norm, as such, for instance, a legal norm, exists in the social reality precisely when it exerts an effect on the institution in its relations with it. The validity of a legal norm rests neither on an expectation based on a prognosis about the future behaviour of the legal staff - as some legal realists believe -, nor on a merely ideal existence based on an assumption, - as pure normativism asserts; instead, it rests on the intrinsic fusion of norm and reality within the institution.

(viii) *The specific "Life" of Institutions*

Institutions are subject to certain social dynamics. Brought about by institutional realities new situations arise, new possibilities for action and potentially new experiences of actions occur. Institutions evolve and branch out, frequently altering their structures and functions in the course of that process. Brought about by the impact of the institution, as a result of the combination of several different institutions, or by means of other socially relevant elements new needs arise; these in turn bring into being new institutions or cause the transformation of existing ones.

---

[13] G.E.M. Anscombe, On Brute Facts, *Analysis* 18, 3, 1958, pp. 69-72; J.R. Searle, *Speech Acts. An Essay in the Philosophy of Language*, Cambridge 1969; O. Weinberger, Ausgangspunkte des Institutionalistischen Rechtspositivismus, D.N. MacCormick, Das Recht als institutionelle Tatsache, both in: D.N. MacCormick/O. Weinberger, *Grundlagen des Institutionalistischen Rechtspositivismus*, Berlin 1985, pp. 11-56; pp. 76-107.

These are not the only dynamics characterising the individual life of the institutions. It is not only a question of new forms and potentials of behaviour coming into being; some forms of procedure, some attitudes and ways of living will equally lose their basis and their function. Under certain circumstances the individual life of the institution may, on the other hand, be reflected in its adherence to established modes of behaviour even after they have lost their function.

(ix) *Institution and System*

Institutions have to be considered as a system of relations and at the same time as having meaningful, functional and informative characteristics.

4. THE ROLE OF THE LAW IN SCHELSKY'S THEORY

The concept of law plays a central role in *Schelsky*'s tenets. I want to focus on three areas where this concept is of fundamental relevance to him:

- the conception of the general theoretical sociology,
- the theory of the institutions,
- the role he ascribes to the law as guarantor of personal freedom.

(i) *Sociology and Law*

For the general sociological theory *Schelsky* postulates that it ought not to regard the law simply as the object of legal sociology but must also consider the law as an essential element of general theoretical sociology.[14] This thesis has certain affinities with my own conception particularly in view of the fact that *Schelsky*'s approach is, like my own, conceived of in terms of a theory of action. In using the observation of man's individual and social actions as a starting-point one inevitably reaches the conclusion that normative rules and other practical informations have to be taken into account for the elucidation of these phenomena. *Schelsky* accords this function to the law which he regards as the conscious regulation and organisation resulting from free and deliberate action. He doubts that the plurality of social norm-systems (customs, traditions, religious norms etc.) have developed from an originally unified system of norms, believing, at any rate, that from the beginning it has been the law alone that has been able to create social institutions through deliberate intentional action and that it is, in fact, even nowadays the sociologically decisive ought-system. In my view, it is not only the law but a variety of normative regulatives and their interplay in society and in the life of the individual that have to be taken into account. This approach results, in my opinion, in a more adequate picture of the legal reality as well as of the actual political world where religious norms and organisations play a not inconsiderable role, for instance. In our society the role of the law can be grasped adequately only, in my view, if the interaction of the

---

[14] Compare H. Schelsky, Systemfunktionaler, anthropologischer und personfunktionaler Ansatz in der Rechtssoziologie, in: the same, *Die Soziologen und das Recht*, Opladen 1980, p. 95.

law and other norm-systems is taken into consideration. This consideration occurs, at least, on two levels: on the level where certain principles of morality, custom, religion etc. become transformed into the legal system, and also on the level where the individual's behaviour - being influenced by the law and other normative regulatives - is determined. The judge, the political functionary and in many situations every individual citizen, they all act not only in accordance with the law but within the sphere of influence of many different normative regulatives. It is important in legal life that a judge regards his acts of deciding not only as a job but as a moral duty. In view of the fact that it is important to expect the simultaneousness and the interaction of a plurality of norm-systems in complex societies my approach is broader and more differentiated compared with *Schelsky*'s references to the role of the law. Moreover, it also takes its orientation from a different theory of action, that is, from a formal theory of action according to which the actions of individuals and social actions are structured in an analogous way while Schelsky seeks to understand the nature of action from studying the individual and human nature.[15]

(ii) *The Law and the Institution*

The concept of the interplay between individual and institution forms the core of *Schelsky*'s institutional theory - if I read him correctly; and this interaction is conceived of in action-theoretical terms. In some ways he continues from *Gehlen*, that is, in as far as he regards the institutions as necessary constituents and as the framework of human behaviour and actions coming into play as a result of the disappearance, or to be more correct, the very much reduced role, of their control by the instincts; he stresses, however, - in opposition to *Gehlen*, as he believes - the influence of the individual on the institution. The subject is not controlled onesidedly by the institutions, but it creates institutions itself which in turn contribute to the determination of the actions of individuals. "Concrete social facts of an institutional kind have a controlling and influencing impact on the individuals' structure of motivation and volition, while conversely, the individuals' subjective will and goal conceptions constantly determine and change the law, and even continually create new laws."[16] In view of the fact that *Schelsky* regards the relationship individual - society - law as a circular process he considers as irrelevant the question whether it is the institutional order or rather the consciousness of the individual engaged in the social action that constitutes the primary basis of the law. *Schelsky* - unlike *Santi Romano*[17], for instance, - does not identify the institution with the law, but recognises clearly the institutional character of the law as well as the role of the law in the development of institutions and in establishing order.

---

15 H. Schelsky, *ibid.*, p. 95.
16 H. Schelsky, *ibid.*, p. 78.
17 S. Romano, *Die Rechtsordnung*, ed. by R. Schnur, Berlin 1975.

The law is a social mechanism for the orientation of the individual's actions; it is a social instrument for the stabilisation of what has evolved as well as being potentially a means of social change. Consequently it is involved in the formation, the change and the development of the institutions.

In basing the definition of his institutional theory on the theories of other authors *Schelsky* does not always make it clear whether he fully endorses the theory which he refers to.

He analyses the institutions from a functional and an institutional point of view. They fulfil anthropological or/and cultural needs. New institutions are brought into existence as a result of the needs created by the primary institutions. There is, in other words, something like a genetic stratification of the institutions.

Governing ideas play a key role for Schelsky as they do in the institutional theories of other scholars like *Malinowsky, Hauriou, Carl Schmitt*. They are the expression of the individual's creative participation in the constituting of institutions. They are not identical with existing needs. They establish functions and make possible a personalistic approach in the institutional theory as well as person-functional and politico-functional analyses of the institutions taking into consideration social functions and core ideas (i.e. possibly ideologies).

I agree that the governing ideas on which the institutions are based must not be identified with purposes and must not simply be regarded as the products of individual or social needs; they are, in fact, programmatic constructs dependent in essence on need-structures and incorporating goal-conceptions.

To produce ideas and models and to call into being institutions are anthropological necessities in *Schelsky*'s eyes.

Schelsky's starting-point is the thesis that sociological theories can, as a matter of principle, be based on two conceptual approaches: either on the notion of the social action or on the idea of the entirety of society.[18] He himself works on the basis of action-theoretical considerations. Among the holistically based theories he also counts - apart from the "organologists" - as he calls them - the system-theoretical approach to sociology. Elsewhere he mentions that it would be possible to formulate a typology of sociological theories by distinguishing between an approach seeking to explain social reality on the basis of the whole of society or on an individual basis. He himself seems to me to be wanting to overcome this alternative of sociological approaches in his own theory of cyclical interaction.

From my point of view there is not only interaction between individual persons and social entities but also a structural relationship between the two manners of explanation in as far as the formal theory of action concerns itself with individual as well as social actions. Neither does the system-theoretical approach appear, in my view, as an opposing position to the action-theoretical

---

[18] H. Schelsky, Zur soziologischen Theorie der Institution, in: the same, *Zur Theorie der Institution*, p. 10.

approach but rather as an attempt to explain individual, collective and social actions in their mutual and complex relations.

The three approaches considered feasible by *Schelsky* in legal sociology (by analogy potentially also generally in sociology): the system-functional approach, the anthropological and the person-functional approach - appear to me more as complementary and partial perspectives than as alternative conceptions.

(iii) *The Law from the Person-functional Point of View and as the Basis of Freedom*

Schelsky's view that the law can also be seen from the person-functional point of view and his demand for it to be considered in this way arise, on the one hand, from his conception of the relationship between individual and institution as a circular process, on the other hand, from his conviction of the anthropological necessity for the existence of ultimate goals for man which determine the nature of the law both functionally and in a certain sense in its content. It is, therefore, not only an anthropological fact that man creates institutions and for their constitution conceives of governing ideas which become social reality in the institutions with the respective laws evolving at the same time; there are also 'person-related governing ideas of the law' with an anthropological foundation protecting - as absolute purposes of the law - the position of the individual vis-à-vis other individuals and vis-à-vis society as well as the legal system. These postulated and immanent anthropologically grounded governing ideas are described by *Schelsky* as:

(a) durable reciprocity,
(b) equality with differentiation,
(c) integrity and autonomy of the person vis-à-vis organisation

This table of the governing ideas of the law is clearly connected with *Schelsky*'s understanding of the law as the basis of personal freedom and with the need to organise it in accordance with this anthropological nature of man. His characterisation of the law in terms of its anthropological function is, therefore, by no means ideologically indifferent and, consequently, also far more specific than, for instance, *Hart*'s anthropologico-functional characterisation of the law which he refers to as 'minimal content of natural law'.[19]

The governing ideas of the law I have mentioned are not regarded by *Schelsky*, not primarily, at least, as principles of legal philosophy or dogmatic principles but, above all, as a sociological characterisation, not as an aspect of legal history but from the point of view of structural logic. He is perfectly aware of the socio-programmatic natur of his theory.

The principle of reciprocity appears to be genetically and functionally of primary importance for the law. It creates the structure for 'giving' and 'receiving' with the tendency to institutionalisation. In addition there are elements of publicity: witnesses, ceremony and active guarantors, especially where the

---

[19] H.L.A. Hart, *The Concept of Law*, Oxford 1961, pp. 189 ff.

interests of third parties are involved and where institutional durability as well as enforceability are the aim.

'Equality with differentiation' is a slogan which defuses the difference between ruler and ruled with the help of the equality of the law; it constitutes the legalisation of power by submitting the power to the law with the resulting distribution of power and the guaranteed freedom for the individual person. The law as means of protecting the individual against the constraints of society in the form of domination has, according to *Schelsky*, largely been lost in the actual world. He considers the transformation of personal rights into organised rights and rights which are collectively institutionalised with the help of specific social organisations as typical for our social structure. From this situation the relevant governing idea arises which *Schelsky* invests with special political relevance nowadays, namely the postulate of the integrity and the autonomy of the individual vis-à-vis the social order. He makes a plea in favour of the free personality and against its disintegration and diffusion into a system of social roles which would imply the control over the individual by the respective role-related institutions.

In my opinion this raises a fundametnal structural and political problem: in order to safeguard particular role-interests and to protect the role-functions as well as the person as the subject of the role particular organisations are required; however, the very existence of these organisations often turns into a far-reaching restriction of personal freedom. Is there a way of combining harmoniously the organised enforcement of interests and the personal independence of the individual from these organisations? It is not, in my view, the dissolution of institutions serving the interests of particular groups that offers a path toward safeguarding personal autonomy, but an appropriate balance of functions between the institutions serving different interests and the general acknowledgement of the postulates stipulating personal autonomy as an element of the democratic way of life. The structure of the institutions has to comply with certain material democratic principles (i.e. the demand for the protection of minorities following a free, opinion-forming discussion).

5. SCHELSKY AND LUHMANN'S SYSTEM-THEORETICAL METHOD

It appears to me that *Schelsky* - on the basis of his pluralist approach - accepts a conflictless coexistence of the anthropological and the person-functional point of view in legal sociology; the same does not apply entirely to the system-theoretical function-analysis which he finds particularly in *Luhmann*'s theory. While he acknowledges the significance of system-theoretical analyses he does so with marked reservations and fundamental doubts about their pragmatic relevance and applicability. Some of these misgivings he has formulated explicitely, others appear to be the implicite cause of his reserved if not dismissive response, without him ever having presented a genuine discussion on the subject. I can't help feeling that *Schelsky*, on the one hand, considers it requisite to deal with *Luhmann*'s theory critically, while having difficulties, on the other hand, in conducting such a discussion convincingly across the entire spectrum of differences of opinion. He has expressed criticism on some of *Luhmann*'s ideas but without arriving at a genuine critique of *Luhmann*'s approach.

Schelsky was not only a theoretical sociologist but also an empiricist. I regard him as an eminent political thinker whose theory was meant to serve as the basis for empirical research whilst offering at the same time a world view with political perspectives. He was not a formal thinker. It is not surprising, therefore, that *Luhmann*'s theory appeared alien and ultimately sterile to him.

Luhmann's theory appears principally as an empirical theory; it is intended to describe structural realities rather than presenting the speculative metaphysics of society and the law. It is not, however, an operational empirical theory. Its basic concepts are not operationally determined. It is a comprehending and explicative system in formal terminology, rather than a system of hypotheses tested step by step by empirical observation. In this respect I fully appreciate *Schelsky*'s doubts.

Schelsky conceives of action in terms of personality, seeing it as a function of conscious volition and autonomous deciding. Consequently he interprets system-theoretical analyses as the opposite position to the action-theoretical point of view. The system-theoretical conception which, according to him reduces the person to one of the environmental facts, and compares functional equivalents without evaluating the differences between functionally equivalent structures appears to *Schelsky* as a formalist game inapplicable in practice and far from the reality of life. This interpretation may be reflected most clearly in the sentence: "In *Luhmann*'s system-theory all cats appear functionally grey."[20] Explications using terms like 'reduction of complexity' appear to him as a kind of magic spell serving to explain everything or nothing. With the emphasis of *Schelsky*'s considerations lying specifically on the sense and forms of life he cannot accept that - according to *Luhmann* - the law is valid only as a result of decisions reached in social and political procedures without taking account of the ideas and values of life encapsulated in the body of the law.

Luhmann's theory leads to the transformation of a number of classical concepts of legal theory and to the reinterpretation of various fundamental juristic problems. *Schelsky* - and many others with him - were taken aback by these two procedures. Is it possible - to mention only one example - to transform the problem of justice into a postulate of adequate complexity without causing amazement and objections? *Luhmann*'s thesis "a system has *adequate* complexity as a legal order to the degree it adapts its other variables to the extent of making it possible for consistent decisions to be taken"[21] means that the entire problem of justice is emptied of values since the consistency of decisions can be maintained on the basis of objectionable as well as of acceptable contents. Even a legal positivist cannot accept this premise in as far as he regards justice as a

---

[20] H. Schelsky, Die Soziologen und das Recht, *op.cit.*, p. 93.

[21] N. Luhmann, Gerechtigkeit in den Rechtssystemen der modernen Gesellschaft, *Rechtstheorie*, vol. 4, 1973, p. 153.

social task and the logical structure of *de-lege-ferenda*-arguments as a problem of analytical jurisprudence.[22]

I want to demonstrate with the help of two examples that *Luhmann*'s conceptual explications are problematical and, in my view, lead to an inappropriate shift of the problem area.

Complexity is defined in his "Legal Sociology" as the existence of more possibilities exist than can be put into practice.[23] Where he refers to the increase and the reduction of complexity, the problem of measurability becomes an important question. In 1973 he himself points out the problems in defining and measuring this concept:

"Any attempt to employ the intellectual means and the previous experiences of system-theory for the task of specification will be faced with the fact that it has not been possible to formulate an unambiguous, one dimensional-concept of complexity and to apply it logically or even empirically."... "In such a highly complex system of decisions in the province of the law where the complexity of its own system is problematical it is possible to distinguish between variables responsible for increasing the complexity and variables which show possibilities of reducing excessive complexity. In the following we have gathered together the most important variables for the purpose of providing an initial survey:
1. *the size of the system* in the sense of the variety of decisions taken or to be taken.
2. *the variety of the system* in the sense of the different kinds of decisions taken and to be taken;
3. *the interdependence within the system* in the sense of dependence between individual decisions;
4. *the degree of generalisation of the system's structure*, in other words, of the programmatic, organisational and personal premisses for the process of decision-taking and, depending on these, the number, variety and inter-dependence of the decisions potentially taken within the system and, depending on those, the extent of the system's self-selectivity; and
5. *the frequency and the tempo of the changes taking place in the premisses of decisions*."[24]

Does this concept provide for the complexity of systems to be measured or compared and ordered according to size? I doubt it, considering there is hardly any meaningful way of weighing up the relevance of the variables on

---

22 Compare O. Weinberger, Jenseits von Positivismus und Naturrecht, in: *Contemporary Conceptions of Law - 9th World Congress* (Basel 1979), *ARSP*, Supplementa, vol. 1 Part I, 1982, pp. 43-56.

23 N. Luhmann, *Rechtssoziologie*, p. 31: "Complexity shall be defined as the existence of more possibilities than can be realized." Similarly, but in greater detail on p. 6: "Here and in the following we shall regard as complexity the entirety of possible experiences and actions the realization of which permits a meaningful connection."

24 N. Luhmann, Gerechtigkeit in den Rechtssystemen der modernen Gesellschaft, *op. cit.*, Hamburg 1972, vol. 1, p. 43.

which the complexity is dependent. I do not, therefore, regard complexity - as *Luhmann* does - as a multi-dimensional concept, but as a kind of family concept which can be made applicable to a structural theory and meaningful for judgements about changes of complexity only where it is used with specific reference to the question to be analysed and to its operationalisation.

Furthermore, it appears to me that this concept of complexity is very different from the one used in *Luhmann*'s "Legal Sociology".

Luhmann tries to eliminate the traditional concept of the norm by a behaviourist-learning-theoretical explication of the concept and to explain it as a kind of expectation. "Norms are expectations which are stabilised contrary-to-fact." According to *Luhmann* there are essentially two kinds of expectations: cognitive and normative ones; there is no distinctive dividing-line between them. "Cognitive expectations are, therefore, marked by a readiness - albeit not necessarily a conscious one - to learn, normative expectations, in contrast, by the determination not to learn from disappointments."[25] Consequently it is, according to *Luhmann*, the manner of treating the disappointed expectation that is crucial. On the basis of this conception there is, of course, no clear differentiation between cognitive and normative expectation, neither, consequently, between 'being' and 'ought'.

When working with the concept of expectation one should always clarify whose expectation is under discussion. While, in principle only individual human beings have expectations it is also possible to refer by analogy to the expectations prevalent within a group. Expectations are essentially the results of learning processes - although the existence of genetically founded expectations cannot be ruled out. While it is possible for one and the same subject to expect a result with greater or smaller probability, normally there would always be only a single approach to the expectation. If somebody expects an event and it does not occur he is going to correct his idea of the regularity of events in this world or he is going to explain the disappointed expectation with the help of a supportive hypothesis. The idea of a contrary-to-fact stabilisation of expectations is, to my mind, preposterous. To decide not to learn from experience has nothing to do with norms but is simply the expression of a lack of common sense as well as being in conflict with the learning-theoretical approach. The fact that there is absolutely no relationship of the kind assumed by *Luhmann* between the social existence of norms and human expectations can be demonstrated in the following reflections: If a norm is valid the expectation - whether or not it is going to be fulfilled - can vary to a considerable degree without this exerting an influence on the validity of the norm. For instance, if in wartime the trading with a certain item is prohibited nobody is going to claim that this norm is not valid as a result of the expectation that there will be a black market. No doubt, there are expectations for individuals to behave in a certain way without allowing the conclusion that there are also equivalent norms. We expect, for instance, that people distort the truth in accordance with their advantages, which does not mean, however, that they ought to behave in this way. This independence of the

[25] N. Luhmann, Rechtssoziologie, *op.cit.*, p. 43.

reasonable expectation and the validity of the norms from each other proves that the norm cannot be defined by the concept of the expectation.

There can be little doubt about the coexistence of several separate social normative systems in a complex modern society. In basing the concept of the norm on the relevant expectation *Luhmann* makes it impossible to separate the normative systems from each other, the expectation being, so to speak, the single result of different factors.

It is a particularly crucial flaw of *Luhmann*'s conception that it does not allow at all for the sociologically important problem of the relationship between the socially valid norm and the assessment of the probability for its fulfilment to be addressed conceptually.[26]

Despite this criticism of the learning-theoretical conception of the norm I should like to emphasise that *Luhmann* deserves great credit for having made this contribution of drawing attention to the question of the expectation in connection with the norms and to have clarified the relevance of the expectations of the partners in the interactive relationship in addition to those of the actors.

The system-theoretical access to an approach to the law can be formulated in different ways:

1. as one of several possible analyses of the legal institutions, or as a theory which alone represents the essence of legal theory;
2. as a theory explaining the interaction of individual and society in the context of action, or as a theory of behaviour in the behaviourist sense, e.g. without taking into account the role of practical informations in the realm of human action;
3. as a theory based on epistemologically differentiated semantics distinguishing between descriptive and practical informations or as a purely behavioural theory attempting to reduce norms, intentions, preferences and values to descriptions of behavioural states.

In each case I plead for the first of the alternatives, *Luhmann* advocates the second.

Cybernetics and system-theory are frequently regarded as theories with a purely behavioural orientation.[27] However, some scientists recognised very early that selective functions, purposes and practical concepts do inevitably occur in these theories.[28] It would seem appropriate to me, therefore, not to conceive of the system-theory in a semantically reductionist manner. For the sociology of law this kind of approach might be more appropriate than the behaviourist reduction permitting as it does the bridging of differences between

---

[26] I have, in the meantime, had the opportunity of discussing the criticised definition of norms with Prof. *Luhmann*. He himself has mentioned a most interesting argument against the reduction of the norm to expectations: Norms are also applied to the past (that is, as value standard and as basis for legal consequences); that would not be possible if norms were nothing but a kind of expectation.

[27] Compare, for instance, R. Ashby, *An Introduction to Cybernetics*, London 1971.

[28] Compare L. Couffignal, *Notions de base*, Paris 1958.

system-theoretical approach, sociological function-analysis and hermeneutical-dogmatic jurisprudence.

6. THESES FOR A THEORETICAL SOCIOLOGY

My reflections have resulted in some fundamental theses about theoretical sociology:

1. The subject of general sociology is human action: the actions of the individual in as far as they are determined by social relations, human interaction, collective action, as well as all kinds of institutions and associated realities.

2. Theoretical sociology is based on a structural theory of action, explaining action as intentional behaviour regulated by informative data. In view of the fact that sociological research considerations require social bodies of different kinds to be studied and social actions to be analysed empirically the sociologist has to proceed from a formal theory of action rather than from the description of the consciousness and behaviour of the acting individuals.

3. Sociology has to employ a language with epistemologically differentiated semantics since the information processes connected with the actions can only be depicted if it is possible to express both descriptive and practical (attitudinal) informations and to distinguish clearly between them conceptually. The behavourist reductionism is to be rejected.

4. Sociology deals with all kinds of institutions, their genesis, functions and changes. Ad hoc institutions as well as permanent ones and all processes of institutionalisation including the question of the destabilisation of institutions all belong into this field of research. A further aspect of institutional analysis is the study of roles and the entirety of institutional realities (of institutional facts, the personal bases of the institutions etc.).

Institutional (i.e. the action-related) reality can only be understood and explained in the context of practical informations, both those constituting them and those inherent within them.

5. Considerations of normative and evaluative systems and their interaction in the social and personal context of action form an indispensible aspect of sociological observations. In these the sociological analysis is dependent on an internal grasp of practical informations on the other hand, it also provides an analysis of the external relations of these systems to social factors.

6. Social analysis is a functional analysis comprising anthropological elements, system-theoretical ones and factors of cultural sense.

7. A system-theoretical analysis is necessary in order to explain the relations and the interactions "individual - society"; it must, however, be conceived of as a structural theory of action and interaction rather than a purely behavioural theory.

8. The analyses of systems are capable of explaining the functions of institutions; they do not replace political comments and programs or their evaluating justifications.

C. TREATISES ON LEGAL POLITICS AND THEORY OF JUSTICE

IX. LEGAL-POLITICAL ANALYSIS OF INSTITUTIONS

1. LEGAL POLICY AS A SCIENTIFIC PROBLEM OF OUR TIME

In our world of today and under the influence of democratic ideas we do no longer believe in the venerability of the law nor do we regard tradition as a sufficient justification for social institutions. On the contrary, we are convinced that man is able to shape and change his own political environment and that legal regulatives and social institutions have to be examined critically and need justifying on the basis of functional and evaluating analyses.

Theoretically this view can be substantiated by anthropological and human-ethological arguments. Man is not the only being living in communities and having "organised states" for his environment. However, the human way of life and human existence in communities are entirely different from the nature of animal communities.

What makes the human position special is the characteristic that fundamentally distinguishes man from other living beings: the fact that the determination of human behaviour by instincts (by behaviour determined by heredity) has been reduced relatively in favour of its determination based on socalled 'free will' and on institutions.[1] It might be assumed that it is only from our - specifically human - perspective that the human situation and human society appear so fundamentally different from those existing in animal communities or that this assessment of the special position of human communities might arise from the religious conception believing man to be the crown of creation. I am of the opinion, however, that fundamental differences between animal groupings and human societies do, in fact, exist. Man is capable of creating a wide variety of modes of life and very different social structures while animal communities possess only minor modifications in their structures. Man and society clearly have comprehensive "degrees of freedom". Man can and must shape his life; having largely lost the guidance provided by the instincts he has to take upon himself the task of decision-making and of establishing political structures. He has to replace the reassuring certainty afforded by the guidance by instincts with the attempt of justifying his actions and the forms of his social institutions in a rational way.

The concept of democracy as the rule of the people for the people and by the people - however vague this concept may be in detail - confronts us with the task of inventing methods of an effective democratic rule and of making political institutions or measures acceptable in a rational way.

These appear to me to be the essential elements which provide the basis for the topicality of the scientific efforts to analyse the legal-political events and legal-political argumentations.

---

[1] A. Gehlen, *Der Mensch. Seine Natur und seine Stellung in der Welt*, Bonn 1955.

2. THE RELEVANCE OF THE LEGAL-PHILOSOPHICAL APPROACH TO LEGAL-POLITICAL ANALYSES

There is no effective practice without the appropriate theoretical basis. This rule applies fairly generally including, undoubtedly, to legal policy and to analyses of political institutions. It is of some importance on the basis of which theories of legal philosophy one proceeds. I want to examine the following legal-philosophical conceptions for their suitability as bases for legal-political analyses: (i) pure normativism, (ii) legal realism, (iii) the approach based on analysis of behaviour, (iv) jurisprudence with a system-theoretical orientation, (v) the theories of natural law, (vi) institutional legal positivism.

(i) The conception of pure normativism according to which only structural theory, legal hermeneutics and dogmatics form the objects of jurisprudence is not suitable as a basis for legal-political investigations. The legal-political analysis demands the examination of the connection between normative content and actual legal and social events, of the kind of relations, in other words, which are inaccessible to pure normativism as a matter of principle. It has to be emphasised that the legal-political analysis forms an essential part of jurisprudence and of the realm of applied law. 'Policies' in the sense of *Ronald Dworkin* are indispensable elements of many argumentations of judicial decisions.[2]

Equally unacceptable is the demand of pure jurisprudence to exclude legal politics from jurisprudence and to treat political science as an entirely separate discipline in relation to the law. Whether or not legal-political investigations are integrated in the legal sciences or treated as a separate science distinct from jurisprudence appears *prima facie* merely as a matter of convention in the way the social sciences are divided. That impression is deceptive, however; mainly so for two reasons: (a) in excluding investigations into legal politics from jurisprudence the implicite assumption is made that legal activities are independent of legal-political investigations and argumentations - while, in fact, this is not the case at all -; (b) in the context of the existing organisation of the sciences and of academic jurisprudence legal-political considerations are *de facto* going to be banished from teaching and research if legal-political investigations are not conducted within the framework of jurisprudence.

(ii) The theories of legal realism do not constitute an adequate basis for legal-political analyses, either. According to them valid law is determined primarily in the practice of judicial decisions taken by the organs of the state and only indirectly by the primary production of norms (legislation) and only those elements which are used in the substantiation of judicial decisions are objects of legal considerations. Although this theory takes into account legal-political factors in so far as the judge's deliberations are affected by them[3] it does not cover the whole breadth of legal implications. The fact is that legal life does not only consist of judicial decisions, but of the entirety of the legal relations, modes

---

[2] Compare R. Dworkin, *Taking Rights Seriously*, London 1977, pp. 22 ff., pp. 90 ff.

[3] The extent to which legal-political arguments are taken into consideration by the judiciary varies in accordance with tradition and with the predominant juristic doctrine.

of life, institutions created by the law. The existence of judges and other organs of the state cannot simply be assumed as given; they are, on the contrary, institutions constituted by legal norms. An analysis evaluating the functions and the legal-political status of institutions cannot, therefore, be conducted from the one-sided point of view held by legal realism.

(iii) In a way similar to pure normativism - only in reverse - legal-political problems are also eliminated from consideration by the kind of sociological approach that concentrates exclusively on descriptions of behaviour, attempting, in other words, to reduce the nature of the law to behaviour and to regularities of behaviour. The questions of legal-political evaluation, in fact, arise precisely if the institutions are regarded as having been established by norms and human behaviour is considered from the point of view of institutionalised norms and values. Those who give only descriptions of behaviour do not penetrate to the relevant legal-political evaluations and decisions.

(iv) The system-theory and system-theoretically orientated analyses are of crucial significance for an important aspect of legal-political considerations: they consider the functional approach to the law and legal institutions as central. Nevertheless, the traditional system-theoretical jurisprudence fails in two areas, in my view, offering, therefore, no adequate basis for legal-political analyses: (a) It is essentially reductionist in the sense of point (iii) having behaviourist foundations and attempting to eliminate the concept of the norm by defining it as a particular kind of expectation, namely, as a "normative", i.e. "contra-factually stabilised" expectation.[4] Expectations which we are determined not to correct on the basis of experience are, in fact, an absurdity rather than a useful means of explaining the concept of the norm. (b) It treats functional relations as mere structural elements and does not enter into discussion on values. In conjunction with the behaviourist-reductionist tendency of system-theoretical analyses this means that the role of governing ideas is not taken into account adequately and consequently no comprehensive functional analyses of the institutions can be achieved.

(v) The theories of natural law are in sympathy with legal-political investigations in as far as they concentrate entirely on the justification of the law from the point of view of its content. Nevertheless, this conception has the effect of limiting and distorting legal-political analyses, in my view. Those advocating natural law inevitably believe certain principles to be valid and just instead of merely recommending them as worthy of recognition on the basis of functional analysis. The postulated validity of fundamental legal principles - whether it rests on religious conviction or phenomenological intuition - in fact, represents a bogus argument (i.e. by attempting to infer material value consequences from formal postulates). To assume - as natural law does - the existence of permanent values or to determine the "correct" type of norm on the basis of the nature of something in the sense of natural law is to restrict the field of possible forms of

---

[4] Compare N. Luhmann, *Rechtssoziologie*, vol. I, Hamburg 1972, p. 30, pp. 42 ff., also my critical response in: O. Weinberger, Soziologie und normative Institutionentheorie, Chap. VIII of *this volume*.

social institutions unjustifiably *a limine*. By making out that the fundamental principles of the law can be substantiated purely by cognition the representatives of natural law disguise the elements of evaluation and decision-making which are necessary aspects of all legal-political considerations.

(vi) Institutional legal positivism represents the broadest starting position for legal-political analyses, in my opinion. It is a kind of normativism focussing particular attention on the possibility of and the necessity for the creative shaping of the forms societies take and of the law. It combines the perspective of the normativist point of view with the observation of sociological facts regarding them as the sphere of activity of practical, especially normative, informations. In considering the institutions and the law from the perspective of the theory of action the examination of the functionality of institutions remains constantly in focus. While institutional legal positivism is in principle based on non-cognitivism it, nevertheless, regards the problems of legal policies as an area for rational and analytical investigations. Analyses of values and of justice are as much the concern of this theory as studying the effects of the law on motivation and investigating the balance of role-relations in social institutions.[5] Being a positivist legal theory it denies the validity of absolute values as a standard for legal policies while finding a useful basis - and one capable of development - for argumentation in respect of evaluations in the *value thesis* which stresses that every human being and every community always adheres to certain (convictions of) values.[6]

3. CHARACTERIZATION OF THE SCIENCE OF LEGAL POLICY

To conceive of the science of legal policy in purely descriptive terms would be misguided in my view; it does more than provide mere descriptions of those political events which are connected with establishing and applying the law. But neither does it undertake the attempt to work out political decisions on a scientific - in other words, purely cognitive - basis. It does not aim at making the taking of political decisions redundant but it does want to support this process, namely by providing clear representations of the logical structure of the decision-making process on the one hand, and by giving directions as to how to conduct the kind of analyses which make it more rational and to demonstrate how to uti-

[5] In the modern theory of justice there is a fundamental lack of reflection on the question in what way a certain legal norm or social institution motivates human actions. The view that justice is one question and motivation an entirely different one is frequently expressed. In contrast, I believe that it is impossible to determine just legal consequences without taking the function of motivation into account. Compare O. Weinberger, Analytisch-dialektische Gerechtigkeitstheorie. Skizze einer handlungstheoretischen und non-kognitivistischen Gerechtigkeitstheorie, in: I. Tammelo/A. Aarnio (eds.), *Zum Fortschritt von Theorie und Technik in Recht und Ethik, Rechtstheorie*, Supplement 3, pp. 307-330.

[6] Compare O. Weinberger, Jenseits von Positivismus und Naturrecht, in: *Contemporary Conceptions of Law - 9th World Congress (Basel 1979), ARSP* 1982, Supplementa, Vol. 1, pp. 43-56.

lize findings for decision-making processes[7], on the other. Furthermore, it deals with the problem of organising institutions, of testing their functionality as well as problems of balance between different roles in the institutions; and finally, it is concerned with the democratic methods of seeking consensus. Consequently, a theory of legal policy in the broad sense, as I envisage it, comprises apart from descriptions of legal-political processes mainly the following three areas: the theory of legal substantiation *de lege ferenda*, the theory of the functionality of the institutions and the theory of justice.

4. RATIONAL THINKING AND PRACTICAL COGNITION

Rationality is regarded as the virtue of legal thinking. It is not clear, however, what the meaning of this term 'rational' is; indeed, there is little doubt, that it is an ambiguous and - I would suggest - frequently misapplied term. The nature of the misuse lies, in my view, in the fact that the concept of rationality is constantly being broadened and that we describe as rational almost all those philosophical, methodological and socio-political conceptions and attitudes which we advocate. We turn rationality into whatever the reasonable person is expected to consider right and proper, and whoever refuses to bow to this rationality - clearly in the interpretation of the respective author -, whoever evaluates matters differently or does not use these "rational" methods is made out to be stupid or evil or both, as the case may be.

There is no denying that this procedure does succeed in exerting a suggestive influence; the postulate of rationality, on the other hand, loses its scientific character, its content becomes blurred and covers a variety of pseudo-argumentations. And, worst of all, the postulate of rationality loses its power as an objective argument against irrational theories. Why? If the content of rationality is conceived as a rational way of thinking declared to be the correct and soul-saving approach and way of thinking those who think differently have the same justification to plead for non-rational, "deeper", or "intuitive" ways of thinking which "go beyond mere rationality". This is particulary the case if a so-called rationalist - who is, in fact, the grave-digger of the analytical rational conception - plays straight into the hands of the irrationalists by claiming to be able to offer rational recipes for the detection of truth, for the right law or the best possible modes of action. These claims allow them to demonstrate that it is, in fact, impossible for these pseudo-rationalists to prove their theses, that they pass off as objective knowledge what is not an incontrovertible, rational conclusion but the result of subjective evaluation. The doubts about so-called rationalism are, indeed, justifiable. Reason alone enables us neither to make discoveries in physics nor to achieve a material axiology. Reason is binding, is an objective critical authority only in as far as it applies to the formally correct operation of thought-processes.

---

[7] O. Weinberger, Zur Theorie der Gesetzgebung, in: J. Mokre/O. Weinberger (eds.), *Rechtsphilosophie und Gesetzgebung*, Wien/New York 1976.

Even *Leibniz*'s almost universally accepted juxtaposition of factual truth (vérité de fait) and rational truth (vérité de raison) suggests that rational truths relate to platonic entities with an independent existence which are grasped in a cognitive process. Under those circumstances it does not seem impossible to regard values, proper ought and similar matters, too, as entities existing in the platonic sense which need only be grasped properly for it to become possible to gain practical (i.e. action-related) knowledge from reason itself. It is only if we come to understand that rational truths are empty (tautological) and represent only structural knowledge that we shall be prepared to turn our backs on the platonic kind of material rationalism.

Furthermore, the question arises how the range of the objects of reason is to be determined. Is it a range that is fixed once and for all or is it possible for several systems of rational truth to coexist or, as the case may be, to constitute themselves in accordance with the conditions i.e. the system by which the language is constituted? Modern logic gives its answer emphatically in the latter sense which also accords with modern constructivist epistemological conceptions. Depending on the stipulated system (the classical two-value system of logic, intuitionistic logic, many-value systems of logic etc.) different rational truths are valid.

What is especially important in the context of practical philosophy is the fact that not only are descriptive (cognitive) thoughts considered appropriate objects of rational truths but, equally, practical sentences - and their meanings - are seen as potential elements in the process of acquiring this structural knowledge.

When considering the different conceptions of rationality in philosophy and in the sciences it becomes obvious that they refer to different kinds of rationality. It is difficult to systematize satisfactorily the types of rationality which philosophers advocate since the connections often remain obscure and the term 'rational' is frequently used as an attribute with a rhetorical function rather than as a definite distinguishing attribute. I shall add some comments on the following types of rationality and the respective postulates of rationality:

(i) logical rationality
(ii) purpose rationality
(iii) economic rationality
(iv) the rationality of the scientific method
(v) the discourse rationality

(i) The essence of rationality and that area where something definite and something relevant in respect of every kind of argumentation can be said is to be found in logical rationality. Logical rationality does not pretend to be able to be a source of material knowledge. Logic is based on the distinction between form and content. Logical arguments are only concerned with form and formal relations. The slogan "Logique oblige" - if understood correctly - encapsulates the essence of logical rationality. Logical rationality compels us to, or rather postulates that we think logically, that we strictly adhere to a fixed system of language-constitution and to the prerequisite conditions of the reflection under consideration. Inconsistency, i.e. logical contradiction, is inadmissable in a system of thought; the detection of contradictions serves as a critical argument which forces us to reconstruct our thought-system in order to transform it into a consistent system. Logical rationality has an instrumental character in our thinking: it serves the purpose of unfolding ideas, to substantiate, refute and test hypotheses. (The latter, obviously, in conjunction with real operations and observations.) This role, above all, is the task of logical deduction. With the help of deducing, e.g. the formal operation for making inferences, we obtain a reliable instrument for the processing of thoughts. This is where the major pragmatic role of the logico-rational analysis lies. *Logical rationality is uncreative.* As an instrument for the processing of informative thoughts it always provides only relative proof and relative substantiation. Proof of informative theses is valid only in relation to the presupposed informative premisses. There is such a thing as pure thruths of reason (although they, too, are relative to the logical system), but they always are in themselves empty of information (tautological). If we reach materially informative conclusions on the basis of a logical operation without informative premisses we can be certain that we have gone wrong in our operation!

(ii) The rationality of purpose is related to actions. Action is considered rational in relation to a given purpose (a system of purposes) when it maximises the probability of achieving its purpose(s). From the point of view of a purpose P_1action $A_1$is rational (in the sense of purpose rationality) if it brings about P_1 or - in the case of the concurrence of different possibilities of action aiming to achieve P_1 - that action which is likely to achieve this goal with the greatest degree of probability or/and to the greatest extent.[8] In complex systems of purposes where both concurrence of purposes and different relevances in relation to several purposes may be present at the same time the choice of action (the choice of the best possible means) frequently depends on additional analyses of preferences. By laying down the purposes the preferences determining the decision are not yet rationally determined. In other words, the socalled rationality of purpose is dependent on preferences (or decisions). This type of rationality does not always imply unequivocal determination - as it does in the case of logical deduction. The analysis of purposes is frequently open to certain decisions. The rationality of purpose is always relative in respect of the actual positing of purposes and to their relative weighing i.e. to decisions of preference.

On the other hand, some logical relations do exist in the realm of purpose-analyses. This is true in particular for the relations between preferences occuring in teleological thought-processes. If preferences are comparable, i. e. if

[8] Even this shows a certain indeterminacy in the rationality of purpose. Let us assume that action A_1 is more likely to fulfil the purpose P_1 than action A_2 but it will do so less thoroughly. If this is so it is uncertain from the logical point of view whether A_1 should be preferred to A_2 or vice versa. For the problem of teleology see O. Weinberger, *Rechtslogik*, Berlin 1989^2, chap. 11.

they are determined in accordance with one and the same criterion, then preferring is transitive: If *'a Pb'* (*'a* is preferred to *b'*) and *'bPc'*, then *'aPc'*.[9]

The logical structure of the rationality of purpose, its connection with causal knowledge and the interaction of analyses of purpose, preferences and decisions have to be explained in terms of a formal theory of teleology (finality).

The teleology (or purpose rationality) is a field of relative considerations: appropriatness to a purpose, teleological deliberation and decision are relative to presupposed purposes. Put more simply: Nothing is useful for its own sake, but only in relation to a given system of purposes.

(iii) Related to the rationality of purpose is economic rationality, representing, one might say, a special elaboration of it. It defines as rational those actions or choices which maximise utility, and as irrational those which are uneconomical, i.e., those which fail to employ the limited means available in the most efficient way in respect of the posited purposes. Economic rationality is seen as the maximisation of effect for the achievement of the purpose combined with the simultaneous minimisation of the means employed.

The question whether the economic analysis is undertaken rationally (correctly) on the basis of the given pre-conditions has to be distinguished from the question whether the action itself is rational. The economic consideration determines the optimum of the action only in relation to those factors (goals, preferences) on which the analysis is based. In as far as economic utility is maximised (maximisation of financial advantage, profit) it can't be ruled out that the action under consideration does not at all represent the best possible action when seen from other points of view. The optimization of the financial advantages could be contrasted, for instance, with the effects on the quality of life which may not be quantifiable in financial terms. The functions of utility which can be determined in financial terms may also change depending on the perspective of time (long-term, short-term advantage).

To equate the act of making a rational choice with the maximisation of utility would be possible only if everything were expressed in terms of utility functions and the preferences in the entire range of potential states and actions were explicitely stated. This is, however, never the case: neither in the practical situations of everyday life experienced by the individual nor in the realm of political decisions. It is certainly not impossible in principle for gains or losses which initially cannot be expressed in terms of money to be subjected to an economic analysis of utility on the basis of certain stipulations. But taken as a whole there will always be elements in the evaluation of actions which are not explicit and therefore not determinable economically. We can, therefore, refer to the essential partiality of the impact on actions by an analysis based on economic rationality. It is, in other words, by no means always irrational to act in a way that is not in accordance with the economic deliberation preceding an action, to act from moral motives, for instance, or as a result of certain factors which have not found their way into economic evaluations. A scientist does not always act

[9] Compare Ch. Weinberger/O. Weinberger, *Logik, Semantik, Hermeneutik*, München 1979, pp. 154 f.; O. Weinberger, *Rechtslogik, op. cit.*, p. 322.

irrationally, for instance, if he devotes his life to science contrary to economic rationality which aims at maximising profit and despite the fact that in many cases he would be able to achieve higher financial rewards if he were to devote the same amount of time to some practical activity.

The fact that it is all but impossible to define the economically rational mode of acting completely results mainly from the following circumstances:

1. We don't know at all what situations and what possibilities for action exist because (a) we have no exhaustive knowledge of the world; (b) our potential for acting depends on institutions which do not simply exist but evolve or are created; (c) actions (the programs for actions) belong, potentially, at least, to the realm of inventions.[10]

2. We cannot know the entirety of all preferences since we do not even know the entirety of all possible states the comparative evaluation of which is expressed in the statement of preference.

3. In my view there is no logical reason for the influence of the time dimension on the preference (e.g. on the discount rate of the utility), there is only a decisionist determination.

4. There are also factors relevant to the evaluation which cannot be determined in terms of utility - neither ordinally nor, even less so, cardinally. Among these are concepts like 'quality of life' and similar global determinants of our decision-making. Certain aspects of our moral attitudes as well decisions of taste also belong into this category.

(iv) In the theory of science the term rationality of the scientific method is used, for instance, where in the experiential sciences *K.R. Popper*'s method of bold hypothesizing and strict endeavours towards their refutation is postulated as the rational path to knowledge. There is no doubt that the scientific method and the explanation of phenomena are closely related to problems of providing logical proof and that this expresses the logical peculiarity of the provability and refutability of general principles of experience (e.d. the problem of induction). Nevertheless, I believe that the principles of scientific methodology ought not to be conceived as postulates of rationality. To determine uniformly and universally how science is to proceed is all but impossible. While it is obviously generally accepted that the forming and testing of hypotheses constitute the essence of empirical research the scientific methods and explications appear so widely different - depending on the formulation of the question and the context of the problem at issue - that a complete reduction to a single - and therefore 'rational' - formula for the scientific approach cannot really be considered appropriate.

It is not in the methodology but in the postulate of consistency and correct logical procedure that the essence of rationality lies. A well-founded analytico-rational and empirical conception of science ought to avoid representing a general recipe for scientific procedure as scientific rationality. For specialised investigations more differentiated working methods appear more appro-

---

[10] It is all but impossible to make a prognosis of future inventions; it is, at least, not possible to characterize them in detail as they would otherwise already have been invented. A general survey over all potential inventions cannot, therefore, be provided at all.

priate than a single "rational" formula. Explications based on models, system-theoretical analyses, linguistic and hermeneutic discussions, all these can be subordinated to a universal scientific "scheme of rationality" only by forcing and distorting them - despite the fact that they create essential elements of experiential science.

(v) Some authors, particularly *Habermas* and *Alexy*, try and employ the concept of the discourse rationality both in the area of theoretical knowledge and in that of action-related thinking. The importance of discourse and of the fair debate of views is indisputable in respect of social problems in the spirit of democracy. However, two theses connected with the discourse rationality (the procedural conception of rationality) have to be rejected most emphatically:

(a) The thesis that truth in the realm of knowledge and correctness in the realm of action, evaluation and ought are determined by consensus (or, more cautiously expressed, by the ability to reach a consensus in an ideal discourse).

(b) The assertion that the ideal discourse (determined by rules of discourse) marks out the path to genuine knowledge and in the practical field defines the nature of objectively correct evaluation and ought, that it leads, in other words, to practical knowledge.

The organisation of the scientific and practical debate is an important problem which the thinkers of Greek antiquity already gave their attention to. To assume that conditions and forms of discourse - be they real or ideal - are capable of defining truth or what is correct in practice and of guaranteeing the path to truth and practical knowledge is, in my opinion, a misguided and a dangerously damaging conception. To suggest that the results of a discourse constitute true theses or correct (rationally based) practical attitudes is both unfounded and extremely confusing. There is no path from the opinions of those participating in the discourse to objective truth or justness. The erroneous belief in the power of the discourse to lead us - provided certain procedural conditions are fulfilled - to truth and correctness diverts us from the essence of scientific argumentation, namely to find methods of establishing proof and substantiation.

In the procedural theories it is always somehow taken for granted that a consensus reached in a discourse held in accordance with rules represents the one and only rational conception: in other words, that it produces a true thesis or - in the case of practical questions - a correct attitude, the just balance of interests, real justice and genuine morality. Discourses[11] can result not only in (a) universal consensus, (b) majority consensus, (c) the discovery of a certain distribution in the frequency of the resulting experiences but also in doubts (expressed by all or some), surprise or/and the realization that as yet no definite basis for the definition of the problem or/and for the substantiation of a thesis has been found. Discourses can be a means of stimulating and advancing reflections, they are meaningful in the *context of discovery*, hardly, though, in the *context of justification*, considering the fact that the acceptance of a justification - be it by general consensus or by a majority - does by no means prove

---

[11] Even in ideal discourses we have no reason to assume that it is possible to reach a universal consensus.

that this substantiation is valid. If everybody agrees there must be a method of representing the length of the circumference of a circle by the use of ruler and a pair of compasses (the problem of the rectification of a circle) that in itself does not at all prove that this opinion is true. The fact that an opinion is held universally has nothing to do with the verity of the thesis. It is not when a consensus is reached but when a new kind of analysis - and therefore, of argumentation - is *discovered* that the opposing thesis (in our case the impossibility of rectification of a circle) becomes not only plausible but provable.

In my view the theory of the discourse rationality is inappropriate in principle. The discourse cannot achieve what the theory expects from it. This theory shifts the processes of scientific thinking and searching involving rational analysis and empirical research onto the level of social opinion-forming processes. In many cases that kind of rules that are laid down for the discourse are not neutral vis-à-vis the content of the theses under discussion; in other words, the existence of justifications is feigned with the help of a metatheoretical stipulation while, in fact, it is only an opinion that is established.

In reality, we can, of course, only conduct real discourses, not ideal ones; discourses cannot be interminable and the impact of personal relations cannot be excluded.

The discourse is not only exposed to being impaired by compulsion and influences of power, but what people, in fact, accept can also be influenced by a multiplicity of other subjective factors like the submission to authority, sympathies and antipathies or modern political slogans and mass-psychological phenomena.

If we define truth and practical correctness on the basis of consensus[12] we can surely regard only those participants of the discourse as rational who accept the results of the discourse and act accordingly. For the scientific view of the world, however, doubt is always permissible, and those who oppose the general consensus and strive for new approaches and new methods of argumentation are the true upholders of intellectual development.

In the scientific discourse there are neither rules about the onus of proof nor is there a *res iudicata*.

There are no rules of discourse capable of ensuring that the crucial arguments are presented and the appropriate methods of substantiation and argumentation are discovered. Consequently discourse constitutes only a heuristic means to an end, not a basis for establishing validity and not the proof of a thesis.

---

[12] This conception cannot be improved by accepting only substantiated consensus as a determinant of verity. As soon as the criterion of substantiation is used the consensus becomes irrelevant (surely, the well-founded thesis remains true even if the participants in the discourse don't accept it due to stupidity or prejudice). What is at issue in the case of the socalled substantiated consensus is, clearly, not that something is presented as a substantiation, nor is it that the participants in the discourse believe they have good reasons for a consensus but it is the question whether the reasons given are in fact sound and adequate reasons.

Furthermore, the concept of discourse rationality, or of discourse verity, obscures the difference between statement and norm since the result of the discourse can lead to norms being justified (true in the sense of the discourse) in the same way as statements.[13] In this way the fundamental difference in significance between the *probandum* and its different ways of justification is disguised: we speak of something that exists when we refer to statements (statements of fact) and the statement must be confirmed by the reality that is described; in the case of the justification of ought (values and sentences related to action) we are dealing with evaluation, and evaluations are the indespensable elements for the justification of norms. If everything is based on consensus the difference between empirical test and deliberate acceptance vanishes.

Finally, it apppears to me that by stipulating the rules of discourse we anticipate the evaluative decisions and attitudes which constitute the content of practical postulates rather than just affecting the manner of the argumentation. Equal treatment and universalization are treated as dictates of reason not as moral and legal requirements. Is it a matter of reason or a matter of morality to treat what is equal equally? When - and this is a question for moral theory as much as for the law - when are two cases to be treated differently? The answer is: when there are *relevant* differences: Since there are always differences - otherwise we would not know that there are two cases (at least the time-space coordinates have to be different) it is always a question of evaluation, of whether the difference is relevant to the ought-consequences. That is not factual knowledge, nor a rational truth, but a normative or a value decision.

While I am no less convinced that discourses are of crucial importance in practical thinking than are the authors whom I have criticised I consider it a distortion of the nature of theoretical and practical argumentation that they believe the discourse itself or the method of conducting the discourse to guarantee truth and correctness: this view obscures the elements of decision-making that occur in practical argumentations; it neglects reflections on the structure of the argumentation because it focusses its attention on the question of consensus.

Discourse rationality is a deception; discourse is a method of searching for the truth and justness not a guarantee for finding them.

A democrat is likely to take account of the views of his fellow-men because of his social attitude and consider their interests as a result of his solidarity and not because of certain principles concerning discourse rationality.

I am reaching the conclusion that logical thinking is relative in principle - provided the term 'rationality' is not only used metaphorically or deceptively as this is the case particularly in the theory of discourse rationality. Rational thinking is, in fact, essentially an operational capacity which can be applied both constructively and critically. Consequently no factual knowledge results from reason, no practical knowledge, no absolute justification of norms, values and purposes.

We may regard practical reason as the structure of action-related argumentations and we may present it in a theory of practical thinking; to consider

[13] Compare R. Alexy, *Theorie der juristischen Argumentation*, Frankfurt a.M. 1978, p. 138.

practical reason as a reservoir of objective values, right ought, objectively valid legal principles of a material nature is an absurdity.

5. TWO TYPES OF LEGAL ARGUMENTATION

Legal theory distinguishes between two kinds of approach to legal norms: the approach of *de lege lata* and considerations *de lege ferenda*. What lies at the centre of this juxtaposition of legal approaches is not the question whether it is valid law or law to be created that is under discussion but the different nature of the respective modes of substantiation and of the logical character of their substantiation. On the one hand, there is the norm-logical substantiation wherein normative conclusions are reached on the basis of normative premisses - mostly also with reference to premisses establishing facts. As a result of certain norms being postulated as valid arguments this context of substantiation corresponds to the *de lege lata* approach. The justification of norms in the teleological perspective or/and on the basis of evaluations represents a substantiation of a totally different kind. It constitutes the core of the *de lege ferenda* approach.

We have to remember, however, that the two modes of argumentation frequently overlap in the solution of legal tasks. In the application of legal norms, for instance, to draw the conclusion from the subsumption is essentially a *de-lege-lata*-operation, while the taking of decisions in the area of the discretionary context is essentially determined by considerations of adequacy of a legal-political nature. *Alf Ross* has described this type of complex deliberation as analysis *de sententia ferenda*.[14]

Despite the fact that normative logic has concerned itself predominently with logical substantiation in contexts of *de lege lata* considerations there is also a need for establishing a theory for the structure of the justification of legal norms *de lege ferenda*. This formal theory of the substantiation of norms could be regarded as a second subject of normative logic[15] unless a separate terminology is assumed. This theory has to be developed on formal lines; it has to introduce rules for the operations of justification into which different determinations of actual purposes, value standards and preferences can be inserted. In other words, like every logical theory this theory distinguishes between forms and rules of operation, on the one hand, and to the determination of the values assumed by the variables occurring within these, on the other.

---

[14] A. Ross, *Law and Justice*, London 1958, p. 46.

[15] O. Weinberger, Zwei Gebiete der Sollsatzlogik, in: the same, *Studie zur Normenlogik*, *Rozpravy* CSVA, Praha 1960; also: the same, *Studien zur Normenlogik und Rechtsinformatik*, Berlin 1974, p. 17.

6. RATIONALITY AND THE LEGAL-POLITICAL DISCUSSION

If reason itself were capable of providing criteria for the correct way of acting or if it were, at least, possible to conduct legal-political argumentations as purely rational operations political deliberations would be simpler and political actions safer and cognitively based on more solid ground. However, reason is not a reservoir for correct political and legal-political conceptions nor does rationality provide an algorithm for legal-political argumentation if it is interpreted in the sense of my conception, that is, as an operative capacity for cognitive and action-related information processing. In other words, there are no rules of the kind we have for calculations guaranteeing the accuracy and effectiveness of the procedure employed in legal-political argumentation. Legal-political investigations comprise a series of different interlocking operations, rational-analytical ones, those that set goals and evaluating ones. In which sequence they occur cannot be determined unequivocally in advance and different procedures in accordance with their chosen approach are justifiable. Only certain aspects of the legal-political argumentation can be conducted in the form of a strictly rational argumentation. We also have to bear in mind that solutions for legal-political problems - such as, the finding of functionally effective forms of organisation or providing compromises capable of achieving a consensus - always contain an element of invention in addition to having their cognitive basis in sociological perceptions. Social problems are solved by the invention of institutional structures in much the same way as the invention of useful machines does not only depend on knowing the laws of nature but also requires ideas for their construction. Inventions, be they technical or socially programmatic, cannot be reduced to rational operations; nevertheless rational operations are fundamentally involved in these processes.

The legal-political analysis and the search for functionally effective solutions has to be conducted on two levels; (a) the effectiveness of the proposed regulations and measures, (b) the democratic acceptability of the proposals have to be examined. I consider the task of harmonizing these two points of view as one of the most important and the most difficult objectives of the practial application of legal-political analyses. This dual approach in the investigation of legal-political problems further calls for an interaction of scientific analyses and political discussions on different levels as well as consultations within the framework of the democratic institutions, particularly on the level of the social sciences and of the mass media.

7. TYPES OF LEGAL-POLITICAL ARGUMENTATION

Legal-political argumentation takes place in the form of two different, albeit variously overlapping processes. It either takes the form of constructive thinking, of the search for viable and acceptable solutions to social problems, or it is critical in the sense of evaluating the political reality and institutions which are either already in existence or planned. With reference to the constructive thinking only little tangible guidance can be given. The same applies to the whole realm of invention as such. There is just one very general rule that is valid for the sphere of constructive thinking: it is always useful to set out as clearly as possible a specific framework for any deliberation and to establish within this framework an exact survey of all the alternatives. In additon computer-based model analyses provide a way of establishing and analysing feasible options. The representations of the alternatives gained in this way can then be contrasted with each other in a process of relative evaluation.

It would be a great advantage for a scientifically based legal policy to be able to draw on a comprehensive typology of legal-political modes of argumentation or, at least, of those which can be applied in a critical function. As far as I can judge the state of scientific advances in this field such a comprehensive typology is as yet not available. On the other hand, there is a general awareness that legal-political substantiation and the critical evaluation of legal-political institutions belong essentially into the realm of teleology. It appears to me, however, that neither the structure of teleological thinking itself nor the methodological problems connected with thinking in terms of purpose have as yet been identiied with sufficient clarity.

I shall not attempt to present a universal typology of legal-political argumentations in this section as this would exceed my possibilities. I shall restrict myself to commenting on the problems involved. In considering some types of argumentation or some factors in the process of legal-political argumentation we are going to leave unanswered the question of the relative weight of individual factors within the argumentation as a whole. This uncertainty about the role played by different types of argumentation and by individual arguments in the argumentation as a whole is a disadvantage that has a greater impact in the realm of constructive legal-political thinking than in that of legal-political criticism. In the critical deliberation every single type of argumentation potentially represents a serious critical objection that deserves to be taken into consideration. The question whether such an objection in itself is sufficient to discredit a social institution with finality can only be answered with reference to a specific case.

Analysis of consequences as legal political arguments

Legal-political investigations of institutions and measures always involve the examination of a variety of consequences caused by the institutions or measures. The field of relevant consequences is varied; it may be a question of economic repercussions, moral implications or motivating influences on the behaviour of people, or the relations between all of these may be at issue. In examining normative regulatives from the legal-political point of view the impact exerted by the norms on actual behaviour always has to be taken into consideration as well as the legal relations and the social consequences of establishing the norms in question. The investigation of the effects of legal norms is by no means limited to the question whether the norms are adhered to or infringed, or how great the chances are for the norms to be effective in a society. In legal-political considerations it is particularly the indirect consequences that the greatest importance is attached to. The motivating effect norms exert on people's behaviour clearly often depends not only on the normative content of the rules but also on a number of other circumstances.[16] The individual lives in a society and within a framework of legal norms in a manner that is determined as much by his interests, personal goals and actual social ties as by the norms of the legal system. Consequently there arises a complex interaction between the motivation of interests and the legal ought. The socio-legal approach has to consider also the fact that people's actions are not only exposed to the controlling influence of the legal system in our modern, complex society but also to other normative systems, such as customs, morality, religious norms and other specific regulatives like the rules relating to different professions or to social status.

The analysis of consequences, on the one hand, comes into its own in legal policy in the realm of *de-lege-ferenda*-considerations, on the other hand, it finds application as an analysis of the actual impact of institutional norms *ex post* in the context of research into legal facts. In the process of investigating the impact of the law it is important not only to examine whether the set goals have been achieved but to study the broadest possible field of actual effects of normative institutions. It appears appropriate, therefore, not to leave it only to bodies subordinate to the legislative institutions to conduct these investigations which fulfil the role of providing feedback-information for the legislature but to charge independent scientific institutions with them, instead. This is the only way of ensuring that these investigations based on socio-legal and legal-political evaluations will be liberated from the tendency to produce successful conclusions and of making sure that the investigations are not restricted to those effects which were set out as the aims of the norms when they were introduced.

In the legal-political approach the analysis of consequences is always connected with evaluations of statements of fact since it is here that it is of particular interest to establish whether or rather to what extent the consequences are welcome or unwelcome. It is only on the basis of this kind of evaluation that the justification or refutation of the regulation under investigation can be achieved.

Reflections on coherence

For the analysis of legal-political questions reflections on the coherence of conceptions appear indispensable. It seems that the postulate of coherence is an important regulative principle; on the other hand, it is all but impossible to reach a general and precise definition of the concept of coherence.[17] Although we are able to define with precision certain elements constituting a lack of coherence these are by no means all the elements which are vital for the assessment of this question. Logical inconsistency is one of these factors that disturb the

[16] See O. Weinberger, Gesetzgebung und Motivation, in: E. Mock/I. Tammelo (eds.), *Rechtstheorie und Gesetzgebung. Festschrift für Robert Weimar*, Frankfurt a.M./Bern/New York 1986, pp. 117-131.

[17] See D.N. MacCormick, Coherence in Legal Justification, in: W. Krawietz et al. (eds.), *Theorie der Normen. Festgabe für Ota Weinberger*, Berlin 1984, pp. 37-53.

coherence; the knowledge that aspects of the investigated field will remain undefined in a certain investigation is another. The question of coherence affects the problem of behavioural norms as well as the value standards and the evaluations and preferences underlying the process of establishing legal norms. To explain the problems of coherence more closely remains a task of prime importance and of significance for the theory of legal-political argumentation as well as for other areas of practical philosophy.

The teleological justification of norms

The justification of norms and the functional analysis of the institutions rests basically on teleological approach.[18] Normative regulatives and institutions exist for certain purposes and have to be investigated from the point of view of social purposes. A theory of the structure of teleological analysis is, therefore, a crucial first step toward a theory of legal-political argumentation.

In view of the fact that all legal-political investigations taking place in a practical context employ complex systems of purposes any teleological assessment made in respect of legal policy must always rely on relative evaluations and evaluative decisions.

Immanent and external evaluation in the context of legal-political consideration

Legal-political analyses frequently involve an evaluation of institutions, of normative rules or measures undertaken from the standpoint of postulated value standards. The application of this kind of standards tends to have the effect of limiting the permissible means. The value standards in conjunction with the respective preferential judgements constitute crucial elements in the determination of the choice between different suitable alternatives. In the application of value standards two matters have to be decided: either the evaluation is conducted on the basis of evaluative criteria which are conceived of as immanent value standards of the legal system or, instead, external standpoints are applied to the evaluation of the legal system, such as the value standards of a particular political persuasion or of a particular religious system. In the latter case external value standards and possibly external normative principles take on the function of standards for the legal-political analysis. No doubt, external assessments of this kind can be conducted and can be significant in certain relations. Whether or not they are depends, however, always on whether these external standpoints are accepted. That alone is the precondition for the relevance of this approach. From the point of view of democratic tolerance and in view of the search for consensus this kind of assessment may, however, also gain importance in an indirect way.

---

[18] See N. Hartmann, *Teleologisches Denken*, Berlin 1951; Ch. Weinberger/O. Weinberger, *Logik, Semantik, Hermeneutik*, München 1979, Chap. 8; O. Weinberger, *Rechtslogik*, 2nd ed. Berlin 1989, pp. 278-297.

8. THE SOURCES OF PRACTICAL DISSENT AND OF THE SEARCH FOR CONSENSUS

Charles Stevenson's reference to the two sources of dissent in practical questions is of fundamental significance for the theory of legal-political argumentation.[19] If two people have two different practical attitudes to a matter the reason for this difference may be found in two fundamentally different areas: 1. in the difference of opinion about facts (about the situation in question, about causal relations or about the probable consequences of certain modes of behaviour); 2. in the difference of values, aims, interests and preferences held by the individuals involved. These elements do not occur separately either in the conscious processes or in the analytical reconstruction of the elements determining the action. Nevertheless, it is a useful methodological guideline to structure the justifications of the different points of view in accordance with these sources of dissent - both for the explanatory explication and for the processes involved in the search for consensus.

In legal-political analyses as in deliberations about political questions it appears advisable in the sense of the quoted distinction between sources of dissent to seek information particularly on two aspects: (i) the mental picture of life held by the participants in the discourse, their awareness of causality, their ideological views, and (ii) their (attitudes to) values and preferences. In view of the fact that the manner of the argumentation has to be different in respect of the treatment of factual questions from the approach taken where different value judgements come into play this is the only way to guarantee that the debate takes on a rational character. As a result the rhetorical argumentation, i.e. the attempt to modify the conviction of the fellow-participant in the discourse by argument, consists of two aspects, namely, of presenting such arguments as are capable of changing the factual basis of the opinions and standpoints at issue, and of introducing the arguments which are capable of influencing attitudes and preferences. Rational deliberation will always involve the analytical discovery of the reasons for dissent and the critical discussion of these reasons.

It appears that it is far more difficult to bring about the acceptance of convincing reasons for the modification of value standards in a discussion than to affect the correction of views on factual matters. It is, however, also possible in principle to change value standards. Apart from using arguments concerning the consistency and the coherence of practical attitudes there is the possibility of introducing evaluative experiences as a means of changing practical convictions.

The discourse about practical questions, whether they concern factual elements or preferences, tend to be long-drawn out and difficult. Frequently the fact that the participants in the discourse have fixed ideological convictions and specific interests gets in the way of modifying practical attitudes. We also have to remember - so as not to be disappointed too often - that one can only convince

[19] Ch. L. Stevenson, *Ethics and Language*, New Haven/London 1944.

those who do not refuse - for whatever reasons, often not even articulated ones - to allow themselves to be convinced: "Nobody is as deaf as he who does not want to hear" as a Spanish saying goes.

9. COMMON FLAWS IN LEGAL-POLITICAL ARGUMENTATIONS

There are certain common types of obstacle to agreement among the participants of a discourse and different types of factor obstructing the successful organisation of legal-political deliberations.

Prejudices

Among the obstacles to rational discourse prejudices and ideological fixation which constitute an important kind of prejudice have to be mentioned first. In some sense everybody has preconceived opinions and ideas which he brings to bear on the discourse. The question is, however, to what extent these attitudes and conceptions are regarded as initial opinions or as unshakable articles of faith. Ideological views are usually based on background-interests and constitute fixed conceptions. They belong to those elements of a world view which it is difficult to modify and which can be changed radically only over a longer period of time and/or by experiences causing deep shock.

Pseudo-substantiations

When following the speeches and the manner of argumentation employed by politicians from a critical distance one discovers that the arguments advanced by them frequently don't represent the true motives and reasons for the standpoint they advocate. It is not uncommon that someone pretends to advance genuine arguments while it is elements of propaganda and power strategy rather than factual ones that count in reality. How are arguments of this kind to be countered? How are we to combat them? Two steps are necessary: (a) to refute the (pseudo-)argumentation and to point out the true motives of the standpoint taken, and (b) to provide a critical analysis of the true motives. On the other hand, in this type of situation there is usually little chance of convincing the opponent in the discourse himself who is not in search of an appropriate solution but in pursuit of different goals and interests. In practical legal-political life - especially in democratic societies - it is often a question of convincing third parties, possibly even a broader audience. If that can be achieved this success may have the indirect effect of forcing the opponent in the discourse to modify his attitude in order to assert himself in the community.

One-sidedness of approach

Institutions and measures are as a rule the result of a certain social idea and pursue a certain purpose. They are thought up for the purpose of fulfilling certain tasks. It is likely therefore that they correspond as a rule - at least to some extent - to the idea and purpose governing them. For a critical legal-political analysis it is important, on the one hand, to examine the extent to which they fulfil their purpose and, on the other hand, to consider the appropriateness of institutions and measures from different relevant perspectives without limiting itself to an assessment only on the basis of the primary goal. In fact, there is an important rule of experience that applies to this situation: The act of establishing institutions and of instituting social measures as a rule has a variety of effects which exceed the original intention.

Thinking in slogans

This term identifies a whole family of practices used in argumentations which are particularly prevalent in practical discourses and especially in legal-political discussion. In view of the fact that this problem takes on a variety of forms the concept of thinking in slogans cannot be defined with precision. It has to be demonstrated with the help of examples. Those who indulge in it state either explicitely or by implication a certain positive or negative idea, they acknowledge a certain authority or consider all their efforts as an expression of a certain preconceived ideology, religious belief or party-political persuasion; in the process of using these preconceived ideas as a standard for their power of persuasion it never occurs to them that the preconceived opinion itself might require justification and that it might - at least in borderline cases - come into conflict with other more important arguments. In view of the fact that thinking in slogans can occur in various forms my examples will illustrate only a general tendency expressed in the practice of legal-political argumentations.

It is a typical aspect of what I call thinking in slogans that certain ideas are invested with a decisive power of argument more as a result of their emotional impact than on the basis of analysing factual relations and of making explicite evaluations. Thinking in slogans usually also leads to one-sidedness of approach. Slogans and their power to convince are also subject to fashion to a not inconsiderable extent, or - if you like - to the "Zeitgeist". Slogans and slogan-type maxims like, for instance, "class-struggle", "common good before individual advantage", "protection of the environment", "democratization", "scientific method", "market economy" are usually based on thoroughly sensible and acceptable ideas; they become slogans and lead to thinking in slogans precisely at the moment when they achieve the characteristic of absolute validity in the practice of argumentations. As a result, searching and testing thought-processes are replaced by dogmatic argumentations. Anybody with a critical mind will be aware of the fact that all principles and rules have their limits. He will avoid taking practical and political decisions on the basis of a single principle. He will prefer multilateral and evaluative thought-processes to the one-sidedness of a dogmatic enthusiasm.

The weighing-up of partial arguments and the juxtaposition of their evaluations

In considering the comments of different political parties to current-affairs questions we frequently notice that they are able to produce comparatively convincing arguments for contradictory opinions. In view of the fact that it is impossible for a thesis and its negation to appear capable of substantiation at the same time in logical argumentations there is clearly a fundamental difference between legal-political argumentations and their logical counter-part. What is the explanation for this difference? Social facts are of such complexity that they may appear in a number of different cross-sections of reality - as one might say -. The results of argumentations will vary in accordance with the level chosen as point of view. A rational and critical analysis has to bear in mind that the argumentations employed are only partial argumentations which have to be developed into a comprehensive argumentation covering the entire field. Here are some relevant examples:

One might, for instance, ask the question whether active and passive bribery should be assessed with equal severity by the law, i.e. should be punishable to the same extent. If one were to plead against the notion of a special status for civil servants in relation to their fellow-citizens this point of view could be used as an argument in favour of an equal judicial assessment. If, on the other hand, one were to take into account the special status as related to competence, the relevance of the civil servant's social task and the protection given to the function of the institution one would support a higher sentence for passive bribery in comparison with active bribery.

To accept even the criteria for a judgement may imply the meritorious decision. The current debate in Austria about the peaceful use of nuclear power which has been taking place since the rejection in a referendum of nuclear power-stations may serve as an example for the possibility that the decision may be taken even at this meta-stage. The following analysis is independent of our position for or against nuclear power-stations.

The frist argumentation: In a democracy the people cannot vote repeatedly until they have achieved the result intended by those in power without destroying democracy itself.

The second argumentation: In view of the fact that in a democracy the people will never abdicate the right to change their minds in the course of time decisions expressed in referenda are in principle subject to being changed as a result of new decisions.

Both arguments are correct in themselves. But the next step is to find reasons for their relative weighing and to come to a decision which takes into account both considerations. The difficulty lies in the fact that in this instance - like in so many where democratic procedure has to be determined - an evaluating preliminary decision has to be taken.

10. THE CONCEPTION OF DEMOCRACY AND LEGAL POLICY

Democracy as autocracy of the people expressed in Abraham Lincoln's formula of "government of the people, by the people, for the people" is a framework concept which is given an emphatically positive evaluation in our society without being clearly defined. The quoted formula expresses, indeed, that in the democratic conception the state is not the dominium of any ruler or of any institution whether profane or sacred. But crucial questions remain unanswered: What is government of the people? In what way can it be realized? Which are the interests of the people? Are they to be interpreted in the collectivist sense or as the sum of individual interests? Nobody really believes that Lincoln's formula constitutes a definition giving an adequate description of the democratic state or guidelines for the organisation of democratic life: it merely expresses a regulative idea.

In my view democratic legal policy rests on the following principles:

(i) Legal institutions have to be judged simultaneously from two points of view: (a) they have to be examined from the point of view of democratic postulates and ideals and (b) the effectiveness of the organisation as well as of the functions of decision-making, of leadership and control has to be analysed.

(ii) Due to the functional differentiation between institutions which demand different structures and mechanisms of control there is no universally valid formula for the best possible democratic organisation.

(iii) Democracy is more than a form of government and control; democracy means inevitably also a way of life; which is reflected in an open category of postulates concerning its content - such as, for instance, tolerance, freedom of opinion and expression, protection of minorities. Without these material democratic convictions being held by broad strata of society and without democratic customs a democratic state would not be viable in the long run.

(iv) We know from history and as a result of function-analyses applied to democratic institutions, that democratic forms can degenerate and that they can on occasion be impaired by undemocratic manipulations. Consequently the stability of democracy requires the existence of open channels for criticism; there have to be formally established opportunities as well as those which are not formally organised for the expression of public criticism and for the discussion of all politically relevant matters.

(v) The democratic state does not rest only on the activities of political parties, of the political and burocratic machine; it is a far more complex structure made up of elements inherent in a democratic society. The legal-political analysis has to take into account the influence of the mass media, the sciences, the different social groups like the professions, ethnic and religious groups and the various pressure-groups in addition to the political parties, the professional politicians and the burocracy. The forms of interaction between the different factors are crucial for the extent to which a society is democratic. The mass media, for instance, may function more as a tool of political propaganda or, they may be employed, instead, for the dissemination of critical information. The sciences - and this applies particularly to the social sciences - may be politically and intellectually more or less constrained or independent. They may stand entirely apart from public life or be fully integrated in the processes of political discourse and decision-making. They may produce "party-specialists" and thereby provide politics with a certain scientific respectability; they may, on the other hand, function as a genuine source of social ideas and as an autoritative channel of criticism. The manner in which the relations between the different factors of democratic life are conducted, in my view, depends less on the character of the people involved than on the institutionalised structures as well as on the democratic customs and traditions.[20]

The actual problem of appropriate remuneration for important work in democratic institutions and of limiting the possibilities for blatent personal enrichment on the basis of functions and positions of power can only be solved by effective institutions providing organisation and control.[21] Elements of motivation, remuneration in accordance with success and, equally, responsibility for failure also have to be institutionalised. Moral factors like, for instance, the misuse of positions for personal enrichment, must not be judged as a petty offence but as a form of misconduct that results in disqualification from political office.

(vi) The subordination of the state and of public life to ideological or religious doctrines and their organisations constitutes a particular danger for democracy.

In view of the fact that it is almost impossible to define the concept of the common good which ought to act as the guideline for democratic policies the theoreticians of democracy on the whole concentrate their attention on the forms of the decision-making processes in the hope that adequate democratic forms will lead to an optimization of the content of decisions. They do so on the assumption that collective decision-making - in contrast to monocratic decisions - is democratic in principle. I do not consider this thesis convincing considering that under certain circumstances monocratic decisions, too, can be recognised as an adequate form of making a democratic decision.

According to Kelsen freedom constitutes the fundamental idea of democracy and the principle of majority acts as a guarantor for minimising potential restrictions imposed on that freedom.[22] The fact that this principle fails to achieve this goal can be demonstrated just as much as that the preferences of the voters do not necessarily find their most comprehensive expression in the casting of votes. What appears to me to be more important than these familiar problems of the processes at work in the shaping of the democratic will is the realization that every collective process of decision-making is dependent on normative regulatives for which an adequate determination is by no means indisputable. Collective processes leading to expressions of intention depend on the selection of candidates, on the formulation of the questions which are to be put to the vote as well as on the way other procedural matters are regulated. There are nearly always alternative ways of establishing norms for democratic processes which lead to non-equivalent results and cannot be justified entirely by

---

[20] In saying this I am by no means underestimating the importance for democratic life of personal courage and I am well aware of the danger posed to the morality of a democracy by the careerist's opportunism.

[21] See O. Weinberger, *Institution, Organisation, Kontrolle*, being printed.

[22] H. Kelsen, *Vom Wesen und Wert der Demokratie*, Tübingen 1929^2.

rational means. The rules for democratic processes cannot be produced democratically.[23]

Democratic life is influenced to a fairly considerable degree by the theories of democracy. There are two wide-spread conceptions which I should like to discuss briefly: the romantic conception of democracy and the model of the competition of elites.

The romantic conception of democracy

This conception is expressed in its crassest form by the thesis "The people are never wrong". The thesis that the will of the people is inherently right is meaningful only in as far as it lays down that social utility is determined by the interests of the people in a democracy. Nevertheless, even here certain restrictions apply. Social problems cannot be solved by the mass of the people, rather, the solutions are produced by individual personalities or by specialised groups. The way social measures are judged depends on the analysis of their potential consequences, on informations and on experience in making value judgements, none of which are as a rule accessible to the mass of the people. Furthermore, the value concepts of the masses are manipulable to a high degree. Crowds can be induced to be enthusiastically in favour of "total war" despite the fact that hunger, millions of dead and other consequences of the war hardly comply with the considered interests of the people. The romantic conception of democracy rests on the entirely implausible assumption that the individual has to make his decisions on the basis of informations and of systematic analyses while collective decisions, on the other hand, are right "purely instinctively" on the basis of something like the principle *"vox populi, vox dei"*. The romantic conception of democracy may be very good at producing effective slogans but, it does, in fact, spell disaster for democracy.

The model of competition of elites in the sense of Schumpeter[24]

This model is based on a realistic view of party-democracy. In reality government is always exercised by elites. In a pluralist democracy they fight for supremacy by competing for votes. The voter expresses his intention by deciding the power of the competing elites through his vote. Party propaganda - including the cult of the personality as an important means of vote-catching - becomes a key element in everyday political life. There is no doubt that this model accurately describes an aspect of democratic reality. I do, however, believe that it only covers a partial aspect of the reality of the party-state. It underestimates functional elements and the power of constructive ideas, of the *idée directrice*, to use the terminology of legal institutional theory. It reduces the complex relationship between different factors of democratic life to the single aspect of the competition for votes.

---

[23] See O. Weinberger, Abstimmungslogik und Demokratie, in: B. Sutter (ed.), *Reformen des Rechts. Festschrift zur 200-Jahr-Feier der Rechtswissenschaftlichen Fakultät der Universität Graz*, Graz 1979, pp. 605-623.

[24] J.A. Schumpeter, *Capitalism, Socialism and Democracy*, New York 1942.

The influence of this theory on the actions of politicians is alarming. What they say and do largely serves the purpose of winning votes. The loss of confidence vis-à-vis politicians and the general weariness with politics have their cause *inter alia* in this factor among others. A politician can only gain the confidence of the people if he is committed to a social goal rather than to his own position of power. Those politicians who represent certain views only in order to gain power instead of seeking power in order to be able to realize political ideas which they consider useful do not deserve the confidence of the people. It is a misconception to believe oneself to be a democrat if one simply goes along with everything the people say. Only those are legitimate political leaders who represent views they believe in themselves and those who know how to establish functionally effective institutions.

11. A FUNCTIONAL ANALYSIS OF INSTITUTIONS AND DEMOCRATIC LEGAL POLICY

The functional analysis enquires into the structures which exist in society and into the way the institutions operate. From the functional point of view legal norms are understood as elements of a context of action as well as being grasped hermeneutically. The functional analysis is institutionally orientated: it regards norms (a) as that which determines the structure and organisation of the institution, (b) as the basis for forms of action determined by the institution, (c) as underlying the interpersonal relations arising from duties and expectations, (d) as the element determining the institutional realities - institutional facts and objects in their institutional function. The functional approach focusses simultaneously on norms, social facts and possibilities of action. The investigation of legal norms in the functional sense represents a holistic approach elucidating also the connections between governing ideas, forms of organisation and modes of action.

The institutional conception, on the one hand, emphasises the need for social stability and the role of the institutions in influencing the actions of the individual, on the other hand, it conceives of the institutions and structures as the work of man and consequently as subject to change affected by the human will.

The institutional approach permits the clarification of some problems facing the theory of democracy.

If democracy is not only regarded as a type of state and a form of government but also as a way of life then the democratic processes which shape the will of the electorate are as important as certain substantive democratic ideas. This can lead to the following dilemma: on the basis of democratic opinion-forming processes certain decisions may come about which conflict with certain material principles of democracy. Democratic processes can be distorted by propaganda, ideological indoctrination or manipulation. Dictatorships are frequently installed democratically or by manipulation on a democratic basis. Consequently we have to ask ourselves how this degeneration of democratic forms, in other words, the collapse of democracy can be prevented.

Any attempt to protect democratic principles by fossilisation or by complicating the conditions of change is doomed to failure, particularly at crucial moments since more difficult conditions for change do not constitute an effective protection against emotional mass movements. To lay down absolute unchangeability is neither effective nor in tune with the democratic conception of life which does not allow the current will of the people to be prevented from shaping the life of society.

It is by no means indisputable which democratic principles can demand absolute validity. Candidates for such a position in the democratic world view are the following: protection of minorities, periodicity of elections and other processes establishing the will of the people, as well as freedom of religious belief.

According to the principle of majority the rights of minorities can be abolished. In the appropriate constellation of interests - e.g. the threat of unemployment - it happens occasionally that measures are taken against individual groups (such as so-called guest-workers, non-members of parties or trade-unions). It is not uncommon that political propaganda employs the method of attacking alleged enemy groups achieving thereby under certain circumstances the kind of majority decision which may lead to the persecution of ethnic or religious minorities.

There are, of course, good reasons, why governments and any organisational leadership ought to be stable; stability increases their power, provides the opportunity for utilizing expertise gained from experience and for realizing long-term plans. The kind of dependence on the will of the people that democratic societies expect is feasible only if the functions are tied to time-limits. The appropriate length of the periods for which the functions are held is, however, a question demanding different solutions in accordance with the respective circumstances.

Religious freedom is a convincing postulate of democracy in principle but we must not forget that systems of religious belief themselves are often extremely intolerant. Commitment to a faith leads not only to the idea of propagation and proselytizing but also to contempt for non-believers or those adhering to a different faith, to fighting other faiths ("heretics") and to war and destruction often connected with particular cruelty.[25] Systems of faith tend to be associated with an ecclesiastical organisation and with claims to domination over public life and the state rather than just influence over the life of the soul and the morals of their members. However much religious freedom ought to be protected we must not forget that religions and religious communities can be undemocratic to an extent that may lead to religious war or to a "Holy War" and to genocide. Where religious freedom is regarded as an absolute principle separate from the substance of the faith and the tolerance of the religious communities themselves this principle can easily deteriorate into a blank cheque for use against freedom and democracy.

---

[25] See O. Weinberger, Angst vor dem menschlichen Wahn, in: A.Grabner-Haider/O. Weinberger/K. Weinke (eds.), *Fanatismus und Massenwahn*, Wien/Graz 1989, pp. 7-19.

The fact that there are dangers which threaten democracy and its material principles does not constitute an objection against democracy itself; it should merely act as a warning: democratic forms and democratic principles of life are constantly under threat. It is, therefore, vital to put every effort into developing democratic habits and convictions and to foster the establishment of institutions through which criticism of public life can be expressed freely and democratively as well as of mechanisms to enable the democratic system to control itself. The postulate of the distribution of power, the adequate organisation of spheres of power and influence and the institution of democratic controls constitute only a part of those measures which contribute to the protection of democratic life. In addition the institutinalization of adequate relations between the state, politicians and bureaucracy, on the one hand, and the sciences, the mass media and literature, on the other, are of crucial importance for the protection of democratic ideas and for the control of their realization.

We have to be prepared for the repeated recurrence of antidemocratic tendencies which need combatting, especially so when they take on organised forms.

The concept of the governing idea plays a key role in the theory of the institutions: the governing idea forms the centre around which institutions crystallize. *Hauriou* regards the governing idea as a given intellectual entity which gives rise to the normative regulative and brings institutions into being.[26] In contrast to *Hauriou* I see the governing ideas as creative ideas which depend on man's social circumstances and on his actual needs.[27] For legal theory the theory of the governing ideas acts as a reminder of the fact that the legal system does not only consist of a multiplicity of behavioural and empowering norms but also correlates with ideas and social aims.

The institutional approach enables us to find a kind of answer to the problem of relations between the forms by which the will of the people is expressed and the material democratic ideals. *The material principles of democracy can be regarded as a kind of governing ideas of the democratic institutions.* They don't constitute strict rules of conduct but goals and regulative ideas developed through concrete analyses. They provide guidelines for evaluating the organisation and for assessing the functionality of the institutions. An appropriate consideration of these material principles is safeguarded only if democracy is conceived of in terms of consultation, discussion and criticism rather than a battle for majorities. The model of the competition among elites as well as related economic theories of democracy[28] fail to give sufficient attention to these ideals, if not always rational elements of the democratic institutions. It is by no means

---

[26] M. Hauriou, *Die Theorie der Institutionen und der Gründung (Essay über den sozialen Vitalismus)*; R. Schnur (ed.), *Die Theorie der Institution*, Berlin 1965, pp. 27-66.

[27] See O. Weinberger, Building Blocks of Institutional Legal Positivism, Chap. I of this volume; also D.N. MacCormick/O. Weinberger, *Grundlagen des Institutionalistischen Rechtspositivismus*, Berlin 1985, pp. 51 ff.

[28] See A. Downs, *An Economic Theory of Democracy*, Harper & Brothers 1957. German translation by L. Walentik, *Ökonomische Theorie der Demokratie*, Tübingen 1968 (1957^1).

true that voters are won over only by measures appealing to their material interests. The behaviour of voters is also determined by their willingness to identify with governing ideas and social goals.

The critical analysis of the institutions has the task of defining the functions of the institutions adequately and of evolving from these definitions viable ideas that are acceptable from the democratic point of view.

The difficulties of defining the governing ideas clearly can be demonstrated in the example of the problems faced by our universities. The university was originally conceived as a community of those who teach, those who learn and those who pursue research: teachers, students and researchers. Essential preconditions for the pursuit of the activities of this community are freedom of thought, of teaching and of learning. Certain developments have lead to restrictions of the transparence, the openess and perhaps even of the plurality of views held within the university. This development was meant to be counteracted by the concept of the so-called group university. Different interest groups were found to exist in the universities and their relations to each other were interpreted in analogy to those between social classes. In my view this approach has overlooked the fact that the university as an institution primarily fulfills a task for the good of the whole of society and stands in the service of the respective governing idea to which group interest must be subordinate. Furthermore I regard the analogy between the groups found in a university and the social classes as a very weak parallel. The problematical interpretation of the governing idea of the universities has lead to the situation where - instead of increasing the transparence of the institution and establishing committees for consultation and co-determination - new bodies for voting have been introduced and mechanisms with totally different functions from those demanded and expected have been set up.

The institutional theory highlights the enormous differences existing between institutions and between the corresponding forms of organisation and of decision-making. It would be pointless as well as destroying functions to want to organise different institutions according to a unified prescription. This is why there are different ways in a democracy for the people to express their will, and the form of the participation in decisions has to be different in different institutions for reasons of functionality.

Three ideas are of particular importance for the process of determining the appropriate forms of decision-making:

(i) Whether decisions that are being taken are functionally the right ones depends on informations as well as on problem-solving concepts.

(ii) Although ideas usually result from interaction between individuals, inerpersonal consultation, they, nevertheless, reflect individual and personal achievements; they cannot be produced by way of a voting process.

(iii) The person that rules is not always the same person as the one taking the decisions and controlling individual actions. There is no need, therefore, for the ruling people to take part directly in every phase of the decision-making process.

These reflections lead to a conception of democracy which I want to describe as "theory of structured democracy". It can be summed up in the following points:

(a) Differentiated forms of decision-making and functionally adequate institutional structures have to be introduced (in some cases even controlled monocratic decisions can be accepted as democratic).

(b) Decisions on the basis of consultation and the right of co-determination are preferable to those reached by mere voting.

(c) Institutions have to be organised in a way that guarantees the effectiveness of their functions, creative forces and informations as well as expertise are to be used in the interest of the community; illusions in the sense of the romantic conception of democracy are to be avoided.

(d) To act creatively in the interest of the people is to be regarded as the function of democratic elites. Elites are the creators and upholders of the governing ideas not the passive mouthpiece for the views held by the masses.

12. DEMOCRACY AND POWER

The questions of power and of the control of power are constant problems of democracy. They are not only concerned with setting limits to power, be it by the division of powers, or by a balanced system of competences and controls, but also with the relations between problems of power and other questions. Among the later the following are of particular importance:

The orientation of power and decisions in accordance with the goals and interests of the people.[29]

The selection of officials with democratic functions on the basis of their previous success in lower functions.

The question of distributing political roles in a wide circle of individuals considering that a large number of people are capable of taking on political roles in our highly developed society.

The healthy practice of selecting officials for leading positions on the basis of their proven efficiency in subordinate roles may be a sensible policy but it does not constitute a perfectly reliable criterion in view of the fact that their activities may be of a totally different kind at a higher level and demand different abilities from those necessary for less important functions.

Connections and positions of power play a significant part in the selection of officials. The fact that the politician has to carve out his position for himself means that he strives to combine a large number of functions, roles and competences in his person. In doing so he proves his abilities while creating at the same time a network of connections and making a reputation for himself. Nevertheless, I believe, that there is a need to restrict the accumulation of roles, offices etc. considerably in a society where such a large number of people are

---

[29] This is an important democratic postulate although the possibility that it might also be realized by a dictator under certain circumstances cannot be ruled out.

able to or - on the basis of specific experiences could be enabled to - take on functions in society.

Here a change of our attitudes is called for: we have to learn to condemn excessive efforts of accumulating functions as undemocratic and the ability to cooperate ought to take the place of the ability of managing many functions simultaneously (as a criterion for the suitability of a candidate).

In the economic sector, too, we find the same urgent postulate to combat the accumulation of occupations or of positions with occupational functions. The respective measures ought to precede the reduction of working hours. I am, of course, aware of the fact that due to the actual power structures there are difficulties in making these conceptions acceptable and that some people will object to restrictions of this kind on the grounds that they imply a limitation of freedom. I do, however, consider legal reforms and the development of a new socio-political awareness of these questions necessary in view of the fact that a highly developed society makes the redistribution of the social functions necessary.

There is no doubt, that democracy faces a certain dilemma in this respect: Positions of power are built up and economically strong positions are achieved by accumulating functions and activities. This means that the necessary process of establishing positions of power comes into almost inevitable conflict with democratic thinking which accords the same ability of taking on important social roles also to a large number of people.

To keep on tried and tested officials for indefinite periods may be simple and effective from the point of view of handling the respective operation; nevertheless, this ought not to be done. Roles mean power, that is why a genuine democracy can only exist if there is a time-limit for holding office. A restriction of power without the rotation of functions is all but impossible. We have to instil the general belief that the exchange of officials is typical of the developed democracy and that the end of a period of holding an office does not mean a *capitis deminutio* for the official who is replaced.

The appropriate space of time for a political function held in a democracy is determined essentially by two factors: the lower limit is set by the fact that every representative has to adjust to his job and that the realization of new ideas which he hopes to put into practice requires a certain period of time; the upper limit results from the necessity, not to allow the existence of fossilized personal domains in a democracy and to give the people the chance to reaffirm their confidence. In most cases a three to five year period with the possibility of one or two re-elections may be considered appropriate.

13. DETERMINANTS OF POLITICAL CONTROL

A scientific analysis of the problems involved in political control must proceed from general considerations of the structure of control. Any form of rational decision-making and effective control is dependent on the following factors:

A. *on cognitive factors*, namely:

1. informations on the actual situation within which actions take place or measures are to be taken;

2. informations on connections resulting from causal laws;

3. programs of action, i.e. rules and regulations about ways of achieving certain goals or of solving actual tasks;

4. the implementation of programs and of political actions requires feed-back informations and the adaptation of the programs (in as far as these are not already conceived as feed-back programs reacting to every conceivable part-result - which is something that in the social sphere can hardly be fully realized due to the maze of factors and of potential developments);

B. *on volitive (evaluative) factors*, namely:

1. on a system of goals and value attitudes, which can be expressed in form of practical informations (the setting of goals, sentences formulating values and preferences, as well as normative principles of action);

2. on the ability of the individuals taking action to make choices, i.e. to make decisions on preferences.

In real life cognitive and volitive factors are not entirely independent of each other. Attitudes depend on the subject's awareness of possibilities and on his value experience; programs are developed for the purpose of satisfying practical goals.

The cognitive factors represent the socalled "expert knowledge" which in the political practice of the democratic state rests with the bureaucracy, with the sciences (namely the experts) and, to some extent, also with the politicians. Expert knowledge is not only a knowledge that can be "applied" but also the capacity to invent or to find solutions.

The volitive elements are these: political will, political programs, social ideals and tendencies of social development. They are represented largely by the politicians, but also by pressure-groups, associations and other institutions of public life.

Democracy - like any other system - needs spiritual leaders. The "will of the people" - if I may use this nebulous expression - determines political activity through the medium of elections and plebiscites; but governing ideas, programs and solutions are found - or better: are evolved - in processes of consultation. The "will of the people" cannot be expressed directly and it cannot be directly constructive; it can only react to proposals, accept them or reject them, in other words, reward the success or failure of measures *ex post* through the medium of its future voting behaviour. These two elements, the need for intellectual leadership elites and the impossibility for the will of the people to be directly constructive leads to the conception of the democratic society which I have already described as "structured democracy". This is a form of democracy which accepts the existence of and the need for leading elites, demands unhindered access to public office, the differentiation of institutions, transparence, balance and control, and - with a view to (the need for) functional efficiency - introduces differentiated forms of organisation for the institutions. This conception emphasises factors like consultation, discussion and control as democratic elements rather than the mere casting of votes and polling.

14. THE ROLE OF THE SCIENCES AND OF EXPERTS IN A DEMOCRACY

The fact that political decisions depend on knowledge and ability raises the question which is the appropriate role for the sciences in a democracy. "To make scientific politics" is a slogan of our time. There are those who represent their political program not only as the result of consultation between politicians and scientists but as the result of scientific research which - in their view - is capable of grasping not only the basic outlines of previous historic developments and of interpreting them but also of predicting key developments of the future and of determining what kind of political goals we ought to be striving for. The communist doctrine uses historic materialism in this way as a "scientific" substantiation of its program. Others base their programs on the views expressed by experts telling their voters explicitely or by implication: what we are doing and what we are planning to do is confirmed as scientifically justified.

Let us ignore the propaganda function of the socalled scientific character of politics for the moment. Starting from fundamental considerations of the theory of science I want to examine the role of the sciences from the point of view of its function and seek out such institutional forms of cooperation between politics and science as correspond to the concept of a structured democracy.

The fact that I am demanding a far more significant role for the sciences in public life should not be interpreted as a plea for a technocratic conception. Neither the sciences nor experts are able to determine what the correct political actions are to be because political decisions are always dependent on evaluations and on the way different interests are brought to bear on them.

Our problem can only be debated adequately if the great differences between scientific disciplines are taken into account. The formal sciences (e.g. logics and mathematics), the natural sciences or the technical sciences relate differently to politics from the social sciences (sociology, jurisprudence, economics etc.) and the historical sciences. This thesis must not, however, be interpreted in the sense that I am suggesting that some sciences - the formal or natural sciences, for instance, - are politically neutral and as such beyond political and ideological controversy. The opposite is the case: any scientific conception or interpretation of political practices can potentially become an arena for ideological conflict.[30]

---

[30] For decades the official Marxist theory, for instance, has opposed logic, especially in its modern form, as well as modern semantics and cybernetics. *Mendel*'s and *Darwin*'s theories have been dismissed while *Lysenko*'s theories have been celebrated as Marxist biology. On other ideological fronts things don't look very different, albeit that it is not necessarily by political decree that the "correct" scientific approach is defined as the relevant one. I want to refer only to two areas where this is the case: (a) The social interpretation of Darwinism produced the familiar political and ideological implications culminating in the racist Nazi ideology. (b) The fight for and against natural law is by no means always conducted without

There is no such thing as *the* scientific point of view, there are always different scientific views which have to be examined and subjected to critical discussions. Science is not capable of providing final truths nor does it offer any perfect recipes for action. This is why the cooperation between politics and the sciences does not take the form of politics adopting scientific results, neither can political measures be fully justified on the basis of a single area of expert knowledge. The cooperation between politics and sciences must be organised as a complex system of consultation. Futhermore, the social sciences must be given *inter alia* the role of an institution of criticism. The number of institutions for free scientific debate must be extended.

The actual role played in politics by experts is largely non-functional and simply provides political actions with a deceptive cloak of scientific justification. The mere choice of experts frequently expresses a bias towards a particular result. The type of expertise that is applied often remains secret and is not exposed to scientific debate, lacking, therefore, the fundamental element of scientific work: its exposure to public criticism.

Scientifically based politics ought to mean cooperation on the basis of consultation between politicians, bureaucracy and scientists. The dual nature of those providing the expert knowledge with the bureaucracy on the one side and the scientists on the other, appears to me to be significant for the processes involved in the optimization of democratic decisions. The fundamental difference in the positions, i.e. the bureaucracy having the greater practical experience, the shorter period of preparation and being more dependent on the politicians; the scientists having greater possibilities for juggling with ideas, for orientation and detailed specialized study - this difference must be utilised institutionally in the consultations. Unfortunately, the bureaucratic establishment tends to regard the scientists as rivals rather than partners for democratic cooperation.

Jurisprudence is only marginally involved in the discussion of current legal-political questions. It restricts its participation on the whole to hermeneutic analyses. Its voice has little impact on the discussions about legal-political reforms. New impulses tend to come from the mass media rather than from jurisprudence.

Decisions must be preceded by democratic consultation. Unfortunately, politicians often follow their unreflected intuition in making decisions or they satisfy some pressure-group or other. In many cases it would be advisable to begin by making preliminary analyses with the open advisory participation of the sciences.

The critical role of the social sciences which must be performed autonomously cannot be fulfilled if they are confronted by a battery of mechanisms ensuring secrecy. I cannot help feeling that much of that secrecy serves, in fact, as a shield against democratic criticism[31], however much it is disguised as pro-

---

emotional envolvement in jurisprudence, on the contrary, it is substantially influenced by religious and ideological considerations.

[31] The fact that somebody is a cobbler or a professor of jurisprudence (and is remunerated in accordance with legally fixed rates of pay) does not count as protected personal data. Infor-

tection of the individual's privacy. There is a need to harmonize personal protection and the transparence of social and political facts.

The scientific ethos ought to oblige the scientist to be prepared to offer this expertise in politically relevant areas only if it is exposed to scientific scrutiny. The notion of the sciences operating in secrecy offends against the scientific ethos, in my view, and conflicts with the role of the scientist in a democratic society.

15. DEMOCRATIC LEGAL POLICY AND THE CONCEPT OF JUSTICE

The passing of just laws may be seen as the immanent task of the legislature. Nobody would deny that the legislature has this task. However, the aim of creating just laws and of institutionalizing just modes of life are not the only aims of the legislature: it also has the task of enabling the members of a society to work effectively and to accumulate wealth, in short of creating a social world where it is possible to live in accordance with moral standards as well as pleasantly and where decent behaviour and achievement do better than socially undesirable behaviour.

There are, however, a great many interpretations of the task of making just laws. The positivists believe that the legislature defines what is just - in terms of the establishment. Those advocating natural law are of the opinion that the kind of laws that we ought to make are laws that are just according to objectively valid criteria. This objective criterion of justice is seen as valid in an absolute sense by some advocates of natural law, while others believe that it can only be defined objectively in relation to the historic situation.

Positivism and the theory of natural law were regarded for a long time as conceptions that are fundamentally mutually exclusive. Nowadays there is, instead, a tendency to bridge the gap between the two conceptions.[32] Positivism acknowledges the need to provide a rational basis for the law which is, in fact, impossible without elements of decision-making; the adherents of natural law are now recognising on the whole, it seems, both the historical and cultural variability of their standards and the difficulty of proving the objectivity of material criteria of justice without having actual experience of the values. This still leaves the question unanswered whether or not this actual experience of the values constitutes an objectively valid knowledge of the values. Nevertheless, the positivist, too, can and must accept that the experience of values as a relevant argument is a social reality and an element of practical argumentation.

---

mation about who sits on which boards and fulfills which official functions, and to what extent the positions and potentials for power are linked and what income and privileges such positions entail, is, on the other hand, regarded as an invasion of privacy.

32 See, for instance, O. Weinberger, Jenseits von Positivismus und Naturrecht, in: *Contemporary Conceptions of Law - 9th World Congress of the IVR (Basel 1979) ARSP*, Supplement, Vol. I Part 1, 1982, pp. 43-56; also the paper by Norbert Leser, "Der Konflikt zwischen Recht und Gerechtigkeit", read at the *12th World Congress of the IVR* in Athens 1985.

If it were possible for us to prove unequivocally and objectively what is just, we could solve the problem referred to earlier of how to protect the material postulates of democracy from being constrained by formal democratic decisions. We could solve it by refraining from subjecting what had been proved objectively (justly, democratively), what is, in other words, unalterable law, to the processes forming the will of the people. This possibility does not, however, exist since there is no objective knowledge of fair ought. Our conviction of what ought to be remains in principle a socially and culturally conditioned factor, or, at least, we cannot know the dividing line between what we currently believe and what is objectively necessary in the practical sphere.

From the point of view of the kind of positivism that regards socalled "practical knowledge" as impossible (non-cognitivism) while emphasising the possibility and the importance of the *de-lege-ferenda*-argumentation the analysis of justice is based on an empirical fact of practical thinking which I want to describe as 'value thesis'. It is a psycho-sociological fact which can be easily verified empirically that every human being has an awareness of values and develops conceptions of justice. Social groups evolve certain communal conceptions of values and of justice. Contrary to the view of those advocating natural law I believe that these conceptions of values themselves can be subjected to scrutiny; they, nevertheless, constitute useful - albeit not permanent - arguments on which a consensus might possibly be found.

I want to put forward some theses concerning justice and the role of the theory of justice in the context of legal policy - although I shall not be able to substantiate them fully in this context.

(i) Justice concerns interpersonal relations. Man being a communal being factors determining the direction of his will and his ought in respect of the community - both in the sense of living together and cooperating and in the sense of taking into account the interests of fellow-human beings (I would describe these as elements of solidarity) are biologically as well as socio-culturally indispensable aspects of the structure of his actions. Normative regulatives and social ideals always aim at constituting fair social relations and to build up a kind of working community. This commitment to the notion of community can take on different forms: it varies between group-solidarity which is coupled with the ideology of hostility to other groups and universal humanist solidarity.

(ii) In our contemporary theory of justice attempts to substantiate social justice by scientific means or, in other words, with rational objectivity (see *John Rawls'* theory) are wide-spread. I am not convinced by these theories. They merely simulate the objective validity of certain ideals of justice. In my view, we have no way of proving what the just society ought to look like.

(iii) I do not believe it is the task of the theory of justice to produce socio-political programs. Instead, it is a means of providing critical analyses. We may expect the theory of justice to define justice and to attempt to determine the criteria for judging human relations, institutions or political measures just or unjust but not to provide a socio-political program.

(iv) Legal policy is to be seen as an interplay of utility - useful measures and institutions - and the realization of ideals of justice. Justice itself must not, in my view, be considered separatedly from questions of motivation. "Just, useful and effective" is the aim of a sensible legal policy. Legal-political evaluations without reference to motivatory effects and without reference to social achievements are, in my opinion, not only naive, they are also the expression of an erroneous theory of justice.

(v) In brief one might say: We can't determine in general terms what is just but we can frequently expound convincingly what is unjust and we are, therefore, able to subject institutions to a critique from the point of view of justice. An example to illustrate this point: it is easy to prove convincingly that it is unjust for the insurance premium of a car to be set in accordance with the value of the car when new although the actual value - and therefore obviously the compensation paid by the insurance company - is often only a fraction of the value of the car when new which means that the yearly premium may even exceed the value of the insured object.

(vi) Formal principles of justice are important instruments for the analysis of justice, but on their own - without additional premisses - they do not provide standards for legal-political decisions. According to the principle of formal justice the same relevant conditions are to result in the same legal consequences. This principle forces us to uncover the reasons for the legal consequences and it demonstrates that legal evaluation is in principle analytically evaluative, in other words, that it has to define the relevant reasons and can never be satisfied with a valuation that is simply globally intuitive.

(vii) According to the principle of universalization an ought is only justified if it is acceptable as a rule that has universal application. This meta-rule of the analysis of justice requires elucidation. Firstly, it does not at all mean an insistence on not-making-any-distinctions; what is to be treated alike and what differently is a matter for decision. It has to be stressed that it does not constitute an independent legal-political principle of justification. (a) Even Kant's formulation of the categorical imperative (which is an expression of this principle)[33] implies that it is a principle for testing normative rules (maxims for action) for their applicability, in other words, *it mut be possible to want them to be universally valid* (relative to the given conditions of application). There is no question, therefore, that this principle could establish an independent objective substantiation. An evaluation from general points of view only constitutes a material substantiation for ought if accompanied by a material evaluation, expressed by Kant as the ability to want. (b) The use of the term 'universalization' is clearly only meaningful if the attribute according to which the universalization is undertaken has been defined. An individual case forming the basis of an analysis always has a number of attributes. If we were to universalize every possible attribute the evaluation would - in accordance with the principle of *identitas indiscernibilium* -, in fact, only apply to this particular case. It is,

---

[33] I am referring, of course, to the sentence: "Act only according to that maxim which you can want to become a general law."

however, a question of selecting and emphasizing the attributes crucial for the legal-political evaluation and to use them as the basis for the generalisation. That means, however, that the principle of universalization is only valid in relation to the decision about the attributes which are relevant to the legal-political analysis, and therefore univerzalisable.

(viii) The postulate of mutuality which plays an important role in the democratic concept appears to be related to the formal principles. As a postulate of equality (equality of value) of services rendered and services received, of the equality of mutual rights and duties of the subjects involved it appears to constitute a formal principle of justice. This appearance of the situation I would question, however. If it were a formal principle it would have to have universal validity. The demand for mutuality does not, however, apply to every relationship between individuals. I believe, it only applies to the kind of relationship which we describe as "partnership". Nor is the principle of mutuality a formal principle of justice. The nature of the postulate of mutuality emerges even from the fact that a material value decision is required to determine whether or not mutuality can be demanded in the respective relationship, also from the fact that the nature of the equality has to be determined: exactly the same activity, or the same value of the service rendered and the service received, or equality of readiness to give assistance etc.

(ix) There are important and very plausible postulates of justice in the application of the law which are independent of other material legal-political conceptions. The postulate of the true determination of facts is a natural demand but it still frequently constitutes a practical and political problem. According to the postulate of realization the legal consequences ensuing from certain facts do not merely constitute evaluative statements but measures to be put into practice. In respect of the research in institutional theory the postulate of the justice of procedure is an area for socio-legal research and for reflections on optimization since it is concerned with organising legal proceedings in such a way as to maximise the probability of just solutions.

(x) Social institutions involve systems of role-playing by the participants. The role-playing constitutes a complex interaction of ought, can (competences) and may, of demands and expectations, of initiative and adaptation. Role-playing is a social fact which we enter into either automatically or by an act of volition. Man is automatically a citizen; one becomes a member of a club or a marriage partner as a result of a specific act of will. Man organises his role-playing partly on the basis of relatively free decisions or he can modify types of institutionalised role-playing by agreement in the course of working out his specific relationships. The existence of communities and of role-playing invariably engenders problems of justice. In this context such problems concentrate on the balance of services rendered and services received among the partners involved in the role-playing.

(xi) We do, in fact, recognise nowadays that questions of justice do not only concern individuals but also groups and their respective freedoms and their interaction. The relative freedom of the individual vis-à-vis the group and his right to leave the group provides a further problem that is both important and difficult. If social freedom is to exist at all the individual's freedom to leave a group must be institutionalized. This freedom of movement must not be restricted except under specific circumstances and for limited periods.

(xii) Justice has a conservative and a reformative aspect. Legal peace, equal judgement of equal cases only with different coordinates of time and the protection of acquired rights represent elements of stability in the life of a society and of our conceptions of justice. At the same time we regard justice as an attempt to make legal relations more just in the course of social developments. As a result we are faced with the need to find a compromise between the two ideals of justice, constancy and progress.

(xiii) The problem of justice in our time is not longer only how to safeguard the interests of the community but how to establish peaceful and co-operative human inter-relations. This is a vital concern both in the individual and in the wider context: it is the pre-condition for the coexistence of different ethnic groups and for the survival of humanity in the face of modern weapons and of the present-day global constellations of power. The ideals of justice of our time have to be placed into the service of these problems. The opening-up of communications between cultures, political systems and communities, tolerance and effort to establish agreement between communities, these ought to be our most important legal-political ideals.

(xiv) The conflict laden world which we inhabit, the arms race to the point of nuclear overkill force us to see the problem of justice not longer primarily as a mechanism for coping with guilt, retribution and oppression, but as a search for viable systems for the future interaction between different human communities. The past is important only in as far as it explains existing structures; we are not, however, concerned with historical claims or retribution - these would only serve to create confusion in the world and would certainly not provide a universal basis for peace -, but we are charged with finding solutions which will harmonize the world in future.

X. THE CONDITIO HUMANA AND THE IDEAL OF JUSTICE

1. THE ROLE OF THE THEORY OF JUSTICE

Who would not stand up for justice? Who does not feel affected by problems of justice? Political systems, religions, the sciences, - and, above all, ethics, jurisprudence and political theory -, they all deal with questions of justice and want to establish a just world in accordance with their precepts. The journalist und the man in the pub alike discuss what is just or fair. Who does not ever ask questions about what is a fair wage, what are fair prices, what makes a fair partnership? We look for just institutions and for justice or fairness in all human relations. In short: *Justice is a ubiquitous problem.*

It is an anthropological fact that man experiences problems of justice and that he develops an awareness of justice. Everybody applies more or less consciously value judgements to human conduct, social processes and institutions. Concepts of justice vary not inconsiderably between individuals and different groups. Bearing that in mind the following questions have to be asked: Is there a common, as it were, universally valid core of justness? Are there certain general principles of justice defining the concept of justice which would mean that differences in the conception of justice are possible only within this general framework? Is justice - or to what extent is it - timeless and independent of social systems? Or, conversely, are conceptions of justice dependent on socio-political systems resulting in different kinds of justice in the feudal, capitalist, socialist and the social market-economy system? Are ideals of justice historical and cultural factors firmly rooted in reality, or are they purely a matter of taste? What, in fact, is just? Is it possible to prove principles of justice, - or, at least, some of them -, scientifically.

I am of the opinion *that nobody knows or can prove objectively and with any finality what the meaning of justice is*. At the same time, I am, however, convinced that problems of justice can be debated rationally, and it appears to me *that sometimes* - at least in relation to certain very plausible presuppositions - *it is possible to prove what is unjust.*

The attributes 'just' and 'unjust' are extremely persuasive terms. As a result they are used rather effectively as arguments in political disputes. References to justice are a legitimate argument in political debates, since, after all, it is undoubtedly the aim of politics to identify and establish just, useful and effective institutions as well as to achieve the same for individual problems. Whether or not the judgment of justice which is used as an argument is well founded, is open to question, however.

A critical theory of justice will inevitably demonstrate that in many cases something which appears as just from a particular point of view does not deserve this attribute when other relevant points of view are taken into account. The principle "equal pay for equal work" will appear just; however, as soon as other parameters are taken into account, i.e. the employee's social contributions, the usefulness of his work, it becomes obvious that this principle does not apply in every case. *Onesidedness in the consideration of the problem and premature reactions are frequent sources of the misjudgment of justice.*

What has the theory of justice to offer to us? Can the scientific investigation of the problems of justice contribute to giving the character of objective validity to definitions of justice, or can it, at least, achieve that certain aspects of the reflections will be made objective and that those parts where value judgements may affect the final decision will be defined and the response made explicit? Is it possible for scientific analysis to transform an argumentation using the terms just or unjust from an instrument of persuasion into a genuinely rational line of argument? The scientific analysis of the problem of justice is meaningful only if we do not organise it as a means of persuasion but as a rational, analytical and critical process and if we clarify what science can and should achieve in this field.

Theories of justice of the type offered by *Rawls* want to provide theoretical foundations for the general criteria of just social institutions;[1] they offer a concept of the just society and believe themselves capable of proving scientifically on what political principles a just society ought to be founded. I do not think that those theories which intend to combine a definition of justice with the plea for a specific political system are able to achieve either goal in a satisfactory manner. In my view, the theory of justice has both a more modest and a more general task. It is meant to show that ideals of justice and reflections about what constitutes 'just' and 'unjust' form necessary elements of human existence. Instead, it tries to tackle the question of justice as an immanent problem of human existence. It bases its argumentation above all on reflections about the *conditio humana*. It does so on two levels: 1. on the general level of anthropological findings, and 2. on observations of humanity's present situation.

2. THE ANTHROPOLOGICAL APPROACH TO THE PROBLEM OF JUSTICE

Postulates of justice always address themselves to subjects capable of action. There are, admittedly, formulations which don't make it immediately clear that the demands are directed to such a person. We demand, for instance, fair wages, or just punishment. It appears, though, that this sort of demand is meant to address itself in reality to persons capable of acting in response to it. The demand for fair wages expresses the wish for society to institutionalise such forms of the economy and of the distribution of wealth as would guarantee the most just reward for any kind of work. Equally, the demand for just punishment is an abbreviated formulation and indicates that the judge is expected to fix a penalty which accords with our criteria of justice and that the state's machinery of criminal proceedings is expected to implement it.

The postulates of justice apply principally to inter-personal relations, i.e. the principles of justice aim at determining the conduct of a person to other sub-

---

[1] J. Rawls, *A Theory of Justice*, Cambridge 1972; German version: *Eine Theorie der Gerechtigkeit*, Frankfurt a.M. 1975.

jects. Here, too, formulations are frequently used which do not explicitely refer to inter-personal conduct; it is, however, not difficult to recognise the true structure of the principles of justice and to prove that they do, indeed, concern interpersonal relations. For instance, we frequently speak of just or unjust people, of just or unjust institutions. A just person is undoubtedly a person acting justly vis-à-vis other human beings. A just social institution is just precisely when it creates just relations between the persons concerned.

The above - pretty well indisputable - characteristics attributed to the postulates of justice, namely that they address themselves to persons capable of action and concern inter-human relations, correspond to two fundamental human characteristics:

(i) *man is a being characterised by the capacity of acting*, and able to determine his conduct and way of life to a large extent freely by his own decisions, and

(ii) *he is a communal being*.

The anthropological approach to the problem of justice which I consider appropriate functions as follows: postulates of justice are seen as determinants of action and *the content of the principles of justice is understood to derive from their function in the life of society*.

3. IDEALS OF JUSTICE AS DETERMINANTS OF ACTION

Actions we understand to mean conduct guided by information, attributed to a subject capable of intervening in the course of events for his own purposes. The process of absorbing information preparatory to deciding and directing actions rests on a factual information: descriptions of the situation, causal knowledge, know-how and practical information, or as we might say, informations expressing voluntary standpoints. The core of these practical informations is formed by an overall framework of objectives within which the agent of an action operates. The acting subject has, in addition, the capability of assessing the relative merits of alternative actions. The term *'utilitarian considerations'* will be used in the following for the analysis which aims at determining decisions of programs of action on the basis of the aims and preferences of the subject.

It is characteristic of human actions that elements other than utilitarian considerations intervene in the determination of an action: fixed intentions, autonomous norms, heteronomous normative regulatives and other factors, like ideological conceptions and - last, but not least - ideals of justice.

A considerable number of those determinants which join the utilitarian considerations have the function of shaping human action with regard to the interests of the community. In my opinion which is confirmed by biology and ethology these elements of the social determination of human action are rooted in our very disposition as communal beings. They are not the product of culture and education but vice versa. Culture and taught ways of living are based on primary hereditary characteristics - this is so in human beings as it is in other organisms living in communities.[2]

It is typical of the *conditio humana* that man while never being without biologically determined tendencies - and consequently never without a value system - has, nevertheless, - uniquely in the world of organisms as far as we know - areas of freedom in which to shape the way of life of individuals and groups.[3]

Not only the individual shapes his life within such a framework of areas of freedom, but institutions and communities can be shaped in different ways too. In other words, their character is not fully determined but merely partially decided by the hereditary programs of the individuals constituting them. There is a fundamental difference in this respect between a swarm of bees, an ant hill or a hord of wild animals and human societies.

Normative regulatives and social ideals are always intended to shape social relations. The autonomous norms of morality determine individual human conduct in respect of the role the individual plays in relation to his fellow-men. Heteronomous regulatives coordinate man's communal life.

What are the implications for the theory of justice of these general anthropological observations on the concept of human action and on the communal character of human existence? Mainly the following:

(a) *Principles and ideals of justice are partly biologically, partly culturally based elements in the determination of actions.*

(b) *Although concepts or ideals of justice have in some sense a biological basis they can, in fact, to a large extent be shaped.* The exact borderline between what cannot be changed and what can be modified is difficult to define. Even inherited characteristics can be modified by cultural influence.

(c) *Man is never a tabula rasa where value judgments are concerned.* The same applies to our spontaneous reactions in terms of justice and to our evaluations of the just or unjust conduct of other individuals and institutions. The fact that every human individual has an awareness of values and develops concepts of justice is psycho-sociologically recognised and empirically easily proved. Social groups evolve certain common value systems and concepts of justice.

(d) *The theory of justice can rely on the existence of a socalled sense of justice.* It has, however, the task of clarifying it, of defining it conceptually and of refining it by its analyses. It has to examine the sense of justice, rationalise it and adapt it to the *conditio humana. In other words it deals with the problem of rational argumentation in matters of justice.*

(e) *Justice is both a moral and a legal problem.* This interplay of morality and law, of ethical considerations and those of the philosophy of law is of vital

---

[2] K. Lorenz, Die angeborenen Formen möglicher Erfahrung, *Zeitschrift für Tierpsychologie* 5 (1943), pp. 235-409; idem, *Die Rückseite des Spiegels. Versuch einer Naturgeschichte menschlicher Erkenntnis*, München/Zürich 1973[2]; idem, *Vergleichende Verhaltensforschung. Grundlagen der Ethologie*, Wien/New York 1978; Ch. Weinberger, *Evolution und Ethologie. Wissenschaftstheoretische Analyse*, Wien/New York 1983.

[3] Ch. Weinberger, *op.cit.*, pp. 174-179.

importance, considering that we are concerned, on the one hand, with making the individual's autonomous acting a just one in respect to his fellow-men, and, on the other hand, with institutionalising a just way of life for the community. The two views of justice complement each other: they are not, however, identical in content. In addition, the perspective of the moral analysis is different from that of legal and political considerations. The ethical reflections will be dominated by the question "How ought I to act?", while the valuation of one's fellow-men's conduct is of secondary importance.[4] In the legal and political context, however, it is precisely the just institution that is of primary importance while the just evaluation of individual relations in specific cases is seen from a broad social point of view.

4. THE ANALYTICAL AND DIALECTIC CHARACTER OF REFLECTIONS ON JUSTICE

Given that the postulates of justice are interpreted as determinants of action the following thesis suggests itself: *Questions of justice always occur in conjunction with utilitarian considerations; ideals of justice combine with utilitarian analyses as well as normative regulatives.* Ideals of justice preclude certain means and methods of action. Normative regulatives are formulated in the spirit of certain concepts of justice, and they are examined critically from the point of view of the ideals of justice. *The manner of the individual's and of society's conduct is determined by a fusion of considerations of justice and utility.*

If I am not mistaken most theories of justice portray the principles of justice as absolute demands quite separate from other elements which determine actions and strictly in a preeminent position regarding all other determinants of action. They draw a sharp dividing line between the question of justice and the motivating influence of institutions.[5] In contrast to this approach I am of the opinion that an adequate understanding of the ethical as well as of the legal and

---

[4] I do not share the view of some authors (e.g. A. *Verdross*), who maintains that morality knows only duties while the legal system acknowledges both duties and rights (compare A. Verdross, *Statisches und dynamisches Naturrecht*, Freiburg 1971, pp. 9, 14, 100). Morality, too, has an impact on our actions and on the inter-play of actions by different persons. Consequently our demands on the conduct of our fellow-men, especially partners, have to be made from the moral point of view, too. Moral norms determine also the relations between individuals, partnerships and joint actions. This task can be fulfilled only by a system of norms which defines both duties and rights. The duty of person *A* in relation to person *B* is not only associated with person *B*'s justified expectation that *A* is likely to conduct himself in accordance with his duty but also with *A*'s moral claim that *B* should behave in this way. As a result I believe that a person has rights from the moral point of view, too, although the primary moral question continues to be "How am I to act?"

[5] e.g. J. Rawls, *op.cit.*, p. 152. "Human society is however, marked by the application of justice. The conditions of its application are not defined by a specific theory of human motivation." Rawls does, indeed, not use the effect of norms and principles of justice as motives for action as an argument in his reflections on justice.

political argumentation can be reached only *if the dialectic interplay of utilitarian analyses and ideals of justice is taken into account. Justice itself must not, in my view, be considered in isolation from questions of motivation.* "Just, useful and effective" is the motto.

The premise of such an analytical and dialectic conception[6] does, however, raise the question, what it is, that sets apart the postulates of justice from the objectives of the utilitarian considerations. Would it not be true to say that the system of social objectives fuses with the principles of justice? I believe, that this question is not an easy one to answer. It may be that a clear distinction between utilitarian goals and legal and political postulates on the one hand and the ideals of justice on the other is, in fact, not feasible. This inter-relationship can be explained approximately in the following way: the ideals of justice are concepts which are seen as yardsticks and constraints for our utilitarian considerations; experience teaches us that individuals and the most divergent social groups alike do have ideals of justice which do not coincide with the respective utilitarian goals. Instead, these ideals imply, on the one hand, a restriction of the means which may be used to achieve these goals and, on the other hand, they represent points of view under which the proposed solutions can be evaluated in addition to the utilitarian analysis. Social objectives, economic and other practical goals form the basic framework for the activities and the creation of institutions. Social institutions are not primarily set up for the sake of justice but in order to realise these objectives are at the same time circumscribed by the ideals of justice.

5. FORMAL POSTULATES OF JUSTICE

Attempts have been made to explain the essence of justice by, as it were, formal principles in contraposition to actual objectives of content. I do not believe, however, that the theory of justice can be defined simply by formal considerations. Inherent ideals of justice must also be taken into account. The formal principles of justice (formal equality, universality, mutuality) as well as ideals of justice (e.g. solidarity, balance of role-play) are above all effective as critical arguments; on their own they are not suitable for giving direction to our actions or to constitute a legal and political program. This conclusion accords with my earlier claim that we are more capable of discerning what is unjust than we are of substantiating a just solution. *The analysis of justice is essentially a critical analysis.*

General points of view of the analysis of justice are, on the one hand, certain formal criteria, on the other, such legal and political postulates as are necessary to ensure the just application of the legal system.

---

[6] See O. Weinberger, Analytisch-dialektische Gerechtigkeitstheorie. Skizze einer handlungstheoretischen und non-kognitivistischen Gerechtigkeitslehre, in: *Zum Fortschritt von Theorie und Technik in Recht und Ethik*, ed. by I. Tammelo, A. Aarnio, *Rechtstheorie,* Beiheft 3 (1981), pp. 307-330.

According to *the principle of formal justice equal legal consequences are to ensue from equal relevant conditions.*

Perelman defines formal justice as follows: "Formal or abstract justice can be defined as a principle of action according to which beings of the same category are to be treated in the same manner."[7]

It is easily demonstrated that this principle equals the postulate that legal judgments must be based on general normative rules.[8]

In my formulation above the link with the relevant conditions is the key element which causes the principle to be empty of content and compatible with every legal and political conception. Knowing that a formal principle cannot on principle offer standards of content the logician will not be surprised by this. The principle of formal justice can only indirectly be meaningful for the *de-lege-ferenda* argumentation, in as much as it forces us to make explicit relevant conditions and the related legal consequences. In this way the basis of the evaluation is made transparent and exposed to a critique.

In *Perelman*'s formulation this principle does not give any indication either about the content of justice since the categories of its substance as well as the legal consequences remain undefined. The concept of the category of sub stance as it is applied by *Perelman* is not an ontological fact but it is left to those setting the norms to define this class. Here, too, - i.e. in the area of the postulates of formal justice -, the critical character of reflections on justice and their dependence on evaluating responses become obvious.

The *principle of mutuality* is a postulate of justice which occurs in various formulations. *Prima facie* it seems that it can be explained as the equality of the inverse relation: equality (e.g. equality of value) of service and return service, equality of the rights and duties of the subjects concerned. In this guise it appears to be a formal principle of justice. I do, however, question this conclusion with - as I believe - good reasons. As a formal principle one would expect it to have universal application. Yet the demand for mutuality does not apply to every kind of human relationship. I believe, it applies only to those relationships which we describe as "partnerships". Consequently the principle of mutuality is not a formal principle. The fact that the principle of mutuality relates to content rather than form is reflected by the fact that the decision whether or not the respective relationship requires mutuality is based on a material or substantive evaluation. It is further reflected by the necessity of defining the nature of the basic equality: exactly the same field of activity, equal value of service and the returned service, equality in the readiness to give assistance etc. Equivalence of mutual services does not mean equality in a strict sense but a

---

[7] Ch. Perelman, *Über die Gerechtigkeit*, München 1967, p. 28.

[8] See O. Weinberger, Gleichheitspostulate. Eine strukturtheoretische und rechtspolitische Betrachtung, *ÖZÖR* 25 (1974), pp. 23-38. The comparatively widespread formulation of the principle of formal justice as: What is equal is to be judged equally; what is unequal is to be judged and treated differently, is incorrect. For instance, the fact that two totally different yet equally grave offences attract the same punishment is by no means to be condemned as unjust.

highly differentiated scale of comparative values in accordance with the circumstances.

It appears advisable to me not to analyse the problems connected with mutuality as an aspect of the formal principle of justice but as one of the problems of relationships in the context of role-play. It has to be said though, that in partnership relations the postulate of mutuality applies in the sense of a tendency toward equivalence of mutual attitudes and services.

Universality in the sense of universal applicability plays a major role in the theory of justice. As long as no more than universality of normative rules is required the principle can be equated with the postulate of formal justice. If one sees universality as a purely formal concept and allows for every possible differentiation of the conditions of subsumption then this postulate does not restrict the admissability of the content of normative rules: it does not, therefore, represent a criterion for the evaluation of justice. Universality is, however, often taken to mean that the postulate of universality implies a demand for "not making distinctions" or, at least, to make an assumption of equality - such as in terms of distribution to equal parts - when there are not good reasons for differentiation. I am, however, of the opinion, that it is always necessary to evaluate what types of persons in what relationships are to be assumed to equal and what differentiations in the conditions of subsumption and of legal consequences have to be fixed. Consequently the demand "not to make distinctions" and the assumption of material equality do not make a contribution to the argumentation *de lege ferenda*, e.g. to the consideration of justice. (They can only be of use as rules of interpretation.) This takes us, in fact, from unrestricted universality to a differentiation of the moral imperative. *The principle of universality has no absolute meaning but is relative to the differentiating conditions which are fixed by every normative order.*

Hare sees the capacity to universalise as such as a constitutive characteristic of the concept of norm.[9] In my view, we are dealing here with a somewhat problematical concept. It is inappropriate to tie the fundamental semantic formulations - here the definition of the concept of norm - to conditions which characterise the moral imperative. In *Hare*'s concept the reading of how the individual norm is universalised is problematical. For instance: "You must pay Mr. N. 100 S". How is this individual norm to be given universal application? "Whoever is identical with you has to pay Mr. N. 100 S" represents a pseudo-universalisation. But the universalisation of other attributes which characterise the addressee can be justified in one case and not in another. "Every person who has borrowed 100 S from Mr. N. has to ..." - "Every person who lives alone in this flat", and let us suppose that both conditions apply to one and the same person. That is to say, that the descriptive function can be the same extensionally but different intentionally. But not every descriptive function leads to a justified universalisation.

---

[9] R.M. Hare, *Freedom and Reason*, Oxford 1967; German version: *Freiheit und Vernunft*, Düsseldorf 1973; see also, *Moral Thinking. Its Levels, Method and Point*, Oxford 1981.

Universality is acceptable as a criterion of correctness only if the term is used in the manner of Kant's formulation, in other words, if one asks oneself whether one can want (wants to, thinks it right and just to want) a certain imperative to be acceptable as a universal rule. Evaluation on the basis of general standards constitutes a substantive foundation for an imperative only if it is supported by a substantive judgment which is expressed by Kant as 'being able to want'. The formal criterion of universality alone does not, however, constitute a sufficient basis for assessments of justice.

6. NATURAL LAW OR CONVICTIONS OF JUSTICE?

What is the source from which the analysis of justice draws its substantive arguments? Some authors refer to natural law in some form or other at this point. In my view that can only lead to pseudo-argumentations as the principles of natural law would have to be defined objectively. That is, of course, not possible. There are, however, factual convictions and ideals of justice which exist in every community and in every human being. (We speak of the existence of a "sense of justice".) Even the relativist in matters of values has to acknowledge that fact. As arguments these convictions of justice play a role analogous to that of the socalled principles of natural law, except for one difference: they appear as opinions and as such they can and ought to be subjected to criticism and refinement.

The positivist has, in my view, no difficulty to conduct rational and evaluating analyses of justice, he can base his investigations on convictions of justice and can support his arguments about content among others on anthropological studies. In addition, let me draw attention at this point to the importance of political postulates for the just application of the law which take up a not inconsiderable position within the totality of the theory of justice.

7. POSTULATES OF THE JUST APPLICATION OF THE LAW

The most important postulates of this kind are:

(a) A genuine fact finding process must form the basis. *The postulate of the genuine establishment of facts* may constitute a banal and self-evident demand. However, those who recall the degenerate legal systems and their show-trials (of the recent past), and those who from their own legal practice know the problems of factual evidence, will have no problems in accepting this postulate as fundamental to a just judicature nor will they underestimate its importance.

(b) *The postulate of realisation.* Moral imperatives do not merely form the basis for legal value judgments they also determine actions: they put into action the legal consequences defined by rational correlations.

(c) *Postulates of just proceedings.* Even within the framework of a theory of relative justice it is certainly meaningful to establish postulates of just procedure. They are founded on our conviction that an appropriate organisation of legal proceedings can maximise the likelihood of reaching just (e.g. lawful) decisions. The principle of just proceedings, in other words, our convictions about the appropriate organisation of legal processes and the effect this organisation has on the likelihood of the substantive justice in any decision ought to be subjected to an empirical verification, even considering that it is not an easy task and, as a result only rarely performed.

8. BALANCED ROLE-PLAY AS A POSTULATE OF JUSTICE

Communities are not based on the fact of coexistence alone, but also on the fact that communities assume forms structured in certain ways as a result of specific imperatives, values and expectations. Individuals and groups take on certain roles in the community which are determined by normative regulatives. *This role-play is a complex mixture of what must be done and what may be done, of tasks and authorisations, of demands and expectations, of taking an active part and adapting to others.*

Role-play is a social condition into which we enter either automatically or by a deliberate act of will. One is automatically a citizen; one becomes the member of a club or a marriage-partner by a specific act of will.

Man organises his role-play partly on the basis of relatively free decisions or possibly by modifying institutionalised role-play in the process of shaping specific relationships.

The existence of communities and of role-play is always connected with problems of justice. *Every role-play is associated with specific moral or legal imperatives and with ideals of justice.*

Role-play as a social institution is subject to a scale of value judgements. The role and its respective value are determined by the social function of the player: compare the ethos of the doctor, the judge, the teacher, the worker.

In this context the problems of justice are above all concentrated in the balance of the quid pro quo of services provided by the partners in the role-play. In some cases it is a matter of a kind of equality, for instance when two farmers promise each other mutual help during the harvest. Sometimes it is not a question of actual equality of services but of equal readiness to render a service, for instance the readiness of siblings to give each other support in emergencies. Often it is a matter of a certain kind of equal value in the general context of material inequality between a service and its return, for instance in the case of an exchange or an acquisition or sale. The assessment of equivalence is based on a relative value judgement. Consequently it depends on a subjective reaction albeit with fundamental factual restrictions. It is also possible to advance sound plausibility arguments for the evaluation in which case the value judgment will depend on institutionalised customs, in particular in those cases which are a matter of institutionalised role-play, e.g. marriage, games, different forms of economic cooperation.[10]

---

[10] The problem of assessing the balance of role-relations being one of the most fundamental questions of justice it requires thorough investigation. Such an analysis cannot, of course, be conducted within the framework of this discourse.

Role-play which is constituted by a partnership agreement conforms to more or less institutionalised types (e.g. marriage, company, club). The criterion of justice for the individual case is provided essentially by the institutionalised ethos or the special agreement which defines the framework of the institution more closely. It is also feasible that within the framework of institutionalised forms a balance of services that differs from the usual one can evolve - corresponding to the agreement or to the situation -. *It is an aspect of the conditio humana that the questions of balance in the roles will constantly be under discussion as a problem of justice.*

9. COLLECTIVE ACTION

Collective action is an aspect of many communities; it means either that the community acts together or that a representative acts as an organ of the community; in other words, he performs acts in the name of the community. In that case he as the representative is required to act exclusively in the interest of the community. While his own interests will, as a rule, to some extent coincide with those of the community, to some extent, however, diverge from them, it is expected of him that he should pursue the interests of the community rather than his own in his position as functionary. We are dealing here with a difficult situation demanding a correct and honourable course of action.

10. PRESENT-DAY ASPECTS OF THE PROBLEMS OF JUSTICE

I should like to point out some problems which arise directly from the present-day *conditio humana*.

a) *Conservative or reforming justice*. It is an essential aspect of the law and of our concepts of justice that we expect that the legal organization grants legal certainty and the effective validity of the rule of law and that what is considered just should not be valid only for today but continues to be recognised as such tomorrow. Acquired rights have to be protected in principle. The general legal situation must offer a basis for people to orientate their actions by. At the same time we expect and demand that our institutions and our ideals of justice should evolve. What is justice if these two postulates conflict with each other (which happens, indeed, in the political area)? No general rules exist for such a situation: in such a case a compromise has to be found with the help of a relative evaluation.

(b) *Communal and supra-communal orientation of justice*. The human ethos is in essence such that moral goodness and justice are characterised by *their orientation on the interests of the community* - no matter how that community may be defined. The ideals of nations, of religious communities and of other collectives and groups based on common interest are of this kind. The fact that in our world of today we all belong to a plurality of communities and the equally undoubted fact that so many different communities coexist with each other throw a totally new light on this attitude. *Our present-day problem lies no longer just in the support we owe to one community but in the need to establish relations between communities*. Both in the smaller and in the larger context this is currently the fundamental pre-condition for the survival of humanity in the face of modern weapons and of the present socio-political constellations in our world. *In our time the ideals of justice must be placed into the service of this problem To open up communications between cultures, political systems and communities in general, and to practice tolerance and to try and achieve understanding between communities should be our highest ideals*. A commitment to conservation of environment appears to me to be only the second most important aim of society, all the more so as progress in matters of peace, disarmament and mutual understanding would also mean that the burden of nature would be eased considerably.

(c) *Prospective justice. From the point of view of the theory of justice the question has to be asked here whether it is not inevitable that the mechanism of guilt, retribution and repression shaped by traditional concepts of justice should in many areas give way to the search for strong and durable systems for future interaction. The past is important only in so far as it explains existing structures, but we are not concerned with historical claims or retribution which would only confuse the world and would with certainty not offer a universal basis for peace. Instead, we are concerned with finding solutions which will bring harmony to the world in the future*.[11]

My observations are summed up briefly in the following propositions:
1. Justice is an ubiquitous problem of humanity.
2. We do not possess the definitive understanding of what is just and unjust.
3. It is strictly not possible to prove what is just, but injustices can be revealed convincingly. Reflections about justice are by their very nature critical analyses.
4. The correctness of judgements of justice is threatened above all by a one-sided approach.
5. Principles of justice have to be seen in their role as determinants of action.
6. The principles of justice have the function of adjusting man's actions to his roles in the community.
7. The problem of justice has a moral as well as legal aspect which can be expressed in the following questions. "How do I act within the precepts of justice?" is the moral question. "How can relations in society be made just?" is the legal question.
8. In considerations which determine actions postulates of justice always occur in conjunction with utilitarian considerations. They are not, therefore, a matter of 'just' or 'unjust' but, as a rule, they are concerned with finding ways of acting which are both just and appropriate to the relevant purpose.

---

[11] It appears to me that there are certain parallels between personal relations - e.g. family relations - and the life of national communities. Neither the family nor the national community is concerned in the first instance to evaluate what has gone before, to draw "just" conclusions from the partner's previous conduct, but wants, instead, to constitute durable ways of life and a balance role-play for the future.

9. The justice of social institutions cannot be assessed as independent of their motivating effect.
10. The formal postulates of justice, formal equality and universality are fundamental instruments of the analysis of justice. They do not, however, constitute, an independent basis for evaluating judgments of justice.
11. It is not in natural law but in convictions of justice that the analysis of justice finds support.
12. The significance of the postulates of the just application of the law - genuine determination of facts, the postulates of realisation and of just procedure - must not be underestimated.
13. Every community is structured by role-play which involves moral imperatives, expectations and ideals of justice. In this context the question of the balance of the roles as a problem of justice is always under discussion.
14. The present-day situation of mankind demands changes in our ideals of justice away from their orientation on the goals of the community we belong to and towards the ideal of inter-community understanding. Not the concepts of guilt, retribution and repression are preeminent but the identification of a system of relatively harmonious interaction.
15. It is an essential aspect of the *conditio humana* that we search for justice, that we don't find it in the world and that we don't even possess fixed standards of justice: justice is a task, both as an eternal problem of defining what justice is, and as an effort to act justly and to create a (relatively) just world.

BIBLIOGRAPHY

A. Aarnio, *On Legal Reasoning*, Turku 1977

-, R. Alexy/A. Peczenik, The Foundation of Legal Reasoning, *Rechtstheorie* 12 (1981), pp. 113-158, pp. 257-279, pp. 423-448; German version: Grundlagen der juristischen Argumentation, in: W. Krawietz/R. Alexy, *Metatheorie juristischer Argumentation*, Berlin 1983, pp. 9-87

R. Alexy, *Theorie der juristischen Argumentation. Die Theorie des rationalen Diskurses als Theorie der juristischen Begründung*, Frankfurt/M. 1978

- see also A. Aarnio/R. Alexy/A. Peczenik

-,W. Krawietz (eds.), *Metatheorie der juristischen Arugmentation*, Berlin 1983

G.E.M. Anscombe, On Brute Facts, *Analysis* 18, 3, 1958, pp. 69-72

Aristoteles, *Politik*, ed. by O. Gigon, München 1973

W.R. Ashby, *An Introduction to Cybernetics*, London 1971^{8} (1956^{1}).

J. Austin, *Lectures on Jurisprudence or the Philosophy of Positive Law*, London 1885

B. Bames, *The Nature of Power*, Oxford 1988

O. Becker, *Untersuchungen über den Modalkalkül*, Meisenheim/Glan 1952

J. Bentham, *An Introduction to the Principles of Morals and Legislation*, ed. by J.H. Burns/H.L.A. Hart, London 1970 (1780^{1})

- *Of Laws in General*, ed. by H.L.A. Hart, London 1970

J. Berkemann/P. Strasser, Bibliographie zur Normenlogik, in: H. Lenk (ed.), *Normenlogik*, Pullach b. München 1974, pp. 207-251

R. Carnap, *Logische Syntax der Sprache*, Wien 1968^{2} (1934^{1})

L. Couffignal, *Notions de base*, Paris 1958

J.T. Delos, La Théorie de l'Institution. La Solution réaliste du Problème de la Personnalité Morale et le Droit à fondement objectif, *Archives de Philosophie du Droit et de Sociologie juridique*, 1931, pp. 98-153

R. Descartes, *Regeln zur Leitung des Geistes*, translated by A. Buchenau, Leipzig 1920

A. Downs, *Ökonomische Theorie der Demokratie*, Tübingen 1968 (orig. 1957)

W. Dubislaw, Zur Unbegründbarkeit der Forderungssätze, *Theorie* 3 (1937), pp. 330-342

R. Dworkin, *Taking Rights Seriously*, London 1977, Harvard 1978[2]

K. Engisch, Der finale Handlungsbegriff, in: *Probleme der Strafrechtserneuerung. FS für Eduard Kohlrausch*, Berlin 1944, pp. 141-179

-, Logische Überlegungen zur Verbrechensdefinition, in: G. Stratenwerth et al. (eds.), *FS für Hans Welzel zum 70. Geburtstag*, Berlin/New York 1974, pp. 343-378

K. Engliš, Nástin národohospodářské noetiky [Outline of Economic Noetics], *Sbornik věd právních a státních*, Praha 1917, pp. 274-300, 1918, pp. 29-55.

- *Malá Logika* (Small Logic), Praha 1947

- *Das Problem der Logik*, Wien 1961

- Die Norm ist kein Urteil, *ARSP* 50 (1964), pp. 305-316

- Kritik der Normativen Theorie, in: V. Kubeš/O. Weinberger (eds.), *Die Brünner rechtstheoretische Schule (Normative Theorie)*, Wien 1980, pp. 176-193

M. Fuchs, *Allgemeine Rechtstheorie Santi Romanos*, Berlin 1979[1]

H.-G. Gadamer, *Wahrheit und Methode. Grundzüge einer philosophischen Hermeneutik*, Tübingen 1972[3].

J.-L. Gardies, Le problème logique et le problème philosophique du passage de l'être au devoir-être, *ARSP* 68 (1982), pp. 281-298

A. Gehlen, *Der Mensch, Seine Natur und seine Stellung in der Welt*, Bonn 1955

-, Probleme einer soziologischen Handlungstheorie, in: the same, *Studien zur Anthropologie und Soziologie*, Neuwied/Berlin 1971, pp. 196-231

H. Grimm/A. Mohlen (eds.), *Einführung in den Konstruktivismus*, München 1985

G. Gurvitch, Les idées-maîtresse de Maurice Hauriou, *Archives de Philosophie du Droit et de Sociologie juridique*, 1931, pp. 155-194

R.M. Hare, *Freiheit und Vernunft*, Düsseldorf 1973

-, *Moral Thinking. Its Levels, Method, and Point*, Oxford 1981

H.L.A. Hart, *The Concept of Law*, Oxford 1961, pp. 189-195

N. Hartmann, *Das Problem des geistigen Seins*, Berlin 1932

-, *Der Aufbau der realen Welt*, Berlin 1940

-, *Teleologisches Denken*, Berlin 1951

M. Hauriou, *Aux sources du droit. Le pouvoir, l'ordre et la liberté*. Paris 1933

-, Die Theorie der Institution und der Gründung. Essay über den sozialen Vitalismus, in: R. Schnur (ed.), *Die Theorie der Institution*, Berlin 1965

A. Höfler, Abhängigkeitsbeziehungen zwischen Abhängigkeitsbeziehungen, in:*Kaiserliche Akademie der Wissenschaften in Wien, Philosophisch-historische Klasse, Sitzungsberichte* 181, vol. 4, pp. 1-56

D. Hume, *Ein Traktat über die menschliche Natur*, Hamburg 1973

G. Jellinek, *Allgemeine Staatslehre*, Bad Homburg/Berlin/Zürich 1966 (1900[1]).

W.J. Jennings, Die Theorie der Institution, in: R. Schnur (ed.), *Institution und Recht*, Darmstadt 1968, pp. 99-177

H.-H. Jescheck, Der strafrechtliche Handlungsbegriff in dogmengeschichtlicher Entwicklung, in: P. Pochelmann and W. Gallas (eds.), *FS für Eberhard Schmidt zum 70. Geburtstag*, Göttingen 1961, pp. 139-155

J. Jørgensen, Imperatives and Logic, *Erkenntnis* 7 (1937/38), pp. 288-296

G. Kalinowski, Théorie des propositions normatives, *Studia Logica* 1 (1953), pp. 146-182

-, *Du métalangage en logique. Réflexions sur la logique déontique et son rapport avec la logique des normes, Documents de Travail et pré-publications*, Università di Urbino, Nr. 48, 1973, Serie A

I. Kant, *Kritik der reinen Vernunft*, ed. by W. Weischedel, vol. IV, Frankfurt a.M. 1968

-, *Grundlegung zur Metaphysik der Sitten*, ed. by W. Weischedel, Wiesbaden 1956

A. Kaufmann, Die ontologische Struktur der Handlung, Skizze einer personalen Handlungslehre, in: the same, *Schuld und Strafe,* Köln et al. 1966, pp. 25-66

H. Kelsen, *Hauptprobleme der Staatsrechtslehre entwickelt aus der Lehre vom Rechtssatz*, Tübingen 1911

-,*Vom Wesen und Wert der Demokratie*, Tübingen 1929[2]

-, *Reine Rechtslehre*, 1st ed., Wien 1934

-, *Reine Rechtslehre*, 2nd ed., Wien 1960

-, *Allgemeine Theorie der Normen*, ed. by K. Ringhofer and R. Walter, Wien 1979

P. Graf Kielmannsegg (ed)., *Legitimationsprobleme politischer Systeme*, Opladen 1976

D. Kienapfel, *Österreichisches Strafrecht*, Allgemeiner Teil, Wien 1979

U. Klug, Der Handlungsbegriff des Finalismus als methodologisches Problem. Prolegomena zu einem axiomatischen Handlungsbegriff, in: U. Klug (ed.), *Philosophie und Recht. FS für C.A. Emge*, Wiesbaden 1960, pp. 34-50

St. Körner, *Erfahrung und Theorie. Ein wissenschaftstheoretischer Versuch*, Frankfurt a.M. 1970

-, *Categorical Frameworks*, Oxford 1974

-, *Experience and Conduct*, Cambridge et al. 1976

W. Krawietz, Begründung des Rechts anthropologisch betrachtet. Zur Institutionentheorie von Weinberger und Schelsky, in: the same/H. Schelsky/G. Winkler/A. Schramm, *Theorie der Normen. Festgabe für Ota Weinberger zum 65. Geburtstag*, Berlin 1984, pp. 541-556

-, see also R. Alexy/W. Krawietz

-, W. Krawietz/O. Weinberger, *Helmut Schelsky als Soziologe und politischer Denker*, Stuttgart 1985
V. Kubeš/O. Weinberger (eds.), *Die Brünner rechtstheoretische Schule (Normative Theorie)*, Wien 1980

K. Larenz, *Methodenlehre der Rechtswissenschaft*, Berlin/Heidelberg/New York 1975[3]

N. Leser, Der Konflikt zwischen Recht und Gerechtigkeit, paper for the *12th Congress of the IVR in Athens 1985, "Das Recht, der Mensch und die Geschichte", Programm und Zusammenfassungen*, pp. 150 f.

J. Loevenstein, *Velká teleologie. Konstrukce hospodářské noetiky [Comprehensive Teleology. Model of a System of Economic Noetics]*, Praha 1933

K. Lorenz, Die angeborenen Formen möglicher Erfahrung, *Zeitschrift für Tierpsychologie* 5 (1943), pp. 235-409

-, *Die Rückseite des Spiegels. Versuch einer Naturgeschichte menschlichen Erkennens*, München/Zürich 1973[2]

-, *Vergleichende Verhaltensforschung. Grundlagen der Ethologie*, Wien/New York 1978

N. Luhmann, *Rechtssoziologie*, vol. 1 and 2, Hamburg 1972[1] (vol. 1/2, Opladen 1980[2])

-, Gerechtigkeit in den Rechtssystemen der modernen Gesellschaft, *Rechtstheorie*, 4th vol., 1973, pp. 131-167

-, Institutionalisierung - Funktion und Mechanismus im sozialen System der Gesellschaft, in: H. Schelsky, *Zur Theorie der Institution*, Düsseldorf 1973, pp. 27-41

D.N. MacCormick, *Law as Institutional Fact*, Edinburgh 1973

-, Coherence in Legal Justification, in: W. Krawietz et al., *Theorie der Normen. Festgabe für Ota Weinberger zum 65. Geburtstag*, Berlin 1984, pp. 37-53

-/ O. Weinberger, *Grundlagen des Institutionalistischen Rechtspositivismus*, Berlin 1985

-/ O. Weinberger, *An Institutional Theory of Law. New Approaches to Legal Positivism*, Dordrecht /Boston/Lancaster/Tokyo 1986

W. Maihofer, *Der Handlungsbegriff im Verbrechenssystem*, Tübingen 1953

W. Mantl, Hans Kelsen und Carl Schmitt, in: W. Krawietz/E. Topitsch/P. Koller (eds.), *Ideologiekritik und Demokratietheorie bei Hans Kelsen, Rechtstheorie*, Beiheft 4 (1982), pp. 185-199

S. Martin-Retortillo, Die Lehre Santi Romanos von der Rechtsordnung und einige ihrer Anwendungen im Bereich des Verwaltungsrechts, in: R. Schnur (ed.), *Institution und Recht*, Darmstadt 1968, pp. 370-420

E. Mayer, *Evolution und die Vielfalt des Lebens*, Berlin/Heidelberg/New York 1979

A. Meinong, Über Gegenstandstheorie, in: the same, *Untersuchungen zur Gegenstandstheorie*, Leipzig 1904

-, A. Meinong, in: R. Schmidt (ed.), *Die Philosophie der Gegenwart in Selbstdarstellungen*, vol. 1, Leipzig 1922, pp. 101-160

A. Merkl, *Die Lehre von der Rechtskraft entwickelt aus dem Rechtsbegriff. Eine rechtstheoretische Untersuchung*, Leipzig/Wien 1923

-, Prolegomena einer Theorie des rechtlichen Stufenbaues, in: A. Verdross (ed.), *Gesellschaft, Staat und Recht, FS für H. Kelsen*, Wien 1931, pp. 252-294

A. Mohler, see H. Grimm/A. Mohler

R. Moos, Die finale Handlungslehre, in: *Strafrechtliche Probleme der Gegenwart*, vol. II, Strafrechtliches Seminar und Vereinigung der österreichischen Richter, Stein 1974, pp. 5-41

W. Niese, *Finalität, Vorsatz und Fahrlässigkeit*, Tübingen 1951

L. Olbrechts-Tyteca, see Ch. Perelman/L. Olbrechts-Tyteca

Ch. Perelman, *Über die Gerechtigkeit*, München 1967

-, L. Olbrechts-Tyteca: *Traité de l'Argumentation*, Bruxelles el 1970^2 (Paris 1958^1)

Platon, *Sophistes*, translated by O. Apelt, Leipzig 1922

W. Platzgummer, *Die Bewußtseinsform des Vorsatzes. Eine strafrechtsdogmatische Untersuchung auf psychologischer Grundlage*, Wien 1964

A. Pöhl, Böser Vorsatz und unbewußtes Wissen, *ÖJZ* 16, 1961, pp. 66-67

K.R. Popper, *Objective Knowledge. An Evolutionary Approach*, London 1973 (1972[1]), (comprises also: On the Theory of the Objective Mind, pp. 152-190)

A. Procházka, Normative Theorie und Rechtserzeugung, in: V. Kubeš/O. Weinberger (eds.), *Die Brünner rechtstheoretische Schule (Normative Theorie)*, Wien 1980, pp. 304-323

J. Rawls, *Eine Theorie der Gerechtigkeit*, Frankfurt/M. 1975 (Engl. original 1971)

G. Renard, *La Théorie des Institutions. Essai d'ontologie juridique*, Paris 1930

N. Rescher, Lawfulness as Mind-dependent, in: the same (ed.), *Essays in Honor of Carl G. Hempel*, Dordrecht 1969, pp. 178-197

J. Rödig, *Die Denkform der Alternative in der Jurisprudenz*, Berlin/Heidelberg/New York 1969

S. Romano, *Die Rechtsordnung*, ed. by R. Schnur, Berlin 1975

A. Ross, Tû-Tû, *Harvard Law Review* 70 (1956-57), pp. 812-825

-, *Law and Justice*, London 1958

-, *Directives and Norms*, London 1968

C. Roxin, Kritik der finalen Handlungslehre, in: the same, *Strafrechtliche Grundlagenprobleme*, Berlin/New York 1973, pp. 72-122 (*ZStW*, vol.74, 1962)

F.C. von Savigny, *System des heutigen Römischen Rechts*, Heidelberg 1814

H. Schelsky, Über die Stabilität von Institutionen, besonders Verfassungen, in: R. Schnur (ed.), *Institution und Recht*, Darmstadt 1968, pp. 265-293

-, (ed.), *Zur Theorie der Institution*, 2nd ed., Düsseldorf 1973

-, *Die Soziologen und das Recht. Abhandlungen und Vorträge zur Soziologie von Recht, Institution und Planung*, Opladen 1980

-, Zur Methode einer empirischen Begriffsbestimmung "des Politischen", in: the same, *Politik und Publizität*, Stuttgart/Degerloch 1983, pp. 38-51

C. Schmitt, *Der Hüter der Verfassung*, Tübingen 1931

-, *Über die drei Arten des rechtswissenschaftlichen Denkens*, Hamburg 1934

-, *Staat, Bewegung, Volk*, Hamburg 1935

-, *Der Begriff des Politischen*, Berlin 1963 (1932[1])

A. Schopenhauer, *Über die vierfache Wurzel des Satzes vom zureichenden Grund*, Rudolstadt 1813

J.A. Schumpeter, *Kapitalismus, Sozialismus und Demokratie*, München 1972[3] (1946[1])

J.R. Searle, How to derive "ought" from "is", *The Philosophical Review* 1964

-, *Speech Acts. An Essay in the Philosophy of Language*, Cambridge 1969

-, A Taxonomy of Illocutionary Acts, in: the same, *Expression and Meaning*, Cambridge et al. 1979, pp. 1-27

-, *Intentionality*, Cambridge et al. 1983

W. Stegmüller, *Wissenschaftliche Erklärung und Begründung (Probleme und Resultate der Wissenschaftstheorie und Analytischen Philosophie,* vol. I) Berlin/Heidelberg/New York 1969

Ch.L. Stevenson, *Ethics and Language*, New Haven/London 1944

P. Strasser, see J. Berkemann/P. Strasser

G. Stratenwerth, Unbewußte Finalität? in: the same et al. (eds.), *Festschrift für Hans Welzel zum 70. Geburtstag*, Berlin/New York 1974, pp. 289-305

R.S. Summers, *Pragmatischer Instrumentalismus und amerikanische Rechtstheorie*, München 1983

I. Tammelo, *Outlines of Modern Legal Logic*, Wiesbaden 1969

A. Verdross, *Statisches und dynamisches Naturrecht*, Freiburg 1971

Th. Viehweg, *Topik und Jurisprudenz*, München 1974[5] (1953[1])

G. Vollmer, *Was können wir wissen?* vol. 1, Die Natur der Erkenntnis, Stuttgart 1985

M. Weber, *Wissenschaft und Gesellschaft*, Tübingen 1972[5]

Ch. Weinberger, *Evolution und Ethologie. Wissenschaftstheoretische Analysen*, Wien/New York 1983

-/ O. Weinberger, Versuch einer neuen Grundlegung der normenlogischen Folgerungstheorie, in: Argumentation und Hermeneutik in der Jurisprudenz, *Rechtstheorie*, Beiheft 1 (1979), pp. 301-324

-/ O. Weinberger, *Logik, Semantik, Hermeneutik*, München 1979

-/ O. Weinberger, Teleonomie und formale Teleologie, in: K. Weinke (ed.), *Logik, Ethik und Sprache. FS für Rudolf Freundlich*, Wien/München 1980, pp. 252-265

O. Weinberger, *Norm und Institution. Eine Einführung in die Theorie des Rechts*, Wien 1988

-, *Rechtslogik*, Berlin 1989[2]

-, Die Sollsatzproblematik in der modernen Logik, *Rospravy CSAV*, 68, 9, Rada SV, Praha 1958 (also in: *Studien zur Normenlogik und Rechtsinformatik*, Berlin 1974)

-, Studie k logice normativních vět [Studies on the Logic of Norms], Praha 1960

-, Théorie des propositions normatives. Quelques remarques au sujet de l'interpretation normative des systèmes K_1 et K_2 de M. Kalinowski, *Studia Logica*, vol. 9, 1960, pp. 7-25; German version: "Zur Theorie der normativen Aussagen. Einige Bemerkungen über die normative Interpretation der Systeme K_1 und K_2 von Georges Kalinowski", in: the same, *Studien zur Normenlogik und Rechtsinformatik*, Berlin 1974, pp. 187-212

-, Der Relativierungsgrundsatz und der Reduktionsgrundsatz - zwei Prinzipien des dialektischen Denkens. Eine logisch-methodologische Studie, *Rozpravy CSAV*, 75/H.5, Rada SV, Praha 1965

-, Probleme der normativ-juristischen Deutung des Modalkalküls von Oskar Becker, *Conceptus* 4 (1970), pp. 22-31

-, Die Norm als Gedanke und Realität, *ÖZÖR* 20 (1970), pp. 203-216 (also in: D.N. MacCormick/O. Weinberger, *Grundlagen des Institutionalistischen Rechtspositivismus*, Berlin 1985)

-, Jurisprudenz zwischen Logik und Plausilibitätsargumentation, *Juristische Analysen* 1971/6, pp. 553-574

-, Der Begriff der Nicht-Erfüllung und die Normenlogik, *Ratio* 14, (1972), pp. 15-32

-, Bemerkungen zur Grundlegung der Theorie des juristischen Denkens, in: H. Albert et al. (eds.), *Rechtstheorie als Grundlagenwissenschaft der Rechtswissenschaften*, Düsseldorf 1972, pp. 134-161

-, Rationale und empirische Kontexte der Rechtsnorm, *Wissenschaft und Weltbild* 26 (1973), pp. 99-108

-, Gleichheitspostulate. Eine strukturtheoretische und rechtspolitische Betrachtung, *ÖZÖR* 25 (1974), pp. 23-38

-, *Studien zur Normenlogik und Rechtsinformatik*, Berlin 1974

-, Kontrafaktualität und Faktentranszendenz. Versuch, die Logik der faktentranszendenten und kontrafaktualen Bedingungssätze mit den Mitteln der extensionalen Logik zu behandeln, *Ratio* 16, 1974, pp. 13-28; English version: Contrary-to-fact and Fact-Transcendent Conditionals. An attempt to deal with the logic of fact-transcendent and contrary-to-fact conditionals by means of truth-functional logic, *Ratio* 16, 1974, pp. 15-32

-, Die Struktur der rechtlichen Normenordnung, in: G. Winkler (ed.), *Rechtstheorie und Rechtsinformatik*, Wien/New York 1975, pp. 110-132

-, Faktentranszendente Argumentation, *Zeitschrift für allgemeine Wissenschaftstheorie* 6/2, 1975, pp. 235-251

-, Zur Theorie der Gesetzgebung, in: J. Mokre/O. Weinberger (eds.), *Rechtsphilosophie und Gesetzgebung*, Wien/New York 1976, pp. 173-198

-, Der nomische Allsatz, in: *Grazer Philosophische Studien* 4 (1977), pp. 31-42

-, Intersubjektive Kommunikation, Normenlogik und Normendynamik, in: *Rechtstheorie* 8 (1977), pp. 19-40 (also in: I. Tammelo/H. Schreiner (eds.), *Strukturierungen und Entscheidungen im Rechtsdenken*, Wien/New York 1978, pp. 235-263)

-, Rationales und irrationales Handeln, in: F. Kaulbach/W. Krawietz (eds.), *Recht und Gesellschaft. FS für Helmut Schelsky zum 65. Geburtstag*, Berlin 1978, pp. 59-89

-, Tiefengrammatik und Problemsituation. Eine Untersuchung über den Charakter der philosophischen Analyse, in: *Wittgenstein und sein Einfluß auf die gegenwärtige Philosophie. Akten des 2. Internationalen Wittgenstein-Symposiums 1977*, Wien 1978, pp. 290-297

-, Die normenlogische Basis der Rechtsdynamik, in: U. Klug et al. (eds.), *Gesetzgebungstheorie, Juristische Logik, Zivil- und Prozeßrecht. Gedächtnisschrift für Jürgen Rödig*, Berlin/Heidelberg 1978, pp. 173-190

-, Kann man das normenlogische Folgerungssystem philosophisch begründen? Überlegungen zu den Grundlagen des juristischen Folgerns, *ARSP* 65/2 (1979), pp. 161-186

-, Abstimmungslogik und Demokratie, in: B. Sutter (ed.), *Reformen des Rechts, FS zur 200-Jahr-Feier der Rechtswissenschaftlichen Fakultät der Universität Graz*, Graz 1979, pp. 605-623

-, Versuch einer neuen Grundlegung der normenlogischen Folgerungstheorie, in: W. Krawietz/K. Opalek/A. Peczenik/A. Schramm (eds.), Argumentation und Hermeneutik in der Jurisprudenz, *Rechtstheorie* Beiheft 1 (1979), pp. 301-324

-, Tatsachen und Tatsachenbeschreibungen. Eine logisch-methodologische Überlegung zu einem Grundlagenproblem der Sozialwissenschaft, in: K. Salamun (ed.), *Sozialphilosophie als Aufklärung. FS für E. Topitsch*, Tübingen 1979, pp. 173-187

-, Handeln und Schließen. Überlegungen zum Begriff der praktischen Inferenz, in: F. van Dun (ed.), *The Law between Morality and Politics, Philosophica* 23 (1979), pp. 5-36 (also in: the same, *Studien zur formal-finalistischen Handlungstheorie*)

-, Das Recht als institutionelle Tatsache. Gleichzeitig eine Überlegung über den Begriff des positiven Rechts, *Rechtstheorie* 11 (1980), pp. 427-442

-, Dialektik und philosophische Analyse, in: E. Topitsch, *Logik der Sozialwissenschaften,* 10th ed., Köngistein/Ts. 1980, pp. 278-309

-, Determinismus und Verantwortung, *Zeitschrift für philosophische Forschung* 34 (1980), pp. 607-620 (also in: the same, *Studien zur formal-finalistischen Handlungstheorie*).

-, *Normentheorie als Grundlage der Jurisprudenz und Ethik,* Berlin 1981

-, Zur Idee eines institutionalistischen Rechtspositivismus, Gleichzeitig eine Auseinandersetzung mit Hans Kelsens Setzungspositivismus, in: *Kelsen et le positivisme juridique, Revue Internationale de Philosophie* 35 (1981), vol. 4, pp. 487-507

-, Analytisch-dialektische Gerechtigkeitstheorie. Skizze einer handlungstheoretischen und non-kognitivistischen Gerechtigkeitstheorie, in: I. Tammelo/A. Aarnio (eds.), *Zum Fortschritt von Theorie und Technik in Recht und Ethik, Rechtstheorie* (1981), Beiheft 3, pp. 307-330

-, Teleologie und Zeitablauf. Gleichzeitig eine Kritik an Wolfgang Stegmüllers Begriff der formalen Teleologie, *Rechtstheorie* 13 (1982), pp. 285-302

-, Ontología de las normas en la perspective de la theoría de la acción, in *Akten des 1. Intern. Kongresses für Rechtsphilosophie in la Plata*, 1982, vol. 2, La Plata 1982, pp. 544-566

-, Jenseits von Positivismus und Naturrecht, in: Contemporary Conceptions of Law, 9th World Congress (Basel 1979), *ARSP*, Supplementa, Vol. I, Part 1, 1982, pp. 43-56

-, Kelsens These von der Unanwendbarkeit logischer Regeln auf Normen, in: *Die reine Rechtslehre in wissenschaftlicher Diskussion. Referate und Diskussion des Internationalen Symposiums zum 100. Geburtstag von Hans Kelsen* (Wien 1981), Wien 1982, pp. 108-121

-, Logische Analyse als Basis der juristischen Argumentation, in: W. Krawietz/R. Alexy (eds.), *Metatheorie der juristischen Argumentation*, Berlin 1983, pp. 159-232

-, *Studien zur formal-finalistischen Handlungstheorie*, Frankfurt/M./Bern/New York 1983

-, Eine Semantik für die praktische Philosophie, in: R. Haller (ed.), *Beiträge zur Philosophie von Stephan Körner, Grazer Philosophische Studien*, vol. 20, 1983, pp. 219-239

-, Die Naturrechtskonzeption von Ronald Dworkin, in: D. Mayer-Maly/P.M. Simons (eds.), *Das Naturrechtsdenken heute und morgen. Gedächtnisschrift für René Marcic*, Berlin 1983, pp. 497-515

-, Self-portrait in "Problemas abiertos en la filosofía del derecho", *Doxa-cuadernos de filosofía del derecho*, vol. I (1984), pp. 257-263

-, 'Is' and 'Ought' Reconsidered. Comment on G.H. von Wright's Lecture "Is and Ought", *ARSP* LXX/4 (1984), pp. 454-474

-, The Expressive Conception of Norms - An Impasse for the Logic of Norms, *Law and Philosophy* 4 (1985), pp. 165-198

-, Freedom, Range for Action, and the Ontology of Norms, *Synthese* 65. No. 2 (1985), pp. 307-324

-, Gesetzgebung und Motivation. in: E. Mock/I. Tammelo (eds.), *Rechtstheorie und Gesetzgebung, FS für Robert Weimar*, Frankfurt/M./Bern/New York 1986, pp. 117-131

-, Der normenlogische Skeptizismus, *Rechtstheorie* 17 (1986), pp. 13-81

-, Rechtstheorie jenseits von Idealismus, Realismus und Materialismus. Ein Plädoyer für den normativistischen Institutionalismus, *ARSP* 1987, pp. 16-26

-, Reine oder funktionalistische Rechtsbetrachtung, in: W. Krawietz/O. Weinberger (eds.), *Reine Rechtslehre im Spiegel ihrer Fortsetzer und Kritiker, Forschungen aus Staat und Recht* 81, Wien/New York 1988, pp. 217-252

-, Skizze einer funktionalistischen Theorie der Demokratie, in: J. Novak, *On Masaryk, Studien zur österreichischen Philosophie*, vol. 12, Amsterdam 1987, pp. 333-360

-, see also: Ch. Weinberger/O. Weinberger

H. Welzel, Kausalität und Handlung, *Zeitschrift für die gesamte Staatswissenschaft* 51, 1931, pp. 703-720

-, *Um die finale Handlungslehre*, Tübingen 1949

-, *Naturrecht und materiale Gerechtigkeit*, Göttingen 1951

-, *Aktuelle Strafrechtsprobleme im Rahmen der finalen Handlungslehre*. Karlsruhe 1953

-, *Das neue Bild des Strafrechtssystems*, Göttingen 1961

-, *Vom Bleibenden und dem Vergänglichen in der Strafrechtswissenschaft*, Marburg 1964

-, *Das deutsche Strafrecht* , 9th ed., Bonn 1965

F. Weyr, Zum Problem eines einheitlichen Rechtssystems, *Archiv für öffentliches Recht* XXIII (1908), pp. 529-580

-, *Základy filosofie právní* [Fundamentals of Legal Philosophy], Brno 1920

-, *Teorie práva* [Theory of Law], Brno/Praha 1936

L. Wittgenstein, *Philosophische Untersuchungen*, in: same, *Schriften* I, Frankfurt a.M. 1969

E.A. Wolff, *Der Handlungsbegriff in der Lehre vom Verbrechen*, Heidelberg 1964

G.H. von Wright, Deontic Logic, *Mind* 60 (1951), pp. 1-15

-, *Norm and Action*, London 1963

-, *Erklären und Verstehen*, Frankfurt a.M. 1974 (1st ed. 1971)

-, *Handlung, Norm und Intention. Untersuchungen zur deontischen Logik*, Berlin/New York 1977

-, Is and Ought, in: E. Bulygin/J.-L. Gardies/I. Niiniluoto (eds.), *Man, Law and Modern Forms of Life*, Dordrecht/Boston/Lancaster 1985, pp. 263-281

W. Wundt, *Ethik. Eine Untersuchung der Tatsachen und Gesetze des sittlichen Lebens*, vols. I-III, Stuttgart 1912

ORIGINAL SOURCES

I." Elements of Institutional Legal Positivism", German title: "Bausteine des Institutionalistischen Rechtspositivismus", written for this volume.

II. "Towards a Formal-Teleological Theory of Action", German title: "Zur Idee einer formal-finalistischen Handlungstheorie", written for this volume.

III. "The Significance of Logic for Modern Legal Theory. Fundamental Problems of Institutionalist Normativism" first published in German: "Die Bedeutung der Logik für die moderne Rechtstheorie. Grundlagenprobleme des institutionalistischen Normativismus", in: G. Kalinowski/F. Selvaggi (eds.), *Les fondements logiques de la pensée normative*. Actes du colloque de logique déontique de Rome 1983, Roma 1985, pp. 109-145.

IV. "Ontology, Hermeneutics and the Concept of Valid Law", German version: "Ontologie und der Begriff des geltenden Rechts", in: Cs. Varga/O. Weinberger (eds.), *Rechtsgeltung, ARSP*, Beiheft 27/1986, pp. 109-126.

V. "Constitutional Theory in the Light of the New Institutionalism", German version: "Verfassungstheorie vom Standpunkt des neuen Institutionalismus"*ARSP*, 1990/LXXVI, pp. 100-118.

VI. "The Formal-Teleological Theory of Action and Criminal Law", German title: "Die formal-finalistische Handlungstheorie und das Strafrecht", in: G. Kohlmann (ed.), *FS für Ulrich Klug zum 70. Geburtstag*, vol. 1 *"Rechtsphilosophie, Rechtstheorie"*, Köln 1983, pp. 199-213.

VII. "Institutional Theory and Institutional Legal Positivism", German version: "Institutionentheorie und institutionalistischer Rechtspositivismus", in: O. Weinberger/W. Krawietz (eds.), *Helmut Schelsky als Soziologe und politischer Denker. Grazer Gedächtnisschrift zum Andenken an den am 24. Februar 1984 verstorbenen Gelehrten*, Stuttgart 1985, pp. 134-172.

VIII. "Sociology and Normative Institutional Theory. Reflections on Helmut Schelsky's Institutional Theory from the Point of View of the Normative Institutional Ontology", German version: "Soziologie und normative Institutionentheorie. Überlegungen zu Helmut Schelskiys Institutionentheorie vom Standpunkt der normativen Institutionenontologie", in: *Recht und Institution*. Helmut

Schelsky-Gedächtnissymposion Münster 1985, ed. by Rechtswissenschaftliche Fakultät der Universität Münster, Berlin 1985, pp. 33-58.

IX. "Legal Political Analysis of Institutions", German version: "Rechtspolitische Institutionenanalyse" in: D. Grimm/W. Maihofer (eds.), *Gesetzgebungstheorie und Rechtspolitik*, Opladen 1988, pp. 246-289

X. "The Conditio Humana and the Ideal of Justice", German version: "Die Conditio Humana und das Ideal der Gerechtigkeit", in: J.M. Broekman/K. Opalek/D.A.A. Kerimov (eds.), *Soziale Gerechtigkeit und individuelle Verantwortlichkeit im Wohlfahrtsstaat, ARSP*, Beiheft 24/1985, pp. 58-70.

Law and Philosophy Library

Publications:

1. E. Bulygin, J.-L. Gardies and I. Niiniluoto (eds.): *Man, Law and Modern Forms of Life*. With an Introduction by M. D. Bayles. 1985 ISBN 90-277-1869-5
2. W. Sadurski: *Giving Desert Its Due*. Social Justice and Legal Theory. 1985 ISBN 90-277-1941-1
3. N. MacCormick and O. Weinberger: *An Institutional Theory of Law*. New Approaches to Legal Positivism. 1986 ISBN 90-277-2079-7
4. A. Aarnio: *The Rational as Reasonable*. A Treatise on Legal Justification. 1987 ISBN 90-277-2276-5
5. M. D. Bayles: *Principles of Law*. A Normative Analysis. 1987 ISBN Hb: 90-277-2412-1; Pb: 90-277-2413-X
6. A. Soeteman: *Logic in Law*. Remarks on Logic and Rationality in Normative Reasoning, Especially in Law. 1989 ISBN 0-7923-0042-4
7. C. T. Sistare: *Responsibility and Criminal Liability*. 1989 ISBN 0-7923-0396-2
8. A. Peczenik: *On Law and Reason*. 1989 ISBN 0-7923-0444-6
9. W. Sadurski: *Moral Pluralism and Legal Neutrality*. 1990 ISBN 0-7923-0565-5
10. M. D. Bayles: *Procedural Justice*. Allocating to Individuals. 1990 ISBN 0-7923-0567-1
11. P. Nerhot (ed.): *Law, Interpretation and Reality*. Essays in Epistemology, Hermeneutics and Jurisprudence. 1990 ISBN 0-7923-0593-0
12. A.W. Norrie: *Law, Ideology and Punishment*. Retrieval and Critique of the Liberal Ideal of Criminal Justice. 1991 ISBN 0-7923-1013-6
13. P. Nerhot (ed.): *Legal Knowledge and Analogy*. Fragments of Legal Epistemology, Hermeneutics and Linguistics. 1991 ISBN 0-7923-1065-9
14. O. Weinberger: *Law, Institution and Legal Politics*. Fundamental Problems of Legal Theory and Social Philosophy. 1991 ISBN 0-7923-1143-4

KLUWER ACADEMIC PUBLISHERS – DORDRECHT / BOSTON / LONDON